The Emergence of ETFs in Asia-Pacific

Adam Marszk • Ewa Lechman • Yasuyuki Kato

The Emergence of ETFs in Asia-Pacific

Springer

Adam Marszk
Gdańsk University of Technology
Gdańsk, Poland

Ewa Lechman
Gdańsk University of Technology
Gdańsk, Poland

Yasuyuki Kato
Kyoto University
Kyoto, Japan

ISBN 978-3-030-12751-0 ISBN 978-3-030-12752-7 (eBook)
https://doi.org/10.1007/978-3-030-12752-7

Library of Congress Control Number: 2019933563

This Springer imprint is published by the registered company Springer Nature Switzerland AG
The registered company address is: Gewerbestrasse 11, 6330 Cham, Switzerland

Foreword

Ever since the first exchange-traded fund (ETF) was launched in the early 1990s, the product has set off an irrepressible wave of change across the global investment landscape. The phenomenon has of course also reached Asia—Japan welcomed its first ETF in 1995, and the market really began to soar after the emergence of ETFs on TOPIX and Nikkei 225 in 2001. Today, Japan is Asia's leading ETF market. As of September 2018, the Tokyo Stock Exchange (TSE) hosts 223 ETFs that command approximately USD 330 billion in assets under management.

Over the years, we have engaged our stakeholders, from regulators to asset managers, brokerages, and investors, to build a market that today serves up a highly diverse offering. Our ETF lineup tracks not only composite equity benchmarks but also specific industries, market tiers, and even distinctive themes. We also have products on foreign equities, bonds, real estate investment trust (REITs), and commodity price indices such as gold to allow exposure to a variety of asset classes. The diversity in our ETF market is apparent, and we can now safely say that Japan has caught up in terms of asset class with more mature markets in Europe and the USA.

The use of ETFs is also growing. A 2017 TSE survey on ETF investment for Japanese financial institutions revealed that most of them hold or invest in ETFs—a clear indication that the product now plays an integral role in professional asset management. Retail take-up has also increased. According to figures from TSE beneficiary surveys that collect and publish data on ETF investment, the number of individual retail investors has more than doubled from just under 360,000 to almost 730,000 in the 5 years since data collection began in July 2012. Meanwhile, retail holdings have surged from about 35.2 million units to more than 233.9 million units over the same period.

ETFs have gained a firm footing among both Japanese institutional and retail investors, but we believe a lot more can be done to develop the market. For instance, liquidity cost used to be a hurdle to investing in ETFs in Japan. In the 2017 TSE survey for financial institutions, we actually found many responses specifically mentioning this aspect—that liquidity tended to gather in a few issues and that the lack of quotes made it difficult to buy issues they wanted to invest in. To improve the liquidity situation, we introduced a market making scheme for ETFs in July 2018. The scheme has greatly improved the range of bid and asks quotes and the amount of orders ready to be filled. The narrower quote spreads, and deeper order books have definitely increased the overall convenience and attractiveness of the market. As we seek to consolidate our position as Asia's top ETF market, we will keep an eye on global regulatory developments and product trends.

Across the world, ETFs present a low-cost, low-entry means of portfolio diversification and asset allocation. By virtue of being traded in real time on public markets just like listed stocks, they are available to all investors. Above all, they have a simple and transparent structure. A survey conducted in 2017 by US consultant Greenwich Associates highlights precisely this aspect as the most important reason behind the rapid take-up of ETFs in the USA. In that survey, "easy to use" garnered the most responses, topping two widely heralded cost-related responses of "attractive management fee" and "speed of execution." In today's low interest rate environment, investors are on the lookout for ways to build assets over the medium to long term, and the convenience that ETFs provide will certainly offer an attractive proposition.

In recent years, the use of ETFs has also been spurred by new technology. For instance, the rise of ETF robo-advisers that design diversified or low-risk portfolios tailored to individual investor needs and better access to such technologies are factors accelerating the shift toward investment in ETFs. With this in mind, I expect technology to make ETFs even more accessible to the public. Indeed, several chapters of this book are devoted to a detailed discussion on how technology ties in with ETF use.

As needs change with technology, TSE will continue to promote ETFs and work to increase market liquidity to raise the appeal of our market, so that we continue to lead the way in Asia in the ETF sphere.

I sincerely hope that this book will contribute to a better understanding of ETFs and perhaps even inspire future initiatives to develop ETF markets both in Asia and in other parts of the world.

Tokyo Stock Exchange, Inc. Koichiro Miyahara
Tokyo, Japan

Acknowledgments

While working on this book, we received the support and constructive criticism from many people. We are profoundly grateful to all of them, and we would like to thank for their intellectual contribution to this work. We are particularly thankful to Professor Tomasz Janowski and the other participants of the seminars and meetings of the Faculty of Management and Economics at Gdańsk University of Technology for their stimulating questions and insightful suggestions concerning our research. Our colleagues were a great source of fresh ideas and inspiration that encouraged us to further work and helped us keep things in right perspective. We would like to express our special gratitude to Money Design Co., Ltd., of Japan for the support of ETF researches. We are also grateful to Mr. Koichiro Miyahara from Tokyo Exchange, Inc., for the excellent foreword. Last but not least, we express our appreciation to our families for their patience and understanding while we were working on the manuscript. They gave us peace of mind and kept us going with this work, which would be impossible without them.

The research presented in this book has been supported by the National Science Centre of Poland [projects no. 2015/19/D/HS4/00399 and 2015/19/B/HS4/03220]. A. Marszk has been supported by the Foundation for Polish Science (FNP).

As always, responsibility for any errors in the book remains our own.

Contents

Chapter 1
Introduction

The centrality of finance and financial markets to economic change has been dramatically reinforced by technological change, (…) and this is leading to (…) a more open and interdependent world.
Philip G. Cerny (1994, p. 320)

1.1 Why ETFs and ICT?

> (…) the new information and communication technology has revolutionized the way that financial products are designed, systems are developed for supporting financial operations, high-risk as well as low-risk transactions are managed, managers and traders understand and interact with each other and interface with technology itself
> Philip G. Cerny (1994, p. 331)

Recently, the world has been rapidly and profoundly transforming due to the explosive growth of the new information and communication technologies. Rapidly boosting demand for the new technologies offering "connection with outside world," mainly due to low-cost, fast distributable, and easily adaptable wireless solutions, has disruptively reshaped the world's landscape. Digital Revolution provides connectivity to geographically isolated and remote regions; it connects individuals and societies that before have been "unconnected." Fast spread of ICT has opened new windows of opportunities for technological catching-up but also for climbing the ladder of economic development. Needless to say that this Digital Revolution has fundamentally reshaped the world we live in, it has changed the way people interact in society, communicate, and do business. New information and communication technologies create new types of networks, social networks, business, and industrial networks, enhancing more dynamic flows of goods, services, money, and even people. Economies are becoming more and more ICT-conditioned.

Rapid expansion of information and communication technologies has created solid foundations for rapid expansion of financial innovations worldwide. ICT and financial innovations diffusion are intimately related. Undeniably, fast spread of such instruments has been facilitated by growing penetration of ICT,

A. Marszk et al., *The Emergence of ETFs in Asia-Pacific*,
https://doi.org/10.1007/978-3-030-12752-7_1

which enables unrestricted and unbounded flows of information and knowledge among geographically separated actors.

For decades, financial products were traded through physical venues where real-world buyers and sellers met to negotiate the prices and finalize transaction. What we read in Kauffman et al. (2015) speaks for itself: "(...) in the history of American financial markets is the 'Buttonwood Agreement' of May 1792, involving 24 stockbrokers in New York. The group established an early basis for the New York Stock Exchange by agreeing to trade with one another and no others (...). They initially met under an American sycamore tree (...) at 68 Wall Street" (Kauffman et al. 2015, p. 2). Today, due to multiple technological solutions, trading on stock exchange has been separated from physical locations. Broad expansion of ICT has led to *de-linking* of financial markets from geography. Technology, for decades, has been transforming the way that financial markets function and enhanced the emergence of various new, innovative financial products (or ways to trade them) (see, e.g., Hendershott et al. (2011), Menkveld (2018)). Most recent discussion in this field focuses on the various aspects of the emerging "fintech" industry that covers the new types of financial companies (Aldridge and Krawciw 2017; Dorfleitner et al. 2017; He et al. 2017). Even though the concept of fintech remains rather vague (i.e., no clear-cut definition is broadly accepted and applied), it can be understood as including companies that offer technology-enabled new or modified types of financial products and services.

One of the most rapidly growing categories of the innovative financial products is exchange-traded funds (ETFs), i.e., investment funds that combine the attributes of various categories of financial institutions and products and offer their users a range of previously unavailable investment possibilities. Shares of ETFs (in contrast with the conventional investment funds—mutual funds) are listed and traded on stock exchanges and can be bought or sold in a similar way as listed stocks, bonds, or derivatives. Growing popularity of ETFs, observable through the increases in the turnover of their units or the value of their assets, is predominantly enhanced by their innovative, distinctive attributes (Ferri 2009; Gastineau 2010; Agapova 2011; Hill et al. 2015; Abner 2016; Madhavan 2016; Meziani 2016; Lettau and Madhavan 2018). Global value of assets invested in ETFs reached in the end of 2017 a record-high value of approximately 4.5 trillion USD (Deutsche Bank 2017).

Growth dynamics of the ETFs markets in various countries differs significantly; and these discrepancies can be attributed to a number of factors, for instance, cross-country differences in the ICT penetration rates. Factors influencing the development of ETFs markets, especially in comparison to the other instruments offering similar investment exposure (e.g., stock index futures and options), remain to a large extent a topic neglected in scientific research (with a few exceptions including Gastineau (2010), Madhavan et al. (2014), Arnold and Lesné (2015), and Madhavan (2016)). It constitutes a significant research gap, especially taking into account growing size of many ETFs markets and the possible impact of these financial innovations on the global, regional, and local financial systems.

Asia-Pacific countries are currently of global interest. They are broadly perceived as those where huge part of global economic growth is "generated." Moreover, across Asia-Pacific region, we observe rapidly growing financial sector, which, undeniably, contributes significantly to the impressive dynamics of economic growth and development that a great majority of countries in these regions are currently experiencing. At a time, we observe rapid and profound transformations of Asia-Pacific financial markets, which, however, is accompanied by growing complexity and interconnectedness of these markets. Undoubtedly, Asia-Pacific financial markets are gaining growing importance in the global financial landscape. With regard to ETFs, this is evidenced by the position of the Asia-Pacific region that is third largest in the world in terms of assets (behind the United States and Europe (Deutsche Bank 2017)); in the country-specific dimension, some of the ETFs markets in this region are among the biggest in the world—the most notable example is Japan, with one of the oldest markets for this category of the financial innovations. However, countries such as China or South Korea have also experienced a substantial development of their ETFs markets.

Asia-Pacific financial systems are interesting for several reasons. In some ways they differ from financial sectors in, for instance, Europe or North America. In most Asia-Pacific economies, financial sectors are effectively dominated by banks that are highly regulated by the governments (see, for instance, China and India), and these banks are more focused on more traditional bank activities (e.g., lending or deposits) than on the capital markets. Asia-Pacific capital markets have also some distinguishing attributes. For example, many stock markets in the region are characterized by relatively high volatility (see, for instance, the Chinese stock market in 2015). In many Asia-Pacific countries, high popularity of the financial products linked to the commodities, e.g., precious metals, can be observed (it includes ETFs based on commodities). Moreover, yet another important feature is the high demand for the financial products with the leveraged returns (e.g., multiples of the stock market index)—one of the most striking examples is geared ETFs in Japan or South Korea that constitute a substantial fraction of the turnover of the ETFs' shares. However, regardless of these differences, Asia-Pacific financial markets demonstrate growing integration with global financial markets. They become more and more connected with the global financial system, which inevitably leads to the growing financial flows. What is important from the perspective of this book's topic is that Asia-Pacific countries are also those where, over the last several years, rapid spread and growth in use of financial innovations, like ETFs, are observed.

Asia-Pacific economies demonstrate enormous potential to develop, but this—to a great extent—is preconditioned by well-structured, stable, and resilient financial sector, which allows mobilizing resources and boosting productivity and, finally, economic growth. Bearing in mind significant changes that are currently observed across Asia-Pacific financial systems, it becomes obvious that these systems grow fast, become more complex, and are linked to financial systems in other regions of the world. In this context, introducing to Asia-Pacific financial markets various financial innovations becomes seminal. They offer not only new possibilities for the domestic investors but also boost integration with global financial markets and enhance international financial flows, thus generating savings allocation possibilities and strengthening financial systems, and hence deserve special interest.

1.2 The Purpose and Focus

The major objective of this book is to contribute to the present state of knowledge by exploring empirical links between the processes of diffusion of financial innovations—exchange-traded funds—and growing deployment of ICT across Asia-Pacific countries, between 2004 and 2017. We examine the evolutionary patterns of ETFs on selected Asia-Pacific stock exchanges and verify the hypothesized relationship between increasing ICT penetration and development of the ETFs markets. More specifically, this study is based on 12 economies from the Asia-Pacific region, namely, Australia, China, Hong Kong, India, Indonesia, Japan, Malaysia, New Zealand, Singapore, South Korea, Taiwan, and Thailand. We exhaustively discuss various issues related to ETFs, and, throughout the empirical parts of the book, we show their diffusion patterns on the selected financial markets in the Asia-Pacific region. In contrast with the existing literature, which concentrates mostly on the benefits and costs of ETFs for investors, we focus on the development of the ETFs markets (used as synonymous term to the diffusion of ETFs); thus we adopt a broader approach to the topic. Financial instruments used for comparison are innovative ones, i.e., ETFs, and conventional ones (more widely recognized and available for a much longer time period), i.e., stock index futures and stock index options. Next, to ensure a broad perspective for the analyzed process of development of financial innovations, we additionally provide the in-depth evidence on relationships between ICT penetration and diffusion of innovative financial instruments—ETFs, across countries in scope.

Put shortly, we examine the process of ETFs and ICT diffusion in the Asia-Pacific region, from four different perspectives, which are:

- Developing financial innovations diffusion trajectories across the Asia-Pacific stock exchanges
- Providing long-term predictions of financial innovations development across examined countries: trying to establish the possible future path of the ETFs market development in Asia-Pacific
- Examining key trends in the growing access to ICT as a prerequisite fostering global development and dynamic diffusion of financial innovations (here, ETFs)
- Verifying the hypothesis on the impact of growing ICT penetration on the development of the ETFs market in countries in scope (including both panel and country-specific estimates)

The time coverage of this study is fully subjected to data availability; exclusively for the period 2004–2017, the balanced dataset is acquirable for all countries included in the analysis. Financial instrument databases used for the research purposes include the dataset provided by the World Federation of Exchanges and data gathered from the local stock exchanges and other sources. The most important financial indicators used to achieve the stated aims are values of turnover (in USD millions) of the examined financial instruments on the selected stock exchanges: ETFs, stock index options, and stock index futures. Additionally, to achieve the empirical goals, we choose a set of variables that approximate each country's individual achievements in access to and usage of information and telecommunication technologies. Henceforth, we propose to use four core ICT indicators, which are exclusively extracted from the World Telecommunication/ICT Indicators database 2017 (20th Edition), namely, mobile-cellular telephony, fixed-broadband Internet, active mobile-broadband networks, and Internet users.

1.3 Structure and Chapters' Outline

This book comprises seven logically structured chapters. The first chapter is the introduction. Chapters 2 and 3 familiarize the reader with the theoretical and contextual background of this study. Next, Chaps. 4–6 demonstrate the results of our empirical analysis. Finally, Chap. 7 contains major conclusions and recommendations.

The following briefly presents main aims and scopes of the consecutive parts of this book.

Chapter 1 is the Introduction itself.

Chapter 2 is designed to provide theoretical framework for the empirical research regarding development of ETFs markets. The special emphasis is put on the innovative funds in the Asia-Pacific region. It discusses the basic mechanisms of ETFs, showing the role of various participants of the ETFs markets and distinguishing between primary and secondary markets. It compares ETFs to their main alternative in the financial system—mutual funds, showing relative advantages and disadvantages of both categories. Additionally, key events of the ETFs' history are described. After the introductory discussion, it presents the main categories of ETFs, classified according to the key criteria, including the replication method, distinction between passive and active funds, approaches to the rate of return in relation to their benchmarks, and types of underlying assets. The third part of the chapter is devoted to discussion of the definition of the ETFs market development, comparisons between ETFs and stock index derivatives (with the focus on the stock index arbitrage complex), presentation of applications of ETFs, and providing some insights into the topic of the determinants of the ETFs market development. Finally, it discusses the main characteristics of the Asia-Pacific ETFs markets—it presents the summary of their history, main market development statistics (in terms of assets, number, and other attributes), their structure, and position of ETFs in the Asia-Pacific investment industries (compared to mutual funds). It should be stressed that the empirical analysis in Chap. 2 is merely the introduction to the comprehensive analysis of the Asia-Pacific ETFs markets, diffusion of ETFs and the impact of ICT, whose results are outlined in the strictly empirical Chaps. 4 and 6.

Chapter 3 introduces the major aspects associated with the role of the new information and communication technologies (ICT) in economy and society, demonstrating channels of their potential impact in these two areas. In the first section, we present ICT as *General Purpose Technologies (GPTs)* (Bresnahan and Trajtenberg 1995)—technologies which, by generating deep structural and qualitative changes, pervasively impact society and economy. Bresnahan and Trajtenberg (1995) underline that broad adoption of General Purpose Technologies fosters radical changes of social norms and structures, which leads to transformation of social systems and ways of doing business, heavily impacting growth of productivity (Helpman 1998) and—at a time—providing solid background for long-term economic growth and development. Importantly to note, also in the context of our study, dynamic diffusion of ICT is broadly observed in countries, which never before have widely adopted "old" technological solutions, and the latter predominantly was a consequence of infrastructural and geographical barriers, lack of financial resources, or lack of knowledge on the use of these technologies. Additionally, inspired by works of, inter alia, Hanna (2003, 2010), we provide brief discussion on how ICT may constitute an important determinant of long-term economic growth and development. We claim that ICT allow for unbounded flows of information (reducing the information asymmetries) and access to global markets and mobilize resources, especially labor force, stimulating economic growth, and all these make these technologies of special importance when various aspects of economic growth and development are considered. After discussing the general role of ICT in the economy, it focuses on the impact of the new technologies on the development of the financial system, in particular with regard to the financial markets. Due to the prevalence of the equity ETFs, the discussion concentrates on the impact of ICT on the stock markets; the effects regarding other parts of the financial system are mentioned briefly. It also presents some of the contemporary issues linked with the ICT adoption in the financial system, such as the broadly understood fintech. The final part of the chapter is devoted to the linkages between the adoption of ICT and development of ETFs markets (i.e., diffusion of ETFs). It starts with the presentation of general remarks concerning factors affecting the diffusion of ETFs, then it discusses the impact of ICT on the demand and supply side of the ETFs market, and, finally, it shows some contemporary examples of the ICT adoption in the investment industry, above all in the selected segments of the fintech sector. Throughout the chapter, both theoretical concepts and results of the empirical research are presented.

Chapter 4 comprises results of the empirical analysis of ETFs markets in the Asia-Pacific region. It provides an overview of the current state of development of ETFs markets (i.e., diffusion of ETFs) in 12 countries: Australia, China, Hong Kong, India, Indonesia, Japan, Malaysia, New Zealand, Singapore, South Korea, Taiwan, and Thailand. First, it presents and compares their level of development in terms of turnover of ETFs and provides short characteristics of all markets, including their structures and features of the key categories of ETFs used in various countries. Additionally, it covers the key trends of the Asia-Pacific regional ETFs market in terms of turnover (and number of listed funds) as well as the inequalities concerning diffusion of ETFs in the region. Second, this part of the research demonstrates the results regarding ETFs diffusion, i.e., ETFs market development. ETFs market development is considered in two perspectives: as the value of turnover of ETFs on the local exchanges (absolute approach) or as the share of ETFs in the total turnover of index instruments on the local exchanges (relative approach). Analysis of the ETFs market development is conducted using the models of diffusion of innovation. In the final part of the chapter, results of projections of the diffusion of ETFs in the Asia-Pacific region are presented. Calculations are based on monthly data for the years 2004–2017. Exclusively the turnover on the stock exchanges is examined.

Chapter 5 is also entirely empirical, and it extensively discusses the process of ICT diffusion across 12 Asia-Pacific economies, between 1990 and 2017. It provides a detailed analysis of country-specific ICT diffusion curves with respect to four core ICT indicators: mobile-cellular telephony, fixed-broadband and active mobile-broadband networks, and Internet users. It shows the unique features of this process in each of examined economies; it demonstrates its dynamic and specific patterns. It also briefly discusses the emerging technological substitution process, which demonstrates gradual switching from "old" technology to "new" technology. All data used in this chapter are exclusively extracted from World Telecommunications/ICT Indicators database 2017 and 2018.

Next, Chap. 6 continues the empirical analysis of the ETFs markets in the Asia-Pacific region by attempting to identify the links between the development of ETFs markets (i.e., diffusion of ETFs) and ICT penetration. Time period of the analysis in this chapter is 2004–2016—calculations are based on annual data. The chapter begins with the brief discussion of the basic evidence on the turnover of ETFs in the annual perspective. In the next part of the chapter, we present the evidence on the relationship between ETFs and ICT on the regional level. Our analysis starts with the discussion of the graphical evidence, and, subsequently, we examine the estimates of the panel models. We focus on the relationships between the value of the turnover of ETFs in USD millions (applied as indicator of the absolute development of the ETFs market) and three indicators of ICT adoption: fixed-broadband subscriptions per 100 inhabitants, active mobile-broadband subscriptions per 100 inhabitants, and Internet users per 100 inhabitants. In the final part of the chapter, we examine the country-level linkages between ETFs and ICT, starting with the brief overview of the graphical evidence, followed by the estimates of the country-specific models. In case of each country, analysis covers the attributes of the diffusion of ETFs and any other issues that may be identified as being significant for the analyzed relationships (in particular the local fintech industries). We devote most attention to the largest ETFs markets in the region: China, Hong Kong, Japan, and South Korea.

This book ends with Chap. 7 discussing main findings and conclusions of the performed analysis (including predictions for the upcoming years).

Arguably the main value of this book consists in presenting the audience joint analysis of both the process of adoption of new information and communication technologies and the fast development and spread of innovative financial products. Undoubtedly, these are closely interrelated, and the evidence from Asia-Pacific markets speaks for itself. We believe that even though the analysis of the ETFs market development and links between ETFs and ICT is conducted using the sample of Asia-Pacific countries, our conclusions may also be applied for countries in other regions of the world as the main trajectory of the processes and their key factors seem rather similar. We also hope that this book paves road ahead for further research and analysis of these important issues.

References

Abner, D. (2016). *The ETF handbook. How to value and trade exchange-traded funds* (2nd ed.). Hoboken, NJ: Wiley.

Agapova, A. (2011). Conventional mutual index funds versus exchange-traded funds. *Journal of Financial Markets, 14*(2), 323–343.

Aldridge, I., & Krawciw, S. (2017). *Real-time risk: What investors should know about FinTech, high-frequency trading, and flash crashes*. Hoboken, NJ: Wiley.

Arnold, M., & Lesné, A. (2015). *The changing landscape for beta replication – Comparing futures and ETFs for Equity Index Exposure*. Boston, MA: State Street Global Advisors.

Bresnahan, T. F., & Trajtenberg, M. (1995). General purpose technologies: 'Engines of growth'? *Journal of Econometrics, Annals of Econometrics, 65*(1), 83–108.

Cerny, P. G. (1994). The dynamics of financial globalization: Technology, market structure, and policy response. *Policy Sciences, 27*(4), 319–342.

Deutsche Bank. (2017, December). *European monthly ETF market review synthetic equity & index strategy*.

Dorfleitner, G., Hornuf, L., Schmitt, M., & Weber, M. (2017). *FinTech in Germany*. Berlin: Springer.

Ferri, R. A. (2009). *The ETF book: All you need to know about exchange-traded funds. Updated edition*. Hoboken, NJ: Wiley.

Gastineau, G. L. (2010). *The exchange-traded funds manual* (2nd ed.). Hoboken, NJ: Wiley.

He, D., Leckow, R., Haksar, V., Mancini-Griffoli, T., Jenkinson, N., Kashima, M., Khiaonarong, T., Rochon, C., & Tourpe, H. (2017). *FinTech and financial services: Initial considerations*. Washington, DC: International Monetary Fund.

Helpman, E. (1998). *General purpose technologies and economic growth*. Cambridge, MA: MIT Press.

Hendershott, T., Jones, C. M., & Menkveld, A. J. (2011). Does algorithmic trading improve liquidity? *The Journal of Finance, 66*(1), 1–33.

Hill, J. M., Nadig, D., & Hougan, M. (2015). *A comprehensive guide to exchange-traded funds (ETFs)*. Charlottesville, VA: CFA Institute Research Foundation.

Kauffman, R. J., Hu, Y., & Ma, D. (2015). Will high-frequency trading practices transform the financial markets in the Asia Pacific Region? *Financial Innovation, 1*(1), 1–27.

Lettau, M., & Madhavan, A. (2018). Exchange-traded funds 101 for economists. *Journal of Economic Perspectives, 32*(1), 135–154.

Madhavan, A. N. (2016). *Exchange-traded funds and the new dynamics of investing*. Oxford: Oxford University Press.

Madhavan, A. N., Marchioni, U., Li, W., & Du, D. Y. (2014). Equity ETFs versus index futures: A comparison for fully funded investors. *The Journal of Index Investing, 5*(2), 66–75.

Menkveld, A. J. (2018). High-frequency trading as viewed through an electron microscope. *Financial Analysts Journal, 74*(2), 24–31.

Meziani, A. S. (2016). *Exchange-traded funds: Investment practices and tactical approaches*. London: Palgrave Macmillan.

Chapter 2
Exchange-Traded Funds: Concepts and Contexts

2.1 Exchange-Traded Funds: History and Features

Section 2.1 focuses on the history and main features of the exchange-traded funds (ETFs). We begin by presenting the context of the launch of world's first ETFs in North America, followed by the brief discussion concerning their spread to other regions. Then we discuss the basic mechanisms of these funds, i.e., their launch, distribution, and turnover, showing the role of various participants of the ETFs markets and distinguishing between primary and secondary markets. Finally, we compare ETFs to their main alternative in the financial system—mutual funds—showing the similarities and differences between the both categories of investment funds.

In order to be able to adequately discuss multiple issues linked with ETFs, it seems necessary to first define them and describe their position in the financial system. There are many definitions of ETFs, some of them slightly different, depending on the feature which is considered as the most significant by the particular author (individual or organization). We do not present the detailed overview of various concepts but rather cite a few most representative (and most often applied) ones.

We start by presenting definitions of some of the most influential organizations linked with the global financial markets. International Monetary Fund defines ETFs as a "type of collective investment vehicle traded on an exchange (…)" (International Monetary Fund 2015, p. 139). Investment Company Institute (ICI), an association of the US mutual funds and similar companies, uses the following definition: "investment company (…) whose shares are traded intraday on stock exchanges at market-determined prices (…)" (see "Glossary" in Investment Company Institute (2017, p. 271)). Very similar definition (yet slightly abbreviated) may be found in the online glossary of The International Investment Funds Association (IIFA) that groups investment company's associations from various countries. ETFs are also defined by the regulatory bodies; for instance, the International Organization of Securities Commissions (IOSCO) states that they are "open ended collective investment schemes (CIS) that trade throughout the day like a stock (…) (g)enerally,

A. Marszk et al., *The Emergence of ETFs in Asia-Pacific*,
https://doi.org/10.1007/978-3-030-12752-7_2

ETFs seek to replicate the performance of a target index (..) investors may trade ETF shares continuously at market prices (…)" (The International Organization of Securities Commissions 2013, p. 1).

The topic of ETFs has been covered in many publications over the recent years, albeit from different perspectives—these differences are evidenced to some extent by the varying definitions adopted by the authors of such publications. In one of the first comprehensive publications on ETFs (the first edition was published in 2002 when ETFs were still rather "exotic" part of the financial system; second in 2010), G. Gastineau claims that they are financial products whose distinguishing feature is the possibility to trade them "throughout the day at market-determined prices that are close to the intraday value of an underlying portfolio or index (…)" (Gastineau 2010, p. 2). In a much more recent, very interesting overview of some of the main issues concerning ETFs, written by the experienced market professionals and published by the CFA Institute, ETFs are defined as "hybrid investment products, with many of the investment features of mutual funds married to the trading features of common stocks" (Hill et al. 2015, p. 2). Another prominent figure of the global ETF industry and academic research in this field, A.N. Madhavan (who held managing positions at the largest providers of ETFs), writes that it is "an investment vehicle that trades intraday and seeks to replicate the performance of a specific index" (Madhavan 2016, p. 3). It is also useful to refer to the definition of the largest financial institution that manages these funds, i.e., BlackRock—very brief and similar in-kind definitions of ETFs may be found on various websites of this company, e.g., "funds that trade like a stock" (website of the Canadian branch) or "a diversified collection of assets (…) that trades on an exchange (like a stock)" (US website).

To supplement the conceptual discussion, it should be added that the widespread inclination to stress the (financial) "innovation" part of the ETFs' definition may be noted in various publications (see, e.g., the description of ETFs in the abovementioned publications such as Gastineau (2010) or Hill et al. (2015) but also Deville (2008), Diaz-Rainey and Ibikunle (2012), Schoenfeld (2015), Hill (2016), Amenc et al. (2017), Ben-David et al. (2017), Dannhauser (2017)).We may thus state that ETFs are regarded by most authors as a category of financial innovations. In-depth discussion regarding the concepts of financial innovations lies outside the scope of this book—we will thus only briefly justify the designation of ETFs as a type of this phenomenon by referring to the main concepts of innovations in the financial sector. It should be stressed that they are usually derived from the more general concepts of innovatory activity, such as the prominent theories of J.A. Schumpeter.

The concept of financial innovation formulated in the time period close to the emergence of first ETFs may be summarized as the launch of securities which offer some novel features (Allen and Gale 1989)—this definition undeniably anticipates well the main idea of ETFs and indicates the trends in the financial industry in the late 1980s and early 1990s. More recently, financial innovations are viewed as the creation and popularization of new financial instruments (as well as new technologies, etc. (Lerner and Tufano 2011; Diaz-Rainey and Ibikunle 2012)) or, in a slightly different approach, as new financial products, services, organizational forms, and production processes (Frame and White 2012). Indisputably, ETFs can be described by these definitions; to emphasize this point, it should be added that they are usually listed as a notable example of financial innovation in the publications on this topic.

Based on the preceding paragraphs, we formulate our own extended definition of ETFs that encapsulates their main attributes but, at the same time, is sufficiently general to be applied in various contexts (in a range of comparative perspectives). ETFs are *innovative investment funds, accessible through their shares which, having the form of equity securities, are listed and usually continuously traded and priced on one or more stock exchanges (or similar trading venues); the creation and redemption of the shares is a continuous process, and their number is not fixed.* Two additional attributes are: first, the returns on the fund's shares are tied to the benchmark, and, second, the name of the fund with "ETF" or similar label indicates its character; there are, though, some exceptions which do not fulfill the extra criteria such as active funds (with regard to the first criterion).

It must be added that we do not designate ETFs unequivocally as "investment companies," "investment vehicles," "(investment) funds," "financial instruments," "securities," "financial products," etc. as in other definitions—we believe that all those denotations are correct, depending mostly on the particular feature of ETFs which is considered as most fundamental in their formulation (e.g., whether the focus is on ETFs as alternatives to mutual funds (then the first three terms seem most correct) or their availability on stock exchanges (then "instruments" or "securities" would be more proper but the other terms obviously remain correct). Throughout the text we use various terms, but "innovative funds" is most prevalent as it refers to the attributes of ETFs (and their full name) or "innovative financial products."

History of ETFs is relatively short, particularly when compared with the other similar products available in the financial sector such as mutual funds or closed-end funds. Even exchange-traded stock index derivatives, which will be contrasted with ETFs in Sect. 2.3, had already been quite established on the major financial markets at the time of the introduction of first ETFs. Interestingly, at the time when the idea of ETFs had been considered by the pioneers which resulted in the first attempts to launch the innovative funds, financial futures or options had still been considered financial innovations (Miller 1986)—nowadays such denotation is rarely used which underlines one of the important (and rather obvious) aspects of the innovations (not only in the financial sector): the passage of time changes the position of various products, and innovative ones sooner or later enter the mainstream of the market and in the next years usually are slowly becoming increasingly outdated which is clearly presented by the diffusion models (see our discussion in Chap. 4 and presentation of the methodological issues in the annex).

The development of the products directly preceding ETFs and first funds which may be included in this category had not taken place in a vacuum—it had been strongly influenced by the discussion of the financial academics and professionals at that time which, most generally, concerned the benefits of "passive" investing, i.e., tracking (mirroring) the returns of selected benchmarks (usually some indexes of financial markets), contrasted with the prevalent concept of "active" investing which focuses on reaching results favorable relative to the benchmark, controlling for the risk level. This debate, with substantial practical implications (such as the launch of first passive mutual funds in the 1970s—called "index funds" (Bogle 2016)), had been spurred by the academic research in the field of portfolio theory and capital market efficiency (groundbreaking concepts regarding efficiency had been suggested by E.F. Fama (1965, 1970) and the famous book that covered the advantages of the indexing investment strategy by B. Malkiel (new editions are still updated and published for the most recent one see Malkiel (2016))). The former, new element of the financial sciences had been initiated by the works of H. Markowitz (1952) and further developed within increasingly more sophisticated models of capital markets—capital asset pricing model (CAPM), arbitrage pricing theory (APT), and Fama-French three-factor model (Sharpe 1964; Ross 1976; Fama and French 1993), just to mention the most famous ones. We do not present them in detail as it is not the topic of this book—we just want to emphasize noticeable theoretical and practical dynamism and innovational wave in the investment industry surrounding the materialization of first ETFs.

Prehistory of ETFs, apart from the abovementioned development of index funds (which were and still are a modification of conventional mutual funds, not a new type of investment vehicle), is associated with the launch of their direct predecessors in the United States: equity market-linked products offered by two US stock exchanges (ultimately regulatory reservations prohibited their listing which stopped further developments) as well as hybrid investment fund called "SuperTrust"; the latter had some features of ETFs, but its limitations (such as a predefined 3 years lifetime of the fund) prevented it from gaining broader recognition and popularity (Ferri 2009). Discussion on the relative benefits and costs of the passive investing as contrasted with the active investing is still one of the important topics for both financial professionals and academics—see, among many, the works of Stein and Narasimhan (1999), Malkiel (2003), French (2008), Pástor and Stambaugh (2012), Foster and Warren (2016), and Pedersen (2018).

Globally, first investment fund which meets the basic requirements of the ETF's concept was launched in Canada in 1990, on the Toronto Stock Exchange (Foucher and Gray 2014); however, initially its name (or marketing materials) did not include "ETF" as this term was announced and popularized a few years later. According to most authors, the start of the global ETFs market should rather be traced back to the early 1993 when SPDR S&P 500 Trust (informally known as "spider"; again, the label "ETF" was not used) was introduced in the United States—currently it is the largest ETF in the world, partially due to the obvious first-mover advantage. The third country, where funds that may be defined as ETFs were introduced as early as in 1995, was Japan (history of ETFs in Asia-Pacific is examined more closely in Sect. 2.4). However, during most of the 1990s, the development of the ETFs markets was limited to the United States. The second US-listed ETF was launched in 1995, and the number of the innovative funds in that country grew substantially a year later when 13 funds linked to the non-US equity markets were launched (Gastineau 2010) which meant a considerable increase in the emerging industry's diversity. Over the next years, the US market experienced even more rapid growth in all dimensions, marked by the launch of funds linked to the fixed-income market (formerly there were exclusively equity ETFs), commodity ETFs, sector ETFs, enhanced indexing ETFs, geared ETFs, and many others (see Sect. 2.2); in 2007 the first active ETF was started in the United States which meant a considerable abandoning of the basic idea of ETFs as passive investing tools—even though active ETFs remain a rather exotic category (with minimal market share), their concept has been expanded, as evidenced by the launch of exchange-traded managed funds (in 2016) which blur the active versus passive distinction even more (Madhavan 2016).

The development of the ETFs markets was not limited to North America (or Japan but in that country for a few years there was only one ETF so it may hardly be marked as an example of significant adoption of innovative funds)—by the end of the 1990s, leading providers of the ETFs in the United States attempted to reproduce their increasingly more noticeable success in other regions. First European-listed ETFs were launched in 1999 (according to other sources in 2000); the expansion of ETFs in Europe started in countries such as Switzerland, Germany, and the United Kingdom (Hill et al. 2015); in Latin America the history of the locally listed ETF started in 2002 in Mexico which over the years has become a significant example of the diffusion of ETFs in an emerging economy. Finally, African ETFs markets are still almost nonexistent (except for one country, i.e., South Africa) which may be explained by their relatively low level of financial system's development. To summarize, it may be stated that less after a decade since their introduction in the first countries, these innovative funds were launched on most major financial markets. Over the next years in almost all cases, substantial development of the ETFs markets has been observed, regardless of the region. Moreover, it is worth mentioning that the trend of increasingly stronger position of ETFs in the world's major financial systems has not been interrupted even by the 2008 global financial crisis or regional-scale events such as eurozone debt crisis.

Now we turn our attention to the basic mechanisms of ETFs—it should be stressed that there are some between-country differences or dissimilarities in case of various categories of these funds. We present, though, some features that are common for most funds; our discussion is based mostly on the ETF model which dominates on the largest market, i.e., in the United States as it serves as the reference point for most other countries. Moreover, we focus on the mechanisms of the most basic and popular group of ETFs—passive equity funds (for the description of the main attributes of the other categories, see Sect. 2.2). Issues specific for the Asia-Pacific region are discussed in Sect. 2.4. Interestingly, fundamental rules of the launch and further operations of the basic ETFs have not changed considerably since the introduction of the pioneering funds.

There are three key entities involved in the creation of the fund and its operation: fund's provider (also labeled "sponsor"—we use both names), authorized participants (APs; plural linked with the fact that there are usually multiple APs for each fund), and, last but not least, investors (financial institutions or retail investors) whose role is crucial for the success of the entire process. ETF landscape is naturally not limited to these participants, but the tasks of the rest are mostly technical and supplementary in relation to the three main groups. In our description we skip the legal, administrative, or similar details as they are not relevant in the context of further theoretical discussion and empirical analysis (with some exceptions that are presented in the subsequent sections).

Decision to launch the fund (usually based on extensive market research or business strategy) is made by the financial corporation which becomes its provider and is responsible for its management, i.e., operations required to reach the financial aims stated in the fund's policy documents (in most cases, tracking the benchmark, see discussion in the next paragraphs). Fund's provider launches an ETF through initial public offering (IPO). This well-known term is also used to describe the process which takes place in case of companies which decide to go public and list their shares—in both cases it is linked with the admission of shares to the listing on exchange and takes place on the "primary" market. During IPO of a company, its shares are sold among investors (institutional or retail) who may later conduct transactions on the stock exchange or other trading venue; even though stock offering is not a one-time event, and the company may offer more shares in the future, due to, e.g., costs, the offerings do not take place on a daily or monthly basis (further offerings can, though, obviously no longer be called IPO). Primary market of the ETFs is radically different as evidenced by two facts (we omit the other, less relevant differences). First, before the ETF's IPO, fund's provider enters agreements with entities which will act as authorized participants. Shares of the fund are distributed during IPO exclusively among APs who later conduct transactions with investors but outside the primary market (details of these processes are described below). Second difference in comparison to company's stocks is the frequency of the offerings on the primary market—in case of ETFs, they take place on continuous basis as it is required for the proper functioning of the funds.

Transactions linked with the fund's IPO or further offerings are not the only activities on the primary market; moreover, the details of the market processes may seem complicated when contrasted with the stock market—therefore, the design of the ETF primary market needs to be presented in detail in order to fully understand the uniqueness of ETFs and explain their innovative character. Majority of key decisions concerning the primary market are made by APs and depend on the trends on the secondary market, i.e., activities of investors who buy or sell the fund's shares. When the demand increases, APs sell the shares from their inventory. However, at some point, they have to replenish their stocks—it is one of the moments when they enter the primary market and creation of the fund's shares takes place. Regardless whether it is the IPO of the fund or transaction during its further lifetime, the course of these transactions, called "creation" of the ETF's shares, is very similar. In order to receive the shares from the provider, APs deliver a prespecified basket of securities ("creation basket"—its composition is established by the provider and in most cases resembles the securities followed by the fund) in exchange for a basket of the fund's shares (Hill et al. 2015). Conducting such transactions too often and using a few shares would be too costly for both sides which means that providers impose certain limits on the minimum number of involved shares—most frequently "creation units," i.e., multiples of the shares (e.g., 50,000), are applied to make the process more cost- and time-efficient. Sometimes cash is also used in these transactions, for instance, to supplement the baskets in case of some minor differences between value of the creation baskets and creation units. What needs to be emphasized is that the transaction may also involve delivery of not only securities but also some other financial or nonfinancial assets, yet such design is rather rare. Another important point in the context of the fund's features is the issue of the net asset value (NAV), one of the key parameters of ETFs. NAV of the ETF's share is calculated as the per share difference between the value of the fund's assets and its liabilities. On the primary market, it is used to indicate the necessary value of the creation basket when converted into creation units, and on secondary market it serves as reference point in assessing the arbitrage opportunities. Intraday indicative value (IIV) is published by the provider of ETF even more frequently than NAV, usually during the trading hours, as it facilitates arbitrage operations (Lettau and Madhavan 2018).

In the preceding paragraphs, we described the process of the fund's shares creation. However, in order to ensure proper functioning of the fund, opposite transactions must take place as well. They are labeled as the "redemption" of the fund's shares (Hill et al. 2015). The basic motivation of the APs to engage in such operation is the decreasing demand for the fund's shares. APs planning to reduce the amount of such securities in their inventory contact the provider in order to redeem the owned shares. In exchange they will receive a basket of securities called "redemption basket" (again the exact amounts of the fund's shares and the other securities are calculated using NAV); its composition usually resembles closely the creation basket. APs may then sell these securities or use them in other way. What is worth underlining is that in fact role of the provider in both creation and redemption of the shares is mostly passive as it simply responds to the actions undertaken by APs and does not initiate them. On some markets APs are also market-makers, while on other there are no such entities or other corporations that are responsible for such operations.

Two types of primary market processes outlined in the preceding paragraphs are together called the ETF's "in-kind" creation and redemption (Gastineau 2010; Elton et al. 2018) and are perceived as one of the most innovative and distinguishing features of these funds in the financial system. In-kind transactions cover an exchange of one particular group of securities (here creation or redemption basket) for the other particular group (shares of the fund). In all other types of investment funds (i.e., other than ETFs), creation or redemption of their units involves cash payments, and in-kind transfer is not allowed; however, as we show later, in case of some groups of ETFs, in-kind transfers are not used.

Strongly linked with the in-kind creation and redemption is another fundamental process concerning ETFs—arbitrage mechanism—regarded also as one of the substantial distinctive aspects of the innovative funds. Central role in this mechanism is played by APs. They can engage in the arbitrage operations if they notice discrepancies between the NAV of the fund's shares (which is a direct function of the tracked securities' prices) and prices of these shares on the secondary ETFs market. If conducted correctly, APs may gain some (usually very limited) profits. For example, in the scenario when secondary market prices of the fund's shares exceed their NAV, APs could buy the tracked securities on the market or use their inventory, form the creation basket, and deliver it to the provider in exchange for the creation unit.

Fund's shares obtained in the creation unit may then be sold to the participants of the secondary ETFs market which would generate gains for the arbitrageur (there may be no gains after accounting for the transaction costs or other expenses (Gastineau 2010; Charupat and Miu 2013)—the reason why very small deviations will not be eliminated due to their unprofitability; arbitrage may also be hindered in case of, e.g., funds that track securities that are listed on the foreign markets (Lettau and Madhavan 2018)). Transaction would be conducted in the reverse manner if opposite discrepancies are noticed. If the arbitrage activity of APs is sufficiently large, market-determined price of the affected shares and their NAV should at least partially converge. However, results of the empirical research conducted by ICI with regard to the US ETFs market (Antoniewicz and Heinrichs 2014) prove that APs tend to access primary market rather infrequently which indicates that the significance of the arbitrage mechanism is overstated. More favorable taxation in some countries is yet another benefit of the in-kind transfer in comparison to the procedures used by conventional investment funds. The issue of the arbitrage linked to ETFs has in the recent years been a subject of many empirical studies whose results are highly inconclusive—see, for example, Aditya and Desai (2015), Swathy (2015), Broman (2016), Kreis et al. (2016), Badenhorst (2017), Petajisto (2017), Kreis and Licht (2018), Piccotti (2018), and Zaremba and Andreu (2018).

There is one issue concerning the basic mechanisms of ETFs which remains to be covered—the responsibilities of the fund's provider. Apart from the obvious marketing and administrative tasks, and participation in the operations with APs, its key role is linked to ensuring that the fund's financial aims are reached (again, in order to simplify the discussion, we focus on the passive equity funds—in other types of funds the activities of providers may differ; their market share is, though, still much lower). First fundamental decision (which must be taken before the fund's inception) is the choice of its benchmark, usually some well-known stock market index, published and calculated by one of the major index providers such as S&P—using selected index requires payments of the licensing fee. Selection of the benchmark influences the basic attributes of the fund: composition of the creation and redemption baskets, securities held in the fund's portfolio, management strategy, its costs, and, above all, the category of market participants interested in investing in its shares (i.e., positioning of the fund on the market—the way it will be classified among other funds) and the fund's attractiveness in comparison to other similar financial products. After the launch of the fund, its provider is responsible for maintaining the returns in the declared relation to the benchmark: in case of elementary passive equity funds presented in this section, it means that the returns on the fund's share should be as close as possible to the returns of the index—they should track them; in case of other types of funds, it may mean, for instance, gaining some multiple of the return on the index (see description of the leveraged ETFs in Sect. 2.2). Two measures can be used by investors to gauge how well the fund's provider is fulfilling this basic task: tracking difference and tracking error. Tracking difference is a very simple measure as it is calculated as the difference between the returns of the benchmark and the returns on the fund's shares (Madhavan 2016). Tracking error is more sophisticated and much more frequently applied indicator. The most common method to calculate it in the ETF sector is to annualize the standard deviation of the differences between the returns of the benchmark and the returns on the fund's shares, computed for each trading day (Kosev and Williams 2011; Nikbakht et al. 2016); for alternative methods of calculation, see Charupat and Miu (2013). Tracking difference and tracking error are frequently used to compare various funds utilized in passive strategies (not only ETFs but also, e.g., index mutual funds) and, in addition to various cost indicators, are among the basic parameters considered in the investment decisions. With regard to both tracking difference and tracking error, lower values are preferred by investors.

Minimization of the tracking difference and error in ETFs is facilitated by the already mentioned arbitrage mechanism, but its proper execution requires adequate management of the fund's portfolio which influences, e.g., the composition of the creation and redemption basket. There are various strategies employed by the providers, and they can be most generally divided into full and optimized replication (Ramaswamy 2011). Full replication is a purchase of the entire basket of securities which are included in the tracked index, with their shares in the total portfolio equal to the ones used in the index calculation. When full replication is too costly or may not be applied for some other reasons, optimized replication is an alternative—instead of purchasing all securities in the exact index proportions, provider buys only selected constituents which are predicted to most accurately follow the index returns (Meziani 2016; Golub et al. 2018). Optimized replication is less expensive than full method, but its drawback is larger tracking difference and error.

Before we discuss further issues, it needs to be stressed that the mechanisms of the ETFs primary market and operations of providers presented in the preceding paragraphs are used in case of the oldest and most popular funds, known as "physical" funds. However, in some regions, an alternative, substantially distinctive approach to the fund's design has emerged (due to, e.g., tracking error reduction attempts)—for more details, see the beginning of Sect. 2.2.

Secondary market is the next segment of the ETFs market, inextricably connected with the primary part—ETFs cannot operate without one or the other. In contrast with the primary market, the secondary market for the shares of ETFs closely resembles its stock counterpart, with some minor differences stemming from the characteristics of the innovative funds such as the activities of APs (Hill et al. 2015). Shares of ETFs may be traded on either regulated exchanges or other trading venues, depending on the local regulations. Participants of the secondary markets (retail and institutional investors as well as other entities such as APs or market-makers) trade in the shares of ETFs, introduced on the market by APs. For most investors transactions are conducted through brokerage accounts and are linked with commissions and other costs. In the vast majority of cases, shares of ETFs are purchased not from other investors but rather from APs, market-makers, or other financial corporations with easy access to large amounts of the fund's shares. Exact structure and mechanisms of the secondary ETFs market are to large extent country-specific. Substantial feature of the trading in the ETF's shares its access to transactions and instruments typical for stocks such as short positions or (in some countries) derivative contracts—futures and options based on the shares of

ETFs (Madhavan 2016); ETF futures are, though, much less popular than options. From the market-broad perspective, operations of the secondary market participants, who notice the differences (usually very small and short term) between prices of the fund's shares and the prices of the tracked assets, and attempt to gain profits by "arbitraging" this discrepancy, contribute to the decrease of the tracking difference and error.

An important, yet frequently neglected feature of the innovative funds, which is a direct consequence of the outlined duality of the ETFs market (with considerably different primary and secondary market), are two types of prices of their shares as it was already indicated in the outline of the APs arbitrage mechanism. The first price is the one applied on the primary market (Ferri 2009). NAV of the fund's shares is calculated (usually by the provider) once a day (with some infrequent exceptions) and is the binding price applied in the creation and redemption process. However, as already noted, the approximation of NAV, IIV, is published much more frequently during trading hours. The second price, the secondary market one, is determined in the course of transactions between various investors, according to the rules of the particular trading venue (in the overwhelming majority of cases, it is determined continuously during trading hours, but it may be calculated, e.g., only once a day)—most generally it depends on the demand and supply which in turn are influenced by a variety of factors (see Sect. 2.3), among them the situation on the markets for the tracked securities and behavior of APs or similar entities. Various arbitrage mechanisms should lead to convergence of the two prices, yet some disparities may persist, for instance, when problems with proper valuation of the tracked securities occur (Lettau and Madhavan 2018).

Due to the historical reasons underlying the launch of first ETFs and, above all, because of their key attributes, these innovative funds are broadly recognized as alternatives to mutual funds, in particular index mutual funds (subcategory of mutual funds whose investment aims place them in the group of passive funds). More formally, in order to avoid unnecessary ambiguities, we start by citing the relevant definition of both mutual funds and index mutual funds. It should be underlined that we regard the terms "mutual fund" and "open-end fund" as synonyms (which may be considered a more "traditional" approach), even though in some (especially relatively recent) classifications mutual funds are a broader category which may also include ETFs. IIFA provides a few definitions, from various member associations—we combine their key elements. Therefore "mutual fund" may be defined as an investment fund that pools funds of unit[1] holders and invests in various securities to meet a specified financial objective; mutual fund stands ready to buy back its units from investors at their current NAV—it means that it continuously issues and redeems units. According to IIFA, "index mutual fund" (or simply "index fund") is a mutual fund designed to track (mirror, duplicate) the performance of a particular market index; its portfolio mirrors the designated market index.

[1] Instead of "units" the term "shares" may also be used, but we decided to use "shares" with reference to ETFs and "units" when discussing mutual funds in order to emphasize the basic difference – shares of ETFs are exchange-traded, while units of mutual funds are not.

Before discussing the differences between ETFs and mutual funds, which are of crucial significance in order to understand some factors strongly influencing the development of ETFs markets, it is first necessary to indicate the common features of both categories. Both ETFs and mutual funds are managed by employees of financial institutions, often parts of large multinational corporations, and need to adhere to extensive regulatory requirements. Furthermore, the basic idea of both categories is identical and common for all types of investment funds—investors may purchase their shares or units in order to become an owner of a proportional part of the managed assets and expect to reach the financial aim stated in the fund's policy. Similar ETFs and mutual funds may be adopted in comparable strategies; the choice of the particular fund depends on, among others, its cost (Hill et al. 2015). Using both groups of funds is not free for investors as various costs are incurred.

The differences between the innovative funds—ETFs and traditional ones—and mutual funds are summarized in Table 2.1. An important point to emphasize is that the rapidly growing diversity of ETFs (see Sect. 2.2) has led to the questioning of the approach which was prevalent until recently, i.e., regarding ETFs as an alternative to exclusively one category of mutual funds—index-tracking. Currently, on major financial markets (particularly in the United States), ETFs have become

Table 2.1 Key dissimilarities between exchange-traded funds and mutual funds

Attribute	Exchange-traded funds	Mutual funds
Distribution channels	Transactions in shares listed at an exchange using brokerage account; available also through other channels, e.g., wealth management companies	Unavailable through brokerage accounts; distributed through other channels, e.g., wealth management companies
Pricing of the fund's shares or units	Two types of prices: on the primary market determined by the managing company; on the secondary market established in the course of market transactions, i.e., depend on the interaction of demand and supply	Single price determined by the managing company
Transparency of portfolio's (holdings) composition	Typically published daily	Generally published monthly or quarterly
Derivatives based on the fund's shares or units	Both futures and options are available	Not available due to lack of exchange-listing feature
Tracking errors/ tracking differences (*refers exclusively to passive funds*)	Arbitrage mechanism of passive ETFs facilitates keeping them at lower level than in index mutual funds	In index mutual funds usually higher than in ETFs
Product range and international availability	Broad product range, available on major advanced markets and some emerging	Very broad product range, available in most countries

Source: Own compilation based on Ferri (2009), Gastineau (2010), Agapova (2011), Charupat and Miu (2013), Cameron (2015), Hill et al. (2015), Abner (2016), Madhavan (2016), Nikbakht et al. (2016), Chang et al. (2018), Farinella and Kubicki (2018), and Lettau and Madhavan (2018)

counterparts of most types of mutual funds; in some areas range of available ETFs is even broader. It means that, with some caveats (regarding aspects typical for passive funds), ETFs may be considered to be substitutes for the entire category of mutual funds.

From the investor's perspective, one of the main differences between ETFs and mutual funds is the way they can be accessed. Shares of ETFs can be bought or sold using brokerage accounts (like listed equities)—this distribution method is unavailable in case of units of mutual funds. This difference influences the accessibility of both categories—investors may buy just one share of the ETF at price determined at any moment during trading hours, whereas some mutual funds impose limits of minimal contribution and their units are valued much less frequently (typically once a day). Moreover, innovative and traditional investment funds differ with regard to the transparency of their portfolio (managed assets)—ETFs are characterized by higher transparency as their portfolios are generally disclosed daily, and mutual funds present their composition on a monthly or even quarterly basis. Among the relative benefits of the mutual funds, an important one is linked to the legal issues—using ETFs is still prohibited in certain investment plans, e.g., in retirement plans in the United States.

Comparison to mutual funds is not the only approach which may be applied to ETFs; other approaches may include comparisons to different types of investment funds, i.e., closed-end funds (shares of both ETFs and closed-end funds are traded on exchanges, but they differ with regard to, for instance, creation and redemption method), or to other financial instruments which offer similar exposure as the main categories of the innovative funds, i.e., stock index derivatives—we present this issue in detail in Sect. 2.3, within the discussion regarding the development of ETFs markets.

2.2 Main Categories of Exchange-Traded Funds

In the previous section, we presented some key attributes of ETFs and the procedures of their launch and further functioning. In this section, we describe various categories of the innovative funds. The "family" of ETFs is currently highly diversified and is no longer limited to the most established funds offering exposure to the main stock market indexes (however, such funds are in most countries still the largest category, regardless whether we consider their assets, turnover of their shares, or the number of available funds)—on a global scale ETFs offer access to numerous asset classes and provide users with many modifications in relation to the simple mirroring of the rates of return. Naturally, in countries with nascent ETF markets, most such modifications are not offered and remain to be launched. We start this section by discussing the differences between physical and synthetic ETFs—funds which use varying mechanisms to provide the declared exposure. Then we present another fundamental distinction, between passive and nonpassive ETFs, which may be regarded as a substantial deviation from the initial basic idea behind the creation of these funds. Next, we show the differences between funds offering various approaches to the rate of return in relation to their benchmarks. The final outlined classification is based on the asset classes tracked by ETFs. We finish this section by briefly showing financial products other than ETFs which together form the category known as exchange-traded products.

The description of the key procedures concerning the operations of ETFs which was one of the main topics of the previous section must be supplemented in order to account for fundamental differences between the funds labeled as "physical" and more recent (in some ways also even more innovative) but definitely less popular ones called "synthetic"; both names are deeply rooted in the ways they operate. First, though, we briefly reiterate some basic facts from the previous section, in which we presented only the design of physical funds, in order to make the distinctions between physical and synthetic ETFs more clear-cut.

Creation and redemption of the fund's shares takes place on the primary market in the course of transactions between the fund's provider and its APs, and it is of in-kind nature (see Fig. 2.1). Fund's provider issues the shares that are bought by APs or, to be more precise, in case of physical funds, received by exchanging certain baskets of securities (i.e., shares of ETF are swapped for creation baskets). Redemption of the physical fund's shares is the exact reverse of the creation mechanism, with some minor terminological differences (i.e., shares of ETF are swapped for redemption baskets). Both creation and redemption basket consist usually of the tracked securities. Provider of the fund may use full replication or optimized replication which means either purchasing and maintaining all tracked securities in its portfolio (using the exact weights of the tracked index) or, in the second method, reaching the tracking aims with only a most representative subset of the securities at the expense of the higher tracking difference and error.

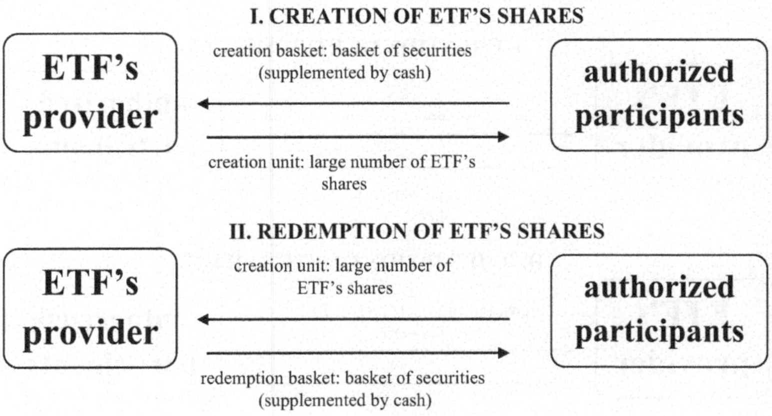

Source: own elaboration.

Fig. 2.1 Creation and redemption of ETF's shares: design of the physical funds

The role of cash in the creation or redemption of the physical fund's shares is usually insignificant; even though it sometimes is used, the key element of these processes is the exchange of securities. Physical design of the ETF's primary market may also be utilized in case of non-equity funds; it is applied even in many commodity ETFs, but the limited liquidity of the markets for non-equity assets represents a considerable barrier. Moreover, most commodity ETFs are not linked to the spot price (current market price applied for transactions settled immediately) of one single commodity but rather its future price (price applied for future deliveries, i.e., transactions settled in the future) or some commodity index. It means that physical replication may be unable to provide investors with the declared performance. These and other reasons have contributed to the development of alternative design of the innovative funds, employed in synthetic ETFs. It should be emphasized that synthetic funds are available mostly in Europe and additionally in some Asia-Pacific countries; in the United States their growth had been halted in 2010 due to regulatory limitations (Aramonte et al. 2017).

Mechanisms and participants of the secondary markets for physical and synthetic ETFs are very close—profound differences can be noticed on the primary market. The general design of the synthetic ETF's creation and redemption mechanism is presented in Fig. 2.2. It is much simpler than the in-kind process applied in physical ETFs—it closely resembles analogical mechanisms in the other categories of investment funds, with the most significant difference being the crucial role of APs, acting again as intermediaries between participants of the secondary market and the fund's provider. For comparison, in mutual funds creation and redemption of the units also involves a swap of cash for the fund's units albeit these transactions are conducted directly between the investors and managing company, without APs.

While the creation and redemption processes in synthetic ETFs are more straightforward than in physical funds, their internal structure (tracking or replication method employed by the provider) is much more complicated. Synthetic ETFs do

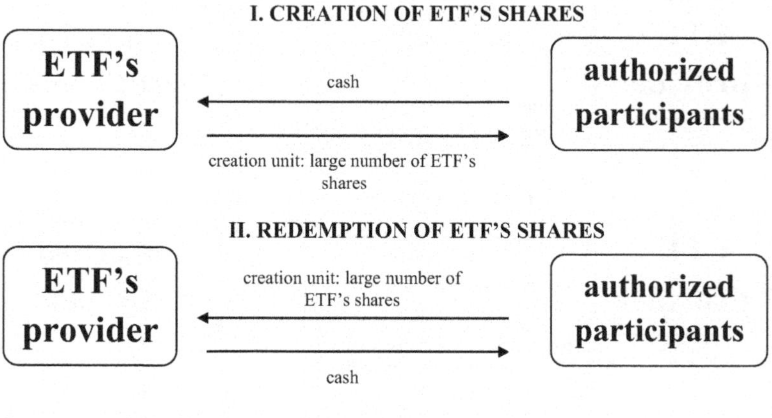

Source: own elaboration.

Fig. 2.2 Creation and redemption of ETF's shares: design of the synthetic funds

not hold the entire or optimized portfolio of the tracked assets but rather employ derivatives to generate the promised performance (Kosev and Williams 2011). Providers of synthetic ETFs typically enter total return swap contracts in which they receive returns on the tracked assets from the counterparty (Ben-David et al. 2017). Swap contract is collateralized (with "collateral basket") which means that provider has access to a basket of securities if counterparty defaults on its obligations (Aramonte et al. 2017). Composition of the collateral basket usually does not resemble the tracked assets. From the perspective of the fund's provider (and, consequently, also the holders of the ETF's shares), a few attributes of this basket are important: its market value (which indicates the level of collateralization), liquidity, and credit quality.

There are two forms of swap-based based replication employed in synthetic funds: unfunded and fully funded swap structure (Awrey 2012); we present below their basic design. Unfunded replication was chronologically the first to be launched and remains much more frequently applied by the providers. In this model, fund's provider gathers cash from APs (exchanged for fund's shares) and uses it to buy a portfolio of securities (typically from the counterparty)—the collateral basket; during the duration of the swap, the provider must deliver returns generated by this portfolio to the counterparty (this portfolio is owned by the provider which means that it may liquidated in case of the financial problems of the counterparty (Aramonte et al. 2017)); some proportion of the cash is forwarded to the counterparty as the swap fee (ETF Securities 2017)

Name of the latter type of the swap-based fund's structure ("fully funded") stems from the fundamental internal process. Cash received by the provider from the investors (with the intermediation of APs) is transferred to the counterparty in the swap contract (Aramonte et al. 2017). Collateral basket is thus not owned by the provider but rather deposited with a third-party custodian. In case of the counterparty's default, fund's provider is entitled to the collateral basket and may liquidate it.

Key advantages of synthetic ETFs in comparison to physical funds include (Kosev and Williams 2011; Omondi 2016; ETF Securities 2017):

- Lower tracking error (at least according to the declarations of the funds' providers)—the exact returns on the tracked benchmark are delivered by the swap counterparty which should result in superior outcomes; however, as Maurer and Williams (2015), Meinhardt et al. (2015), or Mateus and Rahmani (2017) show, when the costs of the synthetic replication are taken into account (especially swap spreads unique for these funds), none of the replication methods offers significant advantage in terms of either tracking error or investment cost.
- Exposure to more asset classes such as illiquid or foreign-listed securities, currencies or commodities, as well as offering funds with modified returns ("geared" funds); for, instance, commodities other than metals are characterized by problems with their storage—managing physical ETF would be in such case difficult and cost-inefficient therefore providers gain the exposure by using swaps.

- Generally, managing synthetic ETFs is relatively cheaper as the provider incurs less transaction costs associated with trades in the held assets, necessary in case of physical funds in order to maintain the declared exposure.

Nevertheless, synthetic funds should be evaluated by either their users or regulators with special caution due to some specific inherent risks (Kosev and Williams 2011; Aggarwal and Schofield 2014; Amenc et al. 2015; IMF 2015; Aguilar et al. 2016). Two main types of risk discussed in the context of synthetic ETFs are counterparty and collateral risk, i.e., the possibility of the swap counterparty's default (counterparty risk) and receiving less inflows than assumed from the sale of the collateral (collateral risk). However, the severity of these problems is limited by various regulatory requirements concerning the swap operations (e.g., concerning the entities that are allowed to act as counterparts or the level and quality of the collateral basket). Moreover, it must be underlined that they are not unique for synthetic funds—currently many physical funds engage into lending of securities in order to increase their profits which may expose them to similar threats (Blocher and Whaley 2016). Due to their complicated structure, synthetic funds are less transparent which may hinder the assessment of their risk. Some additional risks may be linked to certain categories of synthetic funds such as geared ETFs (see, inter alia, Cheng and Madhavan (2009), Charupat and Miu (2011), Li and Zhao (2014), Shum et al. (2015), Madhavan (2016), Ivanov and Lenkey (2018), Zhang (2018)) or volatility ETFs (see, e.g., Bhansali and Harris (2018)).

The early concept of ETFs was to offer them as tools for passive investing, i.e., following (mirroring) the returns of the selected benchmark, usually some type of financial market index, with certain advantages over traditional investment funds—mutual funds and closed-end funds. Apart from a chosen benchmark, passive funds may also track the performance of single selected financial or nonfinancial asset (e.g., gold), yet such construction is rather uncommon (notable exception are the gold ETFs), and it may be stated that in fact they are also tied to a special type of "benchmark."

Various types of passive funds dominate the ETF landscape, regardless of the particular market's history, region, or local regulations. However, as early as a few years since the inception of the first innovative funds, some (initially minor) modifications were made by the ETF providers. 2002 in the United States marked the entrance of one of the current global leading providers—PowerShares. It presented funds tracking not the broad-market, blue-chip, or sectoral indexes as in the previously available funds but rather linked to the indexes constructed using various quantitative methods (quant-based indexes)—these funds were targeted at attempting to outperform the rates of return of the conventional indexes by modifying some of their features (Hill et al. 2015; Meziani 2016). This approach, initially rather infrequent and limited to a certain market niche, after a few years has become one of the most intensively debated and developed innovations in the ETF industry—it has been labeled "enhanced indexing." Most generally, managers of such funds employ customized weighting schemes (distinctive from the benchmark) while deciding about the composition of their portfolios; selection and rules of the weighting scheme are not discretionary during the fund's lifetime—they are declared at its inception. The target of this investment policy is to outperform the benchmark by focusing on some factor evaluated to influence significantly the rates of return of the selected assets (another name of this approach is therefore "factor" investing) (Nikbakht et al. 2016). More technically, factors are defined as equity risk premiums that are identified as being able to deliver returns above average in relation to the market (i.e., positive risk-adjusted) over time (Murphy 2017b). Identification of factor must be based, as A. Ang notices, on "both strong economic intuition and academic evidence" (Murphy 2017b, p. 22). Examples of such factors include value, momentum, size, or dividend yield (Hill et al. 2015; Amenc et al. 2017; Lettau and Madhavan 2018). It must be added that strategies based on single factors are not the only one offered by providers of ETFs—some funds use multi-factor weighting and/or selection schemes. Enhanced indexing is used mostly for equity funds (one important subset of such funds are "smart beta" ETFs whose name refers to the basics of capital asset pricing model and relation between the stock's and its entire market's return); it has been employed rarely for ETFs benchmarked to other asset classes.

Various, more or less passive funds within the enhanced indexing category have been launched, but to some extent they always referred to the predominant perception of ETFs in the financial sector as index-tracking funds whose shares are traded on exchanges. However, in the half of 2010s (we omit first rather unsuccessful attempts halted by the 2008 global financial crisis), some providers launched funds which radically deviate from this concept—active ETFs. This category of innovative funds resembles the largest group of their equivalents in the mutual funds segment. Their managers attempt to generate rates of return superior to the selected benchmark. Active funds remain, though, a niche of the ETFs market. For the time being, the most recent innovation in the field of passive versus active funds, with minimal assets and market recognition, is exchange-traded managed funds, a conjunction of ETFs and mutual funds—their shares are traded on exchanges but with lower transparency and less frequent publication of IIV (Madhavan 2016).

The group of passive ETFs can be further divided based on the criteria of the relation between the rates of return of their shares and rates of return of their benchmarks (tracked indexes—of stock markets or other). The simplest and the most often employed approach, which was presented throughout most of the preceding and current section, is used in the plain vanilla ETFs. It assumes mirroring of the benchmark performance—minimizing the tracking difference and error. For instance, in case of fund tracking DJIA, it means obtaining the rates of return which are as close as possible to the performance of this index. It is, though, not the only design of passive funds in terms of the relation to the benchmark. In 2006 a new type of funds was launched in the United States by ProShares (Hill et al. 2015) (ProShares is still one of the global leading providers of such ETFs)—inverse and leveraged ETFs; similar, chronologically earlier attempts outside the United States had played no significant role as the ex-US market has been still too underdeveloped in order to generate considerable demand and enable gaining the sufficient scale of operations. The new category of funds (including above all leveraged, inverse, and leveraged-inverse ETFs) is sometimes labeled jointly as "geared" funds which indicate their key distinguishing feature—they are aimed at reaching a return of the index modified in a predefined way.

The distinguishing feature of leveraged ETFs is that they are aimed at delivering performance that is a multiple of the returns of the benchmarks, i.e., leveraged returns (Charupat and Miu 2016; Leung and Santoli 2016). For instance, double leverage means that certain fund is targeted at generating doubled performance of the benchmark—return on the benchmark with multiplier of +2. In their most basic form, inverse ETFs are aimed at delivering the reverse (opposite) of the benchmark's performance which means a multiplier of −1. The third subset of geared ETFs are leveraged-inverse or inverse-leveraged funds (both names may be used) that are a blend of leveraged and inverse funds which means that their return multiplier is lower than −1, for example, −3. A common mistake, made by less experienced investors who decide to add geared ETFs to their portfolio, concerns the rates of return of their shares in multiple periods (longer than one day) which may differ substantially from the performance of the benchmarks multiplied by a prespecified factor, due to the compounding effect. Geared performance of ETFs applies to daily returns only, and its results are set to zero after each day. Strong downward or upward trend of the benchmark's returns as well as its high volatility magnifies the deviations between the performances of the benchmarks and fund's shares. For more on this topic see, among other, Shum and Kang (2013), Tang et al. (2014), March-Dallas et al. (2018), or Tsalikis and Papadopoulos (2018).

It should be emphasized that due to their investment target, geared funds need to use derivatives to provide investors with the leveraged or inverse (or combined) returns—they are thus a subset of the synthetic funds (or, more precisely, synthetic passive funds). Geared funds have contributed significantly to the development of some ETFs markets as they are perceived as more accessible (due to, e.g., low required minimal investment and simplicity of entry or withdrawal) and less risky (e.g., maximum loss cannot exceed the initial investment) alternative to the traditional financial instruments offering modified returns such as index futures.

Next classification of ETFs is based on the categories of the underlying assets—assets whose rates of return are references for the financial aims of the particular fund, above all as their benchmarks, and, in most cases, are held in the fund's portfolio. We focus on the equity, bond, and commodity ETFs.

Equity ETFs are the largest category of the innovative funds, and for many years they have been the only one available; in the overwhelming majority of cases, equity funds are the first group launched in the particular country. Their broad-spectrum attribute refers to equities as the tracked assets (in case of passive or enhanced indexing funds) or, even more generally, to some equity indexes as their benchmarks (for active funds as well). Due to the very high number of equity funds (thousands of them are listed worldwide) and their high diversity, there are many classifications. We present one selected, broadly accepted approach to the division of equity ETFs, by focusing on three criteria: market capitalization, index style, and economic coverage (Deutsche Bank 2017b). Additional important classifications focus on, for instance, geographical coverage (examples include emerging markets or all-world funds).

Market capitalization aspect relates to the size of the companies according to the prices of shares, shares which in some way serve as a reference for the fund. The basic division includes the following three groups: small capitalization, mid-capitalization, and large capitalization. The classification is typically based on the broadly accepted stock market indexes which cover one of the aforementioned groups of companies.

The second aspect refers to the style of the index or, more precisely, the style of the shares included in the index which is used by the fund as its benchmark. Style may be understood in this context as particular relation between fundamental features of the company and some characteristics of its stocks. Three major types of style indexes focus on dividend stocks (with high dividend yield, issued by companies which recurrently pay dividends), growth stocks (of the companies with forecasted higher than the market growth of the earnings), and value stocks (relatively cheap considering the fundamental attributes of the issuing companies, measured in terms of, e.g., some earnings or book value indicators).

Economic coverage criterion refers to the fraction of the economy (domestic but it may also apply to multiple countries) that is covered by the index treated as the benchmark. Basic types of such indexes include broad-market (entire stock market), blue-chip (companies with the biggest market capitalization; to some degree this criterion is similar to the large capitalization described earlier) and sector indexes (many varying subclassifications are used, depending on the sector's definition; examples of the covered sectors may include consumer discretionary, financial, industrial, or utilities).

First bond ETF was launched in Canada in 2000 (BlackRock 2011), therefore it is the second oldest type of the innovative funds. Bond ETFs are funds that use as their benchmark indexes calculated based on returns of various fixed-income securities. It should be underlined that these securities are not necessarily bonds (they may also be, e.g., notes), so the most accurate name of this group is "fixed-income ETFs." However, vast majority of these funds offer exposure to bonds, so the simplified name is justified. Most bond ETFs track the indexes comprised of the US Treasury bonds (or notes) due to their highest liquidity. There are, though, also other funds that offer exposure to sovereign bonds (issued by governments of the highly developed economies; apart from the US which is considered separately due to their size), corporate bonds (i.e., issued by companies, not governments), or overall (both sovereign and corporate bonds) as well as a few other categories such as emerging market bonds ETFs (Deutsche Bank 2017b).

Managing and valuating the shares of bond ETFs is linked with a number of problems for their providers (Murphy 2017a). In many cases valid and accurate market prices of bonds cannot be acquired (resulting in the necessity to employ sophisticated bond-pricing models) which is caused by the structure of their turnover—most issues are not actively traded on the exchanges. Furthermore, their liquidity is limited, and most basic full replication cannot be used due to high costs. Finally, it should be emphasized that, similarly to the category of equity funds, high diversification of the bond funds means that our discussion covered only the basic issues concerning this group.

High heterogeneity may also be observed in case of the third major group of innovative funds in terms of the underlying assets—commodity ETFs. Chronologically, commodity ETFs were launched at almost the same time as bond ETFs, in 2001 (BlackRock 2011). In vast majority their underlying assets are commodities (single, some groups, or entire selected markets) such as corn or oil; funds based on the prices of gold are the oldest and the largest in this group. They employ either physical or synthetic replication. The first one is applied much less frequently in terms of the number of funds—it is used usually in funds incepted before the growth of the synthetic structure's popularity, but due to their large assets (particularly of gold ETFs), its significance is substantial. Another subset of commodity ETFs, or rather a crossover category between equity and commodity funds, is ETFs tracking returns on equities of commodity-linked corporations (e.g., owners of gold mines).

Apart from the three key categories of ETFs discussed in the preceding paragraphs, there are also other, less popular types of the innovative funds (they may be labeled as "alternative" funds). Before we discuss them briefly, we first mention the "supplementary" category, i.e., mixed-asset ETFs. Mixed-asset funds, as their name suggests, are funds that offer simultaneous exposure to multiple classes of financial or nonfinancial assets, including equities, fixed-income securities, or commodities—tracked assets may be listed in multiple countries. In other words, their portfolios and benchmarks are some combinations of the three major groups of ETFs.

In the alternative funds category, we can distinguish first currency ETFs. They may be briefly defined as funds that track the performance of selected currencies (single or multiple), by employing either physical or synthetic structure (more often the latter in order to minimize the costs). There are also some other sparse types of innovative funds, which manage currently almost negligible assets, among them real estate ETFs (they invest in shares of real estate investment trusts and provide shareholders with incomes generated from real estate) or money market ETFs (they invest in short-term equivalents of cash, for instance, US Treasury bills (Madhavan 2016)); money market funds have gained considerable popularity in some regions, e.g., Asia-Pacific, as evidenced by their very high turnover (Deutsche Bank 2017a), but on a global scale they are still minor group.

ETFs are currently not the only type of exchange-traded products (ETPs), i.e., financial products (instruments) listed on exchanges, trading like other listed securities, usually tied to some benchmark. Two other major kinds of ETPs are exchange-traded notes (ETNs) and exchange-traded commodities (ETCs); in some countries other categories of ETPs are available, such as exchange-traded vehicles (ETVs) in the United States.

The oldest category of ETPs (apart from ETFs) are ETCs (they had been introduced in 2003; ETNs in 2006), but the global assets of ETNs are slightly larger (data as of 2016 (own estimations based on Deutsche Bank (2017b)). Cumulated assets of both groups are, though, only a small fraction of the total assets of ETFs (moreover, the number of countries with markets for ETN or ETC is much lower than in case of ETFs).

All three types of exchange-traded products have a few common features. Above all, as their name suggests, their units are traded on stock exchanges that serve as the primary distribution channel, which results in the continuously updated prices. Moreover, the predominant type of products is the ones of passive character (Ferri 2009). The most substantial difference between both ETNs and ETCs when contrasted with ETFs concerns the form of securities which are used as their basic component. Shares of ETFs are legally equities, whereas "shares" ("units" would seem a more suitable denotation) of ETNs or ETCs are debt securities—unsecured (without the guarantee of repayment) and unsubordinated (higher in the claims priority than other issued securities) notes issued by the provider, backed by the issuer's credit and of certain maturity (Wright et al. 2010; Rakowski et al. 2017). As a consequence, they are listed and traded analogously to listed sovereign or corporate debt securities. Holders of these notes receive payments which depend on the performance of the tracked benchmark or asset; the replication method used to generate the promised returns is strictly synthetic—providers of ETNs or ETCs do not hold the tracked assets in the product's portfolio. The only exception and, at the same time, a unique (interestingly also the oldest) group among the entire spectrum of ETNs and ETCs is physical ETCs—providers of such products keep the tracked commodities in their portfolios. The usage of physical replication should be discussed in the historical context—when these ETCs had been launched the synthetic structure of ETFs had been almost unknown and limited to a few funds in Europe; very first ETCs, in Australia, had been incepted under the name including "ETFs," and the label "ETCs" was introduced several months later. On most exchanges, the differences between ETNs and ETCs (apart from some country-specific legal or operational issues) apply above all to the category of tracked assets. ETCs offer exposure to commodities, either single assets or market indexes (e.g., indexes of selected commodity sectors). In contrast, ETNs provide investors with returns tied to financial benchmarks or assets such as stock market indexes or currencies as well as other macroeconomic indicator, for example, interest rates. Similarly to ETFs, in both categories, geared products are available.

Less recognized types of ETPs offer investors certain comparative advantages when juxtaposed with ETFs but are also associated with some specific risk factors. The relative benefits of ETCs and ETNs are on average lower tracking error (even zero or close to zero) when comparing products with the same benchmarks (due to the application of synthetic tracking structure), broader access to some market niches, and higher suitability for some hedging strategies. The relative drawbacks of the products offered in a form of notes are associated with the possible default of the issuer (highly improbable yet historically proven to exist, e.g., it affected ETNs issued by Lehman Brothers during the global financial crisis) or losses caused by the credit rating downgrade of the issuer—they may result in significant deviations (unfavorable for the investors) from the benchmark's performance (Ferri 2009; Financial Industry Regulatory Authority 2012). Other risks of most ETCs or ETNs that employ synthetic structure are similar to their counterparts operating as funds.

The number of ETPs other than ETFs in the Asia-Pacific region is very scarce—according to Deutsche Bank (2017a) at the end of 2017, there were only six such products listed, with accumulated assets of only 369 million USD. Therefore we omit them in our analysis.

2.3 Exchange-Traded Funds Market Development Schemes and Determinants

Two previous sections were dedicated above all to the presentation of the specific attributes of ETFs as well as their various categories. In the current section, we adopt a different approach by discussing the development of the ETFs markets. We start by explaining our definition of the ETFs market development, applied in the consecutive chapters. Next, we compare ETFs to stock index derivatives, treating them as (at least partial) substitutes, by adopting the concept of stock index arbitrage complex which constitutes a novelty in the literature about ETFs (particularly with regard to verification based on market data—we apply this concept throughout the empirical Chap. 4). It allows us to conceptualize and define the relative ETFs market development, which is later scrutinized in the section regarding diffusion of ETFs. The next issue presented in this section is applications of ETFs due to their undeniable links to the interest of various market participants in choosing the financial innovations in lieu of alternatives (i.e., it impacts the demand for ETFs). Finally, we extend the issue of factors that determine the ETFs market development by discussing in-depth various demand- and supply-side determinants. The discussion of determinants in this section is rather brief as it is substantially expanded in the next sections, in particular in Sect. 3.3 in which we outline the relationships between diffusion of ETFs and adoption of ICT, one of the leading topics of this book. Development of the ETFs markets was rarely addressed in the previous empirical studies—most similar research focused on the development of the markets for the mutual funds (see, e.g., Klapper et al. (2004), Khorana et al. (2005), Ferreira et al. (2013), Khodayari and Sanoubar (2016)).

In our research we utilize two related approaches to the evaluation of the development of the ETFs markets which we label as "absolute" and "relative"; it should be added that both are used for the purposes of diffusion analysis as we utilize the terms *ETFs market development* and *ETFs diffusion* interchangeably. We define the value (or level) of *absolute ETFs market development* as the *value of the turnover of the shares of ETFs listed on the stock exchanges* (usually on one exchange, but in some countries trading is fragmented among more than one trading facility) *in a particular country*; choice of countries and time span is subject to data availability. In order to ensure between-country consistency, we use data expressed in common currency—US dollars. Due to lack of data on over-the-counter transactions (mostly caused by lack of reporting requirements), we do not consider them in our analysis which may influence the results (it would mean underestimation of development in absolute terms in case of non-zero value of such operations). Alternative approach may be based on the assets of funds—we discuss it in Sect. 2.4. Relative ETFs market development is defined in the further parts of this section as it requires showing alternatives to ETFs in order to measure their market share. It should be emphasized that the absolute approach is the main one adopted throughout the book as it allows for the broader analysis than in the alternative, relative approach (market shares cannot be calculated for some countries due to lack of the competing financial products or insufficient data on their turnover).

In Sect. 2.1 we compared ETFs to their major alternative in the investment funds' segment, i.e., mutual funds (index mutual funds in particular), showing the relative strengths and weaknesses of both categories. Main distinctions, which were presented as the relative benefits of the innovative funds, included different distribution channels (availability through brokerage accounts exclusively in case of ETFs), continuous determination of the ETF's shares prices (in the course of market transactions), higher transparency of ETFs due to more frequent publication of their holdings, availability of derivatives based on the shares of ETFs, and typically lower tracking error in passive ETFs than in index mutual funds. The comparative strengths of traditional investment funds were broader product range (in terms of the offered exposure and countries where they are available) and legal constraints to use ETFs for some asset management purposes.

Innovative investment funds have in the past been contrasted almost exclusively with the other types of investment funds, mostly due to the context of their launch and the business profile of their providers. However, growing popularity and increasing diversity of ETFs attracted the attention of users from the other parts of the financial system. The possibility to apply them in lieu of various financial instruments was discussed in the literature as early as in 2010 by G. Gastineau who suggested using the concept of "equity index arbitrage complex." Gastineau stated that it is the proper way to understand the relationships between transactions in stocks (equities) and trading on stock (equity) derivatives markets, especially the decisions made by users of index financial instruments (it may be applied not only to indexes but also portfolio baskets, yet this approach is irrelevant in the context of our discussion). Arbitrage complex is defined as "a number of related financial instruments or groups of financial instruments based on a common basket of underlying assets" (Gastineau 2010, p. 21). In the context of ETFs, the basic concept is *equity* (or *stock*—we will use the latter term) *index arbitrage complex*—a group of related financial instruments (both domestic and foreign) for which the principal underlying assets are some stock index. Instruments in such complex can have various forms—they may be equities, debt instruments, or derivatives (see the next paragraphs and Table 2.2). For simplicity, in our outline we omit foreign instruments that belong to a certain arbitrage complex and concentrate on the domestic ones.

Table 2.2 presents the list of financial instruments included in the three categories within the stock index arbitrage complex. The first group covers traditional securities—combinations and extensions of the stocks that are considered in the construction and calculation of the particular index. It should be underlined (to avoid terminological misunderstandings) that ETFs are included in this subset because they are traded in a most conventional way and offer rates of return that are very close to the returns of the index (if the tracking error is minimized), not due to absence of innovative attributes. Another important remark is that only index equity ETFs may be included in this complex; however, due to their prevalence it means that it can be applied to the vast majority of the innovative funds.

The second group of instruments consists of three types of derivatives whose basic parameters (e.g., rates of return) are directly and proportionately linked to the corresponding attributes of the stock indexes. This relationship determines the profile of their market risk.

Table 2.2 Major financial instruments included in three categories of stock index arbitrage complex

Category	Financial instruments
Traditional securities	1. Program or portfolio trading of baskets of stocks 2. ETFs
Symmetric derivatives	1. Stock index futures 2. ETF futures 3. Equity index swaps
Nonsymmetric (convex) instruments	1. Stock index options 2. Options on either ETFs or symmetric derivatives 3. Structured notes based on either ETFs or symmetric derivatives

Source: Own elaboration based on Gastineau (2010, p. 21–22)

Finally, nonsymmetric instruments are included in the third group. Their basic parameters are not proportionately linked to the corresponding attributes of the stock indexes. The reason for their asymmetry (convexity) is the option attribute, either stand-alone or embedded. In our further theoretical presentation and empirical analysis, due to, among other, data accessibility, we focus on the instruments from the stock index arbitrage complex which are listed and traded on exchanges—we chose one instrument from each category: *ETFs* (not stocks as they are the most basic instruments), *stock index futures, and stock index options*; we concentrate exclusively on the exchange-listed options due to lack of sufficient data on other groups of these contracts; we label stock index futures and options together as "stock index derivatives" and regard them as traditional instruments (due to, e.g., longer history) when compared to innovative ones—ETFs. Due to the size of their market, we discuss above all futures; however, most of the aspects may be related to options (listed on exchanges) as well. Other instruments, including other stock index derivatives (e.g., swaps), are omitted.

The concept of including some instruments in the stock index arbitrage complex is based not only on the common underlying financial assets but also on their arbitrage relationships. As G. Gastineau (2010, p. 22) states, it means that their pricing relationships are limited by the ability of investors having access to various markets to profit from observed inconsistencies in their prices, as long as they are higher than costs of transactions and other linked expenses. The relationship between growth of the arbitrage complexes on the one side and increasing trading volumes accompanied by decreasing trading costs on the other side is bidirectional—these processes tend to reinforce each other. In broader view, it means that the relationships within the arbitrage complex should limit any significant downward or upward deviations of the prices of instruments from the prices indicated by their counterparts in the same or other categories.

The perception of the potential of ETFs to be used as substitute for stock index derivatives has noticeably evolved since the cited publication by G. Gastineau in 2010. In his book, he describes the possible applications of ETFs, used instead of stock index futures by large investors for short- and long-term risk management. According to the results of his analysis, due to the different structure of their costs,

ETFs are more suitable for long-term applications than futures (they have no rolling costs, i.e., costs of entering a new contract after the expiration of the current one) but in short-term futures are more favorable. Nevertheless, as more recent studies show (see, e.g., CME Group (2016)), the exact choice made by the users of either ETFs or derivatives should depend on the investment strategy in addition to the holding period. In case of the US market, if the user intends to enter short or leveraged position (or is based outside the United States), index futures are relatively more cost-effective, regardless of the holding period.

Over the next few years, new applications of ETFs as substitutes for futures have emerged, to a high degree related to the responses to the 2008 global financial crisis. Various newly imposed regulations aimed at limitation of the risk of the shocks in financial system increased the cost of financial instruments such as stock index derivatives for one of their main group of users—investment banks; significant role was played by the Basel III framework (Madhavan et al. 2014; Arnold and Lesné 2015) and the other similar regulatory initiatives such as the Volcker Rule within the Dodd-Frank Act or reforms in the European Union and United Kingdom (Madhavan 2016). As Lettau and Madhavan (2018) note, since 2008 ETFs have become increasingly popular among institutional investors as substitutes for, among other, futures and swaps, due to the regulation-motivated declines of the banks' balance sheets.

Aforementioned trends mean that the relative costs of ETFs and their attractiveness for various groups of users have been increasing which have been further boosted by the declining costs of the innovative funds, triggered by growing competition among providers (thousands of new funds have been launched, new financial corporations started offering their own funds, etc.). To sum up, Madhavan (2016, p. 82) suggests that there are four main applications for which ETFs and derivatives may be consider substitutes:

1. Investing excess cash
2. Hedging exposures
3. Rapidly shifting exposure ("synthetic" exposure, i.e., not gained by purchasing certain assets)
4. Implementing long-term strategic risk allocation

Regardless of the specific application for which ETFs are considered to be alternatives to futures (or options), it should be stressed that such substitution applies particularly to the institutional segment of the financial markets (i.e., financial institutions as the users of either derivatives or ETFs) due to, for instance, the low recognition of derivatives in the broad investing audience.

Main similarities and differences between the basic type of ETFs—index equity funds—and stock index futures are summarized in Table 2.3 (most of them apply also to stock index options which are traded through exchanges—we do not discuss them separately due to their lower significance in terms of, e.g., turnover). We begin by briefly extending some points concerning the features in which they are alike (see the upper part of Table 2.3) and then proceed to present some distinguishing aspects. Their basic similarities refer to the trading venues—both types of financial instruments are listed and traded on stock exchanges (in case of ETFs it is not,

Table 2.3 Major similarities and differences between index equity ETFs and stock index futures

Attribute	**Similarities**	
Trading venue	Stock exchanges and similar facilities (for ETFs also over-the-counter transactions)	
Liquidity	Usually high or very high	
Pricing	Intraday continuous pricing on exchanges	
Market participants	Multiple participants due to numerous applications	
Counterparty risk	Minimal (some possible in, e.g., synthetic ETFs)	
Attribute	**Differences (I): relative advantages of ETFs**	
	ETFs	**Stock index futures**
Maturity	No predefined—open-ended instruments	Strictly predefined (usually up to 3 months)
Product range	Broad: most major and less popular indexes	Limited mostly to major indexes
Management of the user's position prior to exit	Minimal required (e.g., reinvestment of dividends). In case of ETFs tracking foreign indexes, users usually do not have to manage the foreign exchange component (depending on the attributes of specific fund)	Substantial required (management of margin payments, rolling of the contracts, etc.). In case of contracts based on foreign indexes, management of foreign exchange component is required
Attribute	**Differences (II): relative advantages of futures**	
Minimum initial capital required from investor	Full upfront payment for the ETF's shares	Only a margin, calculated as some percentage of the contract value, must be deposited
Built-in leverage	None, with the exception of leveraged and leveraged-inverse ETFs	Available, typically high or very high
Obtaining short exposure	Short sale of ETF's shares may be regulatory or operationally constrained. Short exposure may also be gained through some geared funds: inverse and leveraged-inverse ETFs	Both long and short positions in futures may be taken

Source: Own compilation based on Ferri (2009), Agapova (2011), Goltz and Schröder (2011), Madhavan et al. (2014), Arnold and Lesné (2015), BlackRock (2015), CME Group (2016), Eurex (2016), Madhavan (2016), and Thomsett (2016)

though, the only trading venue as in many countries a substantial percentage of trades are conducted over the counter). As a result, investors have access to prices which are determined continuously during trading hours by a large number of market participants. In case of most ETFs or stock index futures (especially the most established funds or futures tracking indexes of the world's major equity markets), their liquidity is high or very high, with the exception of the periods of market stress (see the description of the Flash Crash in the further part of this section). Counterparty risk of both categories is severely constrained by their operational structure (clearing house acting as a counterparty and daily marking-to-market for futures) or legal requirements (see the discussion of synthetic ETFs in Sect. 2.2).

There are a number of less or more important (from the point of view of, e.g., their users) differences between index equity ETFs and stock index futures which we divide into relative benefits of, first, ETFs and, second, futures (again, see Table 2.3—its first lower part). Among the crucial dissimilarities that constitute strengths of the innovative funds when contrasted with futures, one was already mentioned—ETFs are open-ended instruments and do not require their rolling which may mean additional costs for the users of futures. Even before the position in certain instrument is closed, managing futures normally is more time-consuming and expensive. Additional relative advantage of ETFs, as stated by Madhavan et al. (2014), is the lack of mispricing of the ETF's shares which is a characteristic for futures contracts when they must be rolled to maintain the desired exposure.

Main relative benefits of stock index futures include following aspects (see the second lower part of Table 2.3): lower initial capital required (this benefit can diminish with the passage of time as further margin deposits may be necessary) as well as broader availability to enter leveraged or short positions on the stock market indexes. It may also be added that ETFs and futures differ with regard to their international availability—due to their longer history and wider recognition futures are available in a higher number of countries. However, the number of ETFs markets has been quickly increasing over the previous several years.

Another distinction between these two categories, not included in Table 2.3, is the different structure of their costs—it may be favorable for either ETFs or futures, depending on the time period, specific application, and other factors (we discussed this issue in the preceding paragraphs of this section). The costs of ETFs (from their user's point of view) consist mostly of commission fees, management fees, and market impact, whereas the costs of futures are above all rolling costs and market impact. Moreover, the exact trading procedures of ETFs (which are traded as equities) and futures (derivatives) differ significantly—we do not cover this issue in detail as it is presented in numerous publications.

The importance of the perspective within which ETFs are regarded as alternatives to stock index derivatives is not purely theoretical or limited to some general comments made by financial professionals. It was proven during one of the most broadly discussed events influenced by the innovative funds—"'Flash Crash" of 6 May, 2010 (it was not the only such event in the recent years, but it is most recognized and has been extensively analyzed by both researchers and regulators). Flash Crash (FC) occurred amidst turbulent environment on the global financial markets (developing eurozone debt crisis), which increased the volatility of the major stock markets; it affected mainly the US equity market. Within a short period of only 15 minutes, prices of many equities (including ETFs) suddenly declined by 40% or more in comparison to their previous transaction prices (Abner 2016); these abrupt decreases were not triggered by any fundamental changes in the issuing companies or funds. Stocks of many companies were unexpectedly traded at very low levels, in some cases the lowest in their history. Some of the strongest collapses were observed for the shares of ETFs which led to emergence of many explanations according to which the innovative funds were not only affected but also contributed to the spread of the crash. Declines had broad-market implications as evidenced by the rapid falls in the prices of the main US stock indexes: in a few minutes S&P 500 decreased by ca. 6% and for Dow Jones Industrial Average it was the sharpest decline in its history—in 20 min it decreased by ca. 1000 points (Ben-David et al. 2012; Madhavan 2012, 2016). Moreover, during the crash, prices were not the only parameter of equities affected—the declines in their liquidity were also substantial.

We do not present the detailed explanation of the sources of the FC and its implications as these issues lie outside the scope of this book (for more on this topic, see, e.g., Zhang (2010), Financial Stability Board (2011), International Monetary Fund (2011), Ramaswamy (2011), Wurgler (2011), Madhavan (2012, 2016), Abner (2016), Ben-David et al. (2017)). We discuss, though, one of the mechanisms which was identified as responsible for the occurrence and aggravation of FC: the links between the stock index futures and ETFs market, based on the publications of Commodity Futures Trading Commission and Securities and Exchange Commission (2010) and Ben-David et al. (2012). FC started on the US stock index futures market with large transactions on the S&P 500 contracts by one of the large market participants. This financial institution began selling increasingly more of a certain type of S&P 500 futures (S&P 500 e-mini contract) which resulted in significant decline of their liquidity. What is important in the context of some of the explanations of FC is that these sales were made using algorithm trading system and were aimed at hedging of the institution's equity position. Due to the arbitrage process between S&P 500 futures on the one side and both the stocks in the S&P 500 index and ETFs tracking this benchmark (as predicted by the concept of stock index arbitrage complex) on the other side, liquidity shocks were transmitted between these markets. According to market data presented by Ben-David et al. (2012), the declines in prices were first observed on the futures market (it was its initial source), then on the ETFs market, and finally they affected the prices of equities. Accordingly, it may be stated that within this explanation of FC, its scale was magnified by the cross-market arbitrage mechanisms enabled by ETFs. First, profits could have been made by selling shares of ETFs and buying futures (which stopped the declines on the futures market but triggered them on the ETFs market). In the next stage, ETFs became underpriced in relation to the tracked index (i.e., to their NAV) which could have been used (according to the mechanisms presented in Sect. 2.1) to gain profits by buying shares of ETFs and selling the stocks included in the S&P 500 index—it resulted in the most serious part of the FC, i.e., substantial declines of the stock prices.

Presentation of the potential substitution between ETFs and stock index derivatives (futures and options) facilitates conceptualization of the *relative ETFs market development*, an approach which is applied in some empirical parts of this book. Level of the relative ETFs market development is defined as the *share of ETFs in the turnover of combined index financial instruments: ETFs, stock index options, and stock index futures*. Analogously to the absolute market development, we need to omit transactions conducted off the exchanges—it cannot be determined, though, whether it results in under- or overestimation of the market development's level as for stock index futures and options we also include only transactions which take place through exchanges.

In order to more adequately analyze the factors that determine the development of the ETFs market (both absolute and relative), it seems necessary to deliberate first about the ways the innovative funds are used by various entities. Since their launch in the United States in the early 1990s, category of ETFs has undergone deep transformation and has become highly diversified, in all possible dimensions (see the previous section). It means that the applications of these funds have also evolved, even though the majority of users still employ them to reach similar aims as more than 20 years ago. We present below some of the main applications of ETFs divided into two categories: uses for individual investors and uses for financial institutions; the list of innovative funds' functions is, though, by no means exhaustive.

The basic, most conventional and on majority of markets the most frequent function of ETFs, typical for both individual and institutional users, is employing them to obtain passive exposure to the particular financial or nonfinancial assets (or slightly modified exposure in case of enhanced indexing funds; we omit active funds because of their negligible recognition), as the part of the investor's asset management strategy. Strengths and weaknesses of ETFs in comparison to the other financial products that facilitate obtaining such exposure (i.e., for which ETFs are replacements) were presented in Sect. 2.1 (ETFs versus index mutual funds) and current one (ETFs versus index derivatives).

Individual investor (usually with the assistance of financial advisors) may use the features of ETFs to reach various aims—we present only some selected applications (Gastineau 2010; Hill et al. 2015; Madhavan 2016):

1. Diversification of the portfolio—obtaining exposure to various asset classes and countries is possible by combining ETFs tracking multiple benchmarks as well as including funds with broad exposure (e.g., to particular global or regional index of the equity markets); portfolio completion (ETFs used to add desired new exposure to the portfolio without substantial modifications) and adding or changing factor exposure (by employing enhanced indexing ETFs based on certain factors) constitute similar applications.
2. Model portfolios—using ETFs in automated portfolio building and rebalancing.
3. Integration and organization of family accounts—separate investment accounts of various family members, with different legal and operational structures, may be managed using ETFs instead of constructing and executing complicated investment plans in order to limit the costs and ensure higher transparency.
4. Gaining tax advantages—higher tax efficiency of ETFs (in comparison to, e.g., mutual funds) in some countries.

Financial institutions (various types of non-ETF investment funds, hedge funds, banks, etc.) employ ETFs for a number of purposes, some of them more or less distinctive compared to the uses of individual investors—we discuss four main types of functions (description is based on Hill et al. (2015) and Madhavan (2016)):

1. ETFs as the part of the managed portfolio of assets—the major long-term application that was already discussed.

2. Selected key short-term applications:
   (a) Shifting exposure to asset classes, for example, as a part of transition management—using ETFs during the process of institutional portfolios' (for instance, portfolios of pension funds in the United States) reallocation due to cost and risk reasons; there may be many causes of the reallocation, e.g., poor performance of the manager or significant desired change in the structure of the held assets (e.g., from stocks only to stocks, bonds, commodities, and other asset classes); during the reallocation process ETFs may be used by the transition manager to obtain short-term exposure to the selected assets without the need to buy other securities, etc.; managers of financial institutions (such as mutual funds) also employ ETFs to modify the exposure gained by investing in various assets in case of some deviations from their declared strategy, e.g., for equity mutual funds, it may mean using ETFs to increase the exposure to certain sector which is underrepresented in the current portfolio in relation to the manager's mandate.
   (b) Cash management—investing excess cash in ETFs instead of deposits in case of time differences between the inflows from investors and outflows related to the purchase of the assets; the main category of ETFs applied for this aim are bond ETFs, but in the future, with the growth of money market ETFs (currently of minimal significance), they may become alternative choice.
3. Gaining short exposure—ETFs may be cheaply and efficiently applied to obtain short exposure to various domestic and foreign assets (this attribute is also crucial in the context of hedging, mentioned below), without the need to employ derivatives.
4. Other applications, such as hedging of positions as well as short-term and medium-term trading purposes, market timing, or tactical trading—ETFs may be used for such purposes due to their low cost, in-built diversification, and possibility of entering and exiting the position quickly; another benefit of specific group of ETFs in this context is their currency hedge feature which facilitates gaining exposure to certain market yet without the need to manage the currency component.
5. Retirement and wealth management strategies of financial advisers—they constitute a separate category which links to some extent retail and institutional users.

In the history of the institutional usage of ETFs on the largest market—in the United States – initially short-term applications were predominant as their early adopters had been attracted by their stock listing feature (the feature which is less relevant for the individual investors). However, over the years they became increasingly popular as tools for long-term investing (similarly to the individual users).

The discussion in the preceding paragraphs highlights the mixture of entities which employ ETFs to reach various aims. Consequently, it may be stated that it is one of the determinants of the demand for these funds—the most basic relationship can be formulated in a following way: a larger number of possible applications (or possibility to apply them at lower cost or with other benefits) leads to more entities attracted to the ETFs market and growing demand. Obviously, it should not be perceived as the sole determinant because the ETFs market development is influenced by many other factors. We discuss below other substantial determinants, divided into two categories: demand- and supply-side factors.

As demand-side factors, we understand financial and nonfinancial determinants which apply to the decisions made by the participants of the secondary ETFs markets to enter or withdraw from this segment of the financial sector, i.e., buy or sell the shares of ETFs. Demand-side determinants should thus be described above all in the comparative context, and the discussion needs to focus on the factors which increase or decrease the relative advantages and disadvantages of ETFs when contrasted with alternative financial products used to reach the aims of their users. Such comparisons were presented in this and the preceding sections; therefore we discuss here only some additional issues.

Relative position of ETFs among other similar financial products depends, inter alia, on the development of the related financial markets (given the domination of equity and bond ETFs it applies mostly to equity and bond markets)—their correct functioning influences the ability to minimize the tracking errors (in case of passive or semi-passive funds) and their costs (for all funds). Moreover, basic parameters of the ETF's shares, such as their risk and return profile, depend on the corresponding attributes of the tracked or managed assets (typically securities or commodities) which means that the demand for ETFs is influenced by the trends on the financial and commodity markets which, in turn, depend at least to some extent on the general economic environment. Demand for the shares of ETFs is also shaped by the accessibility of their distribution channels—costs and availability of brokerage accounts which implies that the development of financial institutions (e.g., banks) must be taken into account. Other important factors are marketing activities of the fund's providers and similar entities as well as much more general aspect—the level of financial education which influences the awareness of the innovative funds' attributes and application.

Supply-side factors are the financial and nonfinancial determinants which influence the decisions of the entities on the other side of the market in comparison to the demand side, i.e., providers of ETFs and other institutions responsible for the proper functioning of the primary (in particular) and secondary market (including distribution of the shares among their final users). In other words, they affect the decisions to launch and further develop the innovative funds, in terms of, for instance, broader product range or more listing and trading locations; we assume that such actions are mostly financially motivated. Four major groups of supply-side factors include:

1. Level of development of the markets for the assets tracked by ETFs or held in their portfolios: developments in this context may be examined in terms of their liquidity, size, and other parameters in order to ensure the correct functioning of the ETFs primary and secondary market, including, for example, the operations of APs.

2. Operational and administrative factors: factors concerning provider's reporting and accounting requirements as well as the distribution of ETF's shares; they may also apply to the regulatory limitations imposed on the providers or users of ETFs, for instance, the way investments in the innovative funds are recorded in the balance sheets of financial institutions (see the example in Hill et al. (2015)).
3. Structure and level of the fee payments from providers of investment fund to the financial advisers or, more generally, structure and level of fees in the investment industry: using the example of the largest world's ETFs market, in the United States, these fees are emblematic for mutual funds, whereas for most ETFs there is no such compensation which makes them less attractive for the advisers;
4. Governmental policy concerning financial markets: it may include regulatory changes encouraging the launch and development of ETFs or, in more direct scenario, launch of the innovative funds as the state-controlled initiative.

Other approaches to the supply-side factors, based on the theories of financial innovation, focus on:

(a) The incentives of the funds' managers to lend some part of the held assets, particularly when ETF are perceived as the common platform in the model of two-sided markets (Blocher and Whaley 2016).

(b) ETFs as an attempt to generate monopolistic profits for innovators by constructing them in a way hindering their commoditization, e.g., in case of synthetic funds (additional motivation in case of unfunded structures, may be linked with the attempts to clean the balance sheets of the swap counterparty by transferring the undesired assets as a collateral to the provider (Awrey 2012)).

Among the array of demand- and supply-side determinants of the development of the ETFs markets, one group requires particular scrutiny due to its potentially high significance and relevance for the modern economy and society—adoption of new technologies, with the key role of information and communication technologies (ICT). Diffusion of ICT (technological innovations) can influence the diffusion of ETFs (financial innovations) through a number of transmission channels, mostly linked to the changes in the financial system triggered by the spread of new or more cost- and time-efficient ways of trading and transferring of securities, accessing financial data, managing assets, etc. These linkages are explored in Sects. 3.2 and 3.3.

2.4 Asia-Pacific Exchange-Traded Funds

In Sects. 2.1–2.3, we discussed various concepts concerning ETFs, referring to both micro and macro perspective (of individual users and entire markets), but we deliberately omitted in most cases region-specific issues, particularly regarding the region being the main topic of this book: Asia-Pacific. In this section we remediate this fully intentional negligence and we concentrate on ETFs in the

Asia-Pacific—we present the summary of their history, main market development statistics (in terms of assets, number, etc.), market's structure, and position of ETFs in the Asia-Pacific investment industries (compared to mutual funds). It should be stressed that the current section serves merely as the introduction to the comprehensive analysis of the Asia-Pacific ETFs markets: diffusion of ETFs and the impact of ICT, whose results are outlined in the strictly empirical Chaps. 4 and 6. Consequently, in the present section, we focus on the regional Asia-Pacific issues, common for at least most economies in scope, as the country-specific analysis is shown in the subsequent chapters. However, summary statistics regarding monthly and annual turnover—the core indicator that we take into account in our study—are presented in Chap. 4 as the preliminary stage in country-specific analysis. In this section we concentrate on a number of dimensions of the Asia-Pacific ETFs markets other than the turnover (the only exception being turnover by asset classes presented here in order to endure the proper flow of the presentation).

Before we begin the presentation of the general overview of Asia-Pacific ETFs markets, we need to address one substantial methodological matter. This chapter as well as the entire book is dedicated to ETFs markets in Asia-Pacific countries[2]. More precisely, we examine Australia, (Mainland) China, Hong Kong, India, Indonesia, Japan, Malaysia, New Zealand, Singapore, South Korea, Taiwan, and Thailand. Explanations of the concept of the ETFs market development as well as some basic remarks about its measurement were outlined in Sect. 2.3. However, what remains to be elaborated is the method we use to combine those two concepts and analyze development of Asia-Pacific ETFs markets. To some extent, we addressed this issue in the preceding section in which we stated that we investigate the absolute or relative turnover of ETFs' shares on the exchanges located in particular countries—in this case it simply means that we consider exchanges in countries in the Asia-Pacific region where ETFs are listed and traded (and enough data are available to conduct robust analysis).

It should be stressed that the turnover of the ETF shares may not be considered the exclusive indicator of the status of the innovative funds' market development. Other equally important measure focuses on the value of the assets or, more precisely, on total net assets or assets under management (i.e., with deducted liabilities). Both indicators have certain relative advantages and disadvantages, yet we decided to focus on turnover; nonetheless, in some parts of the book (e.g., in the current section), we present additional information regarding assets of Asia-Pacific ETFs. It requires, though, making further assumptions. Some funds are listed on exchange in more than one country—we include them in data for the country of their primary listing only (according to the classification in the Thomson Reuters Lipper's database) and exclude them from data for other countries in order to avoid double counting; we do not use data on the domicile of the funds in the calculations as they are highly unreliable in this context. Assets for the entire country are calculated as the sum of assets of individual funds in a given month, using Lipper's

[2] In some cases we analyze territories which are in fact administrative units of other countries, but in order to avoid unnecessary repetitions, we subsequently label all as "countries."

database. For example, assets of ETFs in Japan are understood as total net assets (or assets under management; Lipper uses the former term) of all ETFs with Japan (more technically—Japanese exchanges) provided as their primary listing location. Alternative approach to evaluate assets could be based on exposure by country, but it conveys different information (e.g., it shows links to the financial markets for the underlying assets) which is not highly relevant in the context of this topic.

Strictly technically, Asia-Pacific ETFs markets are among the oldest in the world as the first fund in this region, which complies with our definition of ETF, was launched in Japan in April, 1995, as the fund tracking Nikkei 300 index (Osaki 2001). It was one of the first few ETFs available worldwide, and the earliest one started outside Canada and the United States. The pioneering fund is still listed under the full name "Nomura Nikkei 300 Stock Index Listed Fund" which clearly indicates that it is managed by the asset management arm of one the largest global financial corporations, Nomura. However, as we pointed, the 1995 date may be considered as rather technical starting point of the Asia-Pacific market or, in other words, its "prehistoric" period—until 1999 it had been the only fund in Japan and the entire region (with one exception presented in the next paragraph); the mere concept of ETFs was still under development in the United States where the number of funds and their diversity also remained very low until the turn of the twentieth and twenty-first century. Lack of further development of the Japanese market in the second half of 1990s had to some extent been caused by regulatory policy that prohibited inception of funds linked to indexes other than Nikkei 300, including Nikkei 225 that was much more broadly used and regarded as more representative (Osaki 2001). Further development of the Japanese market is scrutinized in Chap. 4.

First ETF in the Asia-Pacific region outside Japan was launched in New Zealand in 1997 (it was also world's first global equity ETF (BlackRock 2011)), yet in most publications another fund is named the earliest one—Tracker Fund of Hong Kong (known under the abbreviated name "TraHK") listed in 1999 on the stock exchange in Hong Kong (Hill et al. 2015). Non-Japanese part of the Asia-Pacific ETFs market has been growing rapidly in the recent years in terms of both assets and turnover (much faster than in Japan), especially in the period 2008–2012, fueled by, above all, the rise of the markets in Hong Kong, Mainland China, and South Korea. As in case of Japan, the results of the detailed country-specific analysis are discussed in Chap. 4.

Total assets of ETFs with Asia-Pacific countries as their primary listing location have been increasing in the last several years—if we compare the value of assets at the end of 2004 to the value at the end of 2016, it can be noticed that it has grown almost eightfold (see Fig. 2.3). Even more significantly, in this period there was only 1 year when their assets fell—it was 2008 (i.e., outbreak of the global financial crisis)—yet even then the decline was not substantial (less than 15% on a yearly basis). Rate of assets' growth has been particularly high since 2009, with no signs of noticeable slowdown. However, when the position of the Asia-Pacific funds is considered in the context of the global industry, the conclusions to be drawn are less positive—their share in global assets had been declining considerably between 2004 and 2009, and after that period it stabilized at levels of ca. 6–9%, much lower

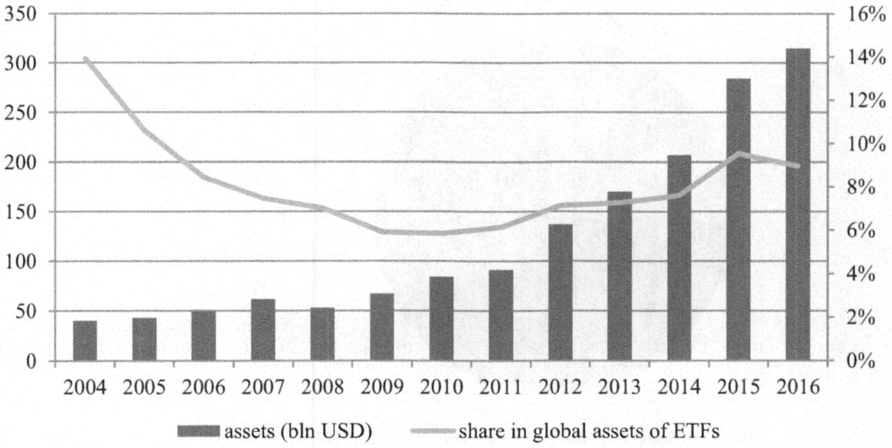

Source: own estimations based on Deutsche Bank (2017a).

Fig. 2.3 Total assets of Asia-Pacific ETFs. Year-end data for 2004–2016

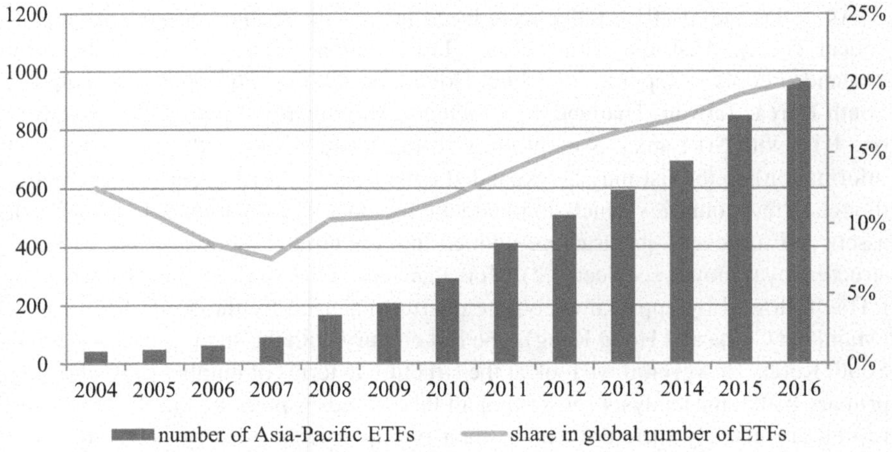

Source: own estimations based on Deutsche Bank (2017a), ETFGI (2016).

Fig. 2.4 Total number of Asia-Pacific ETFs. Year-end data for 2004–2016

than previously noted 10% or more (almost 14% in 2004). It may signal that, even though the whole Asia-Pacific market has grown, in other regions the increases have been even more substantial. Instead of using data on assets, the analysis may focus on the number of funds (see Fig. 2.4). This indicator shows significant growth of the Asia-Pacific market, either considered stand-alone or in the global context. It should be remembered, though, that the mere increase in the number of available funds, if not accompanied by changes in their assets or turnover, cannot be perceived as a sign of market development (here, against the global background).

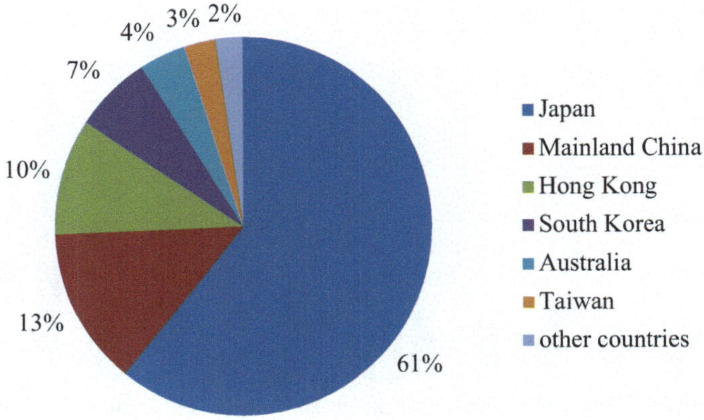

Source: own estimations based on Deutsche Bank (2017a).

Fig. 2.5 Structure of Asia-Pacific ETFs market—assets by country of primary listing. End of October 2017

As of the end of 2016, ETFs were listed in 14 Asia-Pacific countries (in alphabetical order): Australia, Hong Kong, India, Indonesia, Japan, Malaysia, New Zealand, People's Republic of China (Mainland China), Philippines, Singapore, South Korea, Taiwan, Thailand, and Vietnam; additionally, Lipper's database lists one ETF with Sri Lanka as its primary listing location (yet with limited detailed information) so the list may be expanded conditionally to 15 countries. There are, though, a few countries which dominate the regional ETFs market in terms of both assets and turnover—its structure divided into countries is shown in Fig. 2.5 (for structure by turnover, see Sect. 4.2). More than half of the assets are held by Japanese ETFs, followed by approximately one quarter managed by the funds from China (Mainland China and Hong Kong). The last country with the share exceeding 5% is South Korea. However, if we look at the structure in terms of number of funds (only primary listed; the analysis concerning all listed funds is presented in Sect. 4.2), the results are entirely different—more than one quarter is primary listed in South Korea, and there are five countries with between 100 and 200 funds (Australia, Hong Kong, Japan, Mainland China, and Taiwan; Japan is the leader among this group with 176 ETFs). It indicates that the average size of ETF differs considerably among countries in scope.

Figure 2.6 shows the proportions of assets of Asia-Pacific ETFs managed by the five largest providers and other sponsors. Regional market is clearly dominated by the local financial corporations, particularly Japanese ones (due to the size of the ETFs market in this country), and it is highly concentrated, with the three largest companies holding ca. 55% of total assets. Global leaders of the ETF industry, such as State Street or BlackRock, lag behind which differentiates explicitly this region from the North American or European ETFs industries.

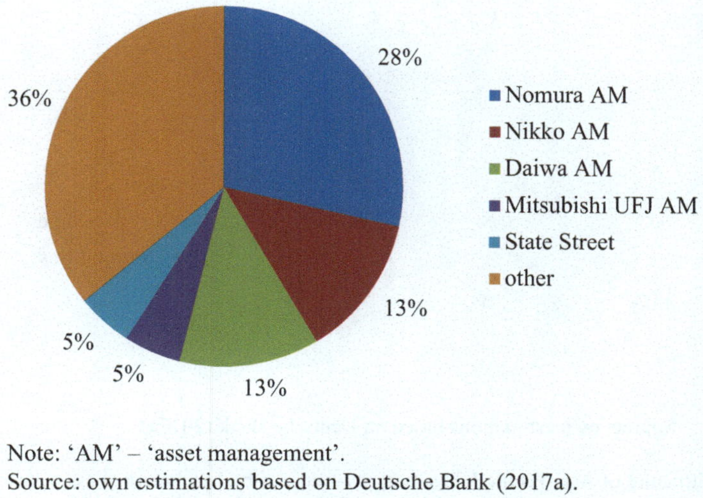

Fig. 2.6 Structure of Asia-Pacific ETFs market—assets by providers. End of October 2017. Note: *AM* asset management

Fig. 2.7 Structure of Asia-Pacific ETFs market—assets by benchmarked asset class. End of October 2017

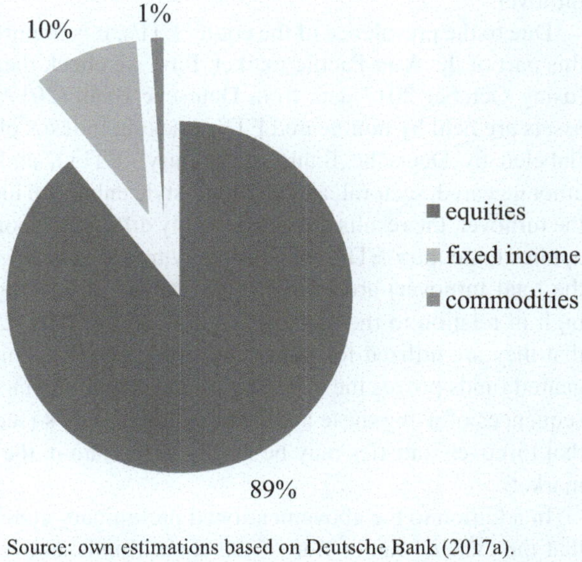

Structure of the Asia-Pacific market in terms of the benchmarked asset classes is presented on Figs. 2.7 and 2.8. Equity funds are the largest group in terms of the managed assets. However, the turnover of fixed-income (i.e., bond and money market) funds slightly exceeds that of funds based on equities. Almost the entire turnover of fixed-income funds has been linked to trades in the shares of money market funds, and their very rapidly increasing popularity (since 2016) has been

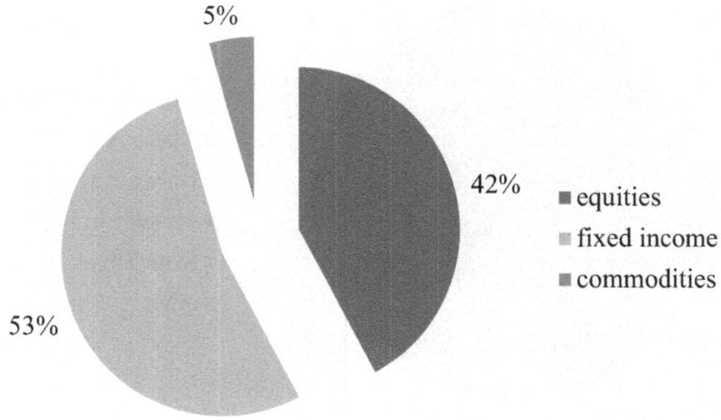

Source: own estimations based on Deutsche Bank (2017a).

Fig. 2.8 Structure of Asia-Pacific ETFs market—turnover by benchmarked asset class. October 2017

caused by very dynamic growth of such ETFs listed in Mainland China. However, prior to 2016 this category had negligible market share in terms of both assets and turnover.

Due to the prevalence of the equity ETFs, it is important to verify the structure of this part of the Asia-Pacific market. First we check their division in terms of assets (using October 2017 data from Deutsche Bank (2017a)). Eighty-seven percent of assets are held by non-geared ETFs tracking indexes of one country's stock market (labeled by Deutsche Bank as "country" ETFs), and the rest is divided mostly among geared, sectoral, and dividend-style enhanced indexing funds. If we consider the turnover, the results are considerably different. About 43% of the value of trades applies to country ETFs. Most actively traded subcategory of equity ETFs (52% of the total turnover) are geared funds (above all leveraged). Their turnover is very high in relation to the managed assets (36.2 versus 12 billion USD) which imply that they are utilized for rather short time periods. This apparent popularity of the geared funds proves the necessity to understand the mechanisms and potential consequences of using these and other synthetic ETFs (see Sect. 2.2). It also indicates that turnover statistics may be more appropriate in the analysis of the Asia-Pacific markets.

In addition to the abovementioned preliminary conclusions, it needs to be stated that the evident domination of the equity funds, above all the ones tracking major stock indexes, shows that the stock index arbitrage complex presented in Sect. 2.3 may be a relevant tool to be used in the analysis of their development patterns and determinants of these processes. The role of the other types of funds, such as bond ETFs, seems negligible, and in the predictable future they cannot be expected to threaten the position of equity funds or, even more importantly, to be an actual competition for other categories of investment funds or financial instruments.

Finally, we briefly discuss the position of ETFs in the context of Asia-Pacific investment industry which means the comparison of their role to that of the much

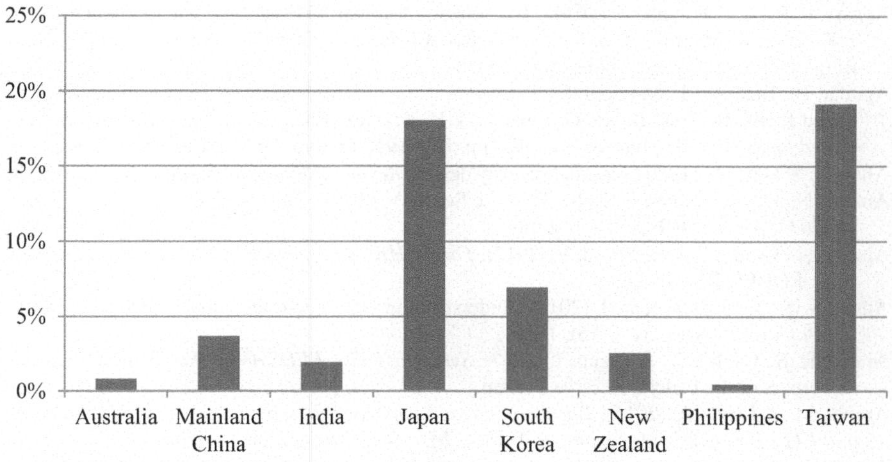

Note: data for Hong Kong not available.
Source: own estimations based on Deutsche Bank (2017a), The International Investment Funds Association (2017).

Fig. 2.9 Assets of ETFs as percentage of the sum of assets of ETFs and mutual funds in the selected Asia-Pacific economies. End of September 2017

more established mutual funds. The report by Deutsche Bank (2017a, p. 11) shows that, in terms of assets (turnover indicators cannot be used here due to lack of exchange-listing feature of mutual funds), the value of assets held by ETFs divided by the value of mutual funds' assets has increased by more than 50% between March 2014 and June 2017. However, total assets of ETFs still account for less than 10% of the combined assets of the two categories (value much higher than in Europe but still far below the one estimated for the US industry). If we consider individual countries (see Fig. 2.9), there are two with exceptionally high value of the assets of ETFs in comparison to mutual funds, Taiwan (ca. 19%) and Japan (ca. 18%; it proves again that it is the region's leader in the ETF landscape), which suggest the relatively strongest position of ETFs; for South Korea it is close to the region's average and in Mainland China several percents below the average level; in other countries the role of innovative funds is negligible against traditional ones.

References

Abner, D. (2016). *The ETF handbook. how to value and trade exchange-traded funds* (2nd ed.). Hoboken, NJ: Wiley.

Aditya, G., & Desai, R. (2015). Pricing efficiency and price discovery of Indian equity ETFs. *The Journal of Index Investing, 6*(3), 67–79.

Agapova, A. (2011). Conventional mutual index funds versus exchange-traded funds. *Journal of Financial Markets, 14*, 323–343.

Aggarwal, R., & Schofield, L. (2014). The growth of global ETFs and regulatory challenges. In J. Kose, A. K. Makhija, & S. P. Ferris (Eds.), *Advances in financial economics* (pp. 77–102). Bingley: Emerald Group Publishing Limited.

Aguilar, B., Bianco, M., Milliken, C., & Spieler, A. C. (2016). Leveraged and inverse exchange-traded funds. In H. K. Baker, G. Filbeck, & H. Kiymaz (Eds.), *Mutual funds and exchange-traded funds: Building blocks to wealth* (pp. 169–194). Oxford: Oxford University Press.

Allen, F., & Gale, D. (1989). Optimal security design. *Review of Financial Studies, 1*(3), 229–263.

Amenc, N., Ducoulombier, F., Goltz, F., & Le Sourd, V. (2015). *The EDHEC European ETF survey 2014*. Nice: EDHEC-Risk Institute.

Amenc, N., Goltz, F., & Le Sourd, V. (2017). *The EDHEC European ETF and smart beta survey*. Nice: EDHEC-Risk Institute.

Antoniewicz, R., & Heinrichs, J. (2014). Understanding exchange-traded funds: How ETFs work. *ICI Research Perspective, 20*(5), 1–20.

Aramonte, S., Caglio, C., & Tuzun, T. (2017). *Synthetic ETFs. FEDS notes*. Washington: Board of Governors of the Federal Reserve System.

Arnold, M., & Lesné, A. (2015). *The changing landscape for beta replication – Comparing futures and ETFs for equity index exposure*. Boston, MA: State Street Global Advisors.

Awrey, D. (2012). Toward a supply-side theory of financial innovation. *Journal of Comparative Economics, 41*(2), 401–419.

Badenhorst, W. M. (2017). Premiums and discounts of exchanged-traded funds. *South African Journal of Accounting Research, 31*(3), 212–222.

Ben-David, I., Franzoni, F. A., & Moussawi, R. (2012). *ETFs, arbitrage, and contagion*. Retrieved July 18, 2017, from https://www.rsm.nl/fileadmin/home/Department_of_Finance__VG5_/LQ5/Franzoni.pdf.

Ben-David, I., Franzoni, F. A., & Moussawi, R. (2017). Exchange traded funds. *Annual Review of Financial Economics, 9*, 169–189.

Bhansali, V., & Harris, L. (2018). Everybody's doing it: Short volatility strategies and shadow financial insurers. *Financial Analysts Journal, 74*(2), 12–23.

BlackRock. (2011). *ETF landscape industry review end H1 2011*. New York: BlackRock Investment Institute.

BlackRock. (2015). *The art of indexing*. New York: BlackRock Investment Institute.

Blocher, J., & Whaley, B. (2016). Two-sided markets in asset management: Exchange-traded funds and securities lending. *Vanderbilt Owen Graduate School of Management Research Paper No., 2474904*, 1–45.

Bogle, J. C. (2016). The index mutual fund: 40 years of growth, change, and challenge. *Financial Analysts Journal, 72*(1), 9–13.

Broman, M. S. (2016). Liquidity, style investing and excess comovement of exchange-traded fund returns. *Journal of Financial Markets, 30*, 27–53.

Cameron, R. (2015). *ETFs exchange traded funds: Everything to know about trading exchanges traded funds*. UK: Amazon.

Chang, C.-L., McAleer, M., & Wang, C.-H. (2018). An econometric analysis of ETF and ETF futures in financial and energy markets using generated regressors. *International Journal of Financial Studies, 6*(1), 2.

Charupat, N., & Miu, P. (2011). The pricing and performance of leveraged exchange-traded funds. *Journal of Banking & Finance, 35*(4), 966–977.

Charupat, N., & Miu, P. (2013). Recent developments in exchange-traded fund literature: Pricing efficiency, tracking ability, and effects on underlying securities. *Managerial Finance, 39*(5), 427–443.

Charupat, N., & Miu, P. (2016). *Leveraged exchange-traded funds*. New York, NY: Palgrave Macmillan.

Cheng, M., & Madhavan, A. (2009). The dynamics of leveraged and inverse exchange-traded funds. *Journal of Investment Management, 7*(4), 43–62.

CME Group. (2016). *The Big Picture: A Cost Comparison of Futures and ETFs*. London: Author.

Commodity Futures Trading Commission, & Securities and Exchange Commission. (2010). *Findings regarding the market events of May 6, 2010*. Washington, DC: Author.

Dannhauser, C. D. (2017). The impact of innovation: Evidence from corporate bond exchange-traded funds (ETFs). *Journal of Financial Economics, 125*(3), 537–560.

Deutsche Bank (2017a). *ETF monthly Asia November 2017*.

Deutsche Bank (2017b). *European monthly ETF market review synthetic equity & index strategy*.

Deville, L. (2008). Exchange traded funds: History, trading and research. In M. Doumpos, P. Pardalos, & C. Zopounidis (Eds.), *Handbook of financial engineering* (pp. 67–98). Berlin: Springer.

Diaz-Rainey, I., & Ibikunle, G. (2012). A taxonomy of the dark side of financial innovation: The cases of high frequency trading and Exchange Traded Funds. *International Journal of Entrepreneurship and Innovation Management, 16*(1), 51–72.

Elton, E. J., Gruber, M. J., & de Souza, A. (2018). *Passive mutual funds and ETFs: Performance and comparison*. Retrieved October 20, 2018, from https://papers.ssrn.com/sol3/papers.cfm?abstract_id=3192164.

ETF Securities (2017). *ETPedia: The educational guide to Exchange Traded Products (ETPs)*. Retrieved November 14, 2017, from https://www.etfsecurities.com/Documents/ETPedia.pdf#zoom=100.

ETFGI (2016). *ETF monthly newsletter June 2016*.

Eurex (2016). *Futures and options on iSahres ETFs at Eurex Exchange*.

Fama, E. F. (1965). The behavior of stock-market prices. *The Journal of Business, 38*(1), 34–105.

Fama, E. F. (1970). Efficient capital markets: A review of theory and empirical work. *The Journal of Finance, 25*(2), 383–417.

Fama, E. F., & French, K. R. (1993). Common risk factors in the returns on stocks and bonds. *Journal of Financial Economics, 33*(1), 3–56.

Farinella, J., & Kubicki, R. (2018). The performance of exchange traded funds and mutual funds. *Journal of Accounting & Finance, 18*(4), 44–55.

Ferreira, M. A., Keswani, A., Miguel, A. F., & Ramos, S. B. (2013). The determinants of mutual fund performance: A cross-country study. *Review of Finance, 17*(2), 483–525.

Ferri, R. A. (2009). *The ETF book: All you need to know about exchange-traded funds. Updated edition*. Hoboken, NJ: Wiley.

Financial Industry Regulatory Authority (2012). *Investor alerts exchange-traded notes – Avoid unpleasant surprises*.

Financial Stability Board (2011). *Potential financial stability issues arising from recent trends in Exchange-Traded Funds (ETFs)*.

Foster, F. D., & Warren, G. J. (2016). Interviews with institutional investors: The how and why of active investing. *Journal of Behavioral Finance, 17*(1), 60–84.

Foucher, I., & Gray, K. (2014). Exchange-traded funds: Evolution of benefits, vulnerabilities and risks. *Bank of Canada Financial System Review*, 37–46.

Frame, S. W., & White, L. J. (2012). Technological change, financial innovation, and diffusion in banking. In A. N. Berger, P. Molyneux, & J. O. S. Wilson (Eds.), *The Oxford Handbook of Banking*. Oxford: Oxford University Press.

French, K. R. (2008). Presidential address: The cost of active investing. *The Journal of Finance, 63*(4), 1537–1573.

Gastineau, G. L. (2010). *The exchange-traded funds manual* (2nd ed.). Hoboken, NJ: Wiley.

Goltz, F., & Schröder, D. (2011). Passive investing before and after the crisis: Investors' views on exchange-traded funds and competing index products. *Bankers, Markets and Investors, 110*, 1–22.

Golub, B. W., Ferconi, M., Madhavan, A., & Ulitsky, A. (2018). Factor-based optimisation and the creation/redemption mechanism of fixed income exchange-traded funds. *International Journal of Financial Engineering and Risk Management, 2*(4), 335–350.

Hill, J. M. (2016). The evolution and success of index strategies in ETFs. *Financial Analysts Journal, 72*(5), 8–13.

Hill, J. M., Nadig, D., & Hougan, M. (2015). *A comprehensive guide to exchange-traded funds (ETFs)*. Charlottesville, VA: CFA Institute Research Foundation.
International Monetary Fund. (2011). Global financial stability report: Durable financial stability. Getting there from here. *World Economic and Financial Surveys, 4*, 1–139.
International Monetary Fund. (2015). Global financial stability report: Navigating monetary policy challenges and managing risks. *World Economic and Financial Surveys*, 1–162.
Investment Company Institute. (2017). *Investment Company Fact Book 2017.*
Ivanov, I. T., & Lenkey, S. L. (2018). Do leveraged ETFs really amplify late-day returns and volatility? *Journal of Financial Markets, 41*, 36–56.
Khodayari, P., & Sanoubar, N. (2016). The Impact of Information and Communication Technology on the assets of mutual funds in D-8 Countries. *International Journal of Contemporary Applied Sciences, 3*(10), 11–19.
Khorana, A., Servaes, H., & Tufano, P. (2005). Explaining the size of the mutual fund industry around the world. *Journal of Financial Economics, 78*(1), 145–185.
Klapper, L., Sulla, V., & Vittas, D. (2004). The development of mutual funds around the world. *Emerging Markets Review, 5*(1), 1–38.
Kosev, M., & Williams, T. (2011). Exchange-Traded Funds. *Reserve Bank of Australia Bulletin, March Quarter*, 51–60.
Kreis, Y., & Licht, J. W. (2018). Trading on ETF mispricings. *Managerial Finance, 44*(3), 357–373.
Kreis, Y., Licht, J. W., & Useche, A. J. (2016). Efficiencies in Latin American ETFs. *Cuadernos de Administración, 29*(53), 7–48.
Lerner, J., & Tufano, P. (2011). The consequences of financial innovation: A counterfactual research agenda. *Annual Review of Financial Economics, 3*, 41–85.
Lettau, M., & Madhavan, A. (2018). Exchange-traded funds 101 for economists. *Journal of Economic Perspectives, 32*(1), 135–154.
Leung, T., & Santoli, M. (2016). *Leveraged exchange-traded funds: Price dynamics and options valuation*. Cham: Springer.
Li, M., & Zhao, X. (2014). Impact of leveraged ETF trading on the market quality of component stocks. *The North American Journal of Economics and Finance, 28*, 90–108.
Madhavan, A. N. (2012). Exchange-traded funds, market structure, and the flash crash. *Financial Analysts Journal, 68*(4), 20–35.
Madhavan, A. N. (2016). *Exchange-traded funds and the new dynamics of investing*. Oxford: Oxford University Press.
Madhavan, A. N., Marchioni, U., Li, W., & Du, D. Y. (2014). Equity ETFs versus index futures: A comparison for fully funded investors. *The Journal of Index Investing, 5*(2), 66–75.
Malkiel, B. G. (2003). Passive investment strategies and efficient markets. *European Financial Management, 9*(1), 1–10.
Malkiel, B. G. (2016). *A random walk down wall street: The time-tested strategy for successful investing*. New York: W.W. Norton & Company.
March-Dallas, S., Daigler, R., Mishra, S., & Prakash, A. (2018). Exchange traded funds: Leverage and liquidity. *Applied Economics, 50*(37), 4054–4073.
Markowitz, H. (1952). Portfolio selection. *The Journal of Finance, 7*(1), 77–91.
Mateus, C., & Rahmani, Y. (2017). Physical versus synthetic exchange traded funds. Which one replicates better? *Journal of Mathematical Finance, 7*(04), 975–989.
Maurer, F., & Williams, S. O. (2015). Physically versus synthetically replicated trackers. Is there a difference in terms of risk? *Journal of Applied Business Research, 31*(1), 131–146.
Meinhardt, C., Mueller, S., & Schoene, S. (2015). Physical and synthetic exchange-traded funds: The good, the bad, or the ugly? *The Journal of Investing, 24*(2), 35–44.
Meziani, A. S. (2016). *Exchange-traded funds: Investment practices and tactical approaches*. London: Palgrave Macmillan.
Miller, M. (1986). Financial innovation: The last twenty years and the next. *Journal of Financial and Quantitative Analysis, 21*(4), 459–471.

Murphy, C. (2017a). 15 Years of bond ETF history in A Nutshell. *ETF Report, October 2017*, 24–26.

Murphy, C. (2017b). Behind factor ETFs' popularity. Highlights from Andrew Ang's presentation at this year's Morningstar ETF conference. *ETF Report, November 2017*, 22–23.

Nikbakht, F., Pareti, K., & Spieler, A. C. (2016). Exchange-traded funds. In H. K. Baker, G. Filbeck, & H. Kiymaz (Eds.), *Mutual funds and exchange-traded funds: Building blocks to wealth* (pp. 153–168). Oxford: Oxford University Press.

Omondi, O. W. (2016). New developments in exchange-traded funds. In H. K. Baker, G. Filbeck, & H. Kiymaz (Eds.), *Mutual funds and exchange-traded funds: Building blocks to wealth* (pp. 449–469). Oxford: Oxford University Press.

Osaki, S. (2001). The development of Exchange-Traded Funds (ETFs) in Japan. *Capital Research Journal, 4*(3), 45–51.

Pástor, L., & Stambaugh, R. F. (2012). On the size of the active management industry. *Journal of Political Economy, 120*(4), 740–781.

Pedersen, L. H. (2018). Sharpening the arithmetic of active management. *Financial Analysts Journal, 74*(1), 21–36.

Petajisto, A. (2017). Inefficiencies in the pricing of exchange-traded funds. *Financial Analysts Journal, 73*(1), 24–54.

Piccotti, L. R. (2018). ETF premiums and liquidity segmentation. *Financial Review, 53*, 117–152.

Rakowski, D., Shirley, S. E., & Stark, J. R. (2017). Tail-risk hedging, dividend chasing, and investment constraints: The use of exchange-traded notes by mutual funds. *Journal of Empirical Finance, 44*, 91–107.

Ramaswamy, S. (2011). Market structures and systematic risks of exchange-traded funds. *BIS Working Papers, 343*, 1–13.

Ross, S. (1976). Arbitrage Theory of Capital Asset Pricing. *Journal of Economic Theory, 13*, 341–360.

Schoenfeld, S. (2015). Foreword. In J. M. Hill, D. Nadig, & M. Hougan (Eds.), *A comprehensive guide to Exchange-Traded Funds (ETFs)* (pp. IX–XIII). Charlottesville, VA: CFA Institute Research Foundation.

Sharpe, W. (1964). Capital asset prices: A theory of market equilibrium under conditions of risk. *The Journal of Finance, 19*(3), 425–442.

Shum, P., Hejazi, W., Haryanto, E., & Rodier, A. (2015). Intraday share price volatility and leveraged ETF rebalancing. *Review of Finance, 20*(6), 2379–2409.

Shum, P. M., & Kang, J. (2013). Leveraged and inverse ETF performance during the financial crisis. *Managerial Finance, 39*(5), 476–508.

Stein, D. M., & Narasimhan, P. (1999). Of passive and active equity portfolios in the presence of taxes. *The Journal of Wealth Management, 2*(2), 55–63.

Swathy, M. (2015). An empirical analysis on pricing efficiency of exchange traded funds in India. *International Journal of Engineering and Management Sciences, 6*(2), 68–72.

Tang, H., Xu, X. E., & Yang, Z. (2014). Can international LETFs deliver their promised exposure to foreign markets? *Journal of International Financial Markets, Institutions and Money, 31*, 30–74.

The International Investment Funds Association (2017). *Worldwide Regulated Open-End Fund Assets and Flows Third Quarter 2017.*

The International Organization of Securities Commissions (2013). *Principles for the Regulation of Exchange Traded Funds.*

Thomsett, M. (2016). *Differences between stock and future options.* Retrieved July 10, 2017, from http://www.investorguide.com/article/12605/differences-between-stock-and-future-options-wo/?gcs=1.

Tsalikis, G., & Papadopoulos, S. (2018). Assessing the performance of American and European leveraged exchange traded funds. *Investment Management and Financial Innovations, 15*(2), 165–182.

Wright, C., Diavatopoulos, D., & Felton, J. (2010). Exchange-traded notes: An introduction. *The Journal of Index Investing, 1*(1), 164–175.

Wurgler, J. (2011). On the economic consequences of index-linked investing. In W. T. Allen, R. Khurana, J. Lorsch, & G. Rosenfeld (Eds.), *Challenges to business in the twenty - first century: The way forward*. Cambridge, MA: American Academy of Arts and Sciences.

Zaremba, A., & Andreu, L. (2018). Paper profits or real money? Trading costs and stock market anomalies in country ETFs. *International Review of Financial Analysis, 56*, 181–192.

Zhang, F. (2010). High-frequency trading, stock volatility, and price discovery. Retrieved December 10, 2017, from https://papers.ssrn.com/sol3/papers.cfm?abstract_id=1691679.

Zhang, L. H. (2018). Leveraged ETFs: Are you prepared for the volatility jumps? Global perspectives on the short-term versus longer-term risk profiles. *The Journal of Index Investing, 9*(1), 19–35.

Chapter 3
Information and Communication Technologies for Financial Innovations

3.1 ICT as General-Purpose Technologies

General-purpose technologies (GPTs—hereafter) are path-breaking innovations, which are one of the most important elements enhancing long-run technological progress, as well as profound changes across economies and societies (Sahal 1981; Bresnahan 2010; Coccia 2017). Rosenberg and Trajtenberg (2004) label such innovations as "epochal innovations," radical innovations which emergence we observe during consecutive technological revolutions and which demonstrate enormous ability to reshape world economy. As claimed in Helpman (1998), general-purpose technologies enforce overwhelming changes in many sectors of national economy; they foster creation and introduction to markets of new products, services, and process. As GPTs possess huge ability to introduce society- and economy-wide structural shifts, Freeman and Soete (1987) claim that these special technologies generate changes in socioeconomic paradigm and thus support the process of economic growth and development (Bresnahan and Trajtenberg 1995; Helpman 1998; Lipsay 2002; Ruttan 2006).

Conceptually speaking, general-purpose technologies may be also defined as revolutionary changes from current patterns (trajectories) of technological change (Bresnahan 2010); and as we read in Calvano (2007), these path-breaking inventions may lead to the "destructive creation" making results of "past technological revolution" out-of-date and obsolete. As argued in Lipsey and Carlaw (1998) or Coccia (2005, 2010), GPTs once come to a wide use of economic agents; they impact pervasively various forms of economic activities and doing business and, hence, drive overall and usually permanent changes in economic structures. Coccia (2005) states that general-purpose technologies are technologies having the highest and the most intensive impact on society and economy. Generally speaking, "GPTs are characterized by pervasiveness, inherent potential for technical improvements, and 'innovational complementarities,' giving rise to increasing returns-to-scale, such as steam engine, the electric motor, and semiconductors" (Coccia 2017, p. 292). Jovanovic

A. Marszk et al., *The Emergence of ETFs in Asia-Pacific*,
https://doi.org/10.1007/978-3-030-12752-7_3

and Rousseau identify three major features of general-purpose technologies. These are pervasiveness, meaning that the impact of these innovations spreads overall all sectors of economy and is assimilated by significant share of social and economic agents; improvements, meaning that GPTs undergo permanent improvements over time, which allows for lowering the cost of their adoption and usage; and innovation spawning, meaning that broad GPT adoption makes it easier to invent and produce new products and process (Bresnahan and Trajtenberg 1995).

Evidently, from historical perspective, certain GDTs demonstrate specific dynamics; existing GPTs compete and replace and then are replaced as new GDTs emerge. The latter is closely related to technological progress and changes that come in waves (Greenwood and Jovanovic 1999). So far, the world has witnessed five technological revolutions, which—to a large extent—marked turning points in economic history of nations. During the eighteenth century, in Britain, the First Technological Wave—First Industrial Revolution (Deane 1979), also labeled the Industrial Revolution—began and gave rise to mechanization of cotton industry, improvements of the water wheel, and refinement of turnpike roads and canals (Lechman 2017). These radical, as for that time, innovations enhanced gradual increases in labor and capital productivity, enabling shifts in overall wealth and living conditions (Jones 2001). Arguably, the First Industrial Revolution was the starting point for long-term and profound reshaping of national economies and gave rise to modern economic growth (Akamatsu 1962; Kuznets 1973; Mokyr 2010). Next, since 1829 onward the world was undergoing the Second Technological Revolution, named the "age of steam and railways" (Wertime 1962; Perez 2010). Those were times of explosive development of railways, postal and telegraph services, ports, and international sailing ships. The time of the Second Industrial Revolution was marked by growing market competition and fast development of railways; newly emerged and introduced to the society, postal and telegraph services gave rise to the increasing importance of networks and communication across social and economic spheres of life (Mokyr 1998; Allen 2009). In fact, those profound changes which started during the Second Industrial Revolution constitute a starting point reshaping the way that economic agents act and do business. The emergence and gradual growth of various types of networks enhance economic activity, which—in long-run perspective—boost labor and capita productivity, and then are embodied in economic growth and welfare. Next, the period spanning from 1875 to 1908 is labeled as the Third Technological Revolution. Those times are sometimes named as age of steel and electricity (Greenwood 1997; Rifkin 2011). Advancements in broad usage of steel and electricity in different sectors of economy enforced further development of global railways and telegraph services (Stearns 2018). Moreover, it perpetuated development of analogue telephony services (Faulhaber 1995; Beniger 2009), which enabled—almost immediate—interpersonal communication. This invention, the analogue telephony, today claimed as "old ICT" was the first *gift* of technological revolutions that helped the society to communicate and transfer knowledge and information. This was crucial from the point of how societies and economies function. Importantly to note that during the Third Industrial Revolution, the use of electricity for industrial purposes become common, which was one of the main drivers of industrial development. Unexpectedly, The Third Technological Revolution was also marked by the emergence of giant companies, trusts, and cartels, which, in turn, induced a growing number of legal antitrust regulations. In 1908 the Fourth Technological Revolution started (Coleman 1956; Christopher and Louca 2001), which today is named the age of oil and mass production (Louca et al. 2001). Further path-breaking innovations allowed dynamic development of roads, automobiles (e.g., Ford plants), ports, and airports (Stern and Kander 2012). People and goods became more "movable and transferable" from different locations, although time needed to transport from place to place was significantly long. Since early years of the twentieth century, electricity was gradually deployed in a growing number of homes, and this created new network—electrical network (Freeman 2013). Also, in the beginning of the twentieth century, analogue modes of communication were gradually becoming more common to the public, as telephone, telegraph, and cablegram were spreading worldwide. These changes mandated the further development of various types of networks, which began to constitute the prime engines of economic development while simultaneously deeply transforming social structures, norms, and attitudes (Rosenberg and Birdzell 2008).

Since the early 1970s of the twentieth century, we witness the Fifth Technological Revolution (Perez 2010), also labeled the Digital Revolution (Dreyer et al. 2006; Abdelgawad and Wheeler 2009), the age of information and telecommunications, encompassing microelectronics, software, computers, and different forms of digital communications, including the Internet (Freeman and Louça 2001). Notably, the Fifth Technological Revolution emerged in 1971 when the first microprocessor developed by Intel saw the daylight, giving rise to wide ranges of path-breaking inventions and—in effect—radical restructuration of economic and social life. The ICT Revolution or the Age of Information and Communications changed the way that people communicate (Cairncross 1997), interact, and do business, and in that sense it changed societies themselves. New information and communication technologies—ICTs—are digital technologies allowing for converting the real-world information and knowledge into binary numeric systems (forms). Importantly, wide introduction of ICT technologies also allows for gradual switching from analogue to digital technologies (Toumazou et al. 1993).

By many ICT are claimed unique technologies. Due to their specific features and technological solutions they offer—specially wireless solution—these technologies are easily and fast installable and distributable among agents; ICT diffuse worldwide and may be adopted even in geographically remote, underserved, and infrastructural-deprived areas. Cairncross (2001) in her seminal book *The Death of Distance* claims that due to the widespread use of this new type of technology, communication and market activities have become distance-free, and this "death of distance" is the evident manifestation of this astonishingly rapid change observable worldwide (Lechman 2015). She writes: "wireless communication (…) is killing location, putting the world in our pocket" (Cairncross 2001, p. 2). ICT may be usually acquired relatively cheaply; hence even low-income societies may afford to buy and use it. Marginal cost of an additional user of ICT tools is close to zero (Bugamelli and Pagano 2004), which is why the growth of number of users does not require any additional investments in backbone infrastructure. All these make ICT tools relatively high affordable for people living in material deprivation. New technologies are easily imitable and deliverable (Lechman 2015); ICTs are rapidly adaptable by low-skilled, poorly educated, or even illiterate people. ICTs are to be "for all" *technologies* (Avgerou and Walsham 2017) as they spread regardless of financial, societal, linguistic, educational, and geographical barriers. What is seminal, ICTs are the prime driver of the development of worldwide network linking physically separated agents (Valente 1996; Castells et al. 2009). The latter suggests that, today, modern economic growth and development are determined by emerging economies of networks (Shapiro and Varian 1998). Katz and Shapiro (1985) and Economides (1996) stress the importance of the "network effects" (Katz and Shapiro 1986, 1994; Grajek 2003), which demonstrates the potential of increasing connectivity and unveils growing utility of certain network as the number of its users increases.

Along with the onset of the Fifth Technological Revolution—the Digital Revolution—multiple radical innovations were introduced to society and economy. The emergence and then gradual diffusion of these innovations gave rise to new products, new services, or even entirely new industries or business models. New types of networks emerged and generated disruptive effects over social, institutional, and economic systems. In that sense, ICT are disruptive (Latzer 2009) technologies; they deliver radical and transformational change to the markets, modifying the landscape. As ICTs produce crosscutting effects on all sectors of the economy, they are argued to be pervasive (ubiquitous) technologies, which are permanently available and network-connected, enrich interactions among entities, and provide effectiveness, efficiency, and empowerment (Lechman 2017). ICTs are hence disruptive and pervasive technologies, generating crosscutting effects in all sectors of the economy; henceforth ICTs are labeled general-purpose technologies (GPTs hereafter). Bresnahan and Trajtenberg (1995) define general-purpose technologies as technologies which are pervasive, having enormous and overwhelming potential to impact economy and social systems. Jovanovic and Rousseau (2005) argue that ICTs by bringing cutting-edge technological improvements evade societies and economies, and in the longtime perspective, they produce capital and labor productivity gains. ICTs are general-purpose technologies, they are endogenously disseminated throughout society, and they not only change the structure of economy but also enforce higher development dynamics. Additionally, GPTs, and to that ICT, are characterized by technological dynamism (Bresnahan and Trajtenberg 1995), which means that innovation efforts are made continuously increasing ICT's intime efficiency. GPTs pave road ahead and open up new opportunities, "as GPTs appear (…) there is a spell a growth, with rising output, real wages, and profits" (Helpman and Trajtenber 1996, p. 4). Bresnahan and Trajtenberg (1995) isolate few characteristics of general-purpose technologies, and evidently ICTs possess all of them. First, and the most important, feature of GPTs is that they are claimed the "enabling technologies" meaning that they open up and offer new opportunities paving roads ahead. They write that "as GPT (…) advance it spreads throughout the economy, bringing about and fostering generalized productivity gains" (Bresnahan and Trajtenberg 1995, p. 4), which spread throughout economy and society. Next, continuous advancements in technological development drive the emergence of innovational complementarities, which strengthen positive productivity gains generated by GPTs. Broad introduction and deployment of GPTs to economic activity enables new downstream inventions and innovations, which before and without those GPTs was not possible. Finally, Bresnahan and Trajtenberg (1995) notice an interesting feature of general-purpose technologies, and as such they claim that those types of technological solutions do not have close substitutes, which obviously distinguishes them from widely used different technologies. In Bresnahan (2010) we read that general-purpose technologies bring revolutionary changes from current technological trajectories, while Calvano (2007) brings the notion that GPTs are transformative in nature and enforce path-breaking shifts to economy and society. Coccia (2010) additionally stresses that different general-purpose technologies have an "ability" to remove and/or omit barriers to wider technological and economic development, which to a large extent impacts social welfare.

Today, as already claimed, ICTs are receiving growing attention; new information and communication technologies are perceived as tools (enablers), which—due to their unique features—foster economic growth and development. Arguably ICTs bring to world countries opportunities to fight underdevelopment and technological deprivation, by improving economic performance and ability to compete on global markets, and they provide means for exploitation of unused labor force and increase social capital (Lipsey et al. 2005).

What seems to be of seminal importance, ICT create effective and cheap ways for information flows opening new possibilities to enhance economic activity on larger scale (Wright 2000; Coccia 2018). The nexus between new technology deployment and achievements of certain "development goals" is recognized, and it is based on mutually shared objectives, which are efficient, scalable, and affordable, and pervasive delivery of goods, services, and information flows between people, government, and firms. ICTs bring open new "opportunity windows" (Perez and Soete 1988; Pérez 2003), despite the fact that exploration of links between technology adoption and economic advancements is not straightforward.

3.2 ICT as Driver of Financial Market Development

In what follows, we focus specifically on the impact of the new technologies on the development of the financial system, drawing special attention to potentially emerging relationships between ICT and financial markets. As the leading topic of the book are ETFs and vast majority of ETFs available globally (including the Asia-Pacific region) are equity funds and, to much lesser extent, bond funds, in our discussion we concentrate on the impact of ICT on the stock markets; the effects regarding other parts of the financial system are mentioned briefly. In the final part of this section, we present some of the contemporary issues linked with the ICT adoption in the financial system, such as the broadly understood fintech. Throughout this section we outline both theoretical concepts and refer to results of the previous empirical research.

It is widely recognized that world economy as such, but also its smaller parts like, for instance, financial systems, is moving rapidly toward global and technology-driven markets. The emergence and broad introduction to society and economy is evidenced by new information and communication technologies, which are blossoming, and are fast, small in scale, precise, cheap, and easy to adopt and use, in particular when compared to "old" technological solutions. Rapid and overwhelming diffusion of ICT to all economy sectors is challenging to social and economic frameworks and seems to have a profound impact of financial rule of law and the mode that, both national and global, financial systems work. By many, the influence of technological progress and specific technological solutions is viewed as a key driving force of change and key to achieve productivity, efficiency, and efficacy increases. As ICTs proliferate all spheres of economy, there emerge new operating schemes, norms, and attitudes that modify our social, economic, organizational, and institutional framework.

Already in 1944, Karl Polanyi underlined the importance of internationalization of finance, calling them the "haute finance." He stressed then in the postwar Bretton Woods system that financial system was undergoing profound transformation, which was catalyzed and accelerated by technological change. This *great transformation*, and as Polanyi (1944) stated this *quantum jump*, in the sensitivity of financial instruments and prices, has attracted both big and small actors to search for profits, which contributed enormously to market expansion. Financial systems seem to be this part of economy that are extremely exposed to being, both positively and negatively, affected, by rapid diffusion on new information and communication technologies. Ad hoc analysis may lead to general understanding of the dynamics between introductions of ICT, contextualizing structural changes that take place across financial systems and also identifying major channels of new technologies that impact on those systems. A massive body of literature emphasizes the role of consecutive technological revolution on the process of development of financial systems. Today, from historical perspective, the most crucial period in history of economic development and development of financial systems seems to be years of the Third Industrial Revolution. The Third Industrial Revolution profoundly reshaped economic structures of production, and, above all, it led to separation of finance capital and the state. Since then onward, capital could "freely" move to sick rent and profits; this was the real beginning of financial system expansion. Moreover, as we read in, inter alia, Krasner (1983), Hamilton (1986), or Rifkin (2011), the changes brought by the Third Industrial Revolution enhanced growing autonomy of financial systems and related state institutions. In the 1930s, the abstract nature of finance became the fact as trade in commodity gold has been broken and trading in financial instruments became virtually instantaneous (Cerny 1994). In this context, the development and broad dissemination of new information and communication technologies seems to have even greater importance, compared to past technological shifts. This enormous expansion of global financial system is marked with growth of variety of transactions among physically separated agents, with no physical commodities to sell or buy, to move or transport. Fast development and society-wide deployment of electronic computer as well as other forms of communication technologies allow, for instance, for fast transferring of money across the globe with no significant time delays and at relatively low cost. Transfer of different financial instruments, without the necessity to record it with paper certificates, is another tremendous change; financial transactions become dematerialized to a large extent. Combing ICT into financial system allows de-linking financial operation from geography. Undeniably, this tremendous change that financial system undergoes as ICTs diffuse worldwide has also far-reaching implications for the "real economy" sectors making the tangible goods better sellable and distributable on global markets. In some sense, these shifts on financial system can even contribute to the overall efficiency of the whole economy.

As stressed in the previous section, ICTs enable fast and unbounded flow of information. This unique feature of new information and communication technologies not only seems to be of crucial importance, from the social or economic perspective, but defines how financial system functions. To a large extent, fast and unlimited flows of information among geographically separated agents may effectively boost both volume and value of financial markets transactions. The "death of distance" in case of financial markets work matters as in none of other cases; we would even risk that it totally redefines and reshapes financial systems. Broad adoption of ICT enhances the emergence of the unique financial system network, which links market agents facilitating exchange of information among them and—to some point—links financial institutions and legal frameworks that seem to influence one another. All these define the environment that the financial system operates. Financial systems may be claimed information systems (Ocampo 2018), and undoubtedly the emergence of such system due to ICT deployment network connectivity effectively strengthens it, makes it work more effectively, and thus increases profits it generates. Fast spread of various types of information across individual entities being part of global, interconnected financial system—in longer time horizon—may lead to total eradication of information inequalities and hence to elimination of one of the market failures that hinders system's effectiveness. Above all, ICT introduction effects to financial system are not limited to eradication of information asymmetries, but above all new technologies bring to financial system new opportunities. These new opportunities are, in the first place, demonstrated through development and diffusion of new financial products (for more see in the consecutive sections) and pricing systems. These create ideal conditions for the emergence of new "specialized" financial markets becoming a substantial part of the whole, global financial system. Introduction of new specialized financial products, by definition, increases demand, makes these new products more tradable, and hence boosts financial transactions. Another aspect of the role of ICT for financial system is that new technologies are thought to make financial markets work more "effectively." That is closely linked to the fact that ICTs allow for information asymmetry elimination, as well as fast spread of various types of information. For functioning of financial systems, the flow of information on pricing is of crucial importance. Efficient pricing systems clear markets and make the financial markets become gradually self-regulated (Asongu and Nnanna 2018). The latter shall inevitably lead to establishing equilibrium on the market, but at the same time dynamic exchange of information among actors drives rapid changes in prices.

The aspects of the relationships between information and communication technologies and financial system development, briefly discussed above, bring to mind the reflection that dynamic progress on the field of technology and gradual emergence on technological innovations drive increasingly transnationalized (globalized) financial system. ICT as none of technology before effectively boosted financial globalization (Neave 2017; Giddens 2018). Cerny (1994) in his influential paper from 1994 wrote that "looking briefly at a range of approaches to the process of financial globalization itself, (…) technological change is the main independent variable, by reducing transaction costs and dramatically increasing the price sensitivity of financial markets across borders, while at the same time making possible a range of economies of scale" (Cerny 1994, p. 319). In the same paper, Cerny (1994) underlines that globalized financial system permanently interacts with different groups of interests of institutional frameworks of states, which leads to "regulatory arbitrage." The latter, however, is usually demonstrated through significant shifts toward the deregulation and liberalization of financial system. Technological change, the rise of network connectivity, drives expansion of financial system structures; it also expands international capital flows, which generates questions on transnational legal and institutional frameworks and regulation policies at national level. New sophisticated technological solutions enhance breakthroughs in international capital mobility, and this inevitably yields new legal frameworks so that these flows may be effectively regulated to ensure the benefits for investors and—at least partially—to escape negative effects in instability and market failure.

But not all gold glitters. This network connectivity that has overwhelmed financial systems due to ICT spread, in some aspects, may lead to negative consequences. In here, it shall be stressed that the more new technologies and financial systems are developed, and the more intensely they are interconnected and interdepended, the broader possible range of market failure emerges. Undeniably, advances in structure and functioning of financial systems, as well as emergence of new and innovative financial products, bring some threats. Indeed, multiple linkages between financial institutions and their interdependency (Eisenberg 1995), paradoxically, may increase financial system volatility, uncertainty, vulnerability, and exposure to external negative shocks. As the global financial system still suffers from different asymmetries, on aggregate level, negative shocks may result in, for instance, bankruptcy cascades across consecutive phases of the business cycle (Cont and Bouchaud 2000). The highly internationalized financial system is composed of huge number of mutual relations both between individuals and between institutions, and the existence of this network itself brings risk of financial contagion of, inter alia, financial crises (see Allen and Gale 2000a, b; Iori et al. 2006; Lenzu and Tedeschi 2012). As stated in Grilli et al., "(…) when the connectivity become too high and things go wrong, financial linkages among highly leveraged agents represent propagation channels for contagion and source of systemic risk" (Grilli et al. 2015, p. 288). Claims similar in kind may be traced in Cabrales et al. (2015), who describe the process of contagion across agents in networks, which enforces negative shock transmission. Financial systems are especially prone to the process of negative shock transmission, under imperfect information and when all agents are highly interconnected. The term "too interconnected" might be correct in that case, as costs of staying in network exceed expected profits. Paradoxically, even though positive gains from ICT adoption for financial system are undeniable, this system becomes more sensitive and exposed to external shocks and instabilities.

When turning to more specific analysis, we claim that the influence of ICT on the financial markets (as stated at the beginning of this section, we focus on the stock markets) can be positive (from the perspective of the impact on their development) or negative, yet it seems that the first type of relationship is more prominent as proven by the previous research; obviously, there are also some areas of influence which may be deemed to be neutral. We devote most attention to the key potential field of impact—infrastructure of the financial markets.

ICT influence the infrastructure of the financial markets, thus deeply impacting their key attributes. According to Essendorfer et al. (2015), infrastructure of the financial markets facilitates trading, processing, and settlement of securities, commodities, and currencies between counterparties as well as provision of other supportive services such as aggregation of data and information from multiple sources.

In case of stock markets (or, more generally, capital markets), exchanges are one of the key elements of the financial markets' infrastructure. Adoption of new technologies means that the position of floor-based exchanges diminishes as market participants begin to opt for exchanges with electronic trading systems due to their time and cost efficiency, the processes that were labeled by Hendershott and Madhavan (2015) as "voice to electronic." It also means that competition among trading venues becomes more intensive as incumbents are challenged by new entrants due to lowered entry barriers—the most noticeable area is derivatives trading (e.g., futures and options), where linked effect was introduction of new types of contracts, unfeasible to trade on conventional exchanges (Lee 2010; Ernkvist 2015), yet it applies to all types of dematerialized securities, i.e., held in the form of digital records at depositary institution (Kauffman et al. 2015b); the benefit of the dematerialization, which does not require physical exchange of the transacted stocks, is reduction of the transactions' costs and duration. As Engelen and Grote (2009) claim, the other effect of the "virtualization" of the stock exchanges is the decline of the second-tier financial centers.

Apart from the growing competition, some other infrastructure-linked effects which may boost the development of the stock markets were identified in the literature. According to Hendershott et al. (2011), who concentrate on algorithmic trading (discussed also below with regard to one of its categories, i.e., high-frequency trading), higher automation of the stock trading processes should be perceived positively from the perspective of the market participants as it reduces trading costs and time delays; in a broader outlook it means that liquidity of the listed stocks increases, and pricing and risk-sharing mechanisms are more efficient. Schmiedel et al. (2006) show that improved cost-effectiveness of the stock depository and settlement systems can be obtained through continuous implementations of new systems and technological upgrades; another benefit is the increased possibility to list and trade stocks on multiple trading venues which may be located even in physically distant locations (also due to more efficient exchange rate risk management). Nishimura

(2010) focuses on the impact of ICT-enabled changes on the microstructure of the stock markets, stating, inter alia, that electronic trading systems are characterized by higher rate of information dissemination than the conventional, floor-based ones (it applies to the both the spread of information between market participants and, more broadly, between markets in various countries). Madhavan (2012) considers the benefits for market participants stating that they can act quickly and use the most recent data. In the broadest perspective, according to Panourgias (2015), adoption of electronic trading system in multiple countries has led to more integrated and globalized capital markets.

One of the most apparent applications of ICT with regard to the turnover on the stock markets (and some other parts of capital markets), enabled by adoption of electronic trading system, is high-frequency trading (HFT) in which computers (based on algorithms—therefore it is a subset of algorithmic trading (Zhang 2010)) are in charge of the assessment of market data (looking for various signals before they are noticed by other market participants) and conduct transactions at low latencies, with fast execution of the orders (McGowan 2010; Prewitt 2012). On many developed financial markets, HFT accounts for substantial share of the transactions on the stock markets which proves their significant role.

Impact of HFT on the financial markets, according to results of various studies, is mixed—as it is an extremely intensively studied topic, we present only selected issues; for an extensive overview, see Menkveld (2016); other notable recent studies include Aldridge and Krawciw (2017), Kirilenko et al. (2017), Leal and Napoletano (2017), Seddon and Currie (2017), Brennan et al. (2018), Brogaard et al. (2018), and Hasbrouck (2018). Brogaard et al. (2014) examined the role of HFT and conclude that it improves the price efficiency through the conducted transaction—made opposite to the transitory pricing errors and in the direction according to the permanent price changes; generally, the direction of their orders is correlated with publicly available information and imbalances in the limit order book. Menkveld (2018) studied the transactions on NASDAQ and states that the risk of price instability inflicted by HFT is highly limited. According to Menkveld and Zoican (2017), the impact of HFT on the liquidity of securities can be both positive and negative, and the net effect depends on the relationship between the updates of the quotes of securities based on the incoming news and the group of market participants that are the main users of these quotes, i.e., whether they are utilized by the speculative or liquidity traders. Some potential threats of the increased adoption of HFT include increased volatility of the equity markets (Diaz-Rainey et al. 2015), lack of adequate control and supervision, for example, by regulatory authorities, and large and irreversible losses of the markets' participants (Kauffman et al. 2015b). Kauffman et al. (2015a) and Zhou and Kalev (2019) examined the HFT in the Asia-Pacific region, focusing on the factors that affect the growth of the computerized trading.

Some authors link the impact of ICT on the financial markets to their influence on the particular country's economic situation (see Sect. 3.1 for in-depth discussion). Gardner et al. (2017) state that there are two reasons for the validity of such approach. First, stock markets mirror the current and, even more importantly in this context, also the expected country's economic performance which means exposure to some level of uncertainty due to lack of access to full information or limited projection capacity. Stock markets may benefit from the adoption of ICT due to reduction of risks associated with deficient information or uncertainty. Second, the rather straightforward reason is the following: as stock markets may be regarded as barometers of the economic situation, any positive impact of ICT on economy is indirectly observed also on the equity markets.

Impact of the new technologies is, though, not unequivocally positive as there are some potential negative effects of the broader ICT adoption in the context of the financial markets; most of them linked to the increasingly computer-based infrastructure of the financial markets. As Preece (2012) states, based on the example of the US equity market, the interactions between market participants have become highly automated, and speed is the critical factor. Johnson et al. (2013) notice that the speed of trading has reached levels which require measurement even in nanoseconds, i.e., impossible to reach in case of fully or even dominantly human-conducted transactions. On the one hand, this may be perceived as the positive effect of the ICT adoption due to, for example, limited time delays. On the other, there are a number of related potentially negative consequences, probably best evidenced by the aforementioned threats associated with HFT.

Two other problematic issues are potentially increasing fragmentation and complexity. Due to the adoption of new technologies but also as a result of regulatory changes and globalization processes, traditional stock exchanges are no longer the dominant stock trading venue—the role of off-exchange trading has strengthened, meaning that liquidity of financial markets (e.g., stock markets) has become increasingly fragmented. Another resulting change, with both positive and negative consequences, is the high complexity of the processes by which the transactions are handled—such processes rely to a high extent on advanced technologies (Preece 2012). Overall, not only with regard to the stock trading, broader adoption of ICT by the participants of the financial markets and in the markets' infrastructure leads to their increasing complexity which may be a barrier, for instance, for the regulatory authorities (Diaz-Rainey and Ibikunle 2012).

Apart from the stock markets, another negative effect of the ICT diffusion, transcending the financial system and connected to some extent to the development of ETFs markets (at least with regard to certain categories of ETFs), is financialization of the commodity markets (Patterson 2012) that may have substantial economic and social consequences (this topic lies outside the scope of our book).

Impact of ICT on the stock markets described in the preceding paragraphs was verified empirically by a number of researchers—we already presented some of these studies that focused on certain specific issues such as the effects of HFT. In the subsequent paragraphs, we discuss the studies that cover the influence of ICT in a broader perspective, i.e., on the development of the stock markets (considered in various dimensions). Generally, results of these studies, which are still relatively scarce, indicate positive influence of the ICT adoption. In order to provide a brief overview, we discuss below studies conducted for various groups of markets, in countries at different level of economic development. Unfortunately, no studies which focus specifically on the Asia-Pacific region could be identified.

Starting with the world's largest equity market, i.e., in the United States, results of the study by the CFA Institute (Preece 2012) prove that it is critically dependent on the adopted technologies; among them the prominent role is played by ICT which enabled the creation and functioning of the decentralized electronic network. Results of another study, by Essendorfer et al. (2015), confirm this conclusion and indicate both positive and negative consequences, showing that unequivocal assessment is impossible. Among the former, they show that stock trading has become faster and less expensive; among the latter, at the same time, it has become more fragmented, and volatility has magnified.

In one of the first studies on this topic, Ngassam and Gani (2003) checked the impact of ICT on the stock market development in a sample of high-income and emerging economies, concluding that in both groups that effect was positive. Rezaie Dolat Abadi et al. (2013) conducted a study that covered all major world's equity markets (in 60 countries). They found positive influence with regard to most indexes (capitalization and turnover) used to determine the stock market's development level (however, the impact on the ease of access to the local equity market seems to be the weakest). Gardner et al. (2017), who used data on almost all active world's stock markets (in 81 countries), observe that expansion of ICT is positively associated with one of the stock market development indicators, i.e., capitalization. Pradhan et al. (2018) analyzed the linkages between the adoption of ICT, development of stock markets, and economic growth in the group of 14 emerging and developing countries—the results of their analysis confirm their long-term relationships.

The effects of ICT adoption have also been tested with the focus on less developed countries. In the country-specific study for India, Bhunia (2011) confirmed the positive impact on the Indian stock market's development in various dimensions. For instance, Okwu (2015) evaluated the discussed relationship on the two major African stock markets (in Nigeria and South Africa) and concluded that application of ICT (mostly in the area of stock transactions) may be described as one of their main development factors.

In the preceding paragraphs, we discussed the impact of ICT on the entire financial system, after which we focused on its role in the context of financial markets. However, it needs to be emphasized that much more extensively researched area is the influence of the new technologies on the banking sector (we omit other parts of the financial sector)—higher interest in that part of the financial system should not be deemed as surprising as on a global scale. The economic significance of the banking sector (measured, for example, in relation to the GDP of particular countries) is much higher. Nonetheless, we mention only a few selected issues related to this topic as it is not highly significant in the context of this book's theme.

Probably some of the most well-recognized results of the new technologies' implementation in the banking sector are credit cards and ATMs. However, their impact is much deeper. ICT influence both the structure and services provided by banks (our discussion draws substantially from Diaz-Rainey et al. (2015)). With regard to the structure of the banking institutions, ICT adoption facilitates more complex task-sharing, e.g., between branches in various countries. It applies above all to various types of back-office tasks which may be located in countries with relatively lower labor costs or other advantages, despite the fact that they are very distant from the bank's major markets. Even more importantly, new technologies have facilitated introduction or development of numerous types of financial services offered by banks, among them electronic payments, online and mobile banking services for retail clients, and electronic processing of financial operations. It should be stressed that the technologically supported banking services are available and popular in various types of countries, not necessarily limited to the most advanced economies (one of the most distinctive examples is the vast popularity of mobile banking in less developed African or Asian countries, in spite of overall underdeveloped financial systems, e.g., in terms of the conventional banking institutions). Moreover, some services traditionally associated with banks are increasingly more often provided by various non-banking companies (see the overview of fintech below).

Current discussion concerning the impact of new technologies on the financial system, including financial markets, concentrates on various types of fintech (alternatively, "FinTech" or "fintech"). Unfortunately, despite substantial attention attracted by this concept, there is no clear-cut definition of fintech which hinders its proper analysis, e.g., in the context of the financial markets. We refer to just two among numerous definitions presented in the scientific literature. First, Schueffel (2016, p. 45), after extensive study on the publications that cover the issue of fintech, defines it as "a new financial industry that applies technology to improve financial activities."[1] And second, Varga (2017, p. 23), also preceded by analysis of various embarked definitions, states that it is "non- or not fully regulated ventures whose goal is to develop novel, technology-enabled financial services (…)." In both definitions fintech companies are clearly distinguishable from the traditional financial institutions, even if they also provide digitalized services. It is also useful to consider the concepts of fintech used among the financial practitioners. R. Edelman in the interview (Bell 2017, p. 16) defines it as "the use of technology for the creation or delivery of financial products or services," and in the context of investment industry he states that it "is created by technology companies and financial service companies for the purpose of creating investment opportunities or for service delivery." He emphasizes that financial technology is a not a new phenomenon as many types of "financial technologies" have been launched over the centuries, including introduction of credit cards or even the currency itself. It may be clearly noticed that this concept differs from the two mentioned previously as it is much broader, covering in fact all types of companies, and it focuses on the product or service provided rather than the responsible entity. Throughout the book (in particular in the Chap. 6), we use the term "fintech industry" or "fintech sector" to denote companies that provide various types of fintech services (see the list in the next paragraph).

Dorfleitner et al. (2017) divide the fintech industry into four categories, according to the function they perform in the financial system:

[1] Similar in-kind definition may be found on the website of *FinTech Weekly*, one of the leading fintech professional magazines: "a business that aims at providing services by making use of software and modern technology" (Fintech Weekly 2018).

1. Financing (both for households and companies)
   (a) Crowdfunding
   (b) Credit and factoring (e.g., innovative online-based factoring solutions)
2. Asset management (discussed in the Sect. 3.3)
   (a) Social trading
   (b) Robo advice
   (c) Personal financial management
   (d) Investment and banking
3. Payments
   (a) Alternative payment methods (e.g., mobile payments)
   (b) Blockchain and cryptocurrencies
4. Other functions
   (a) Insurance
   (b) Search and comparison engines
   (c) Technology and infrastructure
   (d) Other types

One of the most intensively discussed technological solutions linked to the recent developments in the financial system is blockchain—a specific type of data structure in which data are stored and transmitted in packages ("blocks" as in the first part of its name) that are interconnected within a digital "chain" (second part of the name); cryptographic and algorithmic methods are employed by blockchains (Natarajan et al. 2017). Probably the most publicized and recognized application of the blockchain technology is cryptocurrencies, including the most renowned Bitcoin. Cryptocurrencies are a group of digital (virtual) currencies that employ cryptographic techniques (Natarajan et al. 2017); blockchain is used in the cryptocurrency transactions (Dorfleitner et al. 2017). We do not discuss the issue of cryptocurrencies in more detail as it is not related directly to the ETFs markets or investment industry (with some exceptions); however, it should be mentioned that as of early 2018, some ETF providers in the United States are attempting to launch funds with exposure to Bitcoin, yet US regulatory authorities (SEC) object this idea.

Apart from cryptocurrencies, some of the other financial applications linked to blockchains include, inter alia, using the distributed ledger technology (DLT) in which various records are kept and updated for the entire network by users rather than by some central entity to record data on capital market transactions or ownership of assets (He et al. 2017); it means that falsifying the information stored on a number of servers is difficult (Dorfleitner et al. 2017; Natarajan et al. 2017). The impact of blockchains may be also identified in the field of financial advising yet as for now mostly conceptually (Bell 2017); for the empirical study of some example of the new technology's utilization in the investment funds, see Kaal and Dell'Erba (2017). Adoption of blockchains is expected to diminish the number of administrative tasks conducted by financial advisors such as providing information about the value of the client's portfolio or performing periodic or emergency rebalancing of the assets—advisors' responsibilities are predicted to shift toward strategic analysis and personalized advice.

Big data is yet another example of the technological solution regarded as having potential to transform at least some aspects of the economic and financial system. Together with artificial intelligence (AI), it comprises the analysis of complex databases (gathered from, e.g., social networks) that contain attributes and transactions of billions of economic agents with the application of advanced algorithms in order to determine some patterns useful for predictions of behaviors and prices and, ultimately, mimicking human assessment (He et al. 2017); machine learning and predictive analysis are related concepts. Applications in the financial system include automated credit approvals and, with regard to the financial markets, automated trading. Moreover, it may be used to provide highly personalized investment advisory services and marketing campaigns (Madhavan 2016). For the discussion of the potential transformation of the wealth management that can be inflicted by the cognitive computing, (encompassing machine learning, big data, data mining, and many others) see Kliman and Arinze (2019).

It must be emphasized that all aforementioned technological solutions are inextricably linked with the adoption of the basic types of ICT, in particular allowing for more widespread access to the Internet as well as quicker and more stable Internet connection. As He et al. (2017, p. 11) state, the Internet has transformed the financial industry, facilitating accessing a broad range of financial services by billions of consumers through, for instance, mobile devices.

Due to its relatively short period of significant presence in the financial system, the impact of the fintech industry on the economic and financial systems (as well as the societies) remains still to be assessed. Some preliminary findings are presented in the report published by the International Monetary Fund (He et al. 2017)—the following effects may be observed:

- Blurring boundaries between markets, intermediaries, and providers of financial services
- Less reliance on the traditional financial intermediaries (such as banks) and increased role of networks
- Changes in the entry barriers that are becoming lower or higher (in the large closed networks)
- New regulatory challenges

Due to the high diversity of the fintech sectors in various countries, we do not discuss the results of the empirical studies that examined their impact on the financial system (understood broadly or with regard to the specific sectors) or the entire economy (most of these studies focus on the impact of fintech on the financial inclusion). However, in Chap. 6, within the country-specific analysis, we refer to the studies that were performed for the examined Asia-Pacific countries (if available).

3.3 ICT and Exchange-Traded Funds: Tracing Causal Links

In this section we focus on the linkages between the adoption of ICT and development of ETFs markets (i.e., diffusion of ETFs). We focus on the potential role played by the new technologies in the spread of the innovative funds—to some extent our discussion is based on the conclusions presented in the preceding section in which we showed the influence of ICT on the development of financial markets. We start by presenting some general remarks concerning factors affecting the diffusion of ETFs, then we discuss the impact of ICT on the demand and supply side of the ETFs market, and, finally, we show some actual, up-to-date examples of the ICT adoption in the investment industry, related at least to some extent to ETFs (above all selected types of fintech). The impact of ICT on the diffusion of ETFs in the Asia-Pacific countries is verified empirically in Chap. 6.

As discussed in the Sect. 2.3, determinants of the ETFs diffusion may be divided into two broad categories:

1. Demand-side factors: associated with the comparative advantages of ETFs in relation to alternative financial products (e.g., conventional mutual funds or, to lesser extent, stock index futures)
2. Supply-side factors: associated with the motivations of the funds' providers and other institutions taking part in the creation and distribution of the ETFs' units, above all affecting the decisions to enter or withdraw from the ETFs market

Among many factors that may influence the diffusion of ETFs, one group requires particular attention due to its significance—development of the financial markets, in particular stock markets. Explanation behind this statement is rather straightforward—vast majority of globally available innovative funds are equity ETFs, tracking the stock market indexes. On the demand side, ensuring benefits of ETFs such as low costs and tracking errors (in case of passive funds) requires sufficiently developed financial markets. On the other hand, supply side of the ETFs market, the launch and proper functioning of the innovative funds are critically dependent upon developed financial markets (some additional considerations refer to issues such as cross-listing of ETFs or funds offering exposure to foreign assets).

In the next paragraphs of this section, we focus therefore on the effects of ICT adoption on the stock markets (both the ones already discussed in the preceding section and some additional aspects) that may through that channel influence the ETFs markets. It needs to be added that most presented relationships can also be referred to the bond market (bond ETFs are the second-largest group of the innovative funds). Other potential channels are mentioned briefly. Another possible framework of this discussion would involve general analysis of the impact of ICT on financial innovation—such approach can be traced back to, inter alia, Sharpe (1991) who acknowledges that the new technological developments substantially contributed to the spread of financial innovations.

Demand-side factors are to a large extent linked to the costs of investments into ETFs. One of the effects of ICT adoption on the stock markets (here we consider stock trading venues such as stock exchanges) is increasing utilization of electronic trading systems as well as computerized and automated supplementary processing systems necessary for, e.g., the correct settlement of the transactions. At the same time, the role of traditional, open-outcry systems decreases. As the shares of ETFs are listed and traded analogously to the shares of public corporations, most effects of ICT that refer to stock (or generally securities) trading may also be considered with regard to the shares of innovative funds. Trading costs, from the perspective of the ETFs' investors, are important part of the total cost of these financial products. Lower trading costs in the computerized systems of stock trading, settlement, depository, etc. (in comparison with the physical systems) may lead therefore to less expensive transactions in the shares of ETFs. Additionally, as most ETFs are equity-based products, it means that the costs incurred by the entities responsible for the creation and redemption of their shares may also be lowered, leading indirectly to benefits for the ETFs' users.

Further demand-side impact of the adoption of ICT-based trading and related systems on the equity markets may be observed with regard to the other benefit of many ETFs—low tracking errors (deviations of the returns on ETFs from the returns on their benchmarks), facilitated, inter alia, by arbitrage transactions conducted by market participants such as authorized participants. In order to ensure the maximum benefits from the arbitrage operations (i.e., lowest tracking errors), it should be possible to conduct them cheaply and quickly, based on the most recent data on the prices of the ETFs' shares and tracked indexes (or other assets). Moreover, these benefits (e.g., access to the up-to-date market data) extend to other groups of ETFs markets' participants who may be thus able to conduct more informed transactions, for instance, in case of important events. In conjunction with increasingly technologically sophisticated financial services provided for the individual or institutional investors (e.g., online brokerage accounts) and generally broader access to the Internet in the society, it means that users of ETFs can gain access to continuously updated data about ETFs and other assets and be able to act on such information with limited time delays. Consequently, ETFs may attract even more demand from various groups of investors, at the expense of, above all, mutual funds that do not offer such possibilities. The market-broad effect of the outlined changes is the increased rate of the dissemination of information among market participants, higher liquidity of the ETFs' shares, as well as more efficient pricing and risk-sharing mechanisms.

On the supply side of the ETFs market, most substantial effects of the ICT adoption should apply to the transactions conducted on the primary segment or even internal operations of the funds' providers. Shares of ETFs are created and redeemed in the course of transactions between providers and (usually) authorized participants, mostly of the in-kind character. These transactions require transfers of securities whose costs and duration may be reduced by adoption of technologically sophisticated trading, settlement, and depository systems (with the particular role of Internet connections and digitalization (e.g., manifested by dematerialization)). As a result, incentives of these entities to enter the ETFs market and further develop the innovative funds may be affected, increasing their interest in this part of the financial system (due to, for example, higher potential profits). Adoption of the computerized systems can be particularly important in case of more complicated types of ETFs such as geared funds or, more generally, other groups of funds that employ derivatives; it also applies to the possibility to launch and trade derivatives based on the shares of ETFs (e.g., options on ETFs).

Another important supply-side attribute of the ETFs which can be strongly affected by the ICT adoption is the cross-listing of their shares, observed for many funds (it may refer to the listing on two exchanges or other trading venues (dual listing) or more than two (in some cases several) in the same or various countries). In order to facilitate the cross-listing and ensure the cost and time efficiency for investors, trading and related systems on all involved exchanges must be technologically sophisticated so that, for example, the deviations between the prices of certain ETFs' shares are limited and assets can be promptly transferred, sometimes between countries (Calamia et al. 2013).

Most of the ICT-related factors of the ETFs' diffusion discussed in the preceding paragraphs are linked to the benefits of the innovative funds when compared to traditional investment funds. However, there are also some effects related to the relative benefits of ETFs versus stock index futures (for more on this topic, see Sect. 2.3). They affect above all one of the key relative benefits of ETFs in comparison with the stock index futures, i.e., the broader product range, which is in fact another supply-side issue. Category of ETFs covers funds offering exposure to various types of assets, including foreign securities (usually equities). Correct functioning of such funds and attractiveness of their attributes in comparison with competing financial products, similarly to the cross-listed funds, require adoption of ICT-based exchange systems not only in the country of the primary listing of their shares. What is more, the challenges for some categories of funds, including ETFs with exposure to emerging markets, are particularly significant due to on average higher transaction costs and lower liquidity of their financial markets (Blitz and Huij 2012).

Apart from the stock (or bond) market-related perspective, impact of the ICT adoption on the diffusion of ETFs may also be considered with regard to one of the key processes in the investment industry that is linked to the development of the global ETFs markets—increasing popularity of passive investing. As Lettau and Madhavan (2018) observe, managing investment funds with index portfolios with the number of constituents counted in hundreds or thousands was in the past too expensive in relation to more concentrated portfolios of active funds. It changed with the implementation of electronic data delivery and less expensive computing technology.

Further possible relationships between adoption of ICT and development of ETFs markets may be consequences of the changes in other segments of the financial system or overall economy than financial markets or investment industry discussed in the preceding paragraphs. Development of the banking sector, the largest part of most financial systems, may be spurred by the ICT adoption. Broader access to cheaper, faster, and more customer-friendly services provided by banks may lead to general increase in the frequency of the usage of financial services in the local economy, starting from the most basic ones such as savings account. In longer perspective, their clients may begin using more sophisticated services such as financial advising and asset management and consider the purchase of ETFs' shares. Diffusion of ETFs may also be affected by the changes in the overall economic conditions facilitated by the ICT adoption, e.g., higher rate of economic growth, which could impact the attractiveness of stock investments and, consequently, demand for the financial products offering such exposure (including equity ETFs). Due to lack of empirical research linking these processes and verifying its occurrence and significance, the discussion is mostly anecdotal. For general discussion concerning the theoretical linkages between ICT, development of financial systems, and economic growth as well as results of empirical research, see Sects. 3.1 and 3.2.

Following the classification of fintech presented in the preceding section (extracted from Dorfleitner et al. (2017)), we discuss the applications of fintech in the asset management industry as most relevant to the ETFs markets. Accordingly, they are divided into four groups: social trading, robo advice, personal financial management, and investment and banking (i.e., other).

Social trading can be explained as a group of individual investors that access an online community (e.g., established and maintained within some social network) in order to observe, comment and discuss, and, most importantly, copy the investment decisions (i.e., investment strategies or exact portfolios) of other, trusted traders (Gemayel and Preda 2018; Lee and Ma 2018). An important aspect of social trading, which distinguishes it from Internet tools available previously (such as discussion forums), is that the users of social trading platforms may opt for automatic, simultaneous, and unconditional following of the selected other users' investment decisions (either single or multiple, e.g., mirroring all made by particular user); such transactions are executed by the platform (Liu et al. 2014; Oehler et al. 2016; Wohlgemuth et al. 2016; Berger et al. 2018; Glaser and Risius 2018). Social trading platforms (eToro is the world's largest) give their users access to ETF trading; therefore their development may be regarded as one of the mechanisms through which adoption of ICT (resulting in the growth of this category of the fintech sector) can affect the diffusion of ETFs.

Probably the most recognized and discussed example of fintech in the asset management industry is robo advice. According to one of the first reports on the robo-advice phenomenon, published by Accenture (2015, p. 2), it may be defined as "the use of automation and digital techniques to build and manage portfolios of exchange-traded funds (ETFs) and other instruments for investors"—this definition clearly indicates the fundamental role of the innovative funds. More generally, robo advisors can be described as a category of online systems that employ various algorithms in order to provide investment advisory services, for instance, recommendations (Ji 2017; Rogowski 2017; Szpringer 2017); by some authors (e.g., Jung et al. (2018)), they are regarded as the part of the digitalized financial advisory services.

First robo advisors (or, to be more accurate, the robo-advisory platforms) were introduced after the 2008 global financial crisis by independent companies (i.e., not being parts of financial corporations)—in 2010 Betterment, one of the largest independent robo advisor, was launched (overview of the robo-advice history is based on Phoon and Koh (2018)). Initially they were above all tools for automated and inexpensive rebalancing of the clients' portfolios. Growing popularity of the robo advice has attracted large asset management companies, among them leading ETF providers such as BlackRock or Vanguard, with their own platforms of this kind, regarded as a new distribution channel for their financial products (SWFI 2015). As a result, there are currently two categories of robo advisors in terms of their owners: independent (private start-ups) and platforms of established financial institutions (in some cases created by acquisition of the independent platforms). Evaluation of the current size of the robo-advice sector in terms of managed assets is difficult due to lack of relevant data, yet the available estimates imply very rapid growth, in particular in the United States (Phoon and Koh 2018); however, it is still a rather negligible part of the global financial system. Robo-advice services may be linked to the social trading platforms (Rogowski 2017).

Madhavan (2016) and Phoon and Koh (2018) suggest four categories of investment services provided by robo advisors:

1. Model-based portfolio solutions
2. Portfolio rebalancing
3. Portfolio optimization (e.g., in the context of tax liabilities)
4. Portfolio monitoring

Algorithms used by robo advisors are usually based on the principles of passive investing which may be regarded as the reason for utilizing ETFs as one of the primary investment tools—they require limited portfolio management (Jung et al. 2018); exact popularity of the used tools is region- or country-dependent as in some countries the ETFs markets remain too underdeveloped to facilitate their utilization in robo advising. Most robo advisors base their methods of portfolio optimization and asset allocation on the concepts of modern portfolio theory—the other approaches are much less frequent (Beketov et al. 2018). In order to generate higher returns that in similar investment strategies offered by traditional advisors, some robo advisors modify the rebalancing algorithms by introducing tax-saving mechanisms (Sironi 2016). Consequently, the growth of the robo-advice platforms is inextricably linked to the demand side of the ETFs market and may be perceived, particularly in the longer time horizon, as one of the factors potentially contributing to the development of the market for innovative funds (for discussion concerning robo advisors in the Asia-Pacific countries, see our analysis of the linkages between ICT and ETFs in Sects. 6.3 and 6.4).

There is a number of reasons behind the development and growth of the robo-advice platforms (SWFI 2015; Madhavan 2016; Park et al. 2016; Faloon and Scherer 2017; Ji 2017; Rogowski 2017):

- Lower charges and lower minimum required assets (availability for clients with low account balances) than in case of traditional asset management services
- Possibility to avoid some of the biases and errors discussed in the behavioral finance literature (e.g., loss aversion or home bias)
- Avoiding portfolio's drift due to automated routine rebalancing
- Perception of control over investments

Some of the barriers to the increasing adoption of the robo advisory among customers include high expectations of the transparency and problems with making investment decisions (Jung et al. 2018). The report of Accenture (2015) emphasizes that the range of services provided by robo advisors is rather limited and insufficient for more sophisticated investors. However, as Woodyard and Grable (2018) show, using the example of the most developed robo-advisory market, in the United States, the typical users of such services may be willing to accept these inconveniences due to their distrust in the traditional services. Stewart and McDonald (2018) claim that the group of users of robo advisors is evolving and no longer includes exclusively young people but rather broad demographic spectrum. Finally, as Ji (2017) observes, the rising popularity of robo advisors leads to regulatory issues that need to be addressed in order to ensure their long-term viability.

Applications of fintech in the area of personal financial management are in some aspects similar to robo advice as they also include the use of software in order to support personal financial decisions, above all financial planning (Dorfleitner et al. 2017). One example is online investment account aggregators that allow for the aggregate view of the individual's assets held at various institutions (e.g., bank, pension plan, or brokerage account); information from the aggregator may also be used to enhance the quality of financial advisory services (Bell 2017). In addition to assets, liabilities may also be aggregated, e.g., to show loans from various lenders. Some systems are automated as they interact with open-access portals of financial institutions, while others require manual data entry (Dorfleitner et al. 2017).

The fourth group of the fintech applications in the asset management industry includes concepts that cannot be classified as any of the abovementioned categories. The first type of such concepts is digital advisory (online-based asset management) services other than robo advice, i.e., with the active interaction of human advisors who fully or partially automate the investment processes (Dorfleitner et al. 2017). Another subcategory is companies that offer conventional financial services yet supplemented by some additional online (or similar) features in order to lower the fees or better address the expectations of the customers.

Even though robo advisors and other financial services discussed in the previous paragraphs are probably the most recognized type of computer-based investment services connected to the ETFs markets (due to, among other, substantial media coverage), they are not the only example. One of the most recent developments in the area of support to the users of ETFs provided by fintech (or, more generally, new technologies) is linked to the so-called turnkey asset management programs (TAMPs) (our discussion is based extensively on the outline in Crigger (2017)). TAMPs are complex outsourcing services for the financial advisors responsible for management of their clients' investments who wish to delegate this task to third party. Based on the permission and data obtained from the advisor, these programs provide services ranging from establishment of the investment strategies through their implementation to back-office responsibilities (e.g., billing or compliance duties). In some cases, the range of services is extended to communication and interaction with brokers and custodians, which means that they are capable of managing the entire delegated investment strategy. According to the report by Schwab Advisor Services, which offers access to various non-related TAMPs through its platform, these programs may be defined as "an investment service that may provide access to a wide range of managed account services, sales tools, and back-office support for investment advisors and their clients" (Schwab Advisor Services 2013, p. 2). ETFs are used as investment assets in three basic types of accounts available through TAMPs (Schwab Advisor Services 2013; FundChoice 2015):

1. Exchange-traded funds and wrap accounts
2. Unified managed accounts (UMAs)
3. Unified managed households (UMHs)

Wrap accounts are the most simple and consequently the cheapest solution among the above-presented as they are aimed only at delivering the return of the selected benchmark at very low cost. Range of services provided by the programs is much broader in case of UMAs in which professionals who make all decisions are required to manage the client's accounts. UMHs are an extension of UMAs in which services are offered not to one client but rather to more than one person within a particular household.

It must be stressed that TAMPs have been offered since a few decades, yet their popularity began to grow quickly since the early years of the twenty-first century, particularly since the global financial crisis of 2008. According to the report by FundChoice (2015), the value of assets managed with the application of the turnkey programs has increased from under 50 billion USD in 2008 to approximately 300 billion USD in 2014. The cited data apply exclusively to the US market (with Envestnet or AssetMark as some of the largest companies) as in other regions the availability of such services is still highly limited. Among the factors that boosted the popularity of TAMPs a prominent role belongs to the increased implementation of the new technologies by their providers. It allowed for easier and more in-depth integration of the TAMP-type services with the accounting and portfolio accounting systems of the financial advisors who decide to use them; yet another effect is possibility for continuous monitoring of the performance and investment positions (FundChoice 2015). TAMPs facilitate online communication with the client, including mobile services. New technologies are also implemented by advisor service platforms which are an intermediary between financial advisors and the turnkey programs—for example, they act as custodians for the assets of clients and are responsible for management of client's data (Schwab Advisor Services 2013).

Some financial advisors opt, though, not to use the turnkey-type programs for various reasons (e.g., reluctance to lose control over the investment process or the need to use only some part of the complex services offered by the comprehensive programs). A new category of fintechs has emerged in response to the demand from this group of financial professionals, including software for risk analysis, trading operations, and portfolio's rebalancing (Crigger 2017); other examples include tools for customer relation management, in some cases based on cloud data storage. Their growing complexity has made them similar in many aspects to the conventional

TAMPs. However, they offer some features that make them distinctive (apart from the most obvious one—the possibility to customize the level of delegation of the investment services). One of them is access to model portfolio marketplaces, also known as model portfolio exchanges, which enables sharing and buying model portfolios prepared by various categories of investment professionals, typically built using the shares of the largest and cheapest ETFs (Crigger 2017). It may, therefore, be identified as yet another important example of the new technologies' impact on the range of applications of ETFs and, in broader perspective, on the demand for the innovative funds.

In order to supplement the discussion in the preceding paragraphs, it should be added that, despite some apparent similarities between TAMPs and robo-advising solutions, there is one fundamental difference. In case of the asset management programs, the extent of outsourcing is much higher as they cover most duties required from financial advisors, whereas robo advisors do not offer support in the areas such as generation of the financial statements or establishment of the investment strategies.

Empirical verifications of the linkages between ICT and diffusion of ETFs are very scarce, above all due to the relatively short history of the ETFs markets, even in the countries where they are most established such as the United States. Lechman and Marszk (2015) analyzed diffusion of ETFs in five countries, including two in the Asia-Pacific region (Japan, South Korea, Brazil, Mexico, and the United States), over 2002–2012. Results of their evaluation of the effects of ICT on the ETFs market development indicate that adoption of new technologies could be regarded as one of the factors of ETFs' diffusion. In contrast with the research approach adopted in this book, they juxtaposed ETFs with conventional mutual funds rather than stock index derivatives.

To conclude, broad adoption and use of new information and communication technologies can undoubtedly effectively unlock the potential of financial markets, driving its development, giving rise to new innovative products. ICT may boost information flows which may effectively enhance number of transactions, among even geographically dispersed agents. New technologies drive productivity and efficiency of financial systems and financial markets. Apparently, sound combination of technology and innovative financing initiatives also rests on governance, policies and legal regulations, formal and informal institutions, and capability of economic agents to cooperate.

References

Abdelgawad, M., & Wheeler, A. R. (2009). The digital revolution: A new paradigm for microfluidics. *Advanced Materials, 21*(8), 920–925.

Accenture. (2015). *The Rise of Robo-Advice: Changing the concept of wealth management.*

Akamatsu, K. (1962). A historical pattern of economic growth in developing countries. *The Developing Economies, 1*, 3–25.

Aldridge, I., & Krawciw, S. (2017). *Real-time risk: What investors should know about FinTech, high-frequency trading, and flash crashes*. Hoboken, NJ: Wiley.
Allen, F., & Gale, D. (2000a). Financial contagion. *Journal of Political Economy, 108*(1), 1–33.
Allen, F., & Gale, D. (2000b). Bubbles and crises. *The Economic Journal, 110*(460), 236–255.
Allen, R. C. (2009). *The British industrial revolution in global perspective* (Vol. 1). Cambridge: Cambridge University Press.
Asongu, S., & Nnanna, J. (2018). ICT in reducing information asymmetry for financial sector competition. *DBN Journal of Economics and Sustainable Growth* (Forthcoming).
Avgerou, C., & Walsham, G. (2017). *Information technology in context: Studies from the perspective of developing countries: Studies from the perspective of developing countries*. New York: Routledge.
Beketov, M., Lehmann, K., & Wittke, M. (2018). Robo Advisors: Quantitative methods inside the robots. *Journal of Asset Management, 19*(6), 363–370.
Bell, H. (2017). Q+A Ric Edelman: Fintech will change advisory game… *ETF Report, November 2017*, 16–18.
Beniger, J. (2009). *The control revolution: Technological and economic origins of the information society*. Cambridge, MA: Harvard University Press.
Berger, E. S., Wenzel, M., & Wohlgemuth, V. (2018). Imitation-related performance outcomes in social trading: A configurational approach. *Journal of Business Research, 89*, 322–327.
Bhunia, A. (2011). An impact of ICT on the growth of capital market – empirical evidence from Indian Stock Market Exchange. *Information and Knowledge Management, 1*(2), 7–14.
Blitz, D., & Huij, J. (2012). Evaluating the performance of global emerging markets equity exchange-traded funds. *Emerging Markets Review, 13*, 149–158.
Brennan, M. J., Huh, S. W., & Subrahmanyam, A. (2018). High-frequency measures of informed trading and corporate announcements. *The Review of Financial Studies, 31*(6), 2326–2376.
Bresnahan, T. (2010). Ch. 18: General purpose technologies. In B. H. Hall & N. Rosenberg (Eds.), *Handbook of the economics of innovation* (Vol. 2). Oxford: Elsevier.
Bresnahan, T. F., & Trajtenberg, M. (1995). General purpose technologies: 'Engines of growth'? *Journal of Econometrics, Annals of Econometrics, 65*(1), 83–108. https://doi.org/10.1016/0304-4076(94)01598-T.
Brogaard, J., Carrion, A., Moyaert, T., Riordan, R., Shkilko, A., & Sokolov, K. (2018). High frequency trading and extreme price movements. *Journal of Financial Economics, 128*(2), 253–265.
Brogaard, J., Hendershott, T., & Riordan, R. (2014). High-frequency trading and price discovery. *The Review of Financial Studies, 27*(8), 2267–2306.
Bugamelli, M., & Pagano, P. (2004). Barriers to investment in ICT. *Applied Economics, 36*(20), 2275–2286.
Cabrales, A., Gale, D., & Gottardi, P. (2015). Financial contagion in networks. In *The Oxford handbook of the economics of networks*. Oxford: Oxford University Press.
Cairncross, F. (1997). *The death of distance: How the communications revolution will change our lives*. Boston, MA: Harvard Business School Press.
Cairncross, F. (2001). *The death of distance: 2.0: How the communications revolution will change our lives*. Texere.
Calamia, A., Deville, L., & Riva, F. (2013). Liquidity in European equity ETFs: What really matters? *GREDEG Working Paper Series, 10*, 1–26.
Calvano, E. (2007). *Destructive creation, Stockholm School of Economics*. Working Paper Series in Economics and Finance, No. 653.
Castells, M., Fernandez-Ardevol, M., Qiu, J. L., & Sey, A. (2009). *Mobile communication and society: A global perspective*. Cambridge, MA: MIT Press.
Cerny, P. G. (1994). The dynamics of financial globalization: Technology, market structure, and policy response. *Policy Sciences, 27*(4), 319–342.
Christopher, F., & Louca, F. (2001). *As time goes by: From the industrial revolutions to the information revolution*. New York: Oxford University Press.

Coccia, M. (2005). Measuring intensity of technological change: The seismic approach. *Technological Forecasting and Social Change, 72*(2), 117–144.

Coccia, M. (2010). The asymmetric path of economic long waves. *Technological Forecasting and Social Change, 77*(5), 730–738.

Coccia, M. (2017). The Fishbone diagram to identify, systematize and analyze the sources of general purpose Technologies. *Journal of Social and Administrative Sciences, 4*(4), 291–303.

Coccia, M. (2018). A theory of the general causes of long waves: War, general purpose technologies, and economic change. *Technological Forecasting and Social Change, 128*, 287–295.

Coleman, D. C. (1956). Industrial growth and industrial revolutions. *Economica, 23*(89), 1–22.

Cont, R., & Bouchaud, J. P. (2000). Herd behavior and aggregate fluctuations in financial markets. *Macroeconomic Dynamics, 4*(2), 170–196.

Crigger, L. (2017). Tearing up the TAMP. *ETF Report, November 2017*, 8–11.

Deane, P. M. (1979). *The first industrial revolution*. Cambridge: Cambridge University Press.

Diaz-Rainey, I., & Ibikunle, G. (2012). A taxonomy of the dark side of financial innovation: The cases of high frequency trading and Exchange Traded Funds. *International Journal of Entrepreneurship and Innovation Management, 16*(1), 51–72.

Diaz-Rainey, I., Ibikunle, G., & Mention, A. L. (2015). The technological transformation of capital markets. *Technological Forecasting and Social Change, 99*, 277–284.

Dorfleitner, G., Hornuf, L., Schmitt, M., & Weber, M. (2017). *FinTech in Germany*. Cham: Springer.

Dreyer, K. J., Hirschorn, D. S., Thrall, J. H., Mehta, A., & PACS, A. (2006). *A guide to the digital revolution*. New York: Springer Science+ Business Media.

Economides, N. (1996). The economics of networks. *International Journal of Industrial Organization, 14*(6), 673–699.

Eisenberg, L. K. (1995). *Connectivity and financial network shutdown* (No. 95-04-041).

Engelen, E., & Grote, M. H. (2009). Stock exchange virtualisation and the decline of second-tier financial centres—the cases of Amsterdam and Frankfurt. *Journal of Economic Geography, 9*(5), 679–696.

Ernkvist, M. (2015). The double knot of technology and business-model innovation in the era of ferment of digital exchanges: The case of OM, a pioneer in electronic options exchanges. *Technological Forecasting and Social Change, 99*, 285–299.

Essendorfer, S., Diaz-Rainey, I., & Falta, M. (2015). Creative destruction in Wall Street's technological arms race: Evidence from patent data. *Technological Forecasting and Social Change, 99*, 300–316.

Faloon, M., & Scherer, B. (2017). Individualization of robo-advice. *The Journal of Wealth Management, 20*(1), 30–36.

Faulhaber, G. R. (1995). Public policy in telecommunications: The third revolution. *Information Economics and Policy, 7*(3), 251–282.

Fintech Weekly. (2018). *Fintech definition*. Retrieved June 10, 2018, from https://www.fintechweekly.com/fintech-definition.

Freeman, C., & Soete, L. (1987). *Technical change and full employment*. Wiley-Blackwell.

Freeman, C., & Louça, F. (2001). *As time goes by: the information revolution and the industrial revolutions in historical perspective*. Oxford University Press, Inc.

Freeman, C. (2013). *Economics of industrial innovation*. London: Routledge.

FundChoice. (2015). *TAMPS simplified*. LLC: FundChoice.

Gardner, L., Lee, S., Alford, M., & Cresson, J. (2017). The effects of information communication technology on stock market capitalization: A panel data analysis. *Business and Economic Research, 7*(1), 261–272.

Gemayel, R., & Preda, A. (2018). Does a scopic regime erode the disposition effect? Evidence from a social trading platform. *Journal of Economic Behavior & Organization, 154*, 175–190.

Giddens, A. (2018). Globalization. In *Sociology of globalization* (pp. 19–26). New York: Routledge.

Glaser, F., & Risius, M. (2018). Effects of transparency: Analyzing social biases on trader performance in social trading. *Journal of Information Technology, 33*(1), 19–30.

Grajek, M. (2003). *Estimating network effects and compatibility in mobile telecommunications* (No. SP II 2003-26). WZB Discussion Paper.
Greenwood, J. (1997). *The third industrial revolution: Technology, productivity, and income inequality (No. 435)*. Washington, DC: American Enterprise Institute.
Greenwood, J., & Jovanovic, B. (1999). The information-technology revolution and the stock market. *American Economic Review, 89*(2), 116–122.
Grilli, R., Tedeschi, G., & Gallegati, M. (2015). Markets connectivity and financial contagion. *Journal of Economic Interaction and Coordination, 10*(2), 287–304.
Hamilton, A. (1986). *The financial revolution*. New York: The Free Press.
Hasbrouck, J. (2018). High-frequency quoting: Short-term volatility in bids and offers. *Journal of Financial and Quantitative Analysis, 53*(2), 613–641.
He, D., Leckow, R., Haksar, V., Mancini-Griffoli, T., Jenkinson, N., Kashima, M., Khiaonarong, T., Rochon, C., & Tourpe, H. (2017). *Fintech and financial services: Initial considerations*. Washington, DC: International Monetary Fund.
Helpman, E. (1998). *General purpose technologies and economic growth*. Cambridge, MA: MIT Press.
Helpman, E., & Trajtenberg, M. (1996). *Diffusion of general purpose technologies* (No. w5773). National Bureau of Economic Research.
Hendershott, T., Jones, C. M., & Menkveld, A. J. (2011). Does algorithmic trading improve liquidity? *The Journal of Finance, 66*(1), 1–33.
Hendershott, T., & Madhavan, A. (2015). Click or call? Auction versus search in the over-the-counter market. *The Journal of Finance, 70*(1), 419–447.
Iori, G., Jafarey, S., & Padilla, F. G. (2006). Systemic risk on the interbank market. *Journal of Economic Behavior & Organization, 61*(4), 525–542.
Ji, M. (2017). Are robots good fiduciaries? Regulating Robo-Advisors under the Investment Advisers Act of 1940. *Columbia Law Review, 117*(6), 1543–1583.
Johnson, N., Zhao, G., Hunsader, E., Qi, H., Johnson, N., Meng, J., & Tivnan, B. (2013). Abrupt rise of new machine ecology beyond human response time. *Scientific Reports, 3*, 2627.
Jones, C. I. (2001). Was an industrial revolution inevitable? Economic growth over the very long run. *Advances in Macroeconomics, 1*(2), 1–43.
Jovanovic, B., & Rousseau, P. L. (2005). General purpose technologies. In P. Aghion & S. N. Durlauf (Eds.), *Handbook of economic growth* (Vol. 1B). Amsterdam: Elsevier.
Jung, D., Dorner, V., Weinhardt, C., & Pusmaz, H. (2018). Designing a Robo-advisor for risk-averse, low-budget consumers. *Electronic Markets, 28*(3), 367–380.
Kaal, W. A., & Dell'Erba, M. (2017). *Blockchain innovation in private investment funds-A comparative analysis of the United States and Europe*. Retrieved September 12, 2018, from https://papers.ssrn.com/sol3/papers.cfm?abstract_id=3002908.
Katz, M. L., & Shapiro, C. (1985). Network externalities, competition, and compatibility. *The American Economic Review, 75*(3), 424–440.
Katz, M. L., & Shapiro, C. (1986). Technology adoption in the presence of network externalities. *Journal of Political Economy, 94*(4), 822–841.
Katz, M. L., & Shapiro, C. (1994). Systems competition and network effects. *Journal of Economic Perspectives, 8*(2), 93–115.
Kauffman, R. J., Hu, Y., & Ma, D. (2015a). Will high-frequency trading practices transform the financial markets in the Asia Pacific Region? *Financial Innovation, 1*(1), 4.
Kauffman, R. J., Liu, J., & Ma, D. (2015b). Innovations in financial IS and technology ecosystems: High-frequency trading in the equity market. *Technological Forecasting and Social Change, 99*, 339–354.
Kirilenko, A., Kyle, A. S., Samadi, M., & Tuzun, T. (2017). The Flash Crash: High-frequency trading in an electronic market. *The Journal of Finance, 72*(3), 967–998.
Kliman, R., & Arinze, B. (2019). Cognitive computing: Impacts on financial advice in wealth management. In M. Anandarajan & T. D. Harrison (Eds.), *Aligning business strategies and analytics* (pp. 11–23). Cham: Springer.
Krasner, S. D. (1983). *International regimes*. Ithaca: Cornell University Press.

Kuznets, S. (1973). Modern economic growth: Findings and reflections. *The American Economic Review, 63*(3), 247–258.
Latzer, M. (2009). Information and communication technology innovations: Radical and disruptive? *New Media & Society, 11*(4), 599–619.
Leal, S. J., & Napoletano, M. (2017). Market stability vs. market resilience: Regulatory policies experiments in an agent-based model with low-and high-frequency trading. *Journal of Economic Behavior & Organization*, doi: https://doi.org/10.1016/j.jebo.2017.04.013.
Lechman, E. (2015). *ICT Diffusion In Developing Countries*. Cham: Springer International Publishing.
Lechman, E. (2017). *The diffusion of information and communication technologies*. New York: Routledge.
Lechman, E., & Marszk, A. (2015). ICT technologies and financial innovations: The case of Exchange Traded Funds in Brazil, Japan, Mexico, South Korea and the United States. *Technological Forecasting and Social Change, 99*, 355–376.
Lee, R. (2010). *Running the World's Markets: The Governance of Financial Infrastructure*. Princeton, NJ: Princeton University Press.
Lee, W., & Ma, Q. (2018). Discovering expert traders on social trading services. *Journal of Advanced Computational Intelligence and Intelligent Informatics, 22*(2), 224–235.
Lenzu, S., & Tedeschi, G. (2012). Systemic risk on different interbank network topologies. *Physica A: Statistical Mechanics and its Applications, 391*(18), 4331–4341.
Lettau, M., & Madhavan, A. (2018). Exchange-traded funds 101 for economists. *Journal of Economic Perspectives, 32*(1), 135–154.
Lipsey, R. G., & Carlaw, K. (1998). Technology policies in neo-classical and structuralist-evolutionary models. *STI review, 22*, 31–73.
Lipsey, R. G. (2002). Some implications of endogenous technological change for technology policies in developing countries. *Economics of Innovation and New Technology, 11*(4–5), 321–351.
Lipsey, R. G., Carlaw, K. I., & Bekar, C. T. (2005). *Economic transformations: General purpose technologies and long-term economic growth*. Oxford: Oxford University Press.
Liu, Y. Y., Nacher, J. C., Ochiai, T., Martino, M., & Altshuler, Y. (2014). Prospect theory for online financial trading. *PLoS One, 9*(10), e109458.
Louca, I., Freeman, C., Louca, F., Louçã, F., & Iseg, F. L. (2001). *As time goes by: From the industrial revolutions to the information revolution*. Oxford: Oxford University Press.
Madhavan, A. (2012). Exchange-traded funds, market structure, and the flash crash. *Financial Analysts Journal, 68*(4), 20–35.
Madhavan, A. N. (2016). *Exchange-traded funds and the new dynamics of investing*. Oxford: Oxford University Press.
McGowan, M. (2010). The rise of computerized high frequency trading: Use and controversy. *Duke Law and Technology Review, 16*, 1–24.
Menkveld, A. J. (2016). The economics of high-frequency trading: Taking stock. *Annual Review of Financial Economics, 8*, 1–24.
Menkveld, A. J., & Zoican, M. A. (2017). Need for speed? Exchange latency and liquidity. *The Review of Financial Studies, 30*(4), 1188–1228.
Menkveld, A. J. (2018). High-frequency trading as viewed through an electron microscope. *Financial Analysts Journal, 74*(2), 24–31.
Mokyr, J. (1998). The second industrial revolution, 1870–1914. In *Storia dell'economia Mondiale* (pp. 219–245). Rome: Laterza.
Mokyr, J. (2010). *The Enlightened economy an economic history of Britain 1700–1850*. New Haven, CT: Yale University Press.
Natarajan, H., Krause, S., & Gradstein, H. (2017). Distributed Ledger Technology (DLT) and Blockchain. In *World Bank FinTech Note, 1*. Washington, DC: *The World Bank Group*.
Neave, E. (2017). *The economic organisation of a financial system*. New York: Routledge.
Ngassam, C., & Gani, A. (2003). Effect of information and communications technology on stock market development: Evidence from emerging markets and high-income economies. *International Journal of Economic Development, 5*, 1.

Nishimura, K. G. (2010). *Electronic trading and financial markets*. Tokyo: Bank of Japan.

Ocampo, J. A. (2018). International asymmetries and the design of the International Financial System 1. In *Critical Issues in International Financial Reform* (pp. 45–74). New York: Routledge.

Oehler, A., Horn, M., & Wendt, S. (2016). Benefits from social trading? Empirical evidence for certificates on wikifolios. *International Review of Financial Analysis, 46*, 202–210.

Okwu, A. T. (2015). ICT adoption and financial markets: A study of the leading stock exchange markets in Africa. *Journal of Accounting and Management, 2*, 53–76.

Panourgias, N. S. (2015). Capital markets integration: A sociotechnical study of the development of a cross-border securities settlement system. *Technological Forecasting and Social Change, 99*, 317–338.

Park, J. Y., Ryu, J. P., & Shin, H. J. (2016). Robo Advisors for Portfolio Management. *Advanced Science and Technology Letters, 141*, 104–108.

Patterson, S. (2012). *Dark pools: High-speed traders, AI Bandits, and the threat to the global financial system*. New York: Random House Digital Inc..

Pérez, C. (2003). Technological change and opportunities for development as a moving target. In *Trade and development: Directions for the 21st century* (p. 100). Cheltenham: Edward Elgar Publishing.

Perez, C. (2010). Technological revolutions and techno-economic paradigms. *Cambridge Journal of Economics, 34*(1), 185–202.

Perez, C., & Soete, L. (1988). Catching up in technology: Entry barriers and windows of opportunity. In *Technical change and economic theory* (pp. 458–479). *London*: Pinter Publishers.

Phoon, K., & Koh, F. (2018). Robo-advisors and wealth management. *The Journal of Alternative Investments, 20*(3), 79–94.

Polanyi, K. (1944). *The great transformation: Economic and political origins of our time. New York: Rinehart.*

Pradhan, R. P., Mallik, G., Bagchi, T. P., & Sharma, M. (2018). Information communications technology penetration and stock markets–growth nexus: From cross country panel evidence. *International Journal of Services, Technology and Management, 24*(4), 307–337.

Preece, R. G. (2012). *Dark pools, Internationalisation and equity market quality*. Charlottesville, VA: Chartered Financial Analysts Institute.

Prewitt, M. (2012). High-frequency trading: Should regulators do more? *Michigan Telecommunication and Technology Law Review, 19*, 131–161.

Rezaie Dolat Abadi, H., Faghani, F., & Tabatabaee, S. M. (2013). Impact of information technology development on stock market development: Empirical study in the World's leading capital markets. *International Journal of Academic Research in Accounting, Finance and Management Sciences, 3*(1), 382–390.

Rifkin, J. (2011). *The third industrial revolution: How lateral power is transforming energy, the economy, and the world*. New York, NY: Palgrave Macmillan.

Rogowski, W. (2017). Świat wirtualnego doradztwa finansowego (robo-advisor) [World of the virtual financial advising (robo-advisor)]. *E-Mentor, 4*, 71. (in Polish).

Rosenberg, N., & Birdzell, L. E., Jr. (2008). *How the West grew rich: The economic transformation of the industrial world*. New York: Basic Books.

Rosenberg, N., & Trajtenberg, M. (2004). A general-purpose technology at work: The Corliss Steam Engine in the Late-nineteenth-century United States. *Journal of Economic History, 64*, 61–99.

Ruttan, V. W. (2006). *Is war necessary for economic growth? Military procurement and technology development*. New York: Oxford University Press.

Sahal, D. (1981). *Patterns of technological innovation*. Reading, MA: Addison-Wesley Publishing Company, Inc..

Schmiedel, H., Malkamäki, M., & Tarkka, J. (2006). Economies of scale and technological development in securities depository and settlement systems. *Journal of Banking & Finance, 30*(6), 1783–1806.

Schueffel, P. (2016). Taming the beast: A scientific definition of FinTech. *Journal of Innovation Management, 4*(4), 32–54.

Schwab Advisor Services. (2013). *TAMPs may help you gain operational efficiency*. San Francisco, CA: Charles Schwab & Co. Inc..

Seddon, J. J., & Currie, W. L. (2017). A model for unpacking big data analytics in high-frequency trading. *Journal of Business Research, 70*, 300–307.

Shapiro, C. V., & Varian, H. (1998). HR (1999) Information Rules. In *A strategic guide to the network economy. Boston, MA*: *Harvard Business School Press.*

Sharpe, W. (1991). Capital asset prices with and without negative holdings. *The Journal of Finance, 46*(2), 489–509.

Sironi, P. (2016). *FinTech Innovation: From robo-advisors to goal based investing and gamification*. Hoboken, NJ: Wiley.

Stearns, P. N. (2018). *The industrial revolution in world history*. New York: Routledge.

Stern, D. I., & Kander, A. (2012). The role of energy in the industrial revolution and modern economic growth. *The Energy Journal, 33*(3), 125–152.

Stewart, S., & McDonald, B. (2018). The counter-intuitive reality of robo-advice demographics. In S. Chishti & T. Puschmann (Eds.), *The WealthTech Book: The FinTech handbook for investors, entrepreneurs and finance visionaries* (pp. 68–70). Hoboken, NJ: Wiley.

SWFI. (2015). *Everyone wants a Robo-Advisor, Right?* Retrieved January 10, 2018, from https://www.swfinstitute.org/swf-news/everyone-wants-a-robo-advisor-right-8461344/.

Szpringer, W. (2017). *Nowe technologie a sektor finansowy [New technologies and financial sector]*. Warszawa: Poltext Publishing House. (in Polish).

Toumazou, C., Hughes, J. B., Battersby, N. C., & Battersby, N. C. (1993). *Switched-currents: An analogue technique for digital technology* (Vol. 5). Iet). London: Peter Peregrinus Ltd.

Valente, T. W. (1996). Social network thresholds in the diffusion of innovations. *Social Networks, 18*(1), 69–89.

Varga, D. (2017). Fintech, the new era of financial services. *Budapest Management Review, XLVIII*, 22–32.

Wertime, T. A. (1962). *The coming of the age of steel*. Leiden: University of Chicago Press.

Wohlgemuth, V., Berger, E., & Wenzel, M. (2016). More than just financial performance: Trusting investors in social trading. *Journal of Business Research, 69*(11), 4970–4974.

Woodyard, A. S., & Grable, J. E. (2018). Insights into the users of Robo-Advisory firms. *Journal of Financial Service Professionals, 72*(5), 56–66.

Wright, G. (2000). General purpose technologies and economic growth. *Journal of Economic Literature, 38*(1), 161.

Zhang, F. (2010). *The effect of high-frequency trading on stock volatility and price discovery*. Retrieved November 12, 2017, from http://mitsloan.mit.edu/groups/template/pdf/Zhang.pdf.

Zhou, H., & Kalev, P. S. (2019). Algorithmic and high frequency trading in Asia-Pacific, now and the future. *Pacific-Basin Finance Journal, 53*, 186–207.

Chapter 4
Exchange-Traded Funds Market Development in Asia-Pacific Region

4.1 Introductory Notes

In the current chapter, we analyze the development of the ETFs markets in the countries of the Asia-Pacific region.[1] Our analysis consists of two approaches: analysis of the values of the ETFs turnover (first, absolute approach to the evaluation of the ETFs market development (i.e., ETFs diffusion)) and analysis of share of turnover of ETFs in the turnover of index instruments (second, relative approach); for more information on our approach to defining of ETFs market development, see Sect. 2.3. We consider exclusively the turnover on the stock exchanges due to the lack of data on the transactions conducted through other trading venues. It means, therefore, that we analyze in fact the development of the stock exchange-centered ETFs markets (and, consequently, stock exchange-centered markets for the other stock index instruments). Such approach has its flaws as, for instance, OTC transactions (which may account for a substantial share of the total turnover) are not included, yet it is the only one feasible due to data accessibility.

Due to data availability, in the first, absolute approach, our analysis covers 12 countries or administrative units listed in Table 4.1—all countries in the Asia-Pacific region in which ETFs were traded for the majority of the analyzed time period.[2] It means that we use data on ETFs traded on (as of 2017) 14 stock exchanges. In the second, relative approach, the size of our sample is limited by the lack of competing

[1] In some cases we analyze territories that are in fact administrative units of other countries, but in order to avoid unnecessary repetitions, we subsequently label all as "countries" (with some exceptions in the introductory paragraphs).

[2] It should be mentioned that it is not the exhaustive list of the Asia-Pacific countries with local ETFs markets as there are some exchanges which are not the members of the World Federation of Exchanges or there are no data on turnover of ETFs provided in the utilized reports. According to Lipper's database and Deutsche Bank's reports, there are some ETFs listed in the Philippines and Vietnam (their assets or turnover are, though, minimal, so they do not distort our results), and one fund assigned to Sri Lanka. We present them briefly after discussing the least developed ETFs markets in our core analysis.

A. Marszk et al., *The Emergence of ETFs in Asia-Pacific*,
https://doi.org/10.1007/978-3-030-12752-7_4

Table 4.1 Asia-Pacific: countries (and administrative units) with local ETFs markets

Country/administrative unit	Stock exchange(s)
Australia	Australian Securities Exchange
China (Mainland)[a]	Shanghai Stock Exchange
	Shenzhen Stock Exchange
Hong Kong	Hong Kong Exchanges and Clearing
India	BSE India Limited
	National Stock Exchange of India Limited
Indonesia	Indonesia Stock Exchange
Japan	Japan Exchange Group Inc.
Malaysia	Bursa Malaysia
New Zealand	NZX Limited
Singapore	Singapore Exchange
South Korea	Korea Exchange
Taiwan	Taiwan Stock Exchange
Thailand	The Stock Exchange of Thailand

[a]For brevity henceforth "China"

Note: Japan Exchange Group Inc. was formed through the merger of Osaka Stock Exchange and Tokyo Stock Exchange in 2013, previously ETFs were traded separately on those two trading venues

Source: own elaboration based on the reports of the World Federation of Exchanges

instruments on the local exchanges or scarce data on their turnover which precludes calculation of ETFs market shares. As a result, we consider six countries or administrative units, Australia, China, Hong Kong, India, Japan, and South Korea; we use all available data on the turnover of stock index derivatives in the particular country—on all exchanges, not only the places of the ETFs' listing, in order to cover the entire local markets (again, for consistency, we do not consider transactions off-exchanges).

The time period of our analysis in this chapter is January 2004–August 2017. We do not analyze data prior to 2004 due to the minimal size of most ETFs markets or lack of listed funds in the considered economies. We use data extracted from the reports of the World Federation of Exchanges, reports of the local exchanges, as well as additional sources utilized to shed light on some supplementary aspects of the analyzed markets (e.g., data on assets is extracted from Lipper's database that covers world's investment funds—we utilize this database also in case of attributes of individual ETFs such as their name).

4.2 Overview of the Asia-Pacific ETFs Markets

In the current section, we discuss the ETFs market development (i.e., diffusion of ETFs) in the 12 (or 6 using the relative approach) countries of the Asia-Pacific region. The first part of this section covers the key trends of the Asia-Pacific regional ETFs market in terms of turnover (and number of listed funds), and it may be regarded as a supplement to the overview presented in Sect. 2.4 in which we focused on different metrics (e.g., assets). We continue our discussion with the analysis of the country-wise descriptive statistics in order to present the basic attributes of the selected markets and the regional diversity. During our examination we describe briefly the key attributes of the ETFs markets in each country. For selected markets (in particular the most developed), we analyze also the trends in their development in the 2004–2017 time period. We also consider the inequalities concerning diffusion of ETFs in the region.

4.2.1 Main Trends

The total turnover of ETFs listed on stock exchanges in the countries of the Asia-Pacific region has risen over the 2004–2016 period from ca. 36 billion USD to over 1.1 trillion USD (see Fig. 4.1). It should be remembered that to some extent growth has been caused by an increased number of countries in the region with the ETFs markets (i.e., with ETFs listed and traded on the local stock exchanges). In 2004 there were 8 such countries, while in 2016 this number has grown by 50%, to 12.[3] Chronologically, the markets established after 2004 were China, Malaysia (both in 2005), Thailand (in 2007), and Indonesia (in 2008). Growth of the turnover of ETFs in the region was steady until 2009, when the total value stabilized for 2 years at the level of approximately 260 billion USD—lack of expansion between 2009 and 2010 may be attributed to the global financial crisis and its repercussions. Over the next

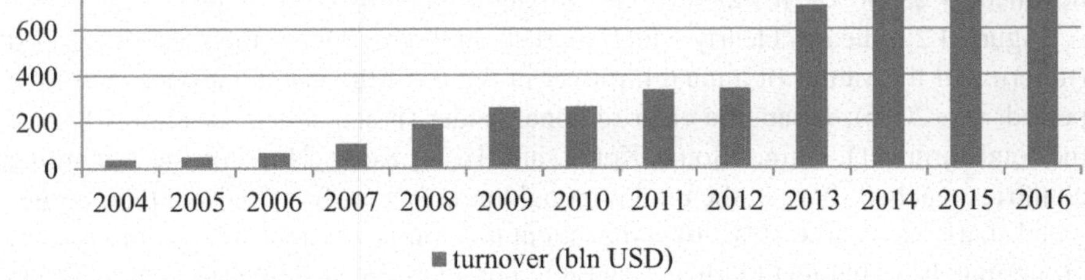

Source: own calculations.

Fig. 4.1 Total turnover of ETFs in the Asia-Pacific countries. Annual data for 2004–2016

[3]According to the data provided by the World Federation of Exchanges.

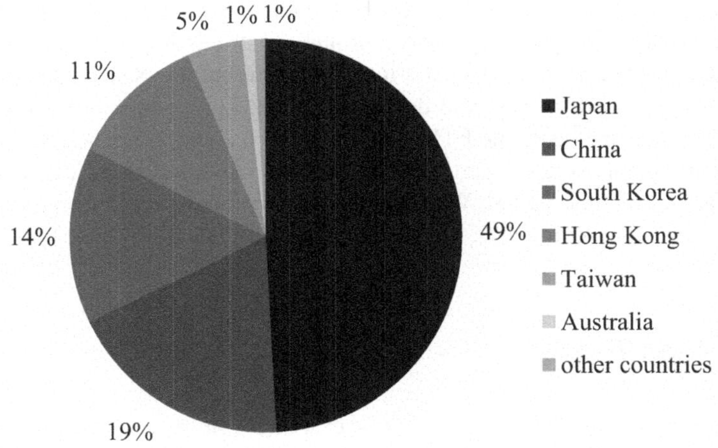

Source: own calculations.

Fig. 4.2 Asia-Pacific ETFs markets—turnover by country, 2016 aggregated annual data

2 years (2010–2012), turnover increased yet at much lower rate than in pre-2009 which may be explained by further turbulences in the global financial system, linked to the events in the eurozone (public debt crisis in some countries). Between 2012 and 2015, the value of ETFs' turnover in the region grew rapidly, at the highest rates in the entire analyzed period—in 2013 (which may be regarded as rebound after the preceding stagnation) and 2015, it increased by about 100% (year-to-year); in 2014 growth was slightly less impressive. In 2015 total turnover of ETFs in the Asia-Pacific exceeded for the first time the level of 1 trillion USD, reaching the historically highest value of approximately 1.7 trillion USD, mostly due to the extremely high turnover in China and Hong Kong (we address this issue in the context of the country-specific analysis of the changes in 2015). However, in 2016 this level (which may be regarded as an "outlier") was not sustained, and total turnover declined by ca. 30%—it was still, though, higher than in any year pre-2015.

Figure 4.2 indicates clearly which markets in the region are the most developed (in terms of the values of annual turnover in the last full year in our analyzed time period, i.e., 2016): Japan, the clear regional leader (it accounted for almost half of the total turnover), China, South Korea, and Hong Kong. None of the remaining countries reached share in the total regional market exceeding 5%, and their aggregated share was below 10%. To some extent the composition of the leading market group may be explained by their economic potential (in particular in case of China or Japan) or the position of the local financial system in the global financial industry (in case of Hong Kong). However, these relationships are not straightforward as proven by the absence of some other major Asia-Pacific economies in this group, for instance, Australia, India, or Indonesia. It should be stressed that we discussed data for 2016; in the preceding years, upper part of the ranking would be substantially different (see Table 4.6).

Trends in the total turnover and its structure may be briefly compared to the parallel features observed for the total assets of ETFs primary listed in the Asia-Pacific region (see Figs. 2.3 and 2.5).[4] Overall trends have been quite alike. Closer scrutiny shows that the growth of the assets has been much more stable (in particular there was no spike in 2015), but the change over the entire period has been much lower than in case of turnover—between 2004 and 2016 total assets have risen by about 700%, while the turnover has grown by about 3100%, proving much more substantial development in the latter dimension. It may, therefore, be concluded that available ETFs have become increasingly more intensively traded on the local stock exchanges. When structure of the regional market is considered, it may be noticed that it is similar regardless of the applied indicator. Japan is the leader in both aspects (yet its position is stronger in terms of assets), followed by China, Hong Kong, and South Korea (reverse to Japan, for these three countries, the shares are higher in terms of turnover than assets). Australia and Taiwan are the biggest among the group of mid-developed markets; the share of the remaining countries is in both dimensions minimal, of 1–2%.

Due to the possible double-counting in case of ETFs whose shares are listed on more than one exchange in the same or multiple countries, the analysis in terms of the number of funds should be conducted by means of the primary listing data (see Sect. 2.4). However, total number of funds listed on exchanges in certain country may also be used in some contexts, for example, to evaluate the trends of this metric in relation to the turnover in order to determine whether the changing total value of transactions has been accompanied by changes in the number of available funds. As Fig. 4.3 proves, in all examined countries, the number of ETFs has increased sharply over 2004–2017; the growth of this indicator has been particularly strong in the most developed ETFs markets identified with regard to Fig. 4.2. It may be, therefore, stated that in these countries the number of ETFs available to investors and traded on local stock exchanges has increased considerably over 2004–2017.

More detailed analysis of data presented on Fig. 4.3 leads to some interesting conclusions. Even though Japan was identified as the most developed ETFs market in the region according to the value of turnover of ETFs (and, additionally, their assets), the number of ETFs listed in South Korea exceeded in some periods the respective value for Japan, especially by the end of the analyzed time period due to the spike in 2017. As of August 2017, there were 302 ETFs listed on the Korea Exchange and 236 on the Japan Exchange Group Inc. It means that Korean ETFs market is much more fragmented than its Japanese counterpart (considering the average fund's turnover (or, referring to Sect. 2.4, average assets)). In other leading ETFs markets in the region, China and Hong Kong, the number of ETFs was 138 and 157, respectively, i.e., much lower than in the two countries discussed previously. Taking into account the values of turnover on the exchanges in these countries, it may be stated that the market in China is more concentrated than in Hong Kong (and in South Korea). However, the average value of individual fund's turnover is still by

[4] Bearing in mind that different classifications were utilized in both cases (all listed funds for turnover versus primary listed funds for assets).

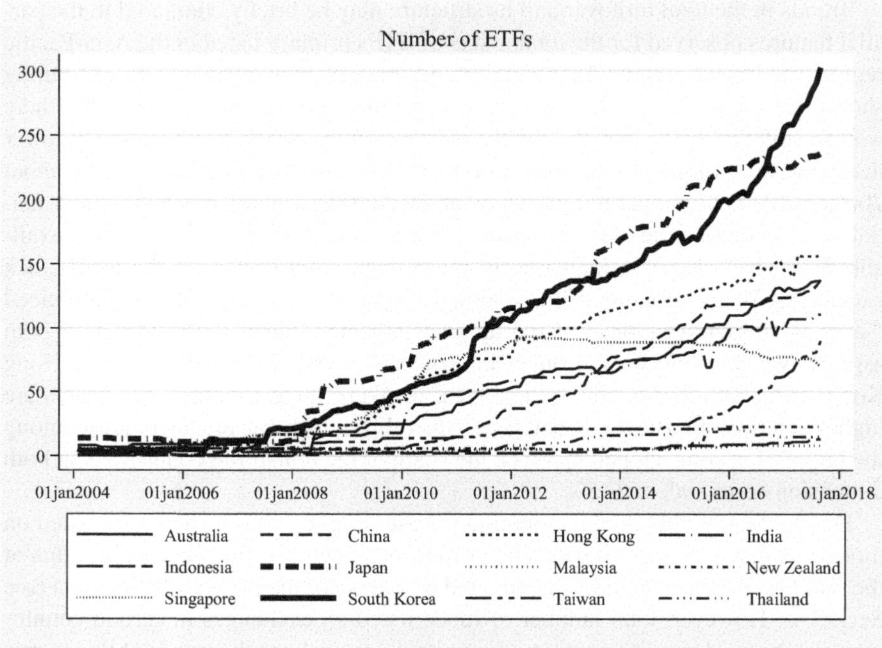

Note: numbers include all funds listed on exchange(s) in certain country, regardless of the location of primary listing (for discussion concerning structure and trends in terms of the primary listing see Section 2.4.). In China, Indonesia, Malaysia, and Thailand ETFs have been traded since a later date than I 2004. For New Zealand lack of data for VI 2010 – XII 2011. In case of China and India possible double-counting due to multiple listing locations.
Source: own elaborations.

Fig. 4.3 Number of ETFs listed on exchanges in the Asia-Pacific countries. Monthly data for January 2004–August 2017

far the largest in Japan. Looking at the remaining countries, there are four with more than 50 ETFs listed: Australia (137—close to the number for China but with substantially lower total and, accordingly, average turnover), India (111), Taiwan (90), and Singapore (69). Malaysia is at the bottom of the analyzed ranking, with merely eight listed funds, but with higher turnover in comparison to countries such as Indonesia. It should be emphasized that we considered all ETFs listed in certain country—the number of the primary listed funds is in most cases lower due to cross-listing.

In terms of the absolute ETFs market development, Japanese ETFs market had been the largest in the early examined years (see Fig. 4.4), and it has remained among the biggest in the region for the most of the analyzed time period (with the most notable exception of 2015 when it was surpassed substantially by China and Hong Kong). In the beginning of the 2004–2017 period, its dominance had been

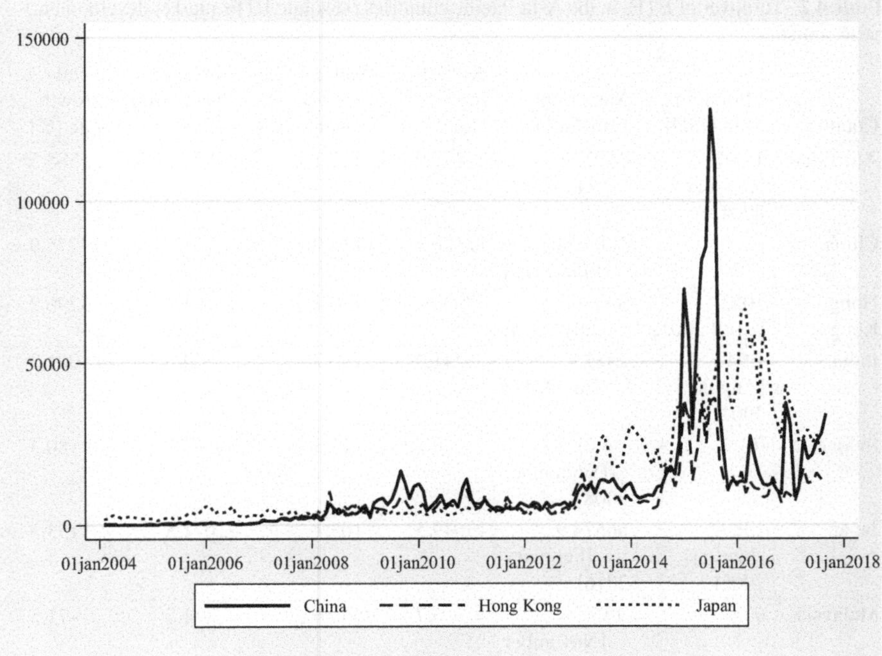

Note: on Y-axis: turnover of ETFs in mln USD.
Source: own elaboration.

Fig. 4.4 Turnover of ETFs in China, Hong Kong, and Japan (three countries with the highest average values in the region). Monthly data for January 2004–August 2017

extremely clear as Japanese market had accounted for almost entire turnover of ETFs in the Asia-Pacific area. However, the launch and rapid growth of the funds in China as well as the expansion of ETFs in two of the oldest markets (apart from Japan), i.e., Hong Kong and South Korea, deeply changed the structure of the regional market (see the final part of this section). As it may be noticed in Table 4.2, maximum values in the region were reached in China, and average turnover in this country has been lower by only ca. 1.5 billion USD than on much more established Japanese market. It means that even though Japan may still for many reasons be regarded as the reference ETFs market (not only in the region but also on a global scale), some of the other countries have been catching up.

4.2.2 Analysis of Absolute ETFs Market Development

After the introductory analysis concerning various aspects of the ETFs markets in the entire region, we now focus on the country-specific evidence. We discuss first the ETFs market development in the 12 Asia-Pacific countries employing the

Table 4.2 Turnover of ETFs in the Asia-Pacific countries (absolute ETFs market development)—basic statistics

Country	Minimum [mln USD]	Maximum [mln USD]	Average [mln USD]	Average monthly dynamic [%]	Absolute change [mln USD]	Total growth rate [%]
Australia	11.07 [October 2004]	1502.3 [June 2017]	492.9	115.1	1071.6	585.5
China	*0*	128,033 [June 2015]	12126.3	112.9	33957.2	13275.9
Hong Kong	105.9 [April 2005]	39056.1 [July 2015]	7029.4	110.4	12691.9	3296.2
India	1.94 [August 2004]	2533.8 [July 2017]	241.3	116.7	624.6	4001.2
Indonesia	*0*	4.21 [September 2008]	0.19	212.3	−3.1	−80.3
Japan	1289.5 [January 2005]	66574.9 [February 2016]	13649.5	105.1	21071.5	1153.3
Malaysia	*0*	135.1 [November 2016]	6.7	*4600.6*	−1.7	−71.5
New Zealand	1.99 [June 2008]	34.9 [September 2016]	7.2	112.8	20.5	859.3
Singapore	0.46 [December 2005]	977.6 [August 2011]	207.2	124.5	159.1	4335.1
South Korea	110.9 [February 2005]	20276.9 [May 2017]	6771.8	107.6	18113.4	9343.5
Taiwan	94.5 [April 2006]	6930.5 [July 2015]	1253.4	110.1	4202.1	2407.5
Thailand	*0*	115.1 [September 2012]	20.0	126.5	−27.2	−81.1

Monthly data for January 2004–August 2017

Note: average monthly dynamic calculated as geometric mean. In China, Indonesia, Malaysia, and Thailand, ETFs have been traded since a later date than January 2004; therefore, multiple minimum values are not reported; total growth rate is calculated by referring to the first positive value. For Malaysia extremely high average monthly dynamic results from multiple and radical ups and downs of ETFs turnover (and possible problems with data reliability that are, though, difficult to determine). For New Zealand lack of data for June 2010–July 2011—this period is not covered in our calculations

Source: own calculations

absolute approach (see Table 4.2), starting with the largest ETFs markets (the ones with the highest average monthly values of turnover expressed in millions of USD). As it may be noticed, the analyzed countries can be classified into three groups of four countries:

1. Most developed ETFs markets (i.e., regional leaders)—China, Hong Kong, Japan, and South Korea.
2. Mid-developed ETFs markets (with some displays of catching-up)—Australia, India, Singapore, and Taiwan.
3. Least developed ETFs markets—Indonesia, Malaysia, New Zealand, and Thailand.

Japan is the oldest ETFs market in the region and one of the most established in the world with the first fund launched in 1995 (see Sect. 2.4). However, for the first few years, Nikkei 300 Stock Index Listed Fund[5] was the single ETF listed in Japan, and its turnover and assets were rather low. What is important (also in the context of much more recent events described below), its launch had been part of the Japanese government's strategy—it had been cautiously prepared through, for instance, implementation of the required laws. The first Japanese ETF offered exposure to the government-promoted Nikkei 300 index, and it was aimed at influencing the trading structure on the local capital markets by decreasing the popularity of Nikkei 225 futures (according to the financial authorities, they had been too strongly impacting the operations on the cash market (Osaki 2001)). The first Japanese ETF had not, though, achieved the expected aim as the Nikkei 300 index remained rather unpopular. Therefore, according to some authors (e.g., Abner 2016), the actual development of the Japanese ETFs market has begun when the funds with exposure to the main stock market's indexes such as Nikkei 225 and TOPIX were launched in the mid-2001 (Seki 2007; Abner 2016). Over the next years, the turnover of ETFs had been steadily increasing until 2005, after which, until 2012, it stabilized at the level of approximately 4 billion USD per month. The stage of rapid growth began in 2013 and lasted until the first half of 2016. In the next months, turnover of ETFs dropped sharply, returning to the 2014 levels.

As it was noticed in the footnote to Table 4.1, structure of the Japanese market has evolved in the considered time period with regard to the listing and trading locations of ETFs. Until 2013 ETFs were traded on the Osaka Stock Exchange and Tokyo Stock Exchange, with the separate statistics on their turnover provided by the World Federation of Exchanges until June 2013. They were integrated in January 2013 and formed a holding company Japan Exchange Group (Ozaki 2013). It means that almost entire ETF trading activity in Japan takes place on the Tokyo Stock Exchange (Osaka now specializes in futures and options), one of the largest in the world in terms of turnover; activity on the other exchanges is extremely low in comparison to the Japan Exchange Group.[6]

---

[5] Full names of the funds were extracted from Lipper's database—we use the names provided as of October 2017.

[6] It is evidenced, in a slightly different perspective, by the fact that according to Lipper's database,

The largest group of ETFs in Japan are equity funds which accounted for more than 95% of the total net assets of the Japanese primary listed ETFs as of August 2017. There were six funds with more than 10 billion USD of managed assets: three tracking TOPIX and the other three with exposure to Nikkei 225; the biggest fund was Nomura TOPIX ETF with more than 50 billion USD in its portfolio. What it is quite exceptional in comparison to almost all other world's ETFs markets, the pioneering Nikkei 300 Stock Index Listed Fund has not remained among the market leaders as its assets were at merely ca. 95 million USD. Despite the domination of the equity funds (driven, inter alia, by the transactions of the Bank of Japan), overall the Japanese ETFs market is one of the most diversified in the world (in many aspects to comparable degree as its US counterpart). It includes not only equity funds (with exposure to equities listed in various countries) but also bond, commodity, and alternative (e.g., currency) funds as well as the other type of ETPs, i.e., ETNs. The growing diversity of the Japanese ETFs market, in particular since 2013, may be regarded as one of the factors contributing to its quick development in that period. Japanese investors may also easily conduct transactions in foreign-listed ETFs (Abner 2016).[7]

Rapidly growing turnover of ETFs in Japan since 2013 onward may also be attributed to another important development—launch of the geared funds in 2012 (CSOP Asset Management 2015). Geared funds have rapidly achieved considerable share in the total turnover—already in 2013 they accounted for about half of the total turnover while 1 year later for ca. 70%; over the next years, their share has increased even further (JPX Tokyo Stock Exchange 2015, 2016, 2017). Geared ETFs have been actively traded, their net assets have remained, though, rather small (in particular in comparison to their turnover). Extremely quickly increasing popularity of this category of ETFs has led to operational problems for some providers (for more on this topic, see JPX Tokyo Stock Exchange (2016)). Due to their fundamental attributes, geared ETFs are considered to be short-term investment solutions, preferred by the individual investors (Abner 2016).

Structure of the main participants of the Japanese ETFs market (in terms of value of turnover) has been substantially changing over the analyzed time period. Share of the two categories has significantly increased: individual investors and, even more substantially, foreign market participants (JPX Tokyo Stock Exchange 2015, 2018). As both groups were less active on the ETFs market in 2017 than in the previous years (possibly due to lack of clear upward or downward trend on the stock market which limited, e.g., the gains from the geared funds), this contributed substantially to the sharp decline in turnover.

However, if the shares in the assets owned by certain groups are considered, the position of the individual investors is radically different as they account for only a

---

there is only one ETF primary listed in Japan, with its primary listing location other than the Japan Exchange Group.

[7]One of the available methods is through ETF-JDRs, i.e., Japanese Depositary Receipts, which allow for transacting in the shares of ETFs primary listed abroad analogically to Japanese securities (Fuhr 2015).

few percents, significantly below 10%, and their share has been declining (based on 2015–2017 data (JPX Tokyo Stock Exchange 2017, 2018)). It implies that individual holders conduct transactions on the ETFs market relatively much more often than the other categories of investors. The largest group of ETFs' shareholders (in terms of assets) is financial institutions, in particular banks, which is caused by the policy issues presented subsequently.

Our discussion of the Japanese market must include a brief overview of one important issue. Despite the high levels of turnover of ETFs in Japan, which imply that the degree of diffusion of the innovative funds in this country is much higher than in all remaining economies, the results obtained for the Japanese market should be perceived to some extent as distorted by the actions of the central bank (i.e., Bank of Japan). Consequently, it is difficult to assess the actual level of the local ETFs market development in either absolute or relative terms as it could include the arbitrary decision concerning the inclusion or exclusion of the transactions conducted with the involvement of the central bank. We decide to analyze the full values of turnover as, through the improvement in the shares' liquidity, operations of the central bank influence positively the ETFs market development (another reason is the fact that, as discussed below, in terms of the share in total value of transactions, the role of central bank's operations is not highly significant).

Bank of Japan has started purchasing the shares of ETFs as an element of the quantitative easing program (Abner 2016). Initial version of the ETFs purchase program was launched in 2010 as an element of the economic stimulus package, and it was modified in 2013, 2014, and 2016 when Bank of Japan increased its scale; according to the data as of December 2017, the total value of the shares of ETFs purchased by Bank of Japan was at ca. 150 billion USD or, in other terms, ca. 70% of the total net assets of the Japanese ETFs (Lee and Urabe 2017). However, when the value of the purchases in each month is compared to particular month's total value of ETFs turnover, it seems that the impact on overall turnover is rather insignificant as they account for below 20% (estimations based on 2016–2017 data (JPX Tokyo Stock Exchange 2018; Lee and Hasegawa 2018)); moreover, the record purchases in 2017 coincided with the period of the strongly declining turnover rather than reverse trend. Some analysts point out in this context that Bank of Japan's purchase program gives some relief against the market downside risk, which is affecting the trading behavior of the investors.

The aim and rules of the ETFs purchase program are presented in the documents of Bank of Japan, including the key one about terms and conditions from 2013, amended in the next years (Bank of Japan 2017a). Its purpose is defined as facilitating money market operations. The range of ETFs to be purchased is restricted to the funds with exposure to the selected Japanese stock market's indexes. Operations are not conducted directly by the central bank but rather by the appointed trust bank. Maximum amounts to be bought are set by the Bank of Japan, taking into account both the aggregate market value of particular ETF and the coverage of the tracked index. Similar (yet smaller) program was introduced in 2016 and is aimed at supporting companies that invest proactively in physical capital and human resources through purchases of ETFs which hold equities of such firms (Bank of Japan 2017b).

Effects of the aforementioned initiative, whose actual aim seems to be supporting the prices of Japanese equities (most purchases of the shares of ETFs are made in the periods of falling prices of equities), are considered to be ambiguous with regard to both the stock and ETFs market. As the program has not been concluded by the end of the analyzed time period, its effects are difficult to evaluate (for more on this topic, see Fueda-Samikawa and Takano (2017), Nangle and Yates (2017), Takeo et al. (2017), Lee and Hasegawa (2018), Petrov (2018), Shimada (2018)).

Apart from the Bank of Japan's program, other government-related plans that could have impacted the development of the ETFs market have been the Nippon Individual Savings Account (NISA), launched in 2014, and the deregulation of DC pension plans for individuals (iDeCo) in 2017, aimed at encouraging investments in securities through tax exemptions on income from capital gains (Japan Securities Dealers Association 2014; Fuhr 2015). Most recently, another important policy implemented by the Tokyo Stock Exchange (in 2018) was the introduction of the market makers system in which registered market makers have to give bid/ask quotes of ETFs. This was because of the relatively lower liquidity excluding some major ETFs such as Nikkei225 or TOPIX ETFs.

Before we discuss the next two ETFs markets, in Hong Kong and China (we discuss them jointly), it is necessary to address the fundamental issue of the complicated structure of the local equity markets (in particular the one in Mainland China) which are strongly interconnected, and their links are unique on a global scale. For many years Chinese financial markets were underdeveloped and substantially restricted for foreign investors. However, in the aftermath of the economic reforms aimed at improving the performance of the Chinese state enterprises (such as improved incentives and factor allocation (Li 1997)), stock exchanges in Shanghai and Shenzhen were established in the early 1990s, initially accessible exclusively for the domestic investors (Ji and Thomas 2003; Wong 2006). By the end of the twentieth century, the only channel, through which foreign investors could buy stocks of the Chinese companies, was equities of the China-incorporated corporations or corporations incorporated outside China yet controlled by the Chinese entities that were listed on exchanges in other countries, above all in Hong Kong (Lystra 2017; actually certain group of Hong Kong-listed equities linked to the Chinese entities had been listed even before the establishment of the stock market in China). It changed with the introduction of special programs designated for foreign investors who wish to access the Chinese stock exchanges. As a result, as of 2017, there are seven distinct classes of shares (in some cases labeled "chips") of Chinese companies and four programs for foreign investors (see Tables 4.3 and 4.4), the only such case among the major global economies.

It should be emphasized that stock connection systems listed in Table 4.4 give also the access to the Hong Kong exchange for the Chinese investors, not only in the reverse direction. However, as of end of 2017, they did not cover ETFs—it was expected to change in the late 2018 (Lord 2018). The two categories of connect initiatives may be described as the programs with potentially high importance for ETFs (due to less stringent restrictions than in case of the other programs and the broadest group of potential users), yet this is still to be observed after their expected

Table 4.3 Classes of shares of Chinese companies

Class	Year introduced	Exchange	Trading currency	Accessibility
A-shares	1990	Shanghai and Shenzhen	RMB	Chinese investors and QFII and RQFII
B-shares	1992	Shanghai and Shenzhen	USD (Shanghai) and HKD (Shenzhen)	Chinese investors (under certain circumstances, i.e., special accounts) and foreign investors
H-shares	1993	Hong Kong	HKD	Chinese investors (through QDII) and foreign investors
N-shares	1992	New York and NASDAQ	USD	Chinese investors (through QDII) and foreign investors
P-chips	2000	Hong Kong	HKD	Chinese investors (through QDII) and foreign investors
Red-chips	1972	Hong Kong	HKD	Chinese investors (through QDII) and foreign investors
S-chips	2001	Singapore	SGD	Chinese investors (through QDII) and foreign investors

Note: QFII, Qualified Foreign Institutional Investor; RQFII, Renminbi Qualified Foreign Institutional Investor; QDII, Qualified Domestic Institutional Investor
Source: own elaboration based on Fowler et al. (2008), Fuhr et al. (2016), Charles Schwab (2017), Lystra (2017)

Table 4.4 Categories of programs for foreign investors on the Chinese stock exchanges

Category	Year introduced	Trading currency of Chinese securities	Eligible investors	Range of available securities
Qualified Foreign Institutional Investor (QFII)	2002	USD and other foreign currencies	Certain institutional investors	Selected A-shares, treasury bonds, and others
Renminbi Qualified Foreign Institutional Investor (RQFII)	2011	RMB	Certain institutional investors	Selected A-shares, treasury bonds, and others
Shanghai-Hong Kong Stock Connect	2016	RMB	All investors	Selected A-shares
Shenzhen-Hong Kong Stock Connect	2016	RMB	All investors	Selected A-shares

Source: own elaboration based on Fuhr et al. (2016), Charles Schwab (2017), Huo and Ahmed (2017)

inclusion. In particular, according to the results of the survey discussed in Lord (2018), it could considerably boost the demand for the shares of the Hong Kong-listed ETFs from the investors in China.

Hong Kong is the oldest ETFs market in the Asia-Pacific apart from Japan—the first innovative fund, the Tracker Fund of Hong Kong ETF, was launched on the exchange in this country in 1999 (Fuhr 2015), followed by iShares MSCI China Index ETF in 2001. The latter fund was in fact the first ETF globally that provided exposure to the Chinese equities (later such funds were listed in the United States and the United Kingdom (in 2004 (Fuhr et al. 2016)). The former fund remains the largest ETF on the local market—it is the only fund whose assets as of August 2017 exceeded 10 billion USD (they were at about 12.3 billion USD).

The biggest category of ETFs in Hong Kong, both in terms of assets and turnover, is equity funds. More specifically, the most actively traded category of the Hong Kong ETFs has been funds which focus on the companies with A-shares, while equity ETFs with exposure to the local stock market have been relatively less popular (CSOP Asset Management 2015). The reason for the popularity of the A-shares ETFs, particularly among foreign investors, is the possibility to gain exposure to the Chinese equities without necessary admission to one of the programs for foreign investors (Fuhr et al. 2016). Due to the legal limitations, initially such funds were exclusively synthetic and employed special derivatives, but later a creation of physical ETFs has been facilitated by the RQFII program—see Table 4.4 (Fuhr 2015). Other categories of ETFs, including bond and commodity funds, are also available in Hong Kong, analogously to Japan. However, one of the most rapidly expanding categories in the other countries of the region, i.e., geared funds, was launched in Hong Kong much later than in, for example, South Korea or Japan due to more restrictive regulation (Fuhr 2015; Lord 2016; Yap 2016; Young 2016; EY 2017). In Hong Kong they remain still relatively less actively traded and have accumulated less assets (to some extent due to narrower range of products offered (Lord 2016)). ETFs market in Hong Kong is highly diversified not only in terms of the available funds but also with regard to the linked financial instruments as investors have access to futures, options, and derivative warrants based on the shares of ETFs, regardless of their underlying exposure (Shum et al. 2014).

Chinese ETFs market was initiated much later than its counterpart in Hong Kong—according to data of the World Federation of Exchanges (and Shanghai Stock Exchange (2012)), the first fund was launched in 2005, known most recently under the name ChinaAMC 50 ETF (or more briefly China 50 ETF), aimed at tracking the SSE 50 index (index of 50 largest companies listed on the Shanghai Stock Exchange). Equity funds are important part of the Chinese ETFs market, yet money market ETFs have become its largest category (an attribute that distinguishes it from all other examined countries). Position of money market ETFs has strengthened after the 2015 events described below that marked the extreme growth in the turnover of equity funds, followed by their strong decline (see total turnover on Fig. 4.4). It led to the withdrawal of investors from this category in lieu of (usually newly launched) money market funds. It is proven very clearly by the ranking of top Chinese ETFs in terms of turnover—in July 2015 eight out of ten funds with the highest turnover were equity ETFs (Deutsche Bank 2015a), whereas 2 years later, in July 2017, nine out of ten were money market ETFs, and the only exception was one bond ETF (Deutsche Bank 2017b). In terms of assets, the largest fund in 2017 was Fortune SGAM Xianjin Tianyi Money Market, with more than twice more assets than the second-largest ChinaAMC 50 ETF (Deutsche Bank 2017a). This move from equity toward money market funds may be attributed mostly to the downfall of the equity prices in 2015. Apart from equity and money market ETFs, a number of bond and commodity (tracking the prices of gold (Pan and Li (2016)) ETFs are also listed in China. There are also some derivatives based on the Chinese-listed ETFs (Wang et al. 2018).

As it may be clearly noted on Fig. 4.4, in both China and Hong Kong, the turnover of ETFs reached historically highest levels in the mid-2015. Such high intensity of transactions in the shares of ETFs may be explained above all by strong fluctuations on the three considered stock exchanges (in Hong Kong, Shanghai, and Shenzhen). In the late 2014 and early 2015, the prices of Chinese equities increased substantially for a number of reasons (detailed discussion lies outside the scope of this book) including internationalization of the local currency, encouraging retail stock investments by the government (despite rapid increase in the popularity of the stock investments in China, they still constitute a marginal part of the households' assets), and growing domestic consumption (ETF Trends 2015). Mainland Chinese stock market consists mostly of the retail individual investors who, in the mentioned time period, attempted to maximize their profits by purchasing stocks of smaller companies using margin. Moreover, in order to further increase the potential gains, some investors applied higher leverage offered by companies operating outside the regulated markets.

Within a few months, the situation changed deeply—the stock prices of Chinese equities dropped substantially. Apart from the macroeconomic factors (which, again, lie outside the scope of our analysis), one of the key mechanisms was the high number of primary and secondary stock offerings conducted in June that attracted investors and led to withdrawal from their previous holdings in the stocks of small companies and, consequently, the fall of their prices (ETF Trends 2015). Another linked mechanism of the decline were margin calls (caused by the declining values of equities of small companies) which caused problems for the investors with too high levels of applied leverage. In order to prevent further aggravation of the decline, regulators allowed to suspend trading in the stocks of many listed (mostly small and mid) companies (almost half on the exchanges in Shanghai and Shenzhen (Maher 2015)). Many Chinese institutions were engaged in the efforts to prevent the further escalation of the crisis: Chinese central bank unexpectedly cut the interest rates and supported the prices of stocks using its reserves, while the financial regulatory authorities influenced the listed companies by suggesting actions such as share buybacks or share purchases by their executives aimed at increasing the prices of their equities (Maher 2015). One of the actions undertaken by the Chinese authorities to mitigate the turbulences on the stock market was purchase of the ETFs' shares by the Chinese state-owned investment fund (Rapoza 2015) which partially explains the extremely high values of turnover in the mid-2015. There are, though, at least two other important reasons for the high activity on the ETFs market. First, investors simply sold their shares of equity ETFs in order to liquidate their exposure to the stock market. Second, ETFs were used as a price discovery tool and provision of liquidity during the abnormal situation on the underlying market (shares of ETFs continued to be traded, while tracked shares were halted (Deutsche Bank 2015a).

After the period of the stock market turmoil, the values of the turnover of ETFs declined to the levels slightly higher than the ones observed before these events—it proves that ETFs markets in China and Hong Kong have continued to grow and, even more importantly, that the levels from 2015 and 2016 should not be perceived as the actual proofs for the strong development of ETFs markets in that period but rather specific outliers. However, the overall trend of changes between 2004 and 2017 is positive in both cases—see absolute changes or total growth rates in Table 4.2.

Key participants of the Hong Kong ETFs market are institutional investors (Fuhr 2015). However, the position of the retail investors is very strong. Even though, due to insufficient data, it is impossible to formulate robust conclusions in this field, Hong Kong may probably be labeled as the world's market with the highest share of residents investing in ETFs—according to the 2014 data, more than one-tenth of adult population held shares of ETFs (CSOP Asset Management 2015).

Chinese ETFs market, despite the higher average turnover than in Hong Kong, may still be perceived as relatively less advanced if aspects such as the diversity of the available funds or availability of linked derivatives are taken into account; this applies also to comparison of their turnover to the size of the local economy. Further growth in the turnover of ETFs in China may be boosted by some of the most recent factors, including the launch of funds which include ETFs in their portfolios, increased presence of institutional investors (using ETFs listed in China for, e.g., risk management or arbitrage), and growing diversity of the China-listed funds with increasingly more ETFs other than the most frequent domestic equity ETFs (Xu 2017). Among the barriers of the development of the Chinese ETFs market are the unfavorable distribution system (with fee structures focused on commissions) and very low share of ETFs in the total investments of retail users due to, inter alia, insufficient education concerning their features (Lord 2018).

Finally, it should be remembered that Chinese ETFs market consists of two stock exchanges (in Shanghai and Shenzhen). The number of ETFs listed in Shanghai is considerably higher than in Shenzhen (in August 2017 it was 85 to 53; some funds are dual-listed), and it includes most of the intensively traded funds (e.g., money market ETFs). As a result, over the period 2004–2017, the value of ETFs turnover in Shanghai has been much higher.

South Korea is the fourth and final Asia-Pacific ETFs market within the category of most developed. Evaluation of the average turnover of ETFs in South Korea shows that in this dimension it lagged significantly behind Japan or China yet only slightly in relation to Hong Kong. In terms of the total growth rate, it was the regional leader among the countries where ETFs have been traded for the full evaluated time period; for a short time, in 2011 and 2012, it was even the country with the highest turnover in the region.

The history of the ETFs traded in South Korea started in 2002 (Yap 2015), with the launch of the equity funds tracking the main index of the South Korean stock market—KOSPI 200, including Samsung Kodex200 Securities ETF which remains the largest ETF primary listed on the Korea Exchange, with almost 5 billion USD of assets as of August 2017. As in most other advanced ETFs markets, the biggest funds (in terms of assets and usually also turnover) are the ones tracking the main indexes of the local stock market—in case of South Korea, it is evidenced by the very strong position of the funds tracking KOSPI 200 index (Park et al. 2014), including geared funds (e.g., leveraged). According to the end of August 2017 data, four out of five funds with more than 1 billion USD in the managed assets tracked KOSPI 200 (including one leveraged and one inverse ETF); the fifth fund in this group tracked KRW Cash Index. Apart from the most established equity ETFs, there are also a few other types of funds traded on the local stock exchange: bond, commodity (not limited to gold as there are also, for instance, funds with exposure to the oil or agriculture market), currency, and mixed-asset ETFs. What is important, these categories (with the exception of multi-asset funds) include also funds with modified returns (leveraged, etc.)—such funds are quite unique[8] even in a global scale as almost all geared listed worldwide are equity ETFs. Examples are funds such as Samsung KODEX 10Y F-LKTB Inverse ETF, KIM KINDEX Synth-Gold Futures Inverse2X ETF, and Kiwoom KOSEF Synth-USD Futures Leverage ETF. The launch of the non-equity-geared ETFs may be regarded as a "side effect" of the very high demand for the geared funds tracking the stock indexes. However, the turnover or assets of such funds have remained significantly below the respective values of the equity-geared funds. Broad range of available funds is proven by the fact that South Korean ETFs market is the largest in the region in terms of the number of listed ETFs (see Fig. 4.3).

Very rapid development of the South Korean ETFs market began in 2011 (in our key approach, i.e., in terms of turnover; the assets of ETFs started growing quickly slightly earlier, in 2009)—the period of the fastest expansion could be observed in the second half of 2011 and first months of 2012, followed by substantial yet short-lived decline. Extremely quick expansion of ETFs in South Korea is proven by the fact that in 2011 and 2012, turnover of ETFs on the local exchange was the highest in the entire region. Over 2013–2016 monthly turnover of South Korean ETFs fluctuated between approximately 10 and 15 billion USD; since late 2016 another period of growth has been noticed, yet its sustainability still remains to be assessed. Negative feature of the South Korean ETFs market is high concentration of the turnover as a small number of funds account for vast majority of the total transactions (Sil 2017).

Analogically to the Japanese ETFs market, the market in South Korea is strictly dominated by the geared equity funds,[9] in particular in terms of turnover. Their launch and increasing popularity may be regarded as one of the causes of the extremely quick absolute ETFs market development in South Korea since 2011. The first South Korean inverse ETF (Samsung KODEX Inverse Exchange-Traded Fund) was launched in 2009 and leveraged ETF (Samsung KODEX Leverage Derivatives ETF) in 2010 (CSOP Asset Management 2015). The pioneering leveraged fund had

[8] In Asia-Pacific they are also offered in Taiwan—see discussion in the further part of this section. However, we identified no such funds on the older and larger markets in Hong Kong and Japan which shows the high level of innovativeness of the South Korean providers.

[9] As we already mentioned, the turnover of the geared non-equity ETFs is much smaller.

very quickly become the leader of the entire market in terms of the turnover (in merely 7 months (Samsung Asset Management 2010)). Initially, this category of South Korean ETFs included exclusively funds tracking the main South Korean equity market's indexes. However, over the further years, it was substantially expanded with the introduction of funds that offer returns based on the stock indexes in, for example, Japan, China, or India. Soon after the introduction of the geared ETFs, they have become the most intensively traded category of ETFs on the Korea Exchange, accounting for the vast majority of the total value of transactions in these securities. One of the consequences of this process has been a substantial increase in the share of individual investors in the total value of ETFs turnover (see the discussion for Japan) and accompanying decline of the share of the institutional investors who had dominated the market in its initial years.

Rapid expansion of ETFs in South Korea has been facilitated by some positive aspects of the regulatory environment and support from the Korea Exchange such as, introduced in the initial years, easement of the rules of ETFs trading in comparison to other securities (Samsung Asset Management 2010; Vaghela 2015) or educational and marketing campaigns. Broad range of measures was announced by the Financial Services Commission in the late 2015 (Korea Financial Investment Association 2016), including, inter alia, shortened fund's registration time or tax incentives (Deutsche Bank 2015b). Other actions were declared in October 2016 by the Korea Exchange in order to attract the institutional investors regarded as a factor of the sustained market development (The Investor 2016). Another factor contributing to the development of the Korean ETFs market in the final part of the analyzed time period has been adoption of ETFs by various types of financial institutions that began utilizing their shares in order to offer indirect investment products, e.g., variable insurance using portfolio managed with ETFs (Sil 2017).

After the discussion concerning the most developed ETFs markets in the Asia-Pacific region, we focus on the group of countries that lag behind the regional leaders, yet some symptoms of the diffusion of the innovative funds could be observed (i.e., the category of mid-developed ETFs markets). It is a highly diverse group as it includes an advanced economy (Australia), one of the world's largest and most populated economies (India), small country which is a global financial center (Singapore), and, finally, Taiwan whose ETFs market resembles in some ways the more developed ones in the region.

Development of the Australian ETFs market has been stable since their launch in 2001, in particular after 2007. Even though the total growth has been much lower than in the remaining mid-developed ETFs markets (see Table 4.2), it should be remembered that at the beginning of 2004, the monthly turnover in Australia was the highest among all countries in this group, except for Taiwan (which, as outlined below, stands out in this group). The first two funds launched in Australia were SPDR S&P/ASX 50 ETF and SPDR S&P/ASX 200 ETF (BlackRock 2011). The latter has remained the market's leader in terms of both turnover and managed assets (among the primary listed ETFs)—as of end of August 2017, it held assets worth approximately 2.7 billion USD; the second-biggest fund was Vanguard Australian Shares Index ETF (assets of ca. 1.7 billion USD). Initially, exclusively equity funds with the exposure to the local stock market as well as one real estate fund (yet with some features of the equity fund) had been listed (Gallagher and Segara 2006), but over the next years (in particular since the enactment of new listing rules in 2008 (Australian Securities and Investments Commission 2012)), the range of traded ETFs has broadened, and it includes all major categories available on the most developed markets in the region, i.e., bond, money market, commodity, and currency ETFs (Enemuwe 2015). Equity ETFs, with either local or foreign exposure, have remained the key category in terms of turnover of assets, yet some bond and money market funds (such as BetaShares Australian High Interest Cash ETF) were also actively traded and gathered substantial funds. The most substantial discrepancy between the Australian and, for example, South Korean ETFs market is underdevelopment of the synthetic funds in Australia, linked to the strict regulations (Cunningham 2017). Cross-listing of ETFs primary listed in the United States contributed to the increasing turnover in the initial years when the number of local ETFs had remained very low. The largest group of users of ETFs in Australia are individual investors (Cunningham 2017); however, some changes in the structure in terms of market participants can be noticed (Rose 2017).

Despite the already quite significant diffusion of ETFs in Australia (labeled even as "seismic shift" in the investment industry (Pash 2018)), there is a number of factors that are expected to contribute to further development of the Australian ETFs market—increasing demand for investment solutions that can be used to diversify the investment's portfolio, growing popularity among investors who manage pensions portfolios on their own, as well as changes in the remuneration structure of the financial planning services in the direction of fee-for-service model, more favorable for ETFs than the competing solutions (BlackRock 2011; Carson 2017; Power 2017; Chandler 2018).

First Indian ETF, known most recently (after a few provider's changes) as Reliance ETF Nifty BeES, was listed in 2002 (and incepted in December 2001) (Samalad 2017; Reliance 2018). In spite of the fact that, based on the average turnover, it may be stated that Indian market is one of the least developed in the region (in the mid group, it surpassed only Singapore), analysis of the most recent trends shows some potential for rapid development. Over the first 8 months of 2017, a total turnover of ETFs increased by about 273% in comparison to the respective period 1 year before; on a monthly basis, it exceeded for the first time the level of 1 billion USD, reaching even more than 2.5 billion USD in July 2017. It means that in that period turnover of Indian ETFs was higher than in any other country of the mid group, except for Taiwan. The rapid diffusion of ETFs in the final part of the analyzed time period (since, approximately, late 2016) has been boosted, in some ways similar to Japan, by the policy of the Indian government (see the next paragraph). Other potential reasons include decreasing costs of investment into ETFs caused by their growing size and investments linked with pension savings (Business Standard 2017). Some of the barriers of their diffusion embrace the distribution and commission structure which favors conventional funds and equities rather than ETFs (Samalad 2017).

A substantial factor of the aforementioned rapid expansion of ETFs since 2016 in India was the launch of one fund which distinguishes itself on a global scale, i.e., ETF aimed at being part of the Indian government's privatization program (Malhotra et al. 2016; Samalad 2017; Shah and Ramarathinam 2017; Kumar, 2018a, b). Fund, under the name "CPSE ETF," invests exclusively in the stocks of ten companies in which the Indian government is the majority owner, including Natural Gas Corp or Rural Electrification Company; it tracks a special stock market index—Nifty CPSE. Its popularity among investors has been driven by high returns on its shares (more than 45% over the first year (Business Standard 2017)). As a result, Indian government decided to launch another "privatization" fund in the late 2017, tracking the index including 22 companies (Bharat 22 ETF (Ghosh 2017, 2018; Kumar, 2018a, b).

Structure of the Indian ETFs market with regard to the funds' exposure is rather typical as equity ETFs have the dominant position. There are in total several bond, commodity (exclusively with exposure to gold), and money market ETFs, yet their role is negligible, with the exception of the single money market ETFs (in terms of turnover) and few gold ETFs (in terms of assets). There is also one very small Shariah-compliant equity fund. Interestingly, Indian ETFs are the topic of intensive academic research—the number of studies devoted to their analysis is among the highest of all Asia-Pacific ETFs markets—see, among the most recent, Banerjee (2015), Narend and Thenmozhi (2016), Purohit and Malhotra (2015), Singh and Seth (2016), Saji (2017), Sarkar (2017), Sarkar (2017), and Kaur and Singh (2018).

Like in China, ETFs in India are traded on two stock exchanges: BSE India Limited ("BSE") and National Stock Exchange of India Limited ("NSE"; both are headquartered in the same city-Mumbai). NSE is the distinct leader when the number of primary listed funds or their aggregated assets is considered (it was also the listing place of the Indian first ETF). Over the analyzed time period, it has also remained the location of much higher value of the ETFs turnover, yet World Federation of Exchanges data for 2017 shows strengthening position of BSE.

Even though, similarly to Hong Kong, Singapore is one of the leading global financial centers (in the 2017 22nd edition of the Global Financial Centres Index, Hong Kong was ranked third and Singapore fourth), its ETFs market is smaller in terms of turnover (and assets). Even among the analyzed mid group, it is the least developed taking into account the value of transactions in the shares of ETFs.[10] The trajectory of changes in the value of turnover of ETFs in Singapore differs from the one observed in the other countries in our sample. It had increased rapidly until reaching the maximum levels in 2011, and afterward significant decline could be observed, followed by stabilization from 2014 onward. As Fuhr (2015) notes, this decline was the result of the more strict regulations and requirements regarding the entities allowed to conduct transaction in the shares of ETFs. Main participants of the ETFs market in this country are private banks and family offices (Fuhr 2015) which may be linked to some degree to the financial regulations which until 2015 hindered retail investments (CSOP Asset Management 2015).

[10] Examination of the development in the relative dimension is impossible due to insufficient data.

SPDR Straits Times Index ETF is the first ETFs in Singapore, launched in 2001 (State Street Global Advisors 2011) and tracking the index of the local stock market. Trading activity in the shares of ETFs on the local exchange has focused on the equity funds with foreign exposure or some non-equity funds (e.g., gold ETFs), including the cross-listed funds (Ivanov and Meshcheryakov 2018) rather than funds tracking local equity indexes.

The fourth and the final country in the second analyzed group, Taiwan, is at the same time the largest ETFs market among the four discussed—with the mean monthly turnover of ca. 1.25 billion USD, it is more than twice bigger than Australia (see Table 4.2). Nevertheless, it is still much less developed in absolute terms than any of the markets that we included in the first group. Turnover of ETFs in Taiwan had been very low over the first analyzed years which led in 2008 to attempts by the local stock exchange aimed at boosting the transactions (CSOP Asset Management 2015). Even though this program impacted positively the value of turnover, period of the rapid growth began a few years later. Another similar program was introduced in 2014 (targeted at, inter alia, increasing the liquidity of the shares of ETFs other than the largest ones (TWSE 2018)), but different, more important reason can be indicated to explain the rapid development since 2015. Similarly to South Korea, the upsurge in the ETFs turnover in Taiwan can to large extent be attributed to the growing popularity of the geared funds; another reason was increasing demand for funds with foreign exposure (CSOP Asset Management 2015; Lord 2016).

History of the Taiwanese ETFs market started in 2003 when first fund, Yuanta/P--Shares Taiwan Top 50 ETF was launched (it is its current name; when it was launched it was known at radically different name as Polaris Taiwan Top 50 Tracker Fund (Lin and Chiang 2005; Lin et al. 2006; Chen and Huang 2010)). Very soon it was accompanied by the introduction on warrants on the fund's shares. Value of the ETFs turnover began to increase rapidly with the launch of the geared funds (Tsai and Lee 2017; Zhang 2018) which soon accounted for almost the entire value of the conducted transactions; what is important, geared funds tracking indexes of the foreign stock markets (e.g., Chinese) are among the most traded. Additionally, Taiwan is (apart from the much bigger South Korean ETFs market) the only Asia-Pacific country with geared funds with exposure other than equity—like in South Korea, geared bond, commodity, and currency ETFs are traded (Deutsche Bank 2017a). Significance of the geared ETFs may also be noticed using data on assets—as of end of August 2017, three out of five largest ETFs were funds from this group.

Next, we focus on the third group of Asia-Pacific countries that clearly lags behind taking into account the absolute development of their ETFs markets. In terms of the size of the local economies or the level of economic development, Indonesia, Malaysia, New Zealand, and Thailand are highly heterogeneous, yet their common attribute is the nascent stage of the local ETFs market development, regardless whether the turnover of innovative funds is considered on a stand-alone basis or in relation to the particular country's GDP or other similar listed instruments (we do not present such values as they are extremely low).

Indonesia is the smallest ETFs market in our sample (see Table 4.2). According to the World Federation of Exchanges, it is also the youngest (data on turnover starts

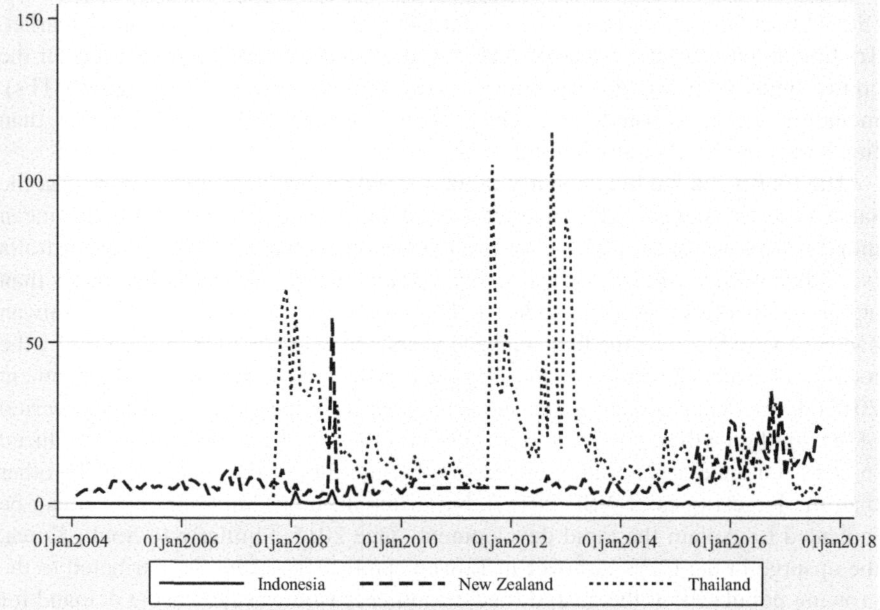

Note: on Y-axis: turnover of ETFs in mln USD. Due to extremely high volatility of the monthly turnover and possible data reliability issues Malaysia is not included.
Source: Authors` elaboration.

Fig. 4.5 Turnover of ETFs in Indonesia, New Zealand, and Thailand (three countries with the lowest average values in the region). Monthly data for January 2004–August 2017

from 2008), but other databases show that some ETFs were primary listed in Indonesia before 2008—according to Lipper's database, there had been two such funds, one listed since 2005 and the other since the late 2007. However, including the pre-2008 period in the time span of our analysis would not change its conclusions as the approximate values of turnover had been similar to the ones observed in further months. Turnover of ETFs on the local stock exchange has remained extremely low over the entire analyzed period (see Fig. 4.5)—the mean value has been at merely ca. 191 thousand USD, and maximum levels of 3.76 and 4.21 million USD were reached in January 2008 and September 2008, respectively. Between 2004 and 2017, there were multiple months in which no turnover of ETFs was recorded—it is the only such case among all selected economies which emphasizes the conclusions concerning the underdevelopment of the local ETFs market. An interesting feature of the Indonesian ETFs market is the fact that the oldest and still the largest fund is not an equity ETF as in almost all other cases but rather a bond ETF: Reksa Dana ABF Indonesia Bond Index Fund ETF (with approximately 300 million USD of managed assets as of end of August 2017).[11] All remaining funds

[11] According to Lipper's database. The report of Deutsche Bank (2017a) implies that Premier ETF

are, however, equity ETFs. Another important attribute is the availability of Shariah-compliant funds (discussed below, with regard to the Malaysian market); their share in the total market in terms of, for example, assets is, though, very low.

According to data extracted from the reports of the World Federation of Exchanges (see Table 4.2), turnover of ETFs in Malaysia has reached the highest maximum value among the four countries included in the least developed category—approximately 135 million USD in November 2016. However, this value should be regarded as an outlier as the mean turnover has been second-lowest in the entire sample—by the end of the analyzed time period, it has dropped even more substantially to the historically lowest levels. Nevertheless, there are some important features of the Malaysian market—its significant part (at least in some segments) are Shariah funds[12]—according to Prakasa (2012), it was the first listing location of such funds in the entire Asia-Pacific region. MyETF Dow Jones Islamic Market Malaysia Titans 25 ETF has been traded since January 2008, and it is aimed at tracking the 25 largest companies domiciled in Malaysia that are evaluated as Shariah-compliant.[13] Shariah ETFs may be perceived within the broad category of Islamic finance industry (or global Islamic wealth management) (Bursa Malaysia 2009; Farouk and Masih 2016). There are a number of requirements that must be met by ETF in order to be able to label itself as Shariah-compliant, which refer above all to the range of possible portfolio holdings and include (for more details see Prakasa (2012), Downes (2016), Rahman (2016), or Gad and Andrikopoulos (2019)):

1. Investing exclusively into securities of companies that adhere to the Shariah principles (e.g., stocks of conventional banks or tobacco companies are excluded).
2. Restricted maximum level of debt or interest income of the company to be included in the portfolio.
3. Fund is not allowed to obtain or provide conventional loans.

Even though Malaysian ETFs market is dominated by the single bond fund, the second remaining group, i.e., funds with equity exposure, consists almost exclusively of Shariah funds (Deutsche Bank 2017a). Most recently, Shariah-compliant gold ETF was listed in Malaysia in December 2017 (Ratna 2017). Overall, two oldest funds in Malaysia are ABF Malaysia Bond Index Fund (listed since July 2005, it accounts for about three-fourths of all funds' assets as end of August 2017) and Malaysia FBM KLCI ETF (available since July 2007). It means that, similarly to Indonesia, the first ETF primary listed in that country was bond fund.

Even though New Zealand is the market with a relatively long history (according to some sources, it is in fact older than the one in Hong Kong (BlackRock 2011)), its role on a regional scale remains negligible due to very low size (Chen et al. 2017;

Indonesia State-Owned Companies is the largest ETF in Indonesia (Reksa Dana ABF Indonesia Bond Index Fund ETF is not covered).

[12] The other used name is "Islamic ETFs."

[13] Shariah ETFs were launched also in other countries, yet according to available data, it had occurred slightly later—for example, in Singapore a few months after Malaysia.

Dang and Jolly 2017). Average turnover of ETFs on the stock exchange in that country over 2004–2017 has been at merely 7.2 million USD, and the maximum monthly value in the late 2016 did not exceed 35 million USD. The size of most ETFs primary listed in New Zealand is very low—as of end of August 2017, assets of only three funds exceeded 100 million USD. The largest fund was NZ Top 50 with assets valued at slightly above 170 million USD and exposure to the domestic equity market; two remaining largest funds were one equity ETF with exposure to the European equity and one bond ETF. Despite its small size, ETFs market in New Zealand is quite diversified as equity funds tracking various domestic and foreign (e.g., Australian or US) indexes are available as well as a few bond funds. The value of the turnover of ETFs has been almost unchanged since 2004 until 2015; between the second half of 2015 and 2017, it has grown considerably, yet it remains very low.

Thailand is the largest ETFs market among the outlined third group of Asia-Pacific countries—the average turnover of ETFs has been close to 20 million USD (see Table 4.2) and maximum level slightly above 115 million USD. However, the period of the highest activity on the Thai ETFs market was observed in 2012 and 2013 (see Fig. 4.5; it can be linked to substantial increases in the stock prices on the Thai stock exchange)—over the next years, turnover has declined to the levels comparable to New Zealand (due to, inter alia, declines on the stock market related to the political situation). Bond ETF is traded on the local stock exchange since 2006 (ABF Thailand Bond Index ETF—it has accumulated most assets) whereas equity ETFs since 2007 (ThaiDex SET50 ETF was the pioneer; turnover data are acquirable since 2007—bond fund is thinly traded, and most transactions are conducted in the shares of the equity funds; local stock exchange regards 2007 as the beginning of the Thai ETFs market (The Stock Exchange of Thailand 2018)). The structure of Thai ETFs market in terms of the assets of the categories of funds listed is similar to the one in Indonesia or Malaysia, with one leading bond ETF and the rest of the market split among a few equity funds (their share was the highest during the upsurge on the local stock market). In contrast with the two previously discussed countries, there are, though, no Shariah-compliant ETFs. However, the third-largest group is gold ETFs (Hoque and Faruqui 2017) with ca. 3.4% share in the total assets as of August 2017.

Apart from the aforementioned ETFs markets, there are (as mentioned in Sect. 4.1) two more stock exchanges in the Asia-Pacific region with the shares of ETFs listed and traded. Their size is very small in all examined dimensions.

In the Philippines, first and still the only ETF was launched in 2013 (its full name: First Metro Philippine Equity ETF, Inc.). It tracks the returns of the blue-chip index of the Philippine Stock Exchange. Both the turnover of its shares and its assets remain very low: according to the World Federation of Exchange's reports for the first 5 months of 2018 (there are no data for the previous years), the mean monthly turnover was at merely two million USD (interestingly, higher than in Indonesia, where there are a few funds listed with much larger assets), and as of August 2017, it managed 24 million USD of assets.

Another similarly small ETFs market is the one in Vietnam. According to the latest available data, there are two funds listed on the local stock exchanges, SSIAM

VNX50 ETF and VFMVN30 ETF, both tracking the indexes of the local equity market and launched in the second half of 2014. World Federation of Exchange's reports include no data about their turnover (according to Deutsche Bank (2017a, b), it is very low yet higher than in Indonesia or the Philippines). In August 2017 their total assets were the highest in the history, exceeding 50 million USD.

4.2.3 *Analysis of Relative ETFs Market Development*

Conclusions concerning country-level ETFs market development that may be drawn using the relative approach are very similar to the ones discussed in the preceding paragraphs (for obvious reasons it is impossible to apply the relative approach on the regional level; therefore, we skip this part of the analysis). Consequently, we focus on between-country comparisons rather than country-specific discussion which were presented with regard to the absolute market development. As in the previous approach, the analyzed countries may be again divided into the following two groups in terms of the average share of ETFs:

1. Hong Kong, Japan, and South Korea.
2. Australia, India, and Taiwan.

Composition of the first group is slightly different than the one shown previously for the absolute development due to the lack of the Chinese market (we omit China in this approach as it is impossible to calculate the share of ETFs because of lack of relevant data on the other index instruments). However, the rest of the leading countries are identical—in Japan the financial markets are characterized by the highest maximum and average share of the innovative funds, followed by South Korea and Hong Kong (see Table 4.5). Considering the size of the Japanese economy and local financial system (and, consequently, their role in the examined region), the results obtained for this country are particularly important as they confirm that the diffusion of ETFs has taken place in this country, in both absolute and relative dimension. At some point in time, the share of ETFs in Japan was close to 7% of the total turnover of index instruments—what is important, it was not simply the month when the turnover of ETFs in absolute terms reached its peak, but rather the period of low turnover of stock index futures. Among many reasons for this occurrence, overall trend on the local stock market could be suggested (substantial decline in the prices of the Japanese equities in the late Spring and early Summer of 2016) and the actions undertaken by the Bank of Japan (see the country-specific discussion in Sect. 4.2.2). Afterward the share of ETFs in Japan has decreased substantially to the pre-2015 levels (see Fig. 4.6).

Since the beginning of 2004, the share of ETFs in the total market for index financial instruments has increased in all three countries in the group of the more developed ETFs markets, but the exact absolute changes (in p.p.) and total growth rates differ considerably (see Table 4.5). Taking into account the latter indicator, it may be stated that the growth has been relatively slower in the countries with the

Table 4.5 Share of turnover of ETFs in the turnover of index instruments in the Asia-Pacific countries (relative ETFs market development)—basic statistics

Country	Minimum share [%]	Maximum share [%]	Average share [%]	Average monthly dynamic [%]	Absolute change [p.p.]	Total growth rate [%]
Australia	0.026 [September 2004]	1.36 [April 2015]	0.44	131.7	−0.11	−10.12
Hong Kong	0.11 [April 2005]	5.39 [December 2014]	1.26	105.8	0.61	108.7
India	0.009 [October 2005]	0.20 [April 2012]	0.049	115.6	−0.03	−51.1
Japan	0.33 [September 2007]	6.93 [July 2016]	1.86	107.0	1.68	118.4
South Korea	0.057 [May 2005]	5.84 [November 2016]	1.54	105.7	4.69	3800.6
Taiwan	0.15 [July 2014]	1.55 [March 2016]	0.49	104.2	0.05	8.21

Monthly data for January 2004–August 2017
Note: average monthly dynamic calculated as geometric mean
Source: own calculations

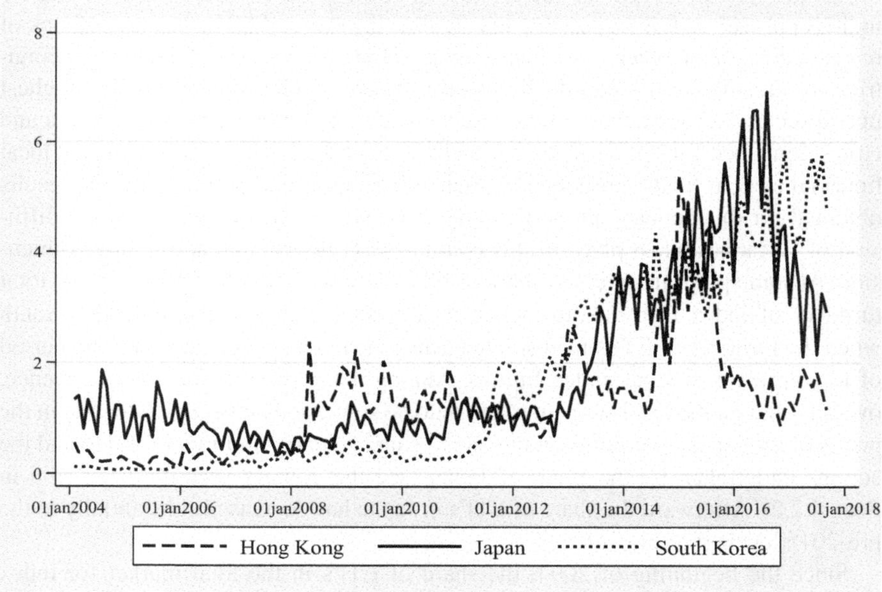

Note: on Y-axis: turnover of ETFs in mln USD.
Source: own elaboration.

Fig. 4.6 Share of turnover of ETFs in the turnover of index instruments in Hong Kong, Japan and South Korea (three countries with the highest average values in the region). Monthly data for January 2004–August 2017

oldest ETFs markets in the region, Hong Kong and Japan, than in South Korea. Development of the South Korean market is particularly significant as in the first analyzed years the share of ETFs in that country had been below levels observed, for instance, in Taiwan. It has increased to almost 6%, i.e., by more than 4.5 p.p.—substantially more than in any other evaluated country. Moreover, Fig. 4.6 proves that the development of the South Korean market in terms of the share of ETFs has been relatively most stable as in the other two countries substantial variability could be observed, in particular after reaching the maximum levels in the final years of the analyzed time period.

Maximum shares of ETFs on the local financial markets, provided in Table 4.5, were reached in 2014 (for Hong Kong) and 2016 (in Japan and South Korea) and ranged between 5 and 7% of the total turnover of index financial instruments. It means that innovative funds in the three analyzed countries have increased their position in comparison to the other instruments regarded in this approach as substitutes, yet in all three cases, the turnover of ETFs is still much lower than the aggregated turnover of stock index derivatives traded through exchanges. However, at least to some extent, the diffusion of ETFs has occurred. Despite the variations presented on Fig. 4.6 (in some cases quite significant), the direction of the changes seems to be quite unambiguous—in all three countries, the turnover of ETFs has been increasing more rapidly than turnover of stock index derivatives which proves the spread of the innovative funds. Not including the periods of temporary surges in the share of ETFs, the least substantial increase in the position of ETFs was observed in Hong Kong. After the period of 2015–2016, when share of ETFs in Hong Kong had exceeded even the level of 5%, it has returned to the previous values of approximately 1–2%, i.e., the average over 2009–2014. It implies that most of the positive change had occurred between 2008 and 2009, and in the remaining years (with the exception of 2015–2016), it has stagnated.

Even though the value of the average share of ETFs in Hong Kong would suggest inferior position of the innovative funds in relation to the two other leading markets, such conclusion would be too far-reaching. It must be added that Hong Kong should be regarded as slightly different case than Japan or South Korea. Despite the rather low size of its economy (in comparison to Japan and South Korea), the size of its financial system is substantial (in particular in relation to its GDP) as it is one of the global financial centers. Consequently, all three considered types of financial instruments are actively traded on the stock exchange in Hong Kong, by both domestic and foreign investors. In contrast with the two other countries in the discussed category, in Hong Kong, monthly turnover of stock index options has amounted to approximately one-third of the corresponding indicator value for futures, whereas in Japan and South Korea, it has been only its small fraction. As a result, in the relative approach, position of ETFs in Hong Kong seems to some extent too weak. In order to shed some light on this issue, we calculate the share of ETFs in these three countries in the total market excluding stock index options (it should be remembered that most recognized substitution is expected to occur between ETFs and stock index futures rather than options—see Sect. 2.3). Using such approach, the obtained average shares of ETFs are very close for all three countries, 1.70% for Hong Kong,

1.88% for Japan, and 1.59% for South Korea, which implies comparable mean level of relative market development.[14]

Finally, data from the final years of the analyzed time period for Hong Kong and Japan may raise some doubts whether these trends are sustainable—we address this issue in Sects. 4.2 and 4.3.

As a supplement to the preceding discussion of the relative development in Hong Kong, Japan, and South Korea, we refer briefly to some approximates for the fourth country among the most advanced ETFs markets in the region—China. World Federation of Exchange's database includes data on the turnover of stock index futures on the China Financial Futures Exchange between April 2010 and August 2017 (there are no data on options as they are not traded on this exchange). Calculation of the share of ETFs in the total turnover of ETFs and stock index futures (taking into account stock exchanges in Shanghai and Shenzhen as well as the future exchange) shows that its mean value was at ca. 4.11% and the maximum levels in 2016 were close to 30% (there has been strong growth trend since the late 2015). Obviously, these data are not directly comparable to the results for the other countries, yet they prove that in China the diffusion of ETFs in the relative perspective has also taken place, and its magnitude could be even stronger than in the remaining countries.

In the group that lags behind in terms of the relative ETFs market development, one country distinguishes itself from the rest of this set, India (the largest economy in this group), with average share close to merely 0.05%; for Australia and Taiwan, the mean values are comparable, at approximately 0.45–0.50%; the same applies to the maximum observed values (see Table 4.5). It may, therefore, be stated that in India the position of ETFs on the market for index instruments has been the weakest among all evaluated economies and no signs of improvement have been observed; actually the share of ETFs has even declined over 2004–2017 by more than 50%. Taking into consideration the increase in the absolute values of the turnover of ETFs in India, its decline in the relative dimension may be explained by even more substantial growth in case of stock index futures and options. Moreover, it means that no substitution between the innovative funds and comparable derivatives has taken place. Despite the rapid growth of the ETFs' turnover on the Indian exchanges in the final months of the evaluated time period (see discussion with regard to the absolute market development), their share has remained extremely low and has not exceeded the historical maximum levels of 0.2% noted in 2012. The reason is quite simple—in 2017 the overall activity on the Indian financial markets in the index instruments segment has increased; during the first 8 months of 2017, it was about 77% higher than in the respective period in 2016 (only the turnover of stock index options declined, yet by merely 5%).

Even though, as it was already stated, Australian and Taiwanese ETFs markets are comparable when average and maximum shares are considered, analysis of the

[14]Apart from that, the remaining conclusions are rather similar. In order to account for the potential substitution between ETFs and options in the further analysis, we use exclusively our main approach, i.e., with all three categories of financial instruments.

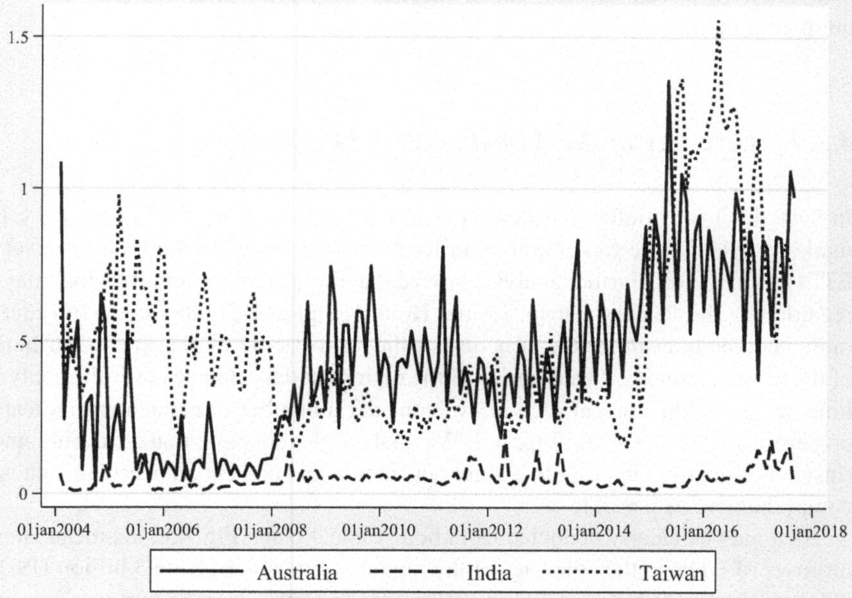

Note: on Y-axis: turnover of ETFs in mln USD.
Source: own elaboration.

Fig. 4.7 Share of turnover of ETFs in the turnover of index instruments of ETFs in Australia, India and Taiwan (three countries with the lowest average values in the region). Monthly data for January 2004–August 2017

dynamics of the changes in the share of ETFs shows substantial differences. In Australia many monthly fluctuations can be clearly noticed (see Fig. 4.7), resulting from the changes in the turnover of the stock index futures which strongly influenced the shares of the remaining categories of financial instruments (we address this issue again in Sect. 4.3 in the context of the diffusion paths). The overall trend in the relative ETFs market development in Australia has been rather positive, in spite of the results presented in Table 4.5—negative total change was caused by very high turnover in 2004 (in particular in the first months); if the turnover in 2016 or 2017 is compared to the respective values in 2006 or 2007, an explicit growth from about 0.1 to 0.7% can be confirmed. It may also be compared to the absolute changes taking place with regard to the turnover of the three analyzed types of index financial instruments—over 2004–2017 the turnover of ETFs has been steadily growing, while turnover of stock index futures, after the stage of growth, has been rather constant since the late 2006 (similar trend could be noticed for stock index options yet since the second half of 2011). In case of Taiwan, changes in the market share of ETFs correspond to high degree with the changes of their absolute turnover. After the rather slight decline in the initial years, market share of ETFs stabilized between 2008 and 2015 when it entered the stage of rapid growth (its reasons were already analyzed). However, the subsequent decline may mean that this process is not unidirectional.

4.2.4 *Diversity of the Asia-Pacific ETFs Markets*

In Sect. 4.2.1 we briefly considered the structure of the Asia-Pacific regional ETFs market by listing the top countries in terms of their share in the total turnover of ETFs in the region. Further analysis proved that there are four countries that may be regarded as the leaders: Japan, China, Hong Kong, and South Korea. In order to more accurately evaluate the structure of the Asia-Pacific market (i.e., distribution of the turnover among the countries of the region) and its changes over the analyzed time period, in the current section, we consider a number of elementary indicators presented in Table 4.6 and Fig. 4.8. We analyze the absolute market development (instead of relative) in order to extend our sample and present an overview that is as comprehensive as possible.

As it may be clearly deducted from both Table 4.6 and Fig. 4.8, the mean annual turnover of ETFs in the countries of the region has increased from 3 billion USD in 2004 to almost 97 billion USD in 2016. Trends of the average turnover's growth have been very similar to the ones observed for the total value (see Fig. 4.1) which may be explained by the strong impact of the few largest markets (above all, China and Japan) on either aggregate or average values—compare Fig. 4.4. The highest average turnover, observed in 2016, was close to 140 billion USD, yet it was linked to some previously discussed extraordinary events on the ETFs markets in China and Hong Kong.

For the initial years of the analyzed time period (2004–2007), the smallest markets in the region were the countries with no ETFs listed on local exchanges (or insufficient data to calculate the required metrics); the first year with full dataset in terms of countries was 2008 (with the exception of New Zealand in 2010 and 2011). Between 2008 and 2016 (2011 not included), Indonesia was the smallest market—in only 1 year (2008) did the annual turnover of ETFs in this country exceed ten million USD. In contrast, the position of the regionally largest market changed a few times. Initially, between 2004 and 2007, it belonged to Japan which was surpassed by Hong Kong in 2008. Over the next years, the top position was occupied interchangeably by China, Japan (most recently), and South Korea. It proves that, in contrast with the bottom part of the regional distribution (i.e., markets in Indonesia, Malaysia, New Zealand, and Thailand), situation in the upper part has been much more dynamic, with frequent switches. Regardless, the difference between the turnover of the most and least developed markets has remained very significant, with no clear signs of catching-up processes.

Finally, we analyze two remaining indicators included in Table 4.6 and Fig. 4.8: Gini coefficient and Atkinson index. Higher values of both indicators may be interpreted as suggesting a more unequal distribution of the analyzed variable. Generally, turnover of ETFs is distributed rather unequally among the stock exchanges in the

Table 4.6 Selected indicators of the Asia-Pacific ETFs market's structure

Year	Average annual turnover [mln USD]	Minimum annual turnover [mln USD]	Maximum annual turnover [mln USD]	Gini coefficient	Atkinson index (for ε = 0.5)
2004	3029.7	0 [China, Indonesia, Malaysia, Thailand]	27247.39 [Japan]	0.82	0.68
2005	4039.7	0 [Indonesia, Thailand]	34599.2 [Japan]	0.80	0.62
2006	5411.7	0 [Indonesia, Thailand]	43668.7 [Japan]	0.79	0.60
2007	8694.1	0 [Indonesia]	42672.5 [Japan]	0.70	0.50
2008	15723.2	10.85 [Indonesia]	56677.9 [Hong Kong]	0.67	0.48
2009	21650.5	0.17 [Indonesia]	112046.6 [China]	0.72	0.52
2010	21936.3	0.55 [Indonesia]	95575.1 [China]	0.69	0.49
2011	27936.2	*0 [New Zealand]*	108914.9 [South Korea]	0.64	0.46
2012	28435.9	0.81 [Indonesia]	120,445 [South Korea]	0.67	0.49
2013	58403.5	2.05 [Indonesia]	236556.3 [Japan]	0.69	0.54
2014	71646.4	0.7 [Indonesia]	306644.2 [Japan]	0.69	0.55
2015	138,729	1.133 [Indonesia]	651605.8 [China]	0.73	0.57
2016	96739.4	2.138 [Indonesia]	570941.8 [Japan]	0.73	0.54
2017	*55740.8*	*2.446 [Malaysia]*	*213,140 [Japan]*	*0.67*	*0.50*

Annual data for 2004–2017
Note: due to data availability for 2017, calculations were made using data for 8 months, i.e., they are not fully comparable to the results for the previous years. For New Zealand lack of data for June 2010–December 2011
Source: own calculations

selected countries—there is a small four-country group of the leaders that accounts for the vast majority of the total turnover, while in the remaining countries, ETFs markets are underdeveloped (see Fig. 4.2 for data as of 2016). More robust conclusions could be drawn based on comparisons with results obtained for other regions, yet it is impossible to due to lack of such research. The preliminary analysis conducted for the European ETFs markets using asset indicators of their development

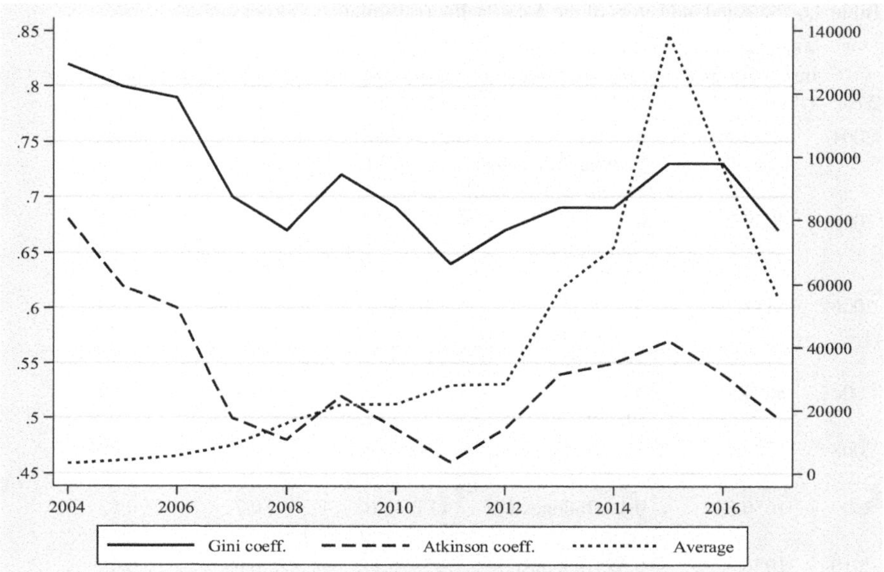

Note: on the left axis – values of Gini coefficient and Atkinson index; on the right axis – average values of ETFs turnover. Due to data availability for 2017 calculations were made using data for 8 months, i.e. they are not fully comparable to the results for the previous years. For New Zealand lack of data for VI 2010 – XII 2011.
Source: own calculations.

Fig. 4.8 Selected indicators of the Asia-Pacific ETFs market's structure: graphical evidence. Annual data for 2004–2017

(see Marszk and Lechman (2019)) implies similar inequalities, with the distinguishable small set of the leading countries; analysis for the North American region would be meaningless (due to obvious domination of the United States), and in the other regions, the number of active ETFs markets is very low.

The trends in time in both Gini coefficient and Atkinson index are highly similar (see Fig. 4.8)—between 2004 and 2016, their values have declined. Decrease was most significant over 2004–2011 when the Gini coefficient declined from 0.82 to 0.64 (Atkinson index from 0.68 to 0.46). Therefore, it may concluded that in this part of the considered period, the turnover of ETFs became more equally distributed among the countries of the region, mostly due to the quick development of the markets in China and Hong Kong which caught up with and eventually surpassed the previous leader—Japan (for instance, in 2004 Japan accounted for almost entire turnover in the region). Since 2012 the direction of the changes has reversed, and inequality in the turnover's distribution has started to increase. However, in the final examined years, the distribution of the analyzed variable has been rather stable and less unequal than prior to 2007.

4.3 ETFs Diffusion Patterns and Dynamics: Country-Specific Evidence

After discussion of the key descriptive statistics concerning the development of the ETFs markets in the Asia-Pacific region, in the current section, we show and interpret the results of analysis conducted using the models of diffusion of innovation. Such models facilitate evaluation of the changes taking place with regard to the innovative funds in the analyzed region (methodology of our analysis is presented in detail in Appendix B). We start our discussion by briefly considering the diffusion patterns of ETFs in the absolute and relative approach and studying the graphical evidence. As the key changes were already outlined in Sect. 4.2, we omit the detailed examination of the observed trends or between-country differences, compiling exclusively some key conclusions. In order to assess the applicability of the diffusion models for the analysis of the Asia-Pacific ETFs markets, it is necessary to take into account the shapes of the diffusion patterns and examine if they are to some degree S-shaped and if the three stages of diffusion may be identified. In the key part of this section, we examine the estimates of the diffusion models. For clarity of presentation, when discussing the diffusion parameters, we use "ETF" to label parameters that refer to the absolute development of ETFs markets and "ETF share" to the ones that were estimated in the relative perspective. Throughout this section we generally discuss the analyzed countries in alphabetical order. For each country we estimate the following parameters of the diffusion for the analyzed period (i is the abbreviated name of the country):

κ_i^{ETF} and $\kappa_i^{ETFshare}$—ceiling ("upper asymptote") that indicates the limit of diffusion (growth).

Tm_i^{ETF} (β_i^{ETF}) and $Tm_i^{ETFshare}$ ($\beta_i^{ETFshare}$)—midpoint that shows the exact time (exact of month) when diffusion reaches half of the ceiling's level.

α_i^{ETF} and $\alpha_i^{ETFshare}$—rate of diffusion that, due to difficulties in interpretation, is used to calculate the derivative parameter, i.e. specific duration (see below).

$\varnothing_i^{ETF}$ and $\varnothing_i^{ETFshare}$—specific duration that shows the time needed for the analyzed diffusion indicator to grow from 10 to 90% of the ceiling's (upper asymptote's) level.

As usual, we report the values of R^2 and number of observations for each model. We use all observations available for the analyzed time period (164 months), with the exception of New Zealand due to data gaps. From the methodological perspective, it needs to be underlined that we assume that the basic assumptions of the diffusion model are met; above all that the diffusion of ETFs follows the S-shaped (sigmoid) trajectory, meaning the logistic growth, characterized by three stages: first and third characterized with the slow rate of growth, whereas second with exponential.

Figures 4.9 and 4.10 present the diffusion patterns of ETFs in the two analyzed dimensions: absolute (value of the turnover of ETFs) and relative (share of ETFs in the total turnover of the index financial instruments). In most cases they are similar. As in the relative approach ETFs are juxtaposed with stock index options and

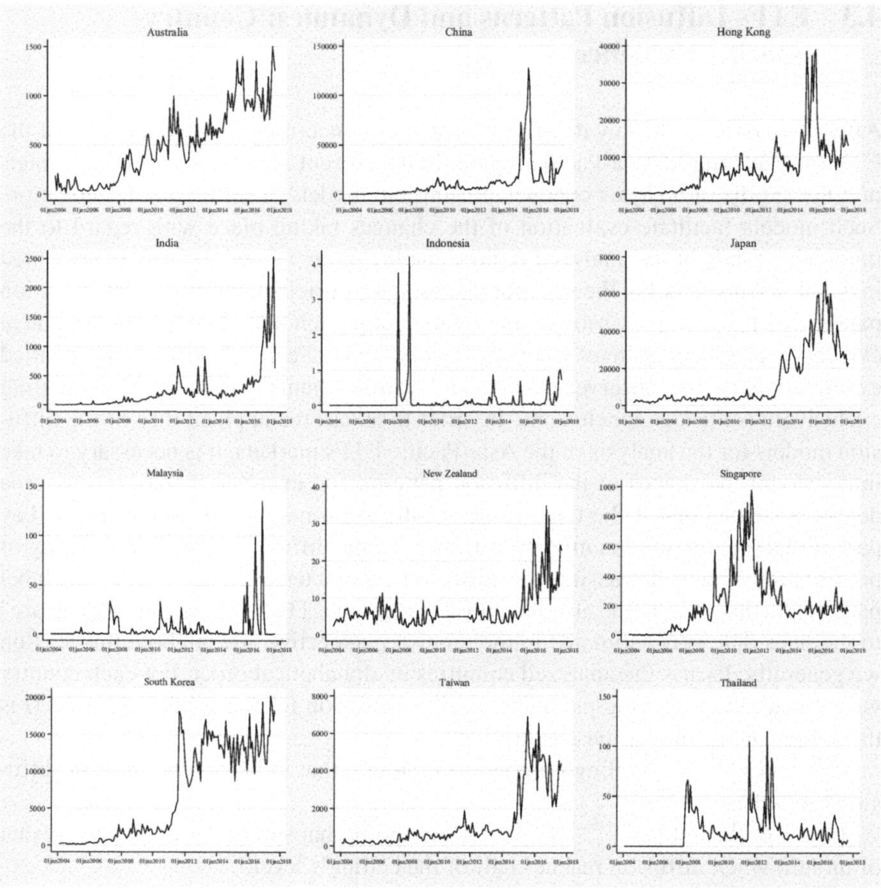

Fig. 4.9 Diffusion patterns of turnover of ETFs in the Asia-Pacific countries. Monthly data for January 2004–August 2017

futures (in all cases only transactions conducted through stock exchanges are taken into account), it would imply that their turnover has been changing at comparable rate both considered on a stand-alone basis and in relation to the potential substitutes. We check the validity of this statement concerning similarity of the diffusion in both approaches by comparing selected parameters of the estimated models (see the discussion concerning models in the relative perspective).

Starting with Fig. 4.9, it may be stated that, as discussed in Sect. 4.2, in most countries the value of turnover of ETFs has grown between 2004 and 2017; the exact rate of the change and in-time variability differ, though, considerably. The country, which distinguishes itself from the rest in terms of the stability of the ETFs market development, is definitely Australia—despite some temporary fluctuations

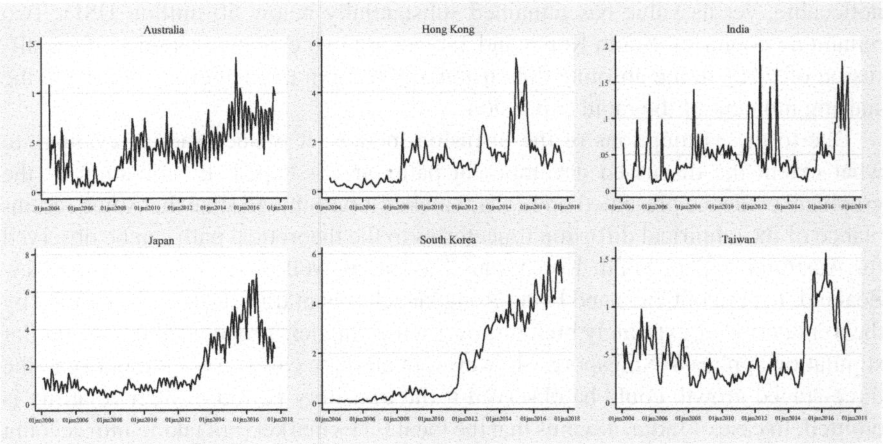

Fig. 4.10 Diffusion patterns of shares of turnover of ETFs in the turnover of index instruments in the Asia-Pacific countries. Monthly data for January 2004–August 2017

(lasting for a few months), the value of the ETFs turnover has increased steadily since 2008. Therefore this specific case requires some closer scrutiny in order to address the issue of its development's stability. Stable growth of the ETFs market in Australia in the final analyzed years (in contrast to most other countries) may be explained by its distinctive regulations regarding the commissions—according to Fuhr (2015), it is the only country in the region where due to the implemented regulations commissions are paid to financial advisors for advice or for implementation of investment decisions, whereas payments for selling certain financial products are forbidden. In the other countries, financial advisors are financially motivated to sell conventional funds or other financial products rather than ETFs.

In the three among leading ETFs markets in the region, China, Hong Kong, and Japan, trajectory of the changes has been comparable, with clearly distinguishable period of rapid upsurge, followed by comparably deep decline. In the two former markets, it may be linked to the events on the local stock markets, whereas in the latter the reasons are more complicated and are linked to, inter alia, actions of the central bank. Similar pattern may be noticed for Singapore, yet the temporary upsurge had occurred much earlier and at much lower levels of turnover—decline in Singapore since the peak levels observed in 2011 can be attributed to the stricter regulations concerning entities allowed to trade shares of ETFs (Fuhr 2015). In India most of the absolute development of the ETFs market has occurred in the last years of the examined time period as previous increases had been short-lived; this growth, similarly to Japan, may be to some extent attributed to the governmental actions. In Indonesia, Malaysia, and Thailand, the value of the ETFs turnover has remained negligent, with short periods (sometimes even only single months) of increased activity. For New Zealand growth in the turnover of ETFs is plainly noticeable, yet its value has remained substantially below 50 million USD. Two remaining countries, South Korea and Taiwan are two evident examples of the diffusion of ETFs in the absolute dimension, differing in the achieved values and the starting moment of the rapid expansion.

Due to the assumptions of the diffusion models, it is necessary to evaluate to what extent the discussed development paths are S-shaped. Examination of the graphical evidence presented on Fig. 4.9 makes it possible to state that some resemblance of the empirical diffusion trajectories to the theoretical path can be observed for Australia, Japan, South Korea, and Taiwan, as well as (to lesser extent) New Zealand. In case of China and Hong Kong, development trajectories are distorted by the joint period of extremely high turnover which hinders proper evaluation; similar stipulation applies to Singapore—however, in all three cases, some similarity to the three-staged growth could be observed if the transitory period of high volatility is omitted. In case of India, it seems that the local ETFs market (not taking into account the turnover from the last month) is in the stage of rapid growth. For obvious reasons, applying diffusion models is questionable for the analysis of the markets where the value of the examined variable has declined or not increased sustainably in relation to the initial value over the considered time period. In here this stipulation applies to three countries: Indonesia, Malaysia, and Thailand.

After discussing the evidence in the absolute approach, we focus on the diffusion understood in the relative perspective. Figure 4.10 shows the diffusion patterns for six countries for which relative ETFs market development can be examined. As it may be noticed by comparing it to Fig. 4.9, for four countries, the diffusion paths are highly similar: Hong Kong, Japan, South Korea, and Taiwan (for their evaluation see the preceding paragraphs). Consequently, the only evident discrepancies can be noticed for Australia and India. In Australia numerous fluctuations of the ETFs' share are evident on Fig. 4.10—it can be contrasted with the substantial stability of the absolute market development. Explanation behind this phenomenon is rather simple—it was caused by the changes in the across the year activity on the futures market resulting from the usual opening or termination of the contracts, on the Australian exchange manifested in the final month of each quarter. For India no trend, either upward or downward, was observed as the share of ETFs remained very low, at only approximately 0.05% over the entire period, with temporary (usually 1-month) surges—turnover of ETFs has been so low in comparison to options and futures that even slight variations in the turnover of the competing financial instruments have influenced strongly the share of the innovative funds. It means that, due to the lack of the S-shaped attributes of the development path, utilization of the diffusion framework for the study of the relative ETFs market development in India is highly questionable.

Tables 4.7 and 4.8 present the estimated parameters of diffusion models for the period 2004–2017—graphical evidence was examined in the preceding paragraphs of the current section. For each country we discuss jointly the parameters obtained using the absolute and relative (if possible to calculate) approach; as stand-alone interpretation of most parameters may be too abstract (apart from, e.g., values of upper asymptotes), we focus on the comparative perspective. The estimates of the

Table 4.7 Estimates of diffusion models of turnover of ETFs in the Asia-Pacific countries

	Australia	China	Hong Kong	India	Indonesia	Japan	Malaysia	New Zealand	Singapore	South Korea	Taiwan	Thailand
κ_i^{ETF} (ceiling/upper asymptote—value of turnover of ETFs; mln USD)	1353	31430.6	17228.9	*2,016,180,826*	*13,083*	40765.4	*1,540,503*	*20365142.6*	300.8	13934.3	4188	19.9
Tm_i^{ETF} (β_i^{ETF}) (midpoint)	109.9 [January 2013]	119.7 [November 2013]	99.3 [March 2012]	*396*	*1866*	114.1 [June 2013]	*901*	*1342.1*	52.3 [April 2008]	88.8 [April 2011]	130.5 [October 2014]	44.3 [August 2007]
α_i^{ETF} (rate of diffusion)	0.027	0.195	0.038	*0.06*	*0.006*	0.119	*0.016*	*0.012*	0.158	0.147	0.397	*26.6 [overestimates]*
$\varnothing_i^{ETF}$ (specific duration)	160.3	22.6	116.8	*73*	*679*	37.1	*282*	*367*	27.7	29.8	11.1	*0.148 [underestimates]*
R^2 of the model	0.842	0.375	0.518	0.68	0.007	0.826	0.067	0.375	0.387	0.887	0.834	0.224
# of obs.	164	164	164	164	164	164	164	145	164	164	164	164

Monthly data for January 2004–August 2017

Note: in italics—misspecifications. For New Zealand, the number of observations is lower than for other countries due to missing observations in 2010 and 2011

Source: own estimates

Table 4.8 Estimates of diffusion models of shares of turnover of ETFs in the turnover of index instruments in the Asia-Pacific countries

	Australia	Hong Kong	India	Japan	South Korea	Taiwan
$\kappa_i^{\text{ETFshare}}$ (ceiling/upper asymptote—share of ETFs; %)	*70527.7*	2.07	*4329.4*	6.4	4.63	*647011.1*
Tm_i^{ETFshare} ($\beta_i^{\text{ETFshare}}$) (midpoint)	*1358.3*	62.8 [Febuary 2009]	*2535.9*	129.2 [September 2014]	111.7 [March 2013]	*2099.1*
$\alpha_i^{\text{ETFshare}}$ (rate of diffusion)	*0.009*	0.038	*0.005*	0.03	0.057	*0.007*
$\varnothing_i^{\text{ETFshare}}$ (specific duration)	*464*	116.8	*945.2*	144.8	76.7	*622.5*
R^2 of the model	0.49	0.46	0.095	0.71	0.95	0.19
# of obs.	164	164	164	164	164	164

Monthly data for January 2004–August 2017
Note: in italics—misspecifications. For New Zealand, the number of observations is lower than for other countries due to missing observations in 2010 and 2011
Source: own estimates

diffusion models for which misspecifications of all parameters were returned are not interpreted. As expected, it applies to Indonesia, Malaysia, and Thailand (countries where the value of ETFs turnover has declined over 2004–2017). Additionally, due to the extremely high values of κ_i^{ETF}, it refers to India and New Zealand in case of the absolute market development and, for the same reason with regard to $\kappa_i^{\text{ETFshare}}$, it applies to Australia, India, and Taiwan. These countries are omitted in the discussion.

The first country in our sample is Australia. Cursory examination of the results presented in Tables 4.7 and 4.8 confirms our intuitions based on the graphical evidence on the diffusion paths from which we concluded that diffusion framework may be used for this country exclusively to analyze the absolute ETFs market development (results for the other approach are not discussed). According to Table 4.7, the estimated upper limit, $\kappa_{\text{Aus}}^{\text{ETF}}$, is at about 1.4 billion USD. Comparison of this result to the maximum value presented in Table 4.2 proves that the theoretical level is approximately 150 million USD lower than the highest value that was actually observed. However, it should not be perceived as surprising because Fig. 4.9 confirms that this level could be temporary and turnover in the final months revolved around slightly lower values. $Tm_{\text{Aus}}^{\text{ETF}}$ was estimated as January 2013 which means that (according to the logistic growth specification) it is the moment when the diffusion observed between 2004 and 2017 was half-complete. It could imply that the process of rapid spread of ETFs in this country started quite late,[15] yet it seems that

[15] Throughout this section we focus on the values of Tm_n^{ETF} and Tm_n^{ETFshare} to compare the approximate time of the diffusion's beginning—it should be remembered, though, that such analysis should take into account also the values of rates of diffusion (or specific durations). However, even considered separately, values of the midpoints can be used to formulate some robust conclusions.

other interpretation is more justified—growth over the entire examined time period has been rather slow. The latter is confirmed by the analysis of further parameters. The value of $\varnothing_{Aus}^{ETF}$ of more than 160 (months) proves that it has taken more than 13 years for the value of turnover to grow from 10 to 90% of the κ_{Aus}^{ETF} (it is the highest result in Table 4.7, misspecifications excluded). What is important in the context of the diffusion model's interpretation and its robustness is the fact its R^2 exceeded 0.84 and was second-highest among all presented in Table 4.7. To sum up, it may be concluded that in Australia the diffusion of ETFs has undeniably occurred between 2004 and 2017 yet at a rate much lower than in all other analyzed countries as proven by the values of α_{Aus}^{ETF} and $\varnothing_{Aus}^{ETF}$.

Development path of ETFs in China in the absolute approach (analysis in relative dimension is not feasible), as already noted, is not distinctively S-shaped due to the temporary period of extremely high trading activity; as a result, R^2 of the estimated diffusion model is among the lowest (see Table 4.7). Nevertheless, no obvious misspecifications were returned which facilitates interpretation of the returned parameters (with the necessary caution). The estimated value of ceiling, κ_{Chi}^{ETF}, is approximately 31.4 billion USD. It is, therefore, much lower than the maximum level actually reached over 2004–2017 time period albeit comparable to the final observed values—it proves thus the temporariness and lack of sustainability of the 2015 extreme turnover. Estimated midpoint for the Chinese ETFs market, Tm_{Chi}^{ETF}, is the highest (November 2013) among all countries, except for Taiwan. Examination of the graphical evidence on Fig. 4.9 (disregarding the 2015 period) confirms that expansion of ETFs on the Chinese stock exchanges started later than in other countries (due to, among others, later launch of the first ETFs). However, the estimated value of $\varnothing_{Chi}^{ETF}$ is extremely low (merely ca. 23 months) which implies that after the late takeoff, further diffusion of ETFs in China has been very rapid as, according to the theoretical specification, growth from 10 to 90% of the upper limit took less than 2 years. Overall, the estimations obtained for the Chinese ETFs market imply that the diffusion of ETFs in that country has taken place—it started later than in other economies and occurred at very high rate. It must be stressed, though, that these results should be regarded with caution due to the discrepancies between the empirical development path and S-shaped trajectory which make applying diffusion model dubious. General conclusion concerning the spread of ETF is, though, rather incontestable.

After China, we consider another country from the group with the most developed ETFs market and, at the same time, strong links to the one previously analyzed—Hong Kong. For Hong Kong, similar stipulations (caused by turnover's fluctuations) concerning the shape of the development path and applicability of the logistic growth model can be formulated; they apply, though, also to the development examined in the relative perspective (compare Figs. 4.9 and 4.10). Relatively higher R^2 of the estimated diffusion model in the absolute approach in comparison to the corresponding value for China indicates lesser problems with the temporary period of very high turnover in the context of the applicability of the diffusion framework. The estimated upper asymptote, κ_{Hon}^{ETF}, is approximately 17.2 billion USD, again below the maximum level but close to the last observed values. The value of the estimated midpoint, $Tm_{\text{Hon}}^{\text{ETF}}$, is below 100 months (starting from January 2004), i.e., approximately in March 2012—it places Hong Kong in the middle of our sample, showing that the diffusion of the local ETFs has started neither at an early nor at late moment; comparison with the most closely linked market in China implies relatively earlier start which should not be deemed to be surprising due to the longer history of the one in Hong Kong. The next two estimates, of $\alpha_{\text{Hon}}^{\text{ETF}}$ and $\varnothing_{\text{Hon}}^{\text{ETF}}$, lead to an interesting conclusion that absolute ETFs market development in Hong Kong (according to the theoretical diffusion specification) has been the slowest in the entire group (apart from Australia)—it may be explained by the already substantial development at the beginning of the analyzed time period.

Estimates of the diffusion parameters in the relative dimension for Hong Kong are very similar (with one exception) to the ones discussed above for the absolute approach (see Table 4.8). $\kappa_{\text{Hon}}^{\text{ETFshare}}$ is estimated at ca. 2.07%, i.e., somewhat higher than the last observed values of the market share of ETFs (analogous situation was noticed for the previously discussed model in the absolute dimension). Values of $\alpha_{\text{Hon}}^{\text{ETFshare}}$ and $\varnothing_{\text{Hon}}^{\text{ETFshare}}$ are identical (after rounding) to the corresponding ones in the former model which implies that the rate of diffusion has been almost identical. Comparison of the three countries for which no obvious misspecifications were retuned, as shown in Table 4.8, proves that the rate of diffusion estimated for Hong Kong is much lower than in South Korea yet somewhat higher than in Japan. It means that in the absolute perspective, ETFs market in Hong Kong has been growing (according to the theoretical specification) much slower than in Japan, yet in the relative perspective, ETFs have more rapidly gained market share in the smaller economy. The only and rather substantial discrepancy between the absolute and relative results concerns the midpoint—$Tm_{\text{Hon}}^{\text{ETFshare}}$ is much lower than $Tm_{\text{Hon}}^{\text{ETF}}$ as its value is at merely ca. 63 months (i.e., February 2009) which could imply that, according to the theoretical specification, diffusion of ETFs in Hong Kong in terms of market share began much sooner than when absolute values are considered. However, examination of the graphical evidence proves that development paths in both perspectives have been very similar—obtained estimates should, thus, be analyzed with caution (differences may be caused by distortions in the period of extreme turnover). R^2 of the estimated diffusion model in the relative approach is slightly lower yet comparable to the one obtained in the absolute approach which further confirms their similarity.

To conclude, according to the results obtained using diffusion models, it may be stated that adoption of ETFs in Hong Kong has been increasing regardless of the employed approach, but the market's development path has not followed the characteristic stages assumed in the logistic growth framework which makes the returned estimated relatively unreliable.

Japan is the next evaluated country (India and Indonesia are omitted). Within the examination of the graphical evidence, we stated that the Japanese ETFs market development path in both absolute and relative dimension may be regarded as bearing some resemblance to the S-shaped trajectory required in the diffusion framework. This conclusion is to some extent weakened by the decline observed in the final months of the evaluated time period, yet our estimates presented in Tables 4.7

and 4.8 prove that this issue is less serious than in case of China and Hong Kong, as indicated by the much higher values of R^2 of the models for the Japanese market (about 0.83 in the absolute approach and lower yet still rather high 0.71 in the relative one).

For Japan, $\kappa_{\text{Jap}}^{\text{ETF}}$ was estimated at 40.8 billion USD, the highest level among all analyzed countries (misspecifications excluded), significantly above values obtained for other countries with the most advanced ETFs markets. Identical observation may be made based on the value of $\kappa_{\text{Jap}}^{\text{ETFshare}}$ (ca. 6.4%). It may be thus concluded that Japanese ETFs market has been the most developed in the Asia-Pacific region when the diffusion over the entire 2004–2017 time period is taken into account, in spite of some subperiods when it was overtaken by the other countries (see Table 4.6). As Figs. 4.9 and 4.10 prove, periodically higher turnover of ETFs in China or Hong Kong were ephemeral and short-lived. In contrast with the countries discussed in the preceding paragraphs, the respective parameters estimated for the Japanese ETFs market development are much higher than values of monthly ETFs turnover or their shares in the total market for index financial instruments in the last months of the examined time series. Such results imply that the final observed values should not be regarded as sustainable ceilings of diffusion reached over 2004–2017 but rather as temporary downward deviations from the higher upper asymptotes. Validity of such conclusions depends, however, to some extent on whether data used for our estimations show their actual development and how strongly their sustainability is distorted by the decisions of Bank of Japan (i.e., it would require conducting counterfactual analysis of its development in the absence of the central bank's transactions; however, such study would be difficult to conduct and based on many arbitrary assumptions such as regarding the indirect impact of the Bank of Japan's operations on the ETFs turnover). Analysis of ETFs turnover data for the period September 2017–May 2018 extracted from the World Federation of Exchanges monthly reports[16] shows a rebound in the value of transactions in the second half of 2017 and first quarter of 2018. However, in the second quarter of 2018, the value of ETFs turnover declined again—it means that it is impossible to state whether the downward trend has been stopped (obviously it is highly dependent upon the decisions of the Bank of Japan).

Values of the next parameters estimated for Japan differ considerably in the absolute and relative perspective. $Tm_{\text{Jap}}^{\text{ETF}}$ is ca. 114, i.e., June 2013, and $\alpha_{\text{Jap}}^{\text{ETF}}$ is about 0.12—both values indicate that diffusion of ETFs in Japan in the absolute perspective has neither began relatively soon (or late) or has taken place at relatively high (or low) rate in comparison to the other countries. Nevertheless, in the group of most developed markets, Japanese market seems to have lagged behind both China and South Korea in both aspects (and, at the same time, to have exceeded Hong Kong).

When the estimated values of both $Tm_{\text{Jap}}^{\text{ETFshare}}$ and $\alpha_{\text{Jap}}^{\text{ETFshare}}$ are considered, it may be clearly noticed that diffusion of Japanese ETFs in the relative perspective is characterized by two attributes. First, it started much later than in Hong Kong or South

[16] For consistency purposes, we do not cover this time period in other parts of our analysis.

Korea (as implied by the respective midpoints)—Fig. 4.10 confirms that the period of quick relative development in Japan began in 2013, whereas in the other two countries, first such trends could be noticed a few years sooner. Second, the speed of ETFs diffusion has been much slower than in South Korea and slightly slower than in Hong Kong. Figure 4.10 shows that most of the relative ETFs market development in Japan took place in a short subperiod since 2013, and when the complete 2004–2017 time period is considered, over its majority, no substantial changes could be observed. Still, regardless of the adopted perspective, diffusion of ETFs in Japan is confirmed by the estimations of our models.

Estimates for Malaysia and New Zealand are not discussed; therefore, the next analyzed country is Singapore, the smallest in the group of ETFs markets classified as mid-developed. Development path of the local ETFs market, with the subperiod of extreme increase, followed by decline (see Fig. 4.9), means that employing logistic growth model is problematic, yet even after exclusion of that subperiod, the overall change between 2004 and 2017 has been positive. As there are no obvious misspecifications, diffusion models may be interpreted yet with required caution as proven by the low R^2, similar to the one obtained for China. Estimated $\kappa_{\text{sin}}^{\text{ETF}}$ (ca. 300 million USD) is much lower than values of turnover during the period of intensive trading between 2009 and 2013 (confirming lack of sustainability of these levels of turnover) but above the final observed values. $Tm_{\text{sin}}^{\text{ETF}}$ is an estimate that distinguishes Singaporean ETFs market due to its very small value (52 on April 2008), meaning that diffusion of ETFs started in this country much sooner than in any other country of the region. It may be associated with the fact that Singapore was the location of quick introduction of the new instruments (Fuhr 2015). Parameters indicating the speed of diffusion imply high dynamics of changes in the ETFs turnover. It should be reminded that due to stipulations regarding the application of diffusion models for the analysis of the ETFs market in Singapore, all presented conclusions must be regarded as to some extent equivocal.

South Korea is the fourth and last discussed country from the group of most developed ETFs markets in Asia-Pacific. It is the most distinct proof of the innovation's framework applicability in the context of the ETFs market development analysis in our sample and probably one of the most explicit such examples among all countries in the world. Examination of the graphical evidence presented on Figs. 4.9 and 4.10 suggests in both cases the high level of resemblance between ETFs market development path and theoretical trajectory, with the clearly distinguishable three stages of growth: initial very slow diffusion, followed by rapid expansion, and finally stabilization at levels much higher than initially; in case of relative approach, one stipulation concerns the growth trend in the final months of the analyzed time period which may mean that in this perspective Korean market is still in the second phase (this issue is investigated in Sect. 4.4). Values of R^2 of both absolute and relative diffusion model are the highest in our sample; in the latter case, it is close to 1 which proves high robustness of the formulated conclusions, in the former relatively lower due to some fluctuations in the absolute values since 2012.

Values of both $\kappa_{\text{Kor}}^{\text{ETF}}$ (13.9 billion USD) and $\kappa_{\text{Kor}}^{\text{ETFshare}}$ (4.63%) confirm the results of the analysis based on descriptive statistics in which we stated that in the former perspective, South Korean ETFs market is the fourth largest while in the latter second largest (behind Japan) in the region (see Sect. 4.2). Both values are close to the means of the respective indicators in the final stage of the diffusion path. $\kappa_{\mathrm{Kor}}^{\mathrm{ETF}}$ is lower than the value of turnover in the last months of the empirical time series as the increase in this subperiod is treated as temporary (no enduring growth is assumed to occur in the third stage of diffusion). $\kappa_{\mathrm{Kor}}^{\mathrm{ETFshare}}$ is almost equal to the mean market share of ETFs for 2016–2017 which may be regarded as the third diffusion's phase.

Dynamics of the diffusion may be analyzed using further parameters. Estimated midpoint, $Tm_{\mathrm{Kor}}^{\mathrm{ETF}}$, is second-lowest among all obtained using data in the absolute dimension and the lowest among the most developed ETFs markets. As a result, it may be stated that the diffusion in terms of the absolute value of ETFs turnover began in South Korea sooner than in the other three leading ETFs markets, and by April 2011 it was approximately half-complete. It was the time of deep change on the South Korean ETFs market, with profound implications for the activity on the local stock exchange, i.e., introduction of the geared funds. $Tm_{\mathrm{Kor}}^{\mathrm{ETFshare}}$ is higher than $Tm_{\mathrm{Kor}}^{\mathrm{ETF}}$ which could suggest that in relative terms diffusion of ETFs started later. However, taking into consideration the values of $\varnothing_{\mathrm{Kor}}^{\mathrm{ETF}}$ and $\varnothing_{\mathrm{Kor}}^{\mathrm{ETFshare}}$, it may be noticed that diffusion in the relative approach has been more spread in time and thus more distant parameter which technically is the inflection point of the diffusion curve. Overall, in both cases rapid expansion started in 2011 (compare Figs. 4.9 and 4.10). $\alpha_{\mathrm{Kor}}^{\mathrm{ETF}}$ was estimated at 0.15 and, consequently, $\varnothing_{\mathrm{Kor}}^{\mathrm{ETF}}$ at 30 months—both values indicate high rate of diffusion (behind only China in the most developed group). It may be therefore concluded that diffusion of ETFs in absolute terms started relatively soon and occurred at comparably quick pace. $\alpha_{\mathrm{Kor}}^{\mathrm{ETFshare}}$ is the highest among all interpretable values in Table 4.8—it implies that in relative terms South Korean ETFs market has been the place of most rapid diffusion of the innovative funds on the local exchange (in other words, in this country, ETFs most quickly increased their turnover at the expense of stock index futures and options).

The last discussed economy is Taiwan (Thailand is omitted)—only analysis in the absolute approach is feasible due to obvious misspecifications returned when relative data are used. Development path of the Taiwanese clearly resembles the theoretical path generated by the logistic growth model which supports application of the diffusion of innovation framework; the only problematic aspect is the very long subperiod with no distinctive diffusion. R^2 of the model confirms this preliminary intuition as it is close to the value for Japan, behind only South Korea (see Table 4.7). $\kappa_{\mathrm{Tai}}^{\mathrm{ETF}}$ is the highest outside the group of most developed ETFs market, at ca. 4.2 billion USD—it is close to the mean monthly turnover observed in 2016 and 2017 which supports its reliability. One of the distinguishing features of diffusion of ETFs in Taiwan is the estimated value of $Tm_{\mathrm{Tai}}^{\mathrm{ETF}}$, at approximately 131 months (October 2014)—the highest in the entire sample. It may be thus stated that diffusion of ETFs in Taiwan started very late in comparison to the other countries (Fig. 4.9 provides additional evidence to support such conclusion). Furthermore, $\alpha_{\mathrm{Tai}}^{\mathrm{ETF}}$ is the highest, and, consequently, $\varnothing_{\mathrm{Tai}}^{\mathrm{ETF}}$ is the lowest in the entire sample which shows that diffusion of ETFs in Taiwan has taken place at a very high rate and, despite its late takeoff, local market reached soon high levels of turnover on a regional scale. Rapid expansion of ETFs, as noted earlier, has been elicited mostly by the introduction of the geared funds. Overall, Taiwan is an important example in our discussion concerning diffusion of the innovative funds as it proves that under favorable circumstances the process of their spread may occur very intensively.

4.4 Future ETFs Market Development: Prospected Pathways

In the current section, we present the results of projections of the diffusion of ETFs in the Asia-Pacific region, i.e., the development of the local ETFs markets, obtained by utilizing the diffusion models. As in the preceding sections, we estimate separate models for each country in both absolute and relative (if possible) approach to the diffusion of ETFs. Due to the estimation procedure in the applied models, values of the upper limits, κ_i^{ETF}, must be arbitrarily selected and imposed in order to obtain values of the other parameters of diffusion. In each case we set the values of $\kappa_{i,n}^{\mathrm{ETF}}$ using rather simple approach yet the one that facilitates comparisons of the results obtained for particular countries. We assume the accelerating diffusion of ETFs in the analyzed countries as in most considered countries the adoption of the innovative funds is still at low or very low levels (see Sects. 4.2 and 4.3); another reason for such choice is to the possibility to examine upper limits progressively more distant in time. Consequently, we impose five increasingly higher levels of $\kappa_{i,n}^{\mathrm{ETF}}$ (in the absolute approach) or $\kappa_{i,n}^{\mathrm{ETFshare}}$ (in the relative approach), with the first one derived from the last observed value, in August 2017:

1. $\kappa_{i,1}^{\mathrm{ETF}} = 1.1 \cdot \mathrm{ETF}_{2017m8}^{i}$ and $\kappa_{i,1}^{\mathrm{ETFshare}} = 1.1 \cdot \mathrm{ETFshare}_{2017m8}^{i}$
2. $\kappa_{i,2}^{\mathrm{ETF}} = 1.25 \cdot \kappa_{i,1}^{\mathrm{ETF}}$ and $\kappa_{i,2}^{\mathrm{ETFshare}} = 1.25 \cdot \kappa_{i,1}^{\mathrm{ETFshare}}$
3. $\kappa_{i,3}^{\mathrm{ETF}} = 1.5 \cdot \kappa_{i,2}^{\mathrm{ETF}}$ and $\kappa_{i,3}^{\mathrm{ETFshare}} = 1.5 \cdot \kappa_{i,2}^{\mathrm{ETFshare}}$
4. $\kappa_{i,4}^{\mathrm{ETF}} = 1.75 \cdot \kappa_{i,3}^{\mathrm{ETF}}$ and $\kappa_{i,4}^{\mathrm{ETFshare}} = 1.75 \cdot \kappa_{i,3}^{\mathrm{ETFshare}}$
5. $\kappa_{i,5}^{\mathrm{ETF}} = 2 \cdot \kappa_{i,4}^{\mathrm{ETF}}$ and $\kappa_{i,5}^{\mathrm{ETFshare}} = 2 \cdot \kappa_{i,4}^{\mathrm{ETFshare}}$,

where i is the abbreviated name of the country (i.e., particular ETFs market) and n is the number assigned to the successive upper limit. As in the preceding section, it should be stressed that we assume that the diffusion path follows the S-shaped (sigmoid) three-staged trajectory as application of diffusion models requires making an assumption of the three-staged development path. Estimated parameters are presented in Table 4.9 (in absolute approach) and 4.10 (in relative approach); countries are presented in the alphabetical order—for each country we discuss jointly the parameters obtained using both approaches (if applicable).

Australia was labeled in Sect. 4.2 as one of the mid-developed ETFs markets in the Asia-Pacific region; estimates of the diffusion models in Sect. 4.3 confirmed the expansion of the innovative funds yet exclusively in the absolute dimension. Estimated parameters for the imposed values of $\kappa_{\mathrm{Aus},n}^{\mathrm{ETF}}$ that range from ca. 1.4 ($\kappa_{\mathrm{Aus},1}^{\mathrm{ETF}}$) to 9.1 ($\kappa_{\mathrm{Aus},5}^{\mathrm{ETF}}$) billion USD imply that the diffusion of ETFs is projected to continue yet

Table 4.9 Estimated parameters of the ETFs diffusion for the selected (predicted) values of the upper limits: absolute approach

Country	Upper limit ($\kappa_{i,n}^{ETF}$)—fixed (value of turnover of ETFs; mln USD)	$Tm_{i,n}^{ETF}$ ($\beta_{i,n}^{ETF}$) (midpoint)—predicted	$\alpha_{i,n}^{ETF}$ (rate of diffusion)—predicted	$\varnothing_{i,n}^{ETF}$ (specific duration)—predicted	R^2 of the model
Australia	1380.2	116 [August 2013]	0.026	163	0.842
	1725.3	131 [November 2014]	0.023	192	0.839
	2587.9	170 [February 2018]	0.019	233	0.832
	4528.8	223 [July 2022]	0.016	269	0.826
	9057.6	285 [September 2027]	0.015	292	0.822
China	37634.3	118 [October 2013]	0.046	95	0.328
	47042.9	133 [January 2015]	0.032	135	0.317
	70564.3	165 [September 2017]	0.025	178	0.307
	123487.5	209 [May 2021]	0.021	212	0.300
	246975.0	259 [July 2025]	0.019	234	0.297
Hong Kong	14384.7	88 [April 2011]	0.045	96	0.51
	17980.9	102 [June 2012]	0.036	123	0.517
	26971.4	136 [April 2015]	0.024	184	0.501
	47199.9	189 [September 2019]	0.018	241	0.486
	94399.9	253 [January 2025]	0.016	277	0.479
India	704.2	118 [October 2013]	0.046	96	0.426
	880.3	144 [December 2015]	0.218	20 *[underestimates]*	0.6
	1320.4	150 [June 2016]	0.249	17 *[underestimates]*	0.691
	2310.7	156 [December 2016]	0.131	33 *[underestimates]*	0.707
	4621.5	170 [February 2018]	0.083	52 *[underestimates]*	0.695

(continued)

Table 4.9 (continued)

Country	Upper limit ($\kappa_{i,n}^{ETF}$)—fixed (value of turnover of ETFs; mln USD)	$Tm_{i,n}^{ETF}$ ($\beta_{i,n}^{ETF}$) (midpoint)—predicted	$\alpha_{i,n}^{ETF}$ (rate of diffusion)—predicted	$\varnothing_{i,n}^{ETF}$ (specific duration)—predicted	R^2 of the model
Indonesia	0.8	*306 [overestimates]*	0.007	*603 [overestimates]*	0.007
	1.0	*350 [overestimates]*	0.007	*619 [overestimates]*	0.007
	1.5	163 [overestimates]	0.188	*23 [underestimates]*	0.04
	2.7	*510 [overestimates]*	0.007	*655 [overestimates]*	0.007
	5.3	*644 [overestimates]*	0.007	*669 [overestimates]*	0.007
Japan	25188.5	Already achieved			
	31485.7	Already achieved			
	47228.5	Already achieved			
	82649.9	152 [August 2016]	0.033	133	0.729
	165299.8	198 [June 2020]	0.025	175	0.705
Malaysia	0.8	Already achieved			
	0.9				
	1.4				
	2.5				
	5.0				
New Zealand	25.2	Already achieved			
	31.5	Already achieved			
	47.3	226 [October 2022]	0.013	334	0.343
	82.8	283 [July 2027]	0.013	347	0.356
	165.5	350 [February 2030]	0.012	357	0.365
Singapore	179.0	Already achieved			
	223.8	Already achieved			
	335.7	Already achieved			
	587.5	Already achieved			
	1175.0	*335 [overestimates]*	0.006	*717 [overestimates]*	0.089

(continued)

Table 4.9 (continued)

Country	Upper limit ($\kappa_{i,n}^{ETF}$)—fixed (value of turnover of ETFs; mln USD)	$Tm_{i,n}^{ETF}$ ($\beta_{i,n}^{ETF}$) (midpoint)—predicted	$\alpha_{i,n}^{ETF}$ (rate of diffusion)—predicted	$\varnothing_{i,n}^{ETF}$ (specific duration)—predicted	R^2 of the model
South Korea	20138.0	Already achieved			
	25172.4	128 [August 2014]	0.028	159	0.793
	37758.7	164 [August 2017]	0.022	204	0.769
	66077.7	213 [September 2021]	0.018	240	0.754
	132155.4	269 [May 2026]	0.017	263	0.746
Taiwan	4814.2	Already achieved			
	6017.8	Already achieved			
	9026.7	160 [April 2017]	0.035	127	0.697
	15796.7	192 [December 2019]	0.029	153	0.689
	31593.5	229 [January 2023]	0.026	170	0.684
Thailand	7.0	Already achieved			
	8.7				
	13.1				
	22.9				
	45.8				

Note: misspecifications in italics. "Already achieved" stands for values already achieved in previous time periods (higher than the level in August 2017 due to declines since the month(s) with the higher values) which leads to misspecifications. However, if certain level was reached only temporary (i.e., in a few months, in particular isolated) and not sustained, it may still be set as the upper limit in the estimations of the diffusion model—see, for example, results for Australia: values higher than $\kappa_{Aus,1}^{ETF}$ were reached only twice over 2004–2017 which does not hinder estimations
Source: own estimates

at increasingly slower rate (estimated values $\varnothing_{Aus,n}^{ETF}$ decline as higher values of upper limit are assumed). It should be remembered that values of the two last imposed upper limits (ca. 4.5 and 9.1 billion USD) are much higher than the last actually observed value; therefore, their reaching may be regarded as highly uncertain, in spite of the stability of the obtained forecasts. We focus, therefore, on the first three levels of $\kappa_{Aus,n}^{ETF}$, imposed at about 1.4, 1.7, and 2.6 billion USD. For the first level, $\kappa_{Aus,1}^{ETF}$, midpoint ($Tm_{Aus,1}^{ETF}$) was estimated at August 2013, and for the second level, $Tm_{Aus,2}^{ETF}$ is at November 2014 which means that in both cases it should have been reached within the historical time period; for $\kappa_{Aus,3}^{ETF}$ its $Tm_{Aus,3}^{ETF}$ slightly exceeds the

Table 4.10 Estimated parameters of the ETFs diffusion for the selected (predicted) values of the upper limits: relative approach

Country	Upper limit ($\kappa_{i,n}^{\mathrm{ETFshare}}$)—fixed (share of ETFs; %)	$Tm_{i,n}^{\mathrm{ETFshare}}$ ($\beta_{i,n}^{\mathrm{ETFshare}}$) (midpoint)—predicted	$\alpha_{i,n}^{\mathrm{ETFshare}}$ (rate of diffusion)—predicted	$\varnothing_{i,n}^{\mathrm{ETFshare}}$ (specific duration)—predicted	R^2 of the model
Australia	1.1	110.8 [March 2013]	0.017	260.0	0.477
	1.3	132.4 [December 2014]	0.015	289.7	0.482
	2.0	190.8 [November 2019]	0.013	349.4	0.488
	3.5	267.1 [March 2026]	0.011	398.2	0.49
	7.1	358.8 [November 2033]	0.011	431.5	0.49
Hong Kong	1.3	Already achieved			
	1.6	Already achieved			
	2.4	Already achieved			
	4.2	Already achieved			
	8.4	245.7 [May 2024]	0.011	397.2	0.389
India	0.0	Already achieved			
	0.0	Already achieved			
	0.1	Already achieved			
	0.1	Already achieved			
	0.2	Already achieved			
Japan	3.2	Already achieved			
	4.0	Already achieved			
	6.0	Already achieved			
	10.6	169.9 [February 2018]	0.022	200.5	0.694
	21.1	227.7 [December 2022]	0.018	241.4	0.686
South Korea	4.9	Already achieved			
	6.1	127.6 [July 2014]	0.039	111.9	0.944
	9.2	154.5 [October 2016]	0.03	148.0	0.931
	16.1	191.4 [December 2019]	0.025	176.9	0.92
	32.3	234.6 [June 2023]	0.022	195.8	0.914

(continued)

Table 4.10 (continued)

Country	Upper limit ($\kappa_{i,n}^{\text{ETFshare}}$)—fixed (share of ETFs; %)	$Tm_{i,n}^{\text{ETFshare}}$ ($\beta_{i,n}^{\text{ETFshare}}$) (midpoint)—predicted	$\alpha_{i,n}^{\text{ETFshare}}$ (rate of diffusion)—predicted	$\varnothing_{i,n}^{\text{ETFshare}}$ (specific duration)—predicted	R^2 of the model
Taiwan	0.7	Already achieved			
	0.9	Already achieved			
	1.4	Already achieved			
	2.5	263.5 [December 2025]	0.008	548.5	0.175
	4.9	381.3 [October 2034]	0.008	585.1	0.187

Note: misspecifications in italics. "Already achieved" stands for values already achieved in previous time periods (higher than the level in August 2017 due to declines since the month(s) with the higher values) which leads to misspecifications. However, if certain level was reached only temporary (i.e., in a few months, in particular isolated) and not sustained, it may still be set as the upper limit in the estimations of the diffusion model—see, for example, results for Australia: values higher than $\kappa_{\text{Aus},1}^{\text{ETFshare}}$ were reached only once over 2004–2017 which does not hinder estimations
Source: own estimates

analyzed period as it is projected as February 2018. All these three values imply that the Australian ETFs market has entered the stage of the rapid exponential growth in the absolute perspective. More accurate determination of the points in time when the set values of $\kappa_{\text{Aus},n}^{\text{ETF}}$ will be approached is possible using their estimated specific durations, $\varnothing_{i,n}^{\text{ETF}}$. In case of the first upper limit, the specific duration of 163 months implies that $\kappa_{\text{Aus},1}^{\text{ETF}}$ should be approximately approached by the end of 2020, i.e., a few years after the end of the historical period; however, for the next levels, it is 2023 and 2029. It means that even though the diffusion of ETFs is projected to continue (evidence for that trend is unequivocal), the anticipated levels of turnover that are expected to be reached in the near future are not considerably higher than the current values. Comparing the estimates of $\alpha_{\text{Aus},n}^{\text{ETF}}$ with the corresponding values obtained for the other countries (not taking into account the misspecifications) shows that the projected growth of the ETFs turnover will be slower than on most other markets—it is in line with the results of the diffusion analysis based on the past data (growth is very stable but relatively slow). Estimates for Australia may be regarded as robust and vastly reliable due to the very high level of R^2 for each of the five models—the highest among all models are included in Table 4.9; it may be explained by the high stability of the observed absolute ETFs market development in this country in the period 2004–2017, which makes it possible to formulate rather certain forecasts.

In case of the relative approach to the ETFs market development, the results obtained for Australia are substantially different due to problems in applying diffusion models for this country in this approach (caused by frequent fluctuations in the ETFs market share over 2004–2017—see Sect. 4.3). Imposed $\kappa_{\text{Aus},n}^{\text{ETFshare}}$ vary from 1.1 to 7.1% (see Table 4.10). Except for the first predicted midpoint, the remaining refer to more distant points in time than the ones discussed in the preceding paragraphs. Moreover, values of $\alpha^{\mathrm{ETFshare}}_{\mathrm{Aus},n}$ are lower, and, consequently, values of $\varnothing^{\mathrm{ETFshare}}_{i,n}$ are higher. As a result, it may be stated that forecasts of the relative ETFs market development in Australia should be perceived as less certain—it means that reaching and maintaining even the levels of market share exceeding 1% are tentative. ETFs in Australia may thus be predicted to remain marginal financial instruments in comparison to the stock index futures and options. The uncertainty of the obtained results is also supported by the values of R^2 that are much lower than for models in the absolute approach.

To sum up our analysis concerning Australia, if the historical trends observed for this market persist (in particular the notable stability of its development in the absolute dimension), projections presented in Table 4.9 indicate highly probable continued quick diffusion of ETFs in this country. However, the values of expected turnover, even though substantially higher than the ones observed in the final months of the 2004–2017 period, are still much lower than in the Asia-Pacific countries with the most developed ETFs markets (unless there are some significant changes on a local or international level that could further boost their diffusion). From the relative perspective (see Table 4.10), the market share of ETFs is predicted to increase slowly and in the upcoming years only slightly exceed 1% of the aggregate turnover of the index financial instruments.

China is one of the most developed ETFs markets in the region in the absolute dimension (analysis in the relative approach is impossible due to lack of sufficient data on the turnover of the other index financial instruments). It is proven by, inter alia, the fact that in this country the historically highest monthly turnover of ETFs among all examined economies was observed—in June 2015 it was close to 130 billion USD. As estimates of the diffusion models discussed in Sect. 4.3 implied, this value and the ones observed in the surrounding months should be perceived as outliers rather than indicators of the upper limit of the turnover over 2004–2017. As those values were reached only in single months, it is possible to impose even lower ones as $\kappa^{\mathrm{ETF}}_{\mathrm{Chi},n}$, between 37.6 ($\kappa^{\mathrm{ETF}}_{\mathrm{Chi},1}$) and 123.5 billion USD ($\kappa^{\mathrm{ETF}}_{\mathrm{Chi},4}$; for details see note below Table 4.9)—all of them are higher than the value of upper asymptote from Sect. 4.3. Estimates for $\kappa^{\mathrm{ETF}}_{\mathrm{Chi},5}$ will not be analyzed as this upper limit exceeds almost by twice the actual maximum level of turnover observed in the past. Estimated values of the midpoint parameters for the four levels of $\kappa^{\mathrm{ETF}}_{\mathrm{Chi},n}$ are very similar to the ones obtained for Australia and may be interpreted analogously as implying that, in case of $Tm^{\mathrm{ETF}}_{\mathrm{Chi},1}$ to $Tm^{\mathrm{ETF}}_{\mathrm{Chi},3}$, they were already reached[17] and diffusion of Chinese ETFs is half-complete, with expected further yet increasingly slower growth. This conclusion is confirmed by the fact that, similarly to Australia, estimated values of the respective $\varnothing^{\mathrm{ETF}}_{\mathrm{Chi},n}$ are increasingly lower when higher imposed values of upper limit are checked. They are, however, much higher (and, consequently, $\varnothing^{\mathrm{ETF}}_{\mathrm{Chi},n}$ are much lower)—among the highest among all countries which implies that the Chinese

[17] For $Tm^{\mathrm{ETF}}_{\mathrm{Chi},3}$ the predicted month is September 2017, i.e., 1 month after the end of the historical time period (the actual difference is several days—values of the estimates in Table 4.9 were rounded).

ETFs market is projected to develop very rapidly. As already outlined in Sect. 4.3, the results obtained with the diffusion framework for China must be interpreted with substantial caution as proven by the low values of R^2 for all estimated models—the lowest among all models without any misspecifications. The main reason is the very short period of extremely high turnover which introduced considerable deviations from the S-shaped trajectory; the overall positive trend and its continuation in the upcoming years may, though, be regarded as feasible despite these stipulations. Comparison of the values for China with the other presented in Table 4.9 suggests that Chinese ETFs market is predicted to be the second- or third-largest in the region, behind Japan (and maybe South Korea).

ETFs market in Hong Kong is older than its closely linked counterpart in China. However, already in the 2004–2017 time period, it has been overtaken by the much more rapidly growing younger ETFs market—estimates for the 2004–2017 period (see Sect. 4.3) show that the rate of absolute diffusion of ETFs in Hong Kong has been one of the slowest in the entire sample. However, as we show below, further diffusion of ETFs in Hong Kong is projected to be rather quick as this market seems to still have potential for future development; it must be stipulated, though, that R^2 of the estimated models are low.

Similarly to China, it is possible to make projections for the levels of $\kappa^{\text{ETF}}_{\text{Hon},n}$ that were already reached yet temporarily; in our case they range from 14.4 to 94.4 billion USD. We concentrate on the predictions for the first four imposed values of $\kappa^{\text{ETF}}_{\text{Hon},n}$ as their reaching is much more certain than in case of the last one used (e.g., $Tm^{\text{ETF}}_{\text{Hon},5}$ is at January 2025 which means that, taking into account the value of $\varnothing t^{\text{ETF}}_{\text{Hon},5}$, turnover of ETFs in Hong Kong is projected to approach the fifth imposed value in the late 2030s or early 2040s—such predictions may not be regarded as reliable).

For the levels $\kappa^{\text{ETF}}_{\text{Hon},1}$ to $\kappa^{\text{ETF}}_{\text{Hon},3}$, their midpoints ($Tm^{\text{ETF}}_{\text{Hon},1}$ to $Tm^{\text{ETF}}_{\text{Hon},3}$) were estimated at April 2011, June 2012, and April 2015, respectively—all of them in the past time period which means that ETFs market in Hong Kong should already have entered the stage of the rapid exponential growth in the absolute dimension. $Tm^{\text{ETF}}_{\text{Hon},4}$ is more distant in time as it is at September 2019. Approximate time when the upper limits will be approached (not reached—it must be emphasized that they are formally upper asymptotes) may be determined with the values of $\varnothing t^{\text{ETF}}_{\text{Hon},n}$. Results of such analysis show that value of the ETFs turnover should increase to levels close to from $\kappa^{\text{ETF}}_{\text{Hon},1}$ to $\kappa^{\text{ETF}}_{\text{Hon},3}$ in the first years of the 2020s—it may be considered possible as such levels were already reached and are not substantially higher than the ones actually observed in China or Japan. Approaching $\kappa^{\text{ETF}}_{\text{Hon},4}$ is much more problematic as it is predicted to occur in the early 2030s. Another important conclusion may be drawn from the comparison of the projections for the four most developed ETFs markets in the region. Despite its strong position in the past and projected quick diffusion, ETFs market in Hong Kong will most probably be the smallest in this group. It may, however, change substantially if there are some new developments on the local market—for example, it seems that it has not yet experienced the boost from the geared ETFs, observed clearly in a few other countries.

What is worth mentioning is the fact that despite their decreasing value, $\alpha^{\text{ETF}}_{\text{Hon},n}$ are high—for each level of the upper limit, they are among the highest among all estimated for the analyzed countries. It suggests that the absolute ETFs market development in Hong Kong is predicted to be much faster than in the past if it occurs in line with the diffusion of innovation specification. It could also imply that, despite its long history, market in Hong Kong has still in fact not reached the final stage of rapid diffusion.

We briefly discuss also the possible future development of the ETFs market in Hong Kong in the relative perspective by examining the projections concerning the share of ETFs in the total turnover of index financial instruments. However, formulating predictions using diffusion models for almost all imposed levels of $\kappa_{Hon,n}^{ETFshare}$ is impossible as they were already reached multiple times over 2004–2017—therefore formulating such predictions would mean violating the assumptions of the diffusion framework (in which no reversal of the growth (other than temporary) is possible). The only level for which estimates are returned is $\kappa_{Hon,5}^{ETFshare}$, but it must be set at 8.4%, i.e., much higher than the maximum observed levels. Additionally, R^2 of this model is very low. As a result, we leave it without interpretation. It may be thus stated that while the diffusion of ETFs in Hong Kong in terms of the absolute value of their turnover is expected to continue and take place quite rapidly, it is difficult to assess the future changes in their market share.

After discussing two of the most developed ETFs markets in the Asia-Pacific, we scrutinize briefly three much less advanced—India, Indonesia, and Malaysia. Despite the rather high values of R^2 of models estimated for the set values of $\kappa_{Ind,2}^{ETF}$ to $\kappa_{Ind,5}^{ETF}$, they include some misspecifications implying that full interpretation is possible exclusively for $\kappa_{Ind,1}^{ETF}$ (for which R^2 is much lower). All estimated midpoints are within the historical data period (except for $Tm_{Ind,5}^{ETF}$ which somewhat exceeds it), showing that Indian ETFs market has already started quick growth (examination of the graphical evidence on Fig. 4.9 supports this view, despite the brief period of extreme changes). Discrepancies between the values of $\alpha_{Ind,n}^{ETF}$ returned for various levels of the upper limit (in particular between $\alpha_{Ind,1}^{ETF}$ and $\alpha_{Ind,2}^{ETF}$) as well as explicit underestimates of most $\varnothing t_{Ind,n}^{ETF}$ hinder determination of the approximate periods when values of ETFs turnover are projected to approach the imposed upper asymptotes. In case of $\kappa_{Ind,1}^{ETF}$, which is set at 704 million USD, returned estimates indicate that it could be approached in the late 2020s—it seems possible taking into account the previous development of the local market and actions undertaken by the Indian government such as launch of special new ETF with exposure to the equities of state-owned companies. Making projections for India in the relative approach is impossible to high variability of the share of ETFs in the total turnover of index financial instruments, with multiple ups and downs, and lack of noticeable upward trend (see Fig. 4.10).

In case of Indonesia, only misspecifications were returned for the absolute market development which means their interpretation is impossible (moreover, R^2 of the models are extremely low). For Malaysia applying diffusion model is impossible as the ETFs turnover has gone through substantial fluctuations and determination of possible values of $\kappa_{Mal,n}^{ETF}$ to be imposed would be highly arbitrary (for all tested values, misspecifications were returned). For both countries no estimates in the relative approach could be made.

In Sect. 4.3 we labeled Japan as the Asia-Pacific country with the highest levels of diffusion of ETFs indicated by the estimates for the 2004–2017 time period. In the current section, we try to determine whether Japan can be projected to maintain its leading position. Due to some fluctuations in the value of ETFs turnover and share of innovative funds in the total turnover of index financial instruments in the final part of the empirical time series, models cannot be estimated for the assumed values of $\kappa_{\mathrm{Jap},n}^{\mathrm{ETF}}$ and $\kappa_{\mathrm{Jap},n}^{\mathrm{ETFshare}}$ for $n = 1$, 2, and 3, calculated using the approach presented at the beginning of this section. As the analysis presented in Sect. 4.3 showed, the decline observed in 2016 and 2017 should be regarded as transitory, and the actual levels of the estimated upper asymptote were higher for both approaches. Consequently, exclusively $\kappa_{\mathrm{Jap},4}^{\mathrm{ETF}}$, $\kappa_{\mathrm{Jap},5}^{\mathrm{ETF}}$, $\kappa_{\mathrm{Jap},4}^{\mathrm{ETFshare}}$, and $\kappa_{\mathrm{Jap},5}^{\mathrm{ETFshare}}$ can be set as the upper limits in the diffusion models utilized in order to obtain predictions.

$\kappa_{\mathrm{Jap},4}^{\mathrm{ETF}}$ was set at about 83 billion USD, i.e., twice higher than upper asymptote estimated for the historical period 2004–2017 (see Table 4.7). Imposed value of $\kappa_{\mathrm{Jap},5}^{\mathrm{ETF}}$ was, as for other countries, twice higher than $\kappa_{\mathrm{Jap},4}^{\mathrm{ETF}}$. Despite their high levels, the returned values of estimated parameters refer to points in time close to the historical time series. Midpoint for the first analyzed upper limit, $Tm_{\mathrm{Jap},4}^{\mathrm{ETF}}$ is August 2016 which means that half of the diffusion process leading to approaching the turnover of more than 80 billion USD should be already completed in approximately mid-2016. For the second upper limit, it is more distant as $Tm_{\mathrm{Jap},5}^{\mathrm{ETF}}$ is at ca. June 2020. Both $\alpha_{\mathrm{Jap},4}^{\mathrm{ETF}}$ and $\alpha_{\mathrm{Jap},5}^{\mathrm{ETF}}$ are high (also in comparison to the other most developed ETFs markets), indicating that diffusion of ETFs in the absolute dimension is projected to continue rapidly. However, the recent downward trend may make this prediction dubious. Additionally, when we take into account the values of $\varnothing_{\mathrm{Jap},4}^{\mathrm{ETF}}$ and $\varnothing_{\mathrm{Jap},5}^{\mathrm{ETF}}$, we may conclude that values of turnover close to $\kappa_{\mathrm{Jap},4}^{\mathrm{ETF}}$ are predicted to be reached in the mid-2020s and $\kappa_{\mathrm{Jap},5}^{\mathrm{ETF}}$ in the late 2020s. It means that, in terms of the absolute ETFs turnover, Japan may be expected to remain the regional leader at least until ca. 2030. R^2 of the both models are rather high, the highest among presented in Table 4.9 except for South Korea which proves their reliability.

In the relative approach, models for $\kappa_{\mathrm{Jap},4}^{\mathrm{ETFshare}}$ of 10.6% and $\kappa_{\mathrm{Jap},5}^{\mathrm{ETFshare}}$ of 21.1% were estimated. $Tm_{\mathrm{Jap},4}^{\mathrm{ETFshare}}$ and $Tm_{\mathrm{Jap},5}^{\mathrm{ETFshare}}$ are higher than respective parameters in the absolute perspective, while $\alpha_{\mathrm{Jap},4}^{\mathrm{ETFshare}}$ and $\alpha_{\mathrm{Jap},5}^{\mathrm{ETFshare}}$ are lower. Their comparison to the respective values estimated for the similar upper limit for South Korea shows that the position of Japan as the country in the region with the highest share of ETFs may be threatened by more rapidly growing South Korean market (it depends on, among other, whether the most recent decline trend in Japan will in fact be temporary). All presented results for the predicted relative diffusion of ETFs in Japan show that it is expected to continue, yet the rate of this process will be probably lower than in terms of the absolute turnover—it implies that gaining increasing share in the total market for index financial instruments by ETFs is more difficult. R^2 of the both models are lower than for the two in the absolute approach yet still the highest except for South Korea.

To conclude, the predictions for Japan in both absolute and relative approach imply that Japanese ETFs market will in the upcoming years be still the leader of the Asia-Pacific region (there are some stipulations concerning the relative dimension), unless there are some substantial changes in the other countries which could substantially boost the speed of diffusion of ETFs on their financial markets. Despite the optimistic forecasts concerning the Japanese market, there are some factors that could hinder its future development. They include the commission structure in the bank's distribution chains which favor competing products such as mutual funds—banks gain sales commissions for their distribution (PwC 2015). In contrast, the factor that could boost the diffusion of ETFs is the possible emergence of independent advisers' community in Japan including robo-advisors, who prefer ETF to mutual funds because of the significant difference in fees and transparency. Currently the market is dominated by the bank and broker-sponsored advisers who prefer high-commissioned mutual funds.

Three models with predictions were estimated for New Zealand. For all three, R^2 is very low which makes their robustness questionable. Moreover, returned values of all $Tm^{\text{ETF}}_{\text{NZe},n}$ parameters refer to points in time outside the 2004–2017 period, and values of $\varnothing t^{\text{ETF}}_{\text{NZe},n}$ suggest that approaching the assumed levels of upper limits is expected to occur in very distant future (in 2030s or even later). It is, therefore, impossible to formulate any reliable interpretation of these results. Based on the graphical evidence (see Fig. 4.9), it may be stated, though, that there are some displays of ETFs diffusion on this market, but its continuation is difficult to evaluate. However, it may be concluded with high level of certainty that it will continue to be one of the smallest ETFs markets in the region (due to, inter alia, the size of the local economy and financial system).

Due to the shape of the ETFs market development, using diffusion models for Singapore is highly problematic. We attempted to utilize this framework to examine the diffusion over the 2004–2017 time period, obtaining some results that are possible to interpret yet with substantial caution. However, as it can be clearly noticed in Table 4.9, formulation of any robust predictions with the diffusion models for this country seems impossible as proven by the overestimates for the only value of $\kappa^{\text{ETF}}_{\text{sin},n}$ that could be imposed. Moreover, R^2 of this single model is extremely low. For both New Zealand and Singapore, conducting the analysis in relative terms is impossible.

In the context of the analysis of diffusion over the 2004–2017 time period, we stated that South Korea is the example of ETFs market for which the application of diffusion framework seems highly fitted. Results presented in Tables 4.9 and 4.10 confirm that previous conclusion as all estimated models seem to be highly robust, in particular in the relative perspective. In both cases models for the first levels of upper limits could not be estimated as they were already reached in some periods in the preceding years.

Imposed upper limits in the absolute approach for South Korea range from $\kappa^{\text{ETF}}_{\text{Kor},\,2}$ at 25.2 billion USD to $\kappa^{\text{ETF}}_{\text{Kor},\,5}$ at 132.2 billion USD. We focus on $\kappa^{\text{ETF}}_{\text{Kor},\,2}$ and $\kappa^{\text{ETF}}_{\text{Kor},\,3}$ as the returned parameters for the other values refer to distant points in time. $Tm^{\text{ETF}}_{\text{Kor},2}$ is estimated at August 2014 and $Tm^{\text{ETF}}_{\text{Kor},3}$ 3 years later, at August 2017. Both values show that Korean ETFs market already started the development leading to approaching the set levels of upper limits (at least if the trajectory implied by the logistic growth model is to be followed). $\varnothing t^{\text{ETF}}_{\text{Kor},2}$ considered in addition to the values of corresponding midpoint suggests that monthly ETFs turnover of about 25 billion USD is projected to be approached in the early 2020s; for the next level (approximately 38 billion USD), $\varnothing_{\text{Kor},3}^{\text{ETF}}$ indicates the mid- or late 2020s. What is worth noticing is the fact that R^2 of all four models, even though high in comparison to the other presented in Table 4.9, are much lower than R^2 of the model of absolute diffusion in the 2004–2017 period (see Table 4.7). These results could imply that, as suggested by, for instance, the graphical evidence concerning the development trajectory, Korean ETFs market has already entered the third stage in the diffusion framework, of stabilization at high levels of turnover (at least temporarily as some disruptive changes may occur in the future). Consequently, assuming that its development will continue is less reliable than using the scenario of lack of future significant changes. This conclusion is to some extent supported by the returned increasingly lower values of $\alpha_{\text{Kor},n}^{\text{ETF}}$. Moreover, over 2004–2017 South Korean ETFs has been one of the most rapidly growing in the entire region, and predictions indicate that the rate of diffusion is expected to slow down substantially, below the one predicted for the other countries in the leading group. Overall, South Korean ETFs market in the absolute dimension can be predicted to stay in this group, and it may be second- or third-largest, depending on the changes on its Chinese counterpart.

For the analysis of the predicted relative ETFs diffusion in South Korea, we use values between $\kappa_{\text{Kor},2}^{\text{ETFshare}}$ of 6.1% and $\kappa_{\text{Kor},5}^{\text{ETFshare}}$ of 32.3%. All of them are higher than shares of ETFs in the total turnover of index financial instruments observed over 2004–2017 (and above the upper limit estimated for the 2004–2017 time period). Returned values of $Tm_{\text{Kor},n}^{\text{ETFshare}}$ are within the historical time period for the second and fourth level of $\kappa_{\text{Kor},n}^{\text{ETFshare}}$, more than 2 years after its end (for the fourth) and as late as in 2023 (for the final). Interpretation is similar to the one presented in the preceding paragraph. Referring to the parameters showing the speed of diffusion in the relative approach, all values of $\alpha_{\text{Kor},n}^{\text{ETFshare}}$ are the highest in the entire sample which proves that South Korean market is projected to continue to develop most quickly in the entire region (when shares of ETFs are taken into account). Another significant conclusion that can be reached based on the values of $\varnothing_{\text{Kor},n}^{\text{ETFshare}}$ is that, in the scenario of the continuation of current trends, South Korean ETFs may have within several years the highest share in the total turnover of index financial instruments in the region, i.e., higher than in Japan. Whether such scenario materializes remains to be seen and depends to a large extent on the situation on the Japanese market (as the growth trend in South Korea seems to be impregnable). In the previous section, while discussing the relative diffusion of ETFs in this country, we mentioned the problems with determining the stage of growth of the South Korean market in this approach (whether it is the final stage of stabilization or rather still the phase of rapid growth). Our predictions show rather unambiguously that diffusion is projected to continue very quickly. It should be emphasized that R^2 of all four models are very high, the highest among all included in Tables 4.9 and 4.10. It means that discussed projections may be perceived to be highly reliable.

For Taiwan the reliability of results obtained in the absolute and relative approach differs considerably. In the former, we obtained models with R^2 comparable to the models for Japan (close to 0.7), whereas in the latter they are below 0.2. We focus, therefore, on the results concerning absolute ETFs diffusion; the projections of relative diffusion indicate some future growth yet highly uncertain and predicted to take place at very low rate.

As the two first levels of $\kappa_{\mathrm{Tai},n}^{\mathrm{ETF}}$ were already achieved, estimations were made for values ranging from 9 to 31.6 billion USD. According to the obtained results, only the midpoint for the third level, $Tm_{\mathrm{Tai},3}^{\mathrm{ETF}}$, was already reached over 2004–2017. $\varnothing t_{\mathrm{Tai},3}^{\mathrm{ETF}}$ of 127 months (in other words, of about 10.5 years) shows that in the theoretical specification, Taiwanese ETFs market is predicted to reach the values of turnover close to 10 billion USD by the mid-2020s. For the fourth and fifth level of $\kappa_{\mathrm{Tai},n}^{\mathrm{ETF}}$, respective parameters imply much more distant points in time, difficult to be regarded as highly reliable. Even though, as in case of most other considered countries, the values of $\alpha_{\mathrm{Tai},n}^{\mathrm{ETF}}$ are increasingly lower, they are quite high—it seems that they are influenced by the quick growth of the Taiwanese ETFs market in the 2014–2016 subperiod. One problematic issue with predictions prepared for this market is its short history in terms of significant ETFs turnover which has started with the introduction of the geared funds. Before 2014 ETFs turnover remained low. It means that these projections are based on relatively short historical trend. We included Taiwan in the group of mid-developed ETFs markets, labeling it as the leading country in this category. Our predictions show that, despite the impressive predicted future diffusion, it will most probably remain in this group as reaching the levels of even the smallest market in the top group (i.e., Hong Kong) is highly uncertain.

For Thailand, identically as in the already discussed case of Malaysia, using diffusion model is impossible as the ETFs turnover has gone through substantial variability—for most of the 2004–2017 time period, it has been very low, yet there were a few months with intensive trading; no sustainable diffusion was observed. Obtaining estimates for any of the levels of $\kappa_{\mathrm{Tha},n}^{\mathrm{ETF}}$ formulated according to the assumed rules is impossible, and imposing higher values of this parameter leads to misspecifications. Predictions in the relative approach could not be made.

References

Abner, D. (2016). *The ETF Handbook. How to value and trade exchange-traded funds* (2nd ed.). Hoboken, NJ: Wiley.

Australian Securities & Investments Commission. (2012). *Regulation of exchange traded funds*. Report 282.

Banerjee, S. (2015). Effectiveness of ETFs in indexing: The mean for equity investments by employees' provident funds in India. *American Journal of Business, Economics and Management, 3*(5), 300.

Bank of Japan. (2017a). *Principal terms and conditions for purchases of ETFs and J-REITs.*

Bank of Japan. (2017b). *Special rules for purchases of ETFs to support firms proactively investing in physical and human capital.*

BlackRock. (2011). *ETF landscape: Celebrating 10 Years of ETFs in Australia.*

Bursa Malaysia. (2009). *Introduction to Sharia Exchange Traded Fund –ETF.*

Business Standard. (2017). *How India's ETF market became the second fastest growing in the world*. Retrieved July 30, 2018, from https://www.business-standard.com/article/markets/how-india-s-etf-market-became-the-second-fastest-growing-in-the-world-117030900426_1.html.
Carson, R. (2017). *Australia loves ETFs – But not as much as the U.S. and Europe*. Retrieved August 03, 2018, from https://www.bloomberg.com/news/articles/2017-11-13/australia-boasts-39-etf-market-boom-but-still-lags-u-s-europe.
Chandler, B. (2018). *Cerulli reports on rapid growth of Aussie ETF market*. ETF Express, 23rd January 2018.
Charles Schwab. (2017). *Understanding Chinese security share classes*.
Chen, J., Chen, Y., & Frijns, B. (2017). Evaluating the tracking performance and tracking error of New Zealand exchange traded funds. *Pacific Accounting Review, 29*(3), 443–462.
Chen, J. H., & Huang, C. Y. (2010). An analysis of the spillover effects of exchange-traded funds. *Applied Economics, 42*(9), 1155–1168.
CSOP Asset Management. (2015). Development of Asian ETFs market.
Cunningham, M. (2017). The Australian exchange-traded funds market. *Reserve Bank of Australia Bulletin, 2017*, 51–56.
Dang, H. D., & Jolly, M. (2017). Red flags for IPO downfalls in New Zealand. *Managerial Finance, 43*(9), 1034–1051.
Deutsche Bank. (2015a). Asia-Pac monthly ETF insights (August 2015).
Deutsche Bank. (2015b). Asia-Pac monthly ETF insights (October 2015).
Deutsche Bank. (2017a). Asia Pac ETF + quarterly directory (Q1 2017 ETPs).
Deutsche Bank. (2017b). ETF monthly Asia (August 2017).
Downes, N. A. (2016). The phenomenon of Shariah compliant funds. *Islamic Finance News*, 20–21.
Enemuwe, N. R. (2015). Dynamic ETF pairs trading system. *Evidence from Australia*. Retrieved July 02, 2018 https://papers.ssrn.com/sol3/papers.cfm?abstract_id=2662258.
ETF Trends. (2015). *The facts on China's June correction*. Retrieved July 12, 2018, from https://www.etftrends.com/2015/07/the-facts-on-chinas-june-correction/.
EY. (2017). *Reshaping around the investor*. Global ETF Research 2017.
Farouk, F., & Masih, M. (2016). Are there profit (returns) in Shariah-compliant exchange traded funds? The multiscale propensity. *Research in International Business and Finance, 38*, 360–375.
Fowler, J., Li, L., & Naughton, T. (2008). Short term equity returns of Chinese IPOs, 1999 to 2004. Excess demand social policy and wealth effects. *Journal of Emerging Market Finance, 7*(2), 197–214.
Fueda-Samikawa, I., & Takano, T. (2017). *BOJ's ETF purchases expanding steadily – How long will the BOJ hold risky assets with no maturity?* Tokyo: Japan Center for Economic Research.
Fuhr, D. (2015). Appendix A: The global footprint of ETFs and ETPs. In J. M. Hill, D. Nadig, & M. Hougan (Eds.), *A comprehensive guide to Exchange-Traded Funds (ETFs)*. Charlottesville, VA: CFA Institute Research Foundation.
Fuhr, D., Li, H., & Rzeszotko, S. (2016). *A guide to China ETFs*. London: Stock Exchange Group.
Gad, S., & Andrikopoulos, P. (2019). Diversification benefits of Shari'ah compliant equity ETFs in emerging markets. *Pacific-Basin Finance Journal, 53*, 133–144.
Gallagher, D. R., & Segara, R. (2006). The performance and trading characteristics of exchange-traded fund. *Journal of Investment Strategy, 1*(2), 49–60.
Ghosh, K. (2017). *Have you heard of passive investing? ETF Market in India doubles AUM in 2017*. Retrieved August 2, 2018, from https://www.moneycontrol.com/news/business/markets/have-you-heard-of-passive-investing-etf-market-in-india-doubles-aum-in-2017-2464669.html.
Ghosh, K. (2018). *A growing ETF market in India*. Retrieved August 2, 2018, from https://seekingalpha.com/article/4136386-growing-etf-market-india.
Hoque, M. A., & Faruqui, M. F. (2017). Equity and commodity market co-movements in Thailand. *International Journal of Business and Social Research, 7*(5), 25–38.

Huo, R., & Ahmed, A. D. (2017). Return and volatility spillovers effects: Evaluating the impact of Shanghai-Hong Kong stock connect. *Economic Modelling, 61*, 260–272.
Ivanov, S. I., & Meshcheryakov, A. (2018). Price discovery of one security traded in several markets around the world. *International Journal of Financial Services Management, 9*(1), 14–21.
Japan Securities Dealers Association. (2014). *NISA: Japan's new tax exemption scheme for investment by individuals*.
Ji, C., & Thomas, S. (2003, Spring). Emerging stock markets in the People's Republic of China. *Financial History*, 28–31.
JPX Tokyo Stock Exchange. (2015). *ETF/ETN Factsheet*.
JPX Tokyo Stock Exchange. (2016). *ETF/ETN Factsheet*.
JPX Tokyo Stock Exchange. (2017). *ETF/ETN Factsheet*.
JPX Tokyo Stock Exchange. (2018). *ETF/ETN Factsheet*.
Kaur, P., & Singh, J. (2018). Testing the tracking efficiency of commodity Exchange Traded Funds (ETFs) across the bearish and bullish market regimes: Evidence from Indian Gold ETFs. *Journal of Asia-Pacific Business, 19*(3), 182–202.
Korea Financial Investment Association. (2016). *Korean capital market annual review 2015*.
Kumar, K. S. (2018a). A study on pricing efficiency and replication strategy of exchange traded funds. *SDMIMD Journal of Management, 9*(2), 1–8.
Kumar, P. (2018b). An investigation of pricing efficiency of CPSE ETF in India. *Journal of Commerce & Accounting Research, 7*(2), 28–33.
Lee, M. J., & Hasegawa, T. (2018). *The Bank of Japan steps up with record buys of local stocks*. Retrieved July 12, 2018, from https://www.bloomberg.com/news/articles/2018-04-03/the-tokyo-whale-steps-up-with-record-purchases-of-japan-s-stocks.
Lee, M. J., & Urabe, E. (2017). *Bank of Japan's $150 Billion ETF binge looks likely to slow next year*. Retrieved July 12, 2018, from https://www.bloomberg.com/news/articles/2017-12-10/the-tokyo-whale-s-150-billion-etf-binge-seen-slowing-next-year.
Li, W. (1997). The impact of economic reform on the performance of Chinese state enterprises: 1980–1989. *Journal of Political Economy, 105*(5), 1080–1106.
Lin, C. C., Chan, S. J., & Hsu, H. (2006). Pricing efficiency of exchange traded funds in Taiwan. *Journal of Asset Management, 7*(1), 60–68.
Lin, C. C., & Chiang, M. H. (2005). Volatility effect of ETFs on the constituents of the underlying Taiwan 50 Index. *Applied Financial Economics, 15*, 1315–1322.
Lord, J. (2016). Leveraged and inverse ETF use on the rise in Asia. *ETF Strategy, 5th April 2016*.
Lord, J. (2018). Stock connect expected to unleash pent-up ETF demand in Greater China. *ETF Strategy, 3rd May 2018*.
Lystra, M. (2017). *China's share class mosaic*. Retrieved July 18, 2018, from http://www.ftserussell.com/blog/chinas-share-class-mosaic.
Maher, J. (2015). China ETFs rally as regulators provide market support. *ETF Strategy, 10th July 2015*.
Malhotra, N., Purohit, H., & Tandon, D. (2016). Price discovery and dynamics of Indian equity exchange traded funds. *International Journal of Business Competition and Growth, 5*(1–3), 91–109.
Marszk, A., & Lechman, E. (2019). *Exchange-traded funds in Europe*. Cambridge, MA: Academic Press.
Nangle, T., & Yates, A. (2017). *Quantifying the effect of the Bank of Japan's equity purchases*. Retrieved July 02, 2018, from https://voxeu.org/article/quantifying-effect-bank-japan-s-equity-purchases.
Narend, S., & Thenmozhi, M. (2016). What drives fund flows to index ETFs and mutual funds? A panel analysis of funds in India. *Decision, 43*(1), 17–30.
Osaki, S. (2001). The development of Exchange-Traded Funds (ETFs) in Japan. *Capital Research Journal, 4*(3), 45–51.
Ozaki, S. (2013). Significance of Japan Exchange Group's formation and future challenges. *Iakyara, 158*.

Pan, W. F., & Li, T. (2016). The measurement of tracking errors of Gold ETFS: Evidence from China. *Applied Finance Letters, 5*(1), 2–11.

Park, J., Byun, Y., & Kang, S. (2014). An empirical study on the relationship between price discovery of ETFs and trading volume: Focused on ETFs of KOSPI200 in Korea. *International Information Institute (Tokyo), 17*(7), 2973–2978.

Pash, C. (2018). *The best, and worst, performing Australian ETFs for 2018*. Retrieved August 24, 2018, from https://www.businessinsider.com.au/best-and-worst-performing-australian-etfs-for-2018-2018-6.

Petrov, A. (2018). *ETFs in Monetary Policy Case Study: Bank of Japan*. State Street Global Advisors.

Power, B. (2017). EFTs in the age of providing service. *Professional Planner, 95*, 20–23.

Prakasa, Y. (2012). The potential for Islamic Exchange Traded Fund (ETF) in Indonesia: A comparative study of development in US, UK and Malaysia. In S. S. Ali (Ed.), *Islamic Capital Markets: Competitiveness and resilience* (pp. 189–218). Jeddah: Islamic Development Bank.

Purohit, H., & Malhotra, N. (2015). Pricing efficiency and performance of exchange traded funds in India. *IUP Journal of Applied Finance, 21*(3), 16–35.

PwC. (2015). *ETF 2020: Preparing for a new Horizon*. Retrieved February 15, 2018, from https://www.pwc.com/jg/en/publications/etf-2020-exchange-traded-funds-pwc.pdf.

Rahman, A. A. (2016). Shariah Parameters on Islamic Exchange-traded Fund (ETF) based on Gold and Silver: A legal perspective on the liabilities of Shariah advisers in Malaysia. *Islam and Civilisational Renewal (ICR), 7*(3), 426–429.

Rapoza, K. (2015). *A timeline of what China's Gov't did to save stock market*. Retrieved July 22, 2018, from https://www.forbes.com/sites/kenrapoza/2015/07/13/a-timeline-of-what-chinas-govt-did-to-save-stock-market/#7d54b4d02a67.

Ratna, I. (2017). First Shariah-compliant ETF debuts on Main Market. *The Malaysian Reserve, 7th December 2017*.

Reliance. (2018). *Reliance ETF Nifty BeES*.

Rose, S. (2017). Institutional investors are catching on to ETFs. *Investment Magazine, 139*, 18–21.

Saji, T. G. (2017). Performance and tracking efficiency of exchange traded funds: An analysis of Indian equity index funds. *Indian Journal of Research in Capital Markets, 4*(2), 7–14.

Samalad, R. (2017). *Do ETFs have a future in India?* Retrieved July 23, 2018, from https://www.morningstar.in/posts/43871/etfs-future-india.aspx.

Samsung Asset Management. (2010). *Overview of Korean ETF Market*. Retrieved March 30, 2016, from www.set.or.th/th/news/download/files/2553/OverviewofKoreanETFMarket.pdf.

Sarkar, S. (2017). Assessing tracking risk of ETFs in India-An Empirical Study on selected index ETFs. *Research Bulletin, 42*(4), 23–37.

Seki, Y. (2007). ETFs and REITs in Japan: Innovation and steps for future growth. In Y. Fuchita & R. Litan (Eds.), *New Financial Instruments and Institutions: Opportunities and policy challenges* (pp. 15–58). New York: Brookings Institution Press & Nomura Institute of Capital Markets Research.

Shah, A. & Ramarathinam, A. (2017). Indian ETF market doubles in three years to $4 billion. *Mint, 9.03.2017, 7*.

Shanghai Stock Exchange. (2012). *Fund market overview: Overview of Shanghai stock exchange fund market development*.

Shimada, Y. (2018). *Bank of Japan shows signs of backpedaling on ETF purchases*. Retrieved August 02, 2018, from https://asia.nikkei.com/Economy/Bank-of-Japan-shows-signs-of-backpedaling-on-ETF-purchases.

Shum, W. C., Kan, A. C., & Chen, T. (2014). Does warrant trading matter in tracking errors of China-focused exchange-traded funds? *The Chinese Economy, 47*(1), 53–66.

Sil, Y. Y. (2017). 300 ETF items listed on domestic stock market. *Business Korea, 31st August 2017*.

Singh, J., & Seth, S. (2016). Investigating stock market Indices of India-empirical analysis. *Oxford Journal: An International Journal of Business & Economics, 10*(2), 29–40.

State Street Global Advisors. (2011). *How ETFs are created and redeemed.*

Takeo, Y., Lee, M. J., & Hasegawa, T. (2017). Japan's Central Bank is distorting the market, Bourse Chief Says. Retrieved July 14, 2018, from https://www.bloomberg.com/news/articles/2017-07-19/japan-bourse-head-turns-surprise-critic-of-kuroda-etf-purchases.

The Investor. (2016). *KRX to encourage ETFs, ETNs for pension funds.* Retrieved June 30, 2018, from http://www.theinvestor.co.kr/view.php?ud=20161013000838.

The Stock Exchange of Thailand. (2018). *ETF FAQs.*

Tsai, C. C., & Lee, T. S. (2017). Liquidity-adjusted value-at-risk for TWSE Leverage/Inverse ETFs: A Hellinger distance measure research. *Journal of Economics and Management, 13*(1), 53–81.

TWSE. (2018). *Liquidity provider program.* Retrieved August 12, 2018, from http://www.twse.com.tw/en/page/ETF/liquidity.html.

Vaghela, V. (2015, February). Seoul doubt. *Risk,* 21–23.

Wang, J., Kang, H., Xia, F., & Li, G. (2018). Examining the equilibrium relationship between the Shanghai 50 stock index futures and the Shanghai 50 ETF options markets. *Emerging Markets Finance and Trade, 54*(11), 2557–2576.

Wong, S. (2006). China's Stock market. A marriage of capitalism and socialism. *Cato Journal, 26*(3), 389–424.

Xu, F. (2017). China's ETF market "booming" putting pressure on active managers. *ETF Stream, 25th November* 2017.

Yap, B. (2015). Korea ETF discrepancies raise liberalisation fears. *International Financial Law Review, 34,* 42.

Yap, B. (2016). HK's first leveraged and inverse ETFs explained. *International Financial Law Review, 35,* 28.

Young, T. (2016). Hong Kong's ETFs deregulation falls short. *International Financial Law Review.*

Zhang, L. H. (2018). Leveraged ETFs: Are you prepared for the volatility jumps? Global perspectives on the short-term versus longer-term risk profiles. *The Journal of Index Investing, 9*(1), 19–35.

Chapter 5
ICT Deployment in the Asia-Pacific Countries: Eliminating Information Asymmetries

5.1 Digital Revolution in Asia-Pacific: A Snapshot

Over the last few decades (since the 1970s onward), the world has witnessed the process of rapid diffusion of new information and communication technologies (ICT), and, undeniably, this process has enforced remarkable changes and structural shifts going far beyond economic sphere of life. At a time, the process of ICT diffusion radically differs, mainly in terms of speed and geographic coverage, from the process of diffusion of "old" technologies (Comin and Hobijn 2011). ICT become fast available widespread and they diffuse at historically unprecedented rate (Comin et al. 2006). The explosive growth of information and communications technologies and rapidly growing demand for all innovative technological solutions ICT offer, particularly the rise of Internet and its related applications, gave rise to unprecedented opportunities to all society members. Interestingly, ICT is fast spreading not only in economically advanced countries but also in economies that lag behind in terms of social, economic, and infrastructural development. An interesting observation arises, showing often materially poorer countries tend to adopt ICT faster than countries that are relatively better off—compare, for instance, estimates of ICT diffusion rates provided in Baliamoune-Lutz (2003) or more recently in Lechman (2017a, b). Now, in 2018, Asia-Pacific economies seem to be fully benefiting from the opportunities offered to each individual but also to companies and whole societies, by the digital revolution. A huge part of Asia-Pacific residents, during last two decades, have gained reliable and affordable (due to rapidly dropping prices of ICT) access to a great variety of ICT solutions. Due to sound telecommunication policies, effective implementation of national e-strategies, and free market competition since the early 1980s of the twentieth century, ICT were diffusing across Asia-Pacific societies.

Time trends demonstrating radical shifts with respect to core ICT indicators, just between 2005 and 2017, speak for themselves (Fig. 5.1).

A. Marszk et al., *The Emergence of ETFs in Asia-Pacific*,
https://doi.org/10.1007/978-3-030-12752-7_5

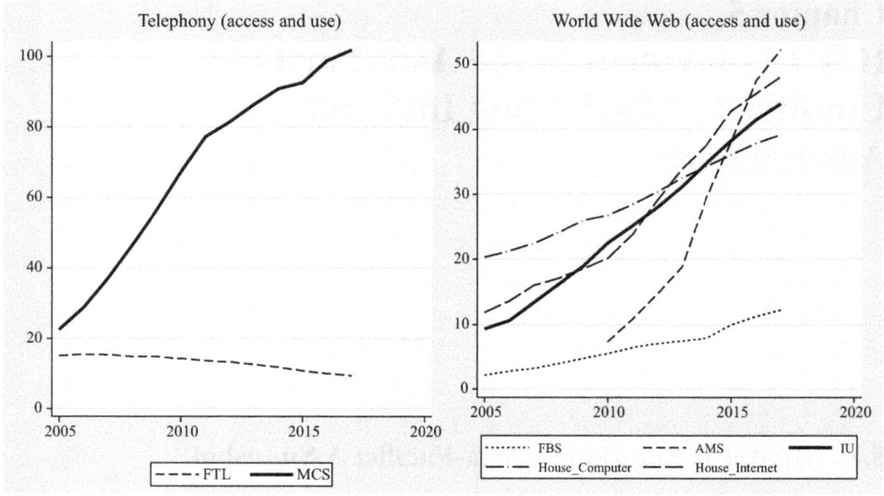

Fig. 5.1 Changes in core ICT indicators. Asia-Pacific Region. Period 2005–2017

In 2005, only 22% of Asian-Pacific societies had access to mobile telephony, and the state of its adoption was comparably low with fixed telephones (slightly above 15% in 2005) (WTI 2018). However, due to rapid expansion of ICT, in 2017, mobile-cellular telephony penetration rate exceeded 100% suggesting that, on average, in this year Asian-Pacific societies has reached full saturation with this type of new technology. Next, between 2010 and 2017, we observe equally dynamic, as in case of mobile-cellular telephony, expansion of active mobile-broadband subscription, which within only 8 years managed to cover more than 50% of societies in Asia-Pacific region. The growth of Internet usage seems to be also very successful, as in 2017, barely 50% of individuals have access to the World Wide Web (WTI 2018). Despite this enormous success in terms of improving access to and use of ICT, still in several Asian countries (especially Southeast Region), due to high prices of access digital networks and poorly developed backbone infrastructure, the ICT penetration rates remain relatively low—see, for instance, countries like Lao PDR, Myanmar, or Cambodia where still in 2017 the share of individuals using the Internet was below 20%. Eliminating such digital gaps is a challenging task (OECD 2017).

However, in the past decades, Asia-Pacific region has been leading in boosting access to and use of technological innovations. Some of the region's ICT-advanced economies are top performers in major ICT indicators—to give an example of Hong Kong with mobile-cellular telephony penetration rate 250 per 100 inhab. or the United Arab Emirates and Maldives with 210 per 100 inhab. and 201 per inhab., respectively. Notably, as noted by Sedik (2018) "Asian players are in the lead in nearly every aspect of digitalization (…) and at any given income level, Asian economies are at the frontier relative to their global peers" (Sedik 2018, p. 31).

In what follows, our empirical evidence focuses on examining the unique characteristics of the process of new information and communication technologies diffusion process across selected Asia-Pacific economies that are in the center of this research. This aims to develop country-specific diffusion patterns and demonstrate both general trends and more specific estimates regarding the process of ICT spread in countries in scope. The latter allows us unveiling the state of adoption and usage of new technological solution in Asia-Pacific economies, and these results are next (see Chap. 6) confronted with the process of development of financial innovations across selected financial markets.

5.2 The Data and Empirical Sample

To stay in line with the major scope of this book, we examine the process of ICT diffusion across selected 12 Asia-Pacific economies, for which empirical evidence on the process of ETFs development was provided in the preceding Chap. 4.

Our database consists of annual data for Australia, China, Hong Kong, India, Indonesia, Japan, Malaysia, New Zealand, South Korea, Singapore, Taiwan, and Thailand; and the empirical sample spans between 1990 and 2017. To ensure international comparison of data, we derived all statistics from the same data source, and we applied the same techniques of numerical analysis. All statistics on core ICT indicators and other indicators related used in the study are exclusively extracted from the World Telecommunication/ICT Indicators database 2017 and 2018 (WTI 2017, 21st Edition; WTI 2018, 22nd Edition). All statistics on ICT adoption, usage, and price that are available in WTI databases are collected from national ministries, telecommunication companies, and other authorities.

To examine ICT profiles of selected countries, regarding intime changes in adoption and usage of new technologies, we have chosen four core ICT indicators[1]: *mobile-cellular telephone* subscriptions per 100 inhabitants (MCS, hereafter), *fixed-broadband* subscriptions per 100 inhabitants (FBS, hereafter), *active mobile-broadband* subscriptions per 100 inhabitants (AMS, hereafter), and *Internet users* per 100 inhabitants (IU, hereafter). ICT data on mobile-cellular subscriptions, fixed-broadband subscription, and active mobile-broadband subscriptions generally tell about ICT accessibility and adoption with country's society. These three ICT indicators also reflect the state of development of ICT backbone infrastructure enabling unbounded access to new information and communication technologies. The Internet users variable rather demonstrates the usage of different ICT solutions that enhance the use of global Internet network. Hence, the IU indicators show the share of society that is "connected" with the World Wide Web using various channels of access and through this gains access to all information and knowledge, usually at low cost, regardless of their physical location (Cairncross 1999).

[1] For detailed explanation of ICT indicators, see Appendix A.

Using these four ICT indicators allows for general analysis of unveiling areas which countries are forging ahead or falling behind with respect to certain ICT achievements. When interpreting ICT statistics, it should be noted that following relationship as "inhabitants > those who have access > users > subscribers" is true. Usually the number of legal subscribers (legal owners of given technology, which are obliged to pay for it) accounts for the smallest number of people, while the number of users is higher than the number of subscribers, and the number of those who have access to ICT usually exceeds the number of its users (those who simply can use certain technology but not necessarily pay for its usage).[2] Only in case of mobile-cellular subscribers we find this simple relationship as untrue, as in many countries the number of subscribers per 100 inhabitants is higher than 100, which suggests that "inhabitants < subscribers < (potentially) users." Additionally, to demonstrate the process of substitution of "old" technologies offering voice communication by "new" solutions, we use statistical data on *fixed-telephone* subscriptions per 100 inhabitants (FTL—hereafter).

Along with core ICT statistical data showing shifts in access to and use of basic new technological solution, we use several data on ICT prices which allows showing major trends in changing economic affordability of ICT solutions. With this aim we have selected the following indicators: mobile-cellular monthly subscription charge (in USD); fixed-broadband Internet monthly subscription (USD); handset_500MB for prepaid tariffs, price of the plan (in USD); and USB_1GB for postpaid tariffs, price of the plan (in USD).

As already emphasized, the time span on our analysis is set for the period 1990–2017. Of course data on mobile-cellular accessibility and fixed-broadband networks trace back to 1980 in some countries; however, still between 1980 and 1990, the state of development on these technological solutions still has been negligible; thus we claim that this period is of little importance for our analysis. Clearly, regarding different ICT indicators, the availability of well-balanced time series may vary. These differences result not only from difficulties with data collection on country level, but they are determined by the time of emergence and introduction to the national market certain type of technology. In case of mobile-cellular telephony, statistics are available without any breaks in time series, with the only exception of India where MCS data start from 1995. Data on fixed-broadband network availability are generally available since 1998 in examined countries; however still in 1998, data on FBS are reported only for Hong Kong, Japan, South Korea, Singapore, and Taiwan. Fully balanced dataset on FBS starts in 2001. First data on active mobile-broadband subscriptions were available in 2007 and only for three countries, Malaysia, Singapore, and Taiwan; next in 2008, these data were available for one more country, South Korea; and fully balanced time series, from 2011 onward. Finally, ICT statistics unveiling the usage of the World Wide Web—Internet users—are fully available since 1994.

Availability of complete time series on prices of ICT is relatively poor. These data are scattered and time spans for which they are reported vary hugely among

[2] The case of people sharing one household is a good example.

different price indicators. Regarding mobile-cellular monthly subscription, charge data are available between 1990 and 2011, with only few observations during next periods. Data for fixed-broadband Internet monthly subscription, handset_500MB for prepaid tariffs, and USB_1GB for postpaid tariffs ranged between 2005–2017 (with breaks in time series), 2012–2017 (with breaks in time series), and 2012–2017 (with breaks in time series) accordingly. Still, data on ICT prices, despite their incompleteness in many cases, allow capturing general trends in changing ICT affordability by individuals.

5.3 ICT Deployment in Asia-Pacific: Descriptive Evidence

This section below throws light on the general trends detectable in the process of ICT diffusion across selected 12 Asia-Pacific countries, being in the scope of this broad study. We do so to show the reader wide context of rapid advances that Asia-Pacific region is undergoing with respect to financial markets restructuration and, above, development and dynamically growing demand for financial innovations, especially ETF which is the central focus of this book. Our aim is to demonstrate that ETFs diffusion has been facilitated and—to a large extent—preconditioned, by growing availability of sophisticated technological solutions offered by ICT to society.

Fast ICT diffusion has been ostensibly observed for the last two decades, not only in Asian economies, but worldwide. What follows uncovers that the process of ICT spread happens at historically unprecedented pace. It also uncovers specific features of this process, its dynamics and patterns, observed across 12 Asia-Pacific economies, between 1990 and 2017. It also sheds light on changing cross-country inequalities with access to and use of new information and communication technologies.

The preliminary evidence of key trends in ICT deployment in examined Asia-Pacific countries is limited to the period spanning from 1990 to 2017. Before 1990, some data on ICT were available; however during that period, ICT penetration rates were negligible and slowly changing, and time series are incomplete; henceforth we believe that years before year 1990 are of minor importance for this analysis. Table 5.1 summarizes the ICT indicators (fixed telephony, FTL; mobile-cellular telephony subscriptions, MCS; fixed-broadband subscriptions, FBS; active mobile subscriptions, AMS; and Internet users, IU), descriptive statistics, and two classical inequality indices. The time span of analysis starts in 1990 regarding FTL, MCS, and IU indicators (although in 1990 not for all countries statistics were available), in 1998 for FBS, and in 2007 for AMS. Figure 5.2 enriches the evidence and graphically demonstrates ICT diffusion trajectories with regard to examined ICT variables (*averaged values*).

The results provided in Table 5.1 and Fig. 5.2 demonstrate how fast and disruptive changes in access to and use ICT are observed in Asia-Pacific economies during examined time period. If we take a closer look at Fig. 5.2, interesting observations arise.

Table 5.1 Core ICT indicators

ICT indicator	# of obs.	Mean	Min. value	Max. value	Lowest percentile [10%]	Upper percentile [90%]	Gini[a] index	Atkinson[a] index [for $\varepsilon = 0.5$]
FTL_{1990}	12	23.7	0.58	45.7	0.58	43.8	0.42	0.26
FTL_{2000}	12	34.7	3.1	58.9	3.1	57.9	0.34	0.15
FTL_{2010}	12	36.6	2.8	71.1	10.2	62.1	0.33	0.11
FTL_{2017}	12	30.2	1.7	57.9	4.2	57.9	0.38	0.16
MCS_{1990}	11	0.78	0.001	2.3	0.009	1.7	0.52	0.28
MCS_{2000}	12	38.6	0.34	81.8	1.7	81.7	0.43	0.22
MCS_{2010}	12	109.1	61.1	196.3	63.2	145.5	0.16	0.02
MCS_{2017}	12	141.8	87.2	249.1	104.6	176.1	0.14	0.01
FBS_{1998}	5	0.11	0.02	0.26	0.02	0.27	0.44	0.17
FBS_{2000}	8	2.3	0.001	8.2	0.001	8.2	0.64	0.44
FBS_{2010}	12	17.8	0.89	34.7	0.94	30.8	0.36	0.16
FBS_{2017}	12	23.1	1.3	41.5	2.3	35.9	0.31	0.12
AMS_{2007}	3	15.4	0.36	40.6	0.36	40.6	0.57	0.37
AMS_{2010}	10	48.3	3.4	98.5	6.3	96.9	0.38	0.14
AMS_{2017}	12	104.3	25.7	148.2	83.6	134.9	0.14	0.03
IU_{1990}	3	0.21	0.21	0.58	0.02	0.58	0.59	0.41
IU_{2000}	12	24.1	0.52	47.4	0.92	46.8	0.41	0.22
IU_{2010}	12	55.4	7.5	83.7	10.9	80.5	0.26	0.08
IU_{2017}	12	74.0	32.9	95.1	32.9	95.1	0.14	0.02

[a]See Appendix B, Method 2
Summary statistics. Period 1990–2017
Source: Authors' calculations

First, regarding mobile-cellular telephony diffusion pattern, we note that from 1990 to 2017, MCS penetration rates were growing dynamically. Initially, in the early 1990s of the twentieth century, average MCS penetration rates increased from 0.78[3] per 100 inhab. in 1990 to 5.3 per 100 inhab. in 1995; hence the growth of access to this form of ICT was changing spasmodically. However, since 1996 we observe abrupt takeoff, and the diffusion path enters exponential growth phase, so that in 2000 the average MCS penetration rate grew until 41.2 per 100 inhab. This dynamic diffusion resulted in achieving average MCS penetration rate slightly above 140.0 per 100 inhab. in 2017. Boosting accessibility of mobile-cellular telephony resulted in another interesting process of gradually proceeding technological substitution between "old" and "new" technology (for theoretical fundamentals see Fisher and Pry 1972; Marchetti and Nakicenovic 1980; Nakicenovic 1987). This switching from fixed telephony to mobile-cellular telephony is apparent, as since 2010 slightly downward trend in average FTL penetration rate is detectable.[4] Note

[3]Authors' calculations.

[4]More empirical evidence on technological substitution may be traced in works of, inter alia,

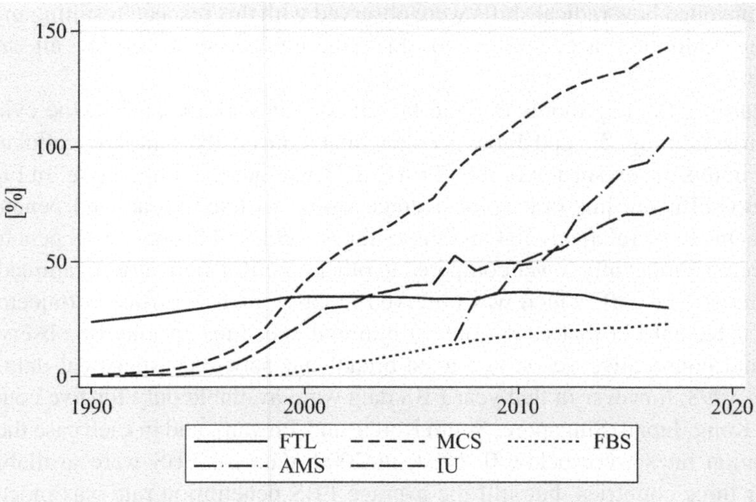

Source: Authors` elaboration

Fig. 5.2 Core ICT indicators. Changes in average values. Period 1990–2017

that in 2010, average MCS penetration rate reached 110 per 100 inhab., hence the fixed to mobile substitution is evidence. In total between 1990 and 2017, the average FTL penetration rate changed from 23.7 per 100 inhab. in 1990, reaching the peak in 2010, 36.7 per 100 inhab., until 30.2 per 100 inhab. in 2017. Calculation summarized in Table 5.1 in brief shows how fast mobile-cellular telephony penetration rates were changing since 1990 onward. In 1990, the average MCS penetration rate was 0.78 per 100 inhab., and in 7 out of 12 examined countries, the MCS penetration rate was below 0. In 1990 the best performing country was Hong Kong with MCS penetration rate slightly above 2.3. per 100 inhab. During the next 20 years, mobile-cellular telephony boosted changing landscape radically. In 2010, the average MCS penetration rate was 109.1 per 100 inhab., while the worst-performing economy was India with MCS = 61.1 per 100 inhab. In 2010 the three top MCS performers were Hong Kong, Singapore, and Taiwan edging with Malaysia, where MCS penetration rates are 196.3 per 100 inhab., 145.5 per 100 inhab., and 120.5 per 100 inhab. Accordingly. Consecutive 7 years resulted continuously increasing accessibility to mobile-cellular telephony, so that in 2017 the average MCS penetration rate achieved 141.8 per 100 inhab., while in Hong Kong the MCS = 249 per 100 inhab. was reported (sic!). In another three countries—Thailand, Indonesia, and Singapore—the MCS penetration rate exceeded the group average. This general overview on changes in deployment to mobile-cellular tele-

Gruber (2001), Sung and Lee (2002), Hamilton (2003), Rodini et al. (2003 and 2004), Banerjee and Ros (2004), Garbacz and Thompson (2005 and 2007), Gunasekaran and Harmantzis (2007), Narayana (2010), Briglauer et al. (2011), Grzybowski (2011), Ward and Zheng (2012), Srinuan et al. (2012), Wulf et al. (2013), Lechman (2016), and Lechman (2017a, b).

phony unveiled how radical shifts were observed with this respect, resulting in guaranteeing unlimited accessibility to this communication form for all society members.

Regarding the key trends in fixed-broadband network expansion, the evidence summarized in Fig. 5.2 and Table 5.1 show that, conversely to mobile-cellular telephony, in this the expansion of this form of ICT was not that impressive. In Fig. 5.2 that FBS diffusion line drawn for average values of fixed-broadband penetration rates seems to be relatively flat and thus suggest achieved average FBS penetration rates were significantly lower compared to other core ICT indicators examined. The characteristic takeoff, which was observed in case of MCS diffusion trajectory, is barely detectable in that case—only a minimal speeding up may be observed in 2000 and consecutive years. For fixed-broadband networks, statistical data trace back to 1998; however in that year FBS data were available only for five countries (Hong Kong, Japan, Singapore, South Korea, and Taiwan), and in each case the FBS penetration rates were below 0. Next, in 2000, data for FBS were available for another three countries, but still the average FBS penetration rate was indecently low—2.3 per 100 inhab. In 2000, the best performing country in this respect was South Korea with FBS penetration rate reaching 8.2 per 100 inhab. South Korea was followed by Hong Kong with FBS = 6.6 per 100 inhab., while in the remaining countries, the FBS penetration rates were below or close to 1 per 100 inhab. The situation changed in 2010, when average FBS penetration rate reached 17.8 per 100 inhab., and the highest results was reported again for South Korea—FBS = 34.7 per 100 inhab. In 2010, still we identify four countries which significantly lag behind; these were India, Indonesia, Thailand, and Malaysia, where FBS penetration rates were 0.89 per 100 inhab., 0.94 per 100 inhab., 4.8 per 100 inhab., and 7.4 per 100 inhab., respectively. During the next 7 years, the state of fixed-broadband development slightly improved, as average FBS penetration rate reached 23.1 per 100 inhab. In 2017 we observe several countries that outstand the examined group of economies—see, for instance, South Korea (FBS = 41.6 per 100 inhab.), Hong Kong (FBS = 35.9 per 100 inhab.), and New Zealand (FBS = 33.6 per 100 inhab.). On the other hand, others heavily lag behind—India (FBS = 1.3 per 100 inhab.) or Indonesia (FBS = 2.3 per 100 inhab.) where state of development of fixed-broadband network, in 2017, was still indecently low and these two countries were still deprived from access to fixed networks offering fast Internet connection. The latter is mainly a negative consequence of poorly developed hard, backbone infrastructure, limited financial resources, and—at least to some extent—unfavorable geographical conditions impeding fixed networks expansion. In another two countries, Malaysia and Thailand, FBS penetration rates also were relatively low—8.5 per 100 inhab. and 11.8 per 100 inhab. accordingly, placing these countries in relatively weak position in terms of broad access to high-speed Internet network.

Despite the fact that until 2017 the fixed-broadband penetration rates did not increase that enormously as we might have expected, since 2007 across examined 12 Asia-Pacific countries, tremendous growth of active mobile-broadband technology is observed. This novel technological solution enabling high-speed Internet connections seems to be an ideal substitute for fixed-broadband network which due to various limitations spread at relatively slow pace compared to other ICT. As we have seen in case of fixed broadband in some of analyzed economies, access to this type of network was highly limited because of multiple country-specific barriers (unfavorable location, poorly developed infrastructure, or even permanent power supply problems). The latter, undoubtedly, fostered pervasive expansion of alternative solution, in our case—mobile (wireless) technology that may be easily installed and adopted for use even in unfavorable environments.

Taking a closer look at Fig. 5.2 unveiling diffusion line for average active mobile-broadband penetration rates in 12 Asia-Pacific countries, it is clearly observable that since 2007 onward, access to mobile-broadband solutions boosted enormously. In the beginning of analyzed period, in 2007, the average AMS penetration rate was 15.4 per 100 inhab.; however in here it should be noted that respective data were available for only three countries, Malaysia, Singapore, and Taiwan where AMS penetration rates were 0.36 per 100 inhab., 40.6 per 100 inhab., and 5.4 per 100 inhab.; hence extraordinarily high differences in this respect are unveiled. Next, in 2010, data on AMS penetration rates were available for ten countries, except India and Thailand, while the average AMS grew up to 48.3 per 100 inhab.; however still huge cross-country disparities were observed—not, for instance, that in China the AMS penetration rate was barely higher than 3 per 100 inhab., while in Singapore, 98.5 per 100 inhab. (sic!). During next 7 years, between 2010 and 2017, the landscape changed significantly, as average AMS penetration rate has almost doubled, achieving 104.3 per 100 inhab. An interesting observation regarding the specific shape of AMS diffusion patterns in that we note direct takeoff into exponential growth; in fact, no early diffusion phase, during which technology spreads slowly, is noted. Such early (initial) diffusion stages are easily recognized in case of mobile-cellular telephony and fixed-broadband networks, where initially the process of diffusion proceeds spasmodically, and then suddenly the curve takes off and ICT starts diffusing at exponential rates. In case of active mobile-broadband technology, this early diffusion phase has been simply omitted. The steepness of the AMS curve, graphically displaying changes in average AMS penetration rate, speaks for itself—during the period 2007–2017, access to mobile-broadband solutions grew even faster compared to mobile-cellular telephony. In fact, since 2007 onward, when mobile-broadband technology started to conquer national telecommunication markets, we observe significant slowdown in the process of fixed-broadband networks expansion. A kind of, although not direct, technological substitution is unveiled, analogously to what was demonstrated in case of mobile-cellular and fixed telephony. The emergence of alternative, favorable technological solution offering relatively cheap, easily installable, and unbounded access to information and knowledge will inevitably lead to the emergence of the process of technological substitution.

The expansion and growing adoption of both fixed-, and mobile-broadband networks resulted in increasing usage of Internet network. Data on Internet users, which trace back to 1990, show average "response" in usage to boosting access of ICT. Not surprisingly, in the beginning of the period, in 1990 the average Internet users penetration rate was just 0.21 per 100 inhab., and please note that in that year relevant data were available exclusively for three countries: Australia, Japan, and

South Korea. Looking at Fig. 5.2, we observe that for the next year, the IU diffusion trajectory was flat suggesting very slow changes in growing usage of Internet networks by individuals. However in the late 1990s of the twentieth century, the IU diffusion curve elevates suggesting the speedup in terms of Internet usage. Next, in 2000, the average IU penetration rate was 24.1 per 100 inhab., and during the next 10 years, it has more than doubled reaching average IU penetration rate 55.4 per 100 inhab. Finally, in 2017, the average IU penetration rate resulted to achieve 74.0 per 100 inhab., which may be interpreted that barely ¾ of society uses Internet network through various ICT devices.

Regarding the year 2017, data on average AMS and IU penetration rates may surprise, as hypothetically average IU shall be higher than average AMS penetration rate. Number of legal subscribers should, in fact, exceed number of users. However, in that case of observed reverse tendency and for each individual country, access to mobile broadband outdistances usage of Internet network. This may suggest that across examined countries, access to mobile broadband is still a kind of luxury good and is affordable only for a relatively small part of society relatively materially better off, while each entity (individual or company) legally owns more than one subscription of active mobile broadband. On the other hand, this part of society that is materially deprived and may not afford subscribing active mobile broadband remains excluded from access to Internet network. Evidently, higher AMS subscription rates do not directly convent into growing Internet usage among individuals—see Fig. 5.3 to compare (examples of India, Indonesia, China, and Thailand are particularly glaring).

Rapid advances in access to and use of ICT were accompanied by falling cross-country inequalities with this regard. Figure 5.4 graphically explains intime evolution in distribution of fixed telephony, mobile-cellular telephony, fixed broadband, mobile broadband, and Internet users in 12 Asia-Pacific countries between 1990 and 2017, while Fig. 5.5 displays Lorenz curves for analogous ICT variables report on changes in cross-country inequalities.

This graphical evidence is enriched by Gini and Atkinson coefficients summarized in Table 5.1. In case of mobile-cellular telephony, we have drawn density lines for 4 years: 1996, 2000, 2010, and 2017 (see Fig. 5.4). In 1990 the MCS density line resulted to be highly leptokurtic, while for consecutive time periods, these density lines become gradually more platykurtic. Such evolution supports our previously discussed evidence on fast-changing MCS penetration rates in countries in scope of this research. Highly unequal distribution in 1990 is confirmed by relatively high values of both Gini and Atkinson coefficients (see in Table 5.1—0.52 and 0.28 accordingly). However, this unequal distribution has been radically changed into more equal during consecutive years. In 2017, the respective Lorenz curve is close to 45° line, while the Gini and Atkinson coefficients fell until 0.14 and 0.01, respectively. Analogous tendencies in changes in distribution and falling cross-national disparities are easily observable with regard to the remaining three ICT indicators. Changes in FBS distribution lines and IU distribution lines resemble the dynamics of the process observed for mobile-cellular telephony. In all cases, initially highly leptokurtic distribution became highly platykurtic—especially in case of fixed-

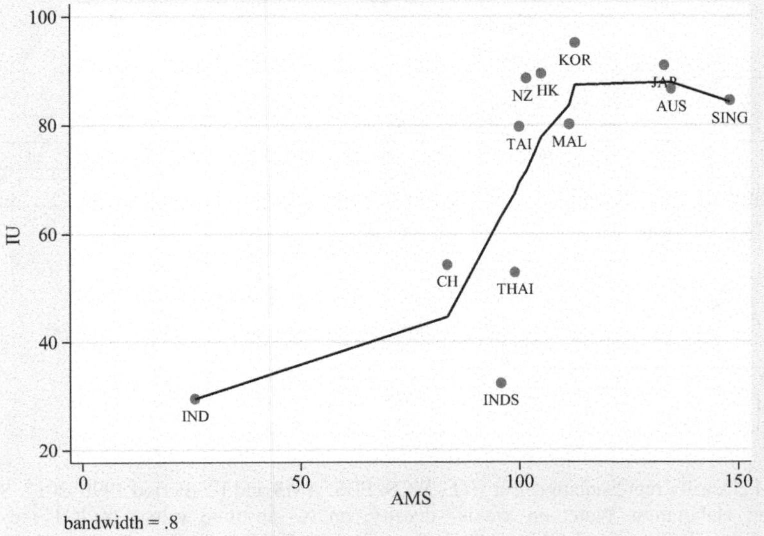

Source: Authors` elaboration. Note: for India, New Zealand and Taiwan IU data are for 2016; AUS – Australia; CH – China; HK – Hong Kong; IND – India; INDS – Indonesia; JAP – Japan; KOR – South Korea; MAL – Malaysia; NZ – New Zealand; SING – Singapore; TAI – Taiwan; THAI – Thailand; Locally weighted polynomial smoother applied[1].

Fig. 5.3 Internet users versus active-mobile broadband penetration rates. Year 2017. See Appendix B, Method 4

broadband networks. Reported in Table 5.1 values of Gini and Atkinson coefficients along with respective Lorenz curves displayed in Fig. 5.5 ostensibly demonstrate radical drops in cross-country inequalities. The situation in case of active mobile-broadband penetration rates slightly differs, especially when looking at distribution line drawn for 2007, 2010, and 2017. In here we have moved from highly platykurtic distribution in 2010 to perfectly leptokurtic in 2017; however still significant falls in cross-country relative inequalities are demonstrated—see inequalities indices and Lorenz curves.

5.4 ICT Diffusion Patterns: Country-Wise Evidence

In Sect. 5.3, we have briefly discussed a general overview of the process of ICT diffusion across selected 12 Asia-Pacific countries, demonstrated between 1990 and 2017. In each of examined economies, we have observed rapidly growing ICT penetration rates, which have radically shifted societies' access to and use of new technological solutions enabling fast and unlimited communication, information, and knowledge sharing. The dynamics of ICT diffusion was unprecedentedly high; relatively highest average diffusion rate could be noticed in case of mobile-cellular

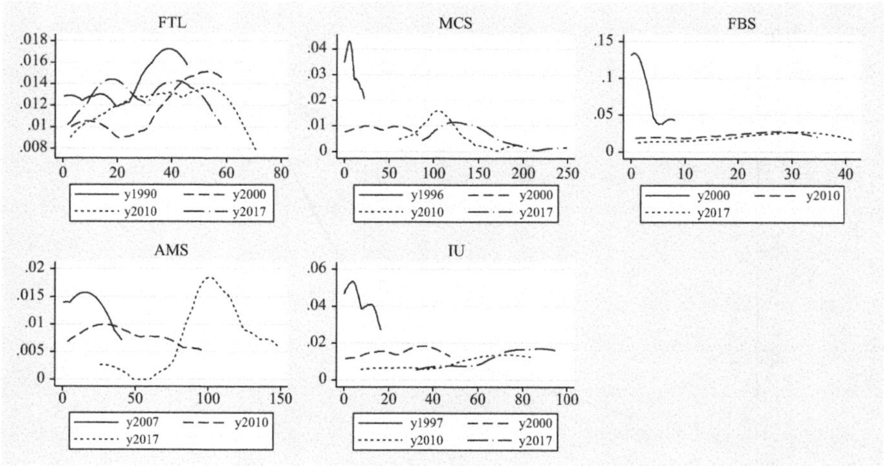

Fig. 5.4 Density representations for FTL, MCS, FBS, AMS and IU. Period 1990–2017. Source: Authors` elaboration. Note: on Y-axis—density; on X—absolute values of ICT indicators; kernel=epanechnikov; bandwidth—default. See Appendix B, Method 1

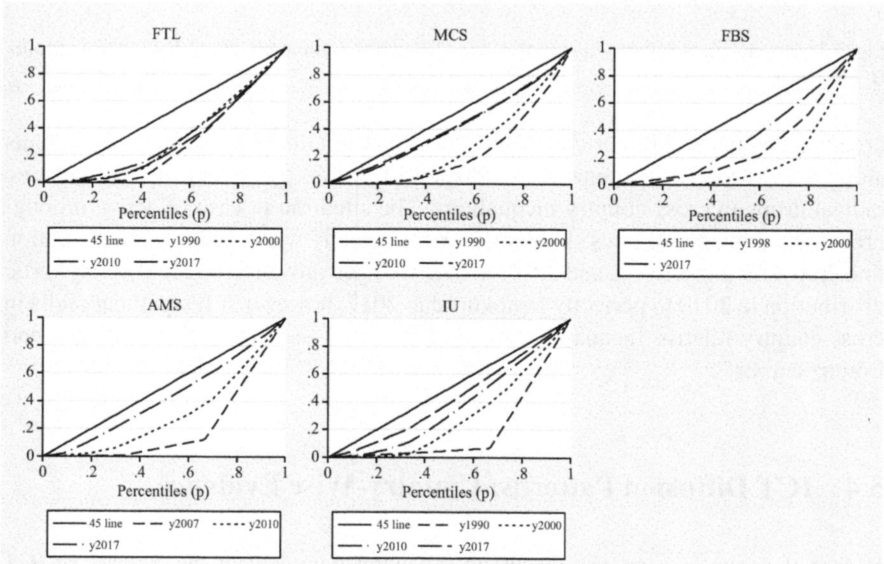

Fig. 5.5 Lorenz curves for FTL, MCS, FBS, AMS and IU. Period 1990–2017. See Appendix B, Method 2

telephony and mobile-broadband networks. Additionally, a visible drop in cross-country relative technological inequalities was reported. This preliminary evidence summarized in Sect. 5.3, in fact, suggests that new information and communication technologies spread society-wide regardless of country's per capita income, institutional or legal frameworks, social norms, and attitudes. Moreover, we have noticed that ICT spread even in countries suffering from infrastructural constrains and located in unfavorable geographical environment. All these observations may even lead to more general conclusion that ICT diffusion process is strongly endogenously driven, enhanced by emerging network effects that boost demand, at least to some extent, regardless of the costs of access to and use of those technologies. Faced with the challenge of identifying the unique features of the process of information and communication technologies diffusion, in what follows we take a closer look at the process in each of examined countries individually. To this aim, we deliberately disaggregate our initial sample and develop country-specific ICT diffusion profiles in regard to mobile-cellular telephony and fixed telephony and fixed-broadband and active mobile-broadband networks along with Internet users. The time span of analysis is analogous as in the previous Sect. 5.3. To provide the in-depth insight into each country's changing ICT deployment, in case of each considered core ICT indicator, we consider for the analysis the longest available time series in respect to certain ICT indicators. The latter mean that for different countries and ICT indicators, the span of analysis may differ, as ICT data availability varies in terms of length of completeness. By drawing ICT profiles for individual economies, we get a clear picture of how new technologies are deployed; we unveil individual characteristics of this process, and also this enables us to identify some similarities and/or regularities if exist.

The first part of this section is entirely dedicated to presenting the results of our analysis of mobile-cellular telephony trajectories in 12 Asia-Pacific countries, between 1990 and 2017. Figure 5.6 display country-specific MCS diffusion paths, while Table 5.2 summarizes the results of estimated logistic growth models[5] that allow explaining the specific characteristics of the process in each country being in scope of this study. In Fig. 5.6, in each picture that visualizes the process of MCS spread, purposely, we have added diffusion line showing changes in adoption of fixed telephony; this allows us enriching the picture by demonstrating the unique process of technological substitution (in this case—fixed telephony to cellular-mobile telephony substitution).

First considering exclusively the evidence on mobile-cellular telephony diffusion, between 1990 and 2017, in examined 12 Asia-Pacific countries, the first and impressive observation is that in all economies the shift in adoption of this telecommunication mode was disruptive. At the beginning of analyzed period, all countries were equally "ICT poor" and suffered from access to this form of communication. Note that, in 1990, the state of fixed-telephony adoption was not impressive—countries like China, India, and Indonesia were totally deprived from access to fixed telephony. However, during next 27 years, rapid expansion of telecommunication companies, offering access to mobile-telephony, enhanced its broad adoption by all society members.

[5] See Appendix B, Method 3.

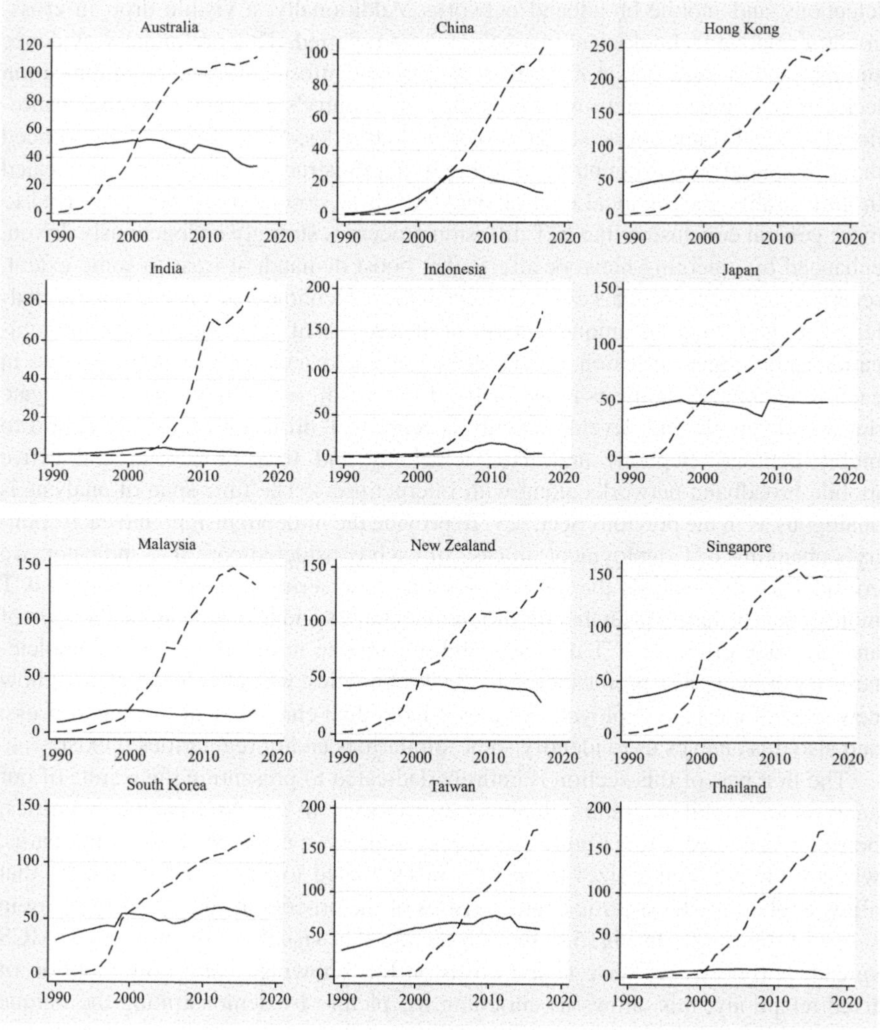

Fig. 5.6 MCS and FTL diffusion patterns. Period 1990–2017

Each country, being in scope, until 2017, has reached the level of MCS saturation exceeding 100% (100 per 100 inhab.), while in Hong Kong, Indonesia, and Thailand, these shifts in mobile-telephony penetration rates were the most impressive. In 2017, the three "bottom" countries were India, China, and Australia achieving 87.3 per 100 inhab., 104.6 per inhab., and 112.7 per 100 inhab. accordingly.

Logistic growth estimates for mobile-cellular telephony summarized in Table 5.2 unveil specific characteristics of the diffusion process in each individual country. Notably, with only one exception of India, the estimated κ parameters explaining upper ceiling (saturation, growth limit) exceed 100 per 100 inhab., suggesting that the

Table 5.2 MCS logistic growth estimates

Country	κ (ceiling/upper asymptote)	*Tm* (midpoint)	α (rate of diffusion)	Δt (specific duration)	R^2 of the model	Root MSE	# of obs.
Australia	110.6 [1.6]	2000.8 [0.14]	0.35 [0.01]	12.1	0.99	2.34	28
China	117.8 [3.7]	2008.9 [0.24]	0.26 [0.01]	15.4	0.99	1.86	28
Hong Kong	306.5 [21.3]	2004.6 [0.45]	0.18 [0.02]	19.2	0.99	7.4	28
India	81.1 [2.6]	2008.7 [0.18]	0.62 [0.06]	7.1	0.99	3.53	23
Indonesia	172.9 [8.4]	2010.1 [0.34]	0.35 [0.03]	11.9	0.99	5.29	28
Japan	*354.5* *[233.1]*	*1999.4* *[6.1]*	0.06 [0.04]	n.a.	0.98	4.86	28
Malaysia	149.2 [4.6]	2005.4 [0.23]	0.32 [0.02]	10.1	0.99	4.69	28
New Zealand	127.6 [6.4]	2001.9 [0.37]	0.28 [0.03]	13.4	0.98	5.41	28
Singapore	165.7 [8.6]	2001.9 [0.38]	0.27 [0.03]	14.5	0.98	6.69	28
South Korea	143.7 [14.1]	2000.5 [0.73]	0.21 [0.03]	14.7	0.98	6.2	28
Taiwan	115.9 [3.9]	1999.3 [0.18]	1.05 [018]	4.2	0.97	8.07	28
Thailand	197.3 [11.8]	2008.8 [0.48]	0.25 [0.02]	15.6	0.99	5.61	28

Period 1990–2017
Source: Authors' estimates. Note—four-parameter logistic function applied (see Appendix B, Method 3); SE, below coefficients; constant included, not reported; estimation method, NLS; in italics, results statistically insignificant.

countries in question have achieved full saturation with mobile-cellular telephony. The latter might speak in support of the hypothesis that mobile-cellular telephony became broadly available to society members in examined 12 Asia-Pacific countries. The highest values of κ are reported for Hong Kong, κ=306.5; Thailand, κ=197.3; and Indonesia, κ=172.9. These three best performing countries are followed by Singapore with κ = 165.7 and Malaysia with κ = 149.2. For the remaining countries, κ parameter is slightly lower but still demonstrating full society's saturation with this form of ICT. Taking into account another estimated parameter, *Tm* (midpoint), indicating the specific time period (in here, year) when the process of diffusion is half-completed (the countries have reached 0.5κ), we see that it ranges from 1998 in Taiwan to 2010 in Indonesia. The latter means that during this 12-year period, all analyzed countries have reached at least 50% of expected (modeled) saturation with mobile-cellular telephony. Economies which passed the earliest this specific inflection point (midpoint) are Taiwan (1998) and Australia and South Korea (both in 2000). In contrast, the midpoint was reached much latter in Indonesia, in 2010, and China, India, and Thailand—in 2008. Another estimated parameter—see Table 5.2—is specific duration Δt, which explains the time needed to pass from 10 to 90% of modeled saturation. According to our country-specific estimates, these values differ extensively among countries. The lowest estimated specific duration is reported for Taiwan, $\Delta t = 4.2$ years, and for India, $\Delta t = 7.1$ years. These relatively low values of specific duration are directly related to the intrinsic growth rate, α, that shows the speed of intime diffusion process. In case of these two countries, the specific α for Taiwan was 1.05, suggesting 105% per annum intrinsic growth rate of MCS diffusion, while for India, 0.62, hence intrinsic growth rate of 62% per annum. For the remaining ten countries, the estimated specific duration was longer than 10 years, which was a direct consequence of significantly lower estimated rates of diffusion. The lowest estimated α is demonstrated for Hong Kong ($\alpha = 0.18$), Thailand ($\alpha = 0.25$), and China ($\alpha = 0.26$). In effect, in these economies, the highest values of Δt are noted for Hong Kong ($\Delta t = 19.2$ years) and then China and Thailand—slightly more than 15 years.

Taking a closer look at country-wise MCS diffusion curves that graphically approximate mobile-cellular telephony development patterns (see Fig. 5.6), the first striking observation is impressive similarity of MCS diffusion lines among countries. Although developed MCS diffusion trajectories naturally differ, they all unveil certain regularities in shape. In each case the three characteristics of diffusion stages are identifiable: early (initial) phase during which the pace of diffusion is usually low, the specific sudden takeoff that precedes entering the exponential growth phase when the process of diffusion proceeds at high rate, and finally the saturation (stabilization) phase when the telecommunication market approaches full saturation with given technology and during which the process of diffusion slows down. Obviously, the length of consecutive diffusion stages varies among countries, which is directly conditioned by the pace at which ICT is assimilated. In case of our countries studied, the longest early diffusion stage is observed with respect to Indonesia, Taiwan, and Thailand, where it took almost 10 years to take off along diffusion trajectory, while the relatively short, in Australia, Hong Kong, Japan, Singapore, and South Korea, where countries shortly after the mobile-cellular telephony was introduced to the market entered exponential growth rate.

As already noticed in Sect. 5.3, in examined 12 Asia-Pacific countries, rapidly boosting demand for mobile-cellular telephony gave rise to the emergence of the technological substitution process. Plotted fixed-telephony diffusion lines for each individual country show that in all cases, except Hong Kong, accelerating deployment of mobile telephony caused drop in fixed-telephony usage. This is especially visible in China, New Zealand, Singapore, and Taiwan. Evidently, briskly expanding new communication technology "immediately" became the more favorable alternative compared to traditional telephony. In countries like India, Indonesia, and Thailand, and—to some extent—Malaysia, the process of switching from fixed to mobile telephony is illusive, as in these countries the state of development of fixed telephony was negligible in and before 1990 and remained as such until 2017.

Table 5.3 FBS logistic growth estimates

Country	κ (ceiling/upper asymptote)	*Tm* (midpoint)	α (rate of diffusion)	Δ*t* (specific duration)	R^2 of the model	Root MSE	# of obs.
Australia	29.1 [3.2]	2005.4 [0.43]	0.71 [0.19]	5.1	0.96	67.7	16
China	Not applicable—misspecification returned						
Hong Kong[a]	69.1 [25.1]	1998.3 [2.6]	0.25 [0.05]	10.1	0.98	61.6	20
India	1.34 [0.04]	2009.0 [0.14]	0.62 [0.05]	6.8	0.99	0.04	17
Indonesia	*4.6* *[3.3]*	*2016.2* *[6.4]*	0.19 [0.09]	13.7	0.97	0.13	18
Japan	37.8 [3.1]	2003.3 [0.47]	0.33 [0.04]	9.2	0.99	1.05	20
Malaysia	9.70 [0.72]	2007.8 [0.34]	0.59 [0.11]	7.4	0.97	0.65	17
New Zealand	34.5 [2.3]	2006.6 [0.31]	0.46 [0.06]	7.9	0.98	1.49	18
Singapore	28.9 [1.4]	2004.3 [0.25]	0.44 [0.04]	9.1	0.99	0.91	20
South Korea	Not applicable—misspecification returned						
Taiwan	34.1 [8.3]	2002.1 [1.4]	0.37 [0.17]	8.3	0.94	2.42	20
Thailand	20.6 [5.7]	2013.8 [2.01]	0.19 [0.05]	13.3	0.99	0.35	16

Period 1998–2017
Source: Authors' estimates. Note—four-parameter logistic function applied (see Appendix B, Method 3); SE, below coefficients; constant included, not reported; estimation method, NLS; in italics, results statistically insignificant; [a]overestimates

Analogous evidence however demonstrating changes in access to and use of Internet network is presented and discussed below. In what follows we address the empirical results explaining the process of growing access to fixed-broadband and mobile-broadband networks enabling usage of the World Wide Web and—what is closely related—the growing share of individuals using Internet network. As in case of mobile-cellular telephony, we present country-wise evidence. Figure 5.7 illustrates fixed-broadband and mobile-broadband penetration rates and Internet users diffusion trajectories. Consecutive Tables 5.3, 5.4 and 5.5 summarize the results of logistic growth estimates for each ICT indicator, respectively.

To visualize fixed-broadband network diffusion paths, we use data tracing back to 1998—before that year, data on this ICT indicator are unavailable or state of deployment of such types of networks was close to zero. Statistics for active mobile-broadband penetration rates are available since 2007 onward, while data explaining changes in share of population using Internet (IU) trace back to 1990. Before 1998, individual could access Internet network using fixed-narrowband (low-speed con-

Table 5.4 AMS logistic growth estimates

Country	κ (ceiling/upper asymptote)	Tm (midpoint)	α (rate of diffusion)	Δt (specific duration)	R^2 of the model	Root MSE	# of obs.
Australia	Not applicable—misspecification returned						
China	108.5 [16.7]	2014.8 [0.44]	0.59 [0.11]	6.7	0.99	2.46	9
Hong Kong	75.1 [3.67]	2011.5 [0.11]	1.47 [0.20]	2.8	0.99	2.61	9
India	66.5 [17.9]	2017.7 [0.68]	0.68 [0.07]	7.1	0.99	0.24	7
Indonesia	Not applicable—misspecification returned						
Japan	*149.2* *[129.7]*	*2008.1* *[4.08]*	0.35 [0.15]	n.a.	0.99	1.79	9
Malaysia	112.6 [17.13]	2013.6 [0.44]	0.82 [0.26]	5.4	0.96	9.00	11
New Zealand	72.03 [19.7]	2012.2 [0.58]	1.01 [0.52]	3.3	0.95	7.04	8
Singapore	120.5 [12.9]	2009.8 [0.31]	0.79 [0.15]	7.5	0.98	5.03	11
South Korea	Not applicable—misspecification returned						
Taiwan	Not applicable—misspecification returned						
Thailand	100.4 [9.13]	2012.8 [0.16]	1.55 [0.34]	2.4	0.99	4.57	7

Period 2007–2017
Source: Authors' estimates. Note—four-parameter logistic function applied (see Appendix B, Method 3); SE, below coefficients; constant included, not reported; estimation method, NLS; in italics, results statistically insignificant

nection) network; however, this technological solution has never become widely available. Once fixed broadband (fast-speed connection) emerged, societies immediately switched from analog forms of accessing Internet to "fiber-optic" high-speed connections. Fixed-broadband networks are far more advantageous technological solution compared to fixed narrowband; in 2017, still this type of ICT was a kind of "luxury" good not unboundedly available society-wide. These restrictions in access reported in some countries are—at least to some extent—caused by poorly developed backbone infrastructure and lack of sufficient financial resources. Moreover, needless to emphasize that access to fixed networks depends on physical location of an agent wishing to use this network. All these obstacles usually constitute important impediments in broad expansion of fixed-broadband networks and disable these regions to advance technologically and then economically. However, new wireless (mobile)-broadband technological solution that in 2007 started to expand over telecommunication markets offers favorable and "technically better"—compared to fixed networks—solution offering access to the Internet network regardless of physical location. Mobile-broadband technology can be installed relatively

Table 5.5 IU logistic growth estimates

Country	κ (ceiling/upper asymptote)	*Tm* (midpoint)	α (rate of diffusion)	Δt (specific duration)	R^2 of the model	Root MSE	# of obs.
Australia	94.6 [8.13]	1999.5 [0.64]	0.27 [0.05]	14.7	0.97	5.25	25
China	55.8 [1.11]	2009.1 [0.13]	0.39 [0.02]	11.1	0.99	0.95	25
Hong Kong	93.8 [6.4]	2001.4 [0.48]	0.25 [0.03]	13.2	0.98	3.82	27
India	81.1 [21.2]	2017.8 [1.5]	0.29 [0.02]	15.6	0.99	0.51	25
Indonesia	Not applicable—misspecification returned						
Japan	93.5 [3.1]	2001.7 [0.25]	0.32 [0.03]	11.7	0.99	3.23	28
Malaysia	84.1 [9.1]	2002.3 [0.73]	0.24 [0.04]	13.7	0.97	4.73	26
New Zealand	111.9 [15.2]	1998.2 [1.06]	0.24 [0.04]	13.5	0.98	4.38	25
Singapore	88.8 [5.2]	2000.4 [0.43]	0.28 [0.03]	11.9	0.98	3.57	27
South Korea	88.0 [2.8]	2000.4 [0.23]	0.56 [0.06]	7.2	0.98	4.75	28
Taiwan	81.7 [2.7]	2001.2 [0.23]	0.35 [0.03]	11.1	0.99	2.61	26
Thailand	Not applicable—misspecification returned						

Period 1990–2017

Source: Authors' estimates. Note—four-parameter logistic function applied (see Appendix B, Method 3); SE, below coefficients; constant included, not reported; estimation method, NLS; in italics, results statistically insignificant

fast and cheaply even in infrastructural undeserved areas, providing access to Internet network in remote, rural, and geographically isolated regions. Obviously, introduction to the telecommunication markets of mobile-broadband technologies radically shifted Internet penetration rates empowering individuals and whole societies. Undoubtedly, according to ITU 2018 data, since 2007 mobile-broadband technology has been the most dynamically developing telecommunication market segment, and its average pace of diffusion grew more than 12-fold between 2007 and 2017.

Let us first take a more detailed look at country-specific diffusion trajectories, which visualize the process, with respect to fixed-broadband and mobile-broadband networks (see Fig. 5.7), thus two different technological solutions that enable Internet usage. As claimed before, data on FBS trace back to 1998, while on AMS—to 2007. When analyzing FBS country-specific lines, the first impression is that between 1998 and 2017, the state of deployment of this technology, in 12 analyzed Asia-Pacific countries, remained relatively low compared to mobile cellular and mobile broadband. FBS country-specific diffusion paths' shapes suggest that only a

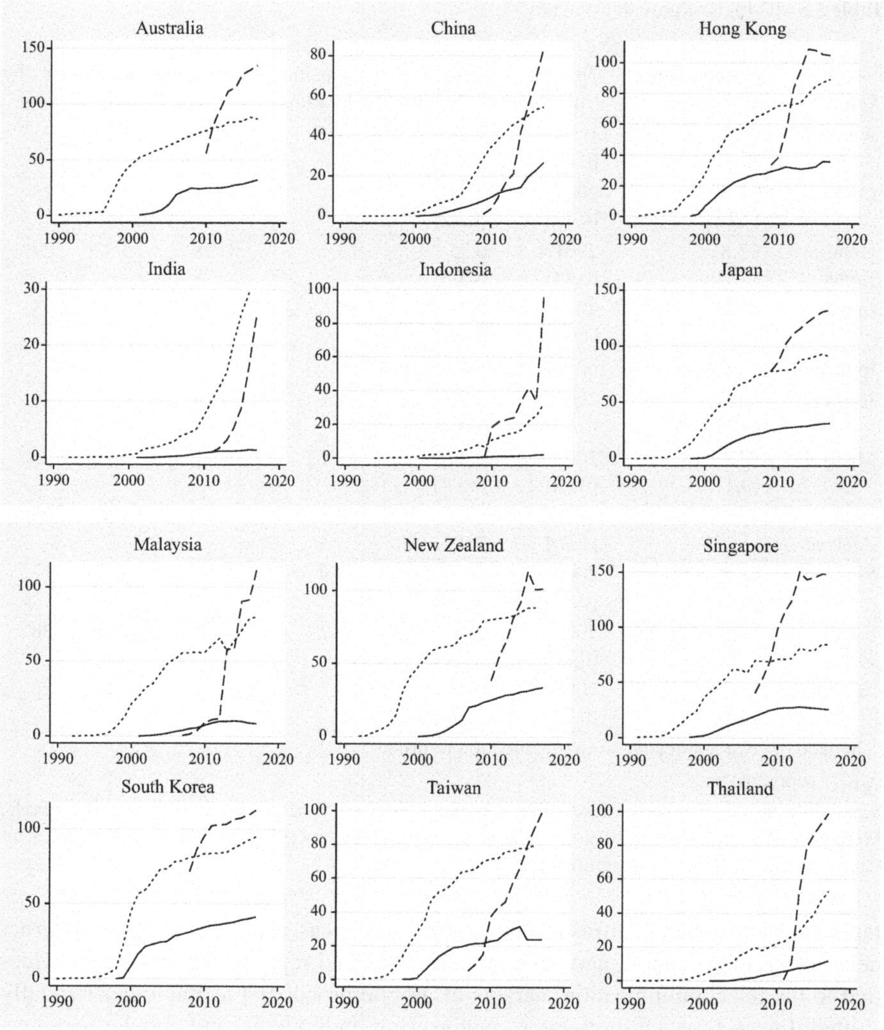

Fig. 5.7 FBS, AMS and IU diffusion patterns. Period 1990–2017

small share of societies, until 2017, gained access to fixed-broadband networks offering high-speed Internet connection.

In case of four economies, namely, India, Indonesia, Malaysia, and Thailand, FBS development paths show that these countries did not even manage to take off and until 2017 were "locked" in early diffusion stage. Note that in India and Indonesia, in 2017, the fixed-broadband penetration rates were still indecently low—1.3 per 100 inhab. and 2.3 per 100 inhab., respectively. In remaining countries, slightly better achievements in terms of installing fixed-broadband networks are reported. In these eight economies, FBS diffusion paths suggest that that takeoff took place, and countries entered exponential growth phase. However, to a large extent, this takeoff is rather illusive. Although a kind of takeoff is detectable—see, for instance, FBS curves for New Zealand or South Korea—in fact, the FBS deployment never proceeded at exponential rate in these countries. Apparently, the process of fixed-broadband diffusion visibly slows down as new advantageous technology—mobile broadband—emerged. Logistic growth estimates for fixed broadband—see Table 5.3—confirm our initial conclusions on relatively poor deployment of this form of ICT. The highest estimated upper ceilings, κ parameters, are reported for Japan ($\kappa = 37.8$), New Zealand, ($\kappa = 34.5$) and Taiwan ($\kappa = 34.1$). Unreliably high estimates of upper asymptote are for Hong Kong ($\kappa = 69.1$), but this should be rather treated as overestimates. The shortest specific duration—Δt—is returned for Australia (Δt = 5.1 years), followed by India (Δt = 6.8 years) and then Malaysia and New Zealand, $\Delta t = 7.4$ years and $\Delta t = 7.9$ years accordingly; however for India these estimates shall not be treated as valid, as between 1998 and 2017, the state of deployment of FBS remained negligible. Obviously, the shortest specific duration in countries mentioned above is a direct consequence of relatively high FBS intrinsic growth rates—the higher for Australia—$\alpha = 0.71$, thus 71% annually.

However, relatively poor deployment of fixed-broadband networks in examined 12 Asia-Pacific countries is not that surpassing after looking at the astonishingly proceeding spread of mobile-broadband networks. Apparently, since 2007 onward, the individual demand for this newly introduced ICT boosted rapidly overwhelming national and global telecommunication markets. Note that between 2007 and 2017, the average mobile-broadband penetration rated shifted from 15.4 per 100 inhab. to 104.3 per 100 inhab. In 2017, in fact, only India heavily lagged behind, as it achieved only AMS = 25.7 per 100 inhab. Other "laggard" countries were China, Indonesia, and Taiwan; however even there the mobile-broadband penetration rates suggested barely full saturation (in China, 83.5 per 100 inhab.; in Indonesia, 95.6 per 100 inhab.; and in Taiwan, 99.9 per inhab.). The three outstanding countries, still in 2017, were Singapore, Australia, and Japan in which mobile-broadband penetration rates significantly exceeded 100 per 100 inhab. Plotted in Fig. 5.7, country-specific mobile-broadband diffusion patterns unveil several attractive features. First, in a great majority of cases, the developed mobile-broadband diffusion curves do not follow standard sigmoid diffusion trajectories, hence in terms of shape that differs from what was observed, for instance, in case of mobile-cellular telephony, to give an example. In fact, in none of analyzed countries, the early (initial) diffusion stage is clearly distinguishable; instead, the AMS diffusion curve "beings" directly in the exponential growth stage. This striking characteristic has not been observed in case of other technologies' spreading process, and this suggests that immediately after introduction of mobile-broadband technology, the effective demand boosted enormously. Another catching observation is that in some cases—see, for instance, China, India, Indonesia, Malaysia, Taiwan, and Thailand—the shape of AMS diffusion pattern does not suggest heading toward the saturation (stabilization) stage, even though the AMS penetration rates in 2017 were very high. Only the shape of AMS diffusion paths in Hong Kong, Japan, New Zealand, Singapore, and South Korea may suggest that national telecommunication markets head toward stabilization phase. Logistic growth estimates—see Table 5.4—summarize results for mobile-broadband expansion for each individual country. Estimated parameters on intrinsic rates of diffusion and specific durations differ significantly from analogous estimates however for mobile-cellular telephony and fixed-broadband networks. In this case we witness unprecedentedly high intrinsic growth rates (α). We notice the fastest increases in the case of Thailand with $\alpha = 1.55$ (155% per annum), Hong Kong with $\alpha = 1.47$ (147% per annum), and New Zealand with $\alpha = 1.01$ (101% per annum), which, by definition, resulted in extremely short specific duration times—2.4 years, 2.8 years, and 3.3 years for Thailand, Hong Kong, and New Zealand accordingly. The "worst" performer in the group was Singapore, with intrinsic growth rate "only" 79% annually and specific duration 7.5 years. When analyzing jointly fixed-broadband and mobile-broadband networks diffusion paths in each country being in scope of this research, another striking observation arises. Consider that in a given country, the process of diffusion of network technology enabling access to Internet might be decomposed into subprocesses. Put differently, we might claim that the diffusion process of network technology is transformable into two-growth "pulses" process, where the first "pulse" is the growth of fixed-broadband network, while the second "pulse" is the growth of mobile-broadband network. In such case the *component logistic curve* is generated, with two clearly distinguishable growth phases—in our case the fixed-broadband growth impulse and mobile-broadband growth impulse. Then the "new" diffusion curve is observed that would be the approximated sum of two discrete wavelets (growth impulses). Such *component logistic curve* may be easily traced in China, Hong Kong, India, Indonesia, Malaysia, New Zealand, Singapore, Taiwan, and Thailand. In each of the countries listed above, we observe that the emergence of mobile-broadband technology actually impedes further expansion of fixed broadband; and the first boosts off rapidly gaining the telecommunication market, while the growth of fixed networks significantly slows down.

The presented above evidence on the process of diffusion of fixed-broadband and mobile-broadband networks allows concluding that accessibility of ICT has been continuously shifting between 1998 and 2017, in all 12 examined Asia-Pacific countries. All analyzed economies made enormous efforts toward broader assimilation of different forms of into societies and changed their telecommunication market structure giving more space for wireless technological solutions. The great merit of this abrupt upswing in ICT adoption is that it has created solid fundaments for broader usage of Internet network, at a time creating new opportunities, particularly for societies living in countries, in the past, suffering from relative technological backwardness. The results of our research on changes of Internet penetration rates (IU) suggest that its development follows the familiar S-shape pattern in each examined country. Except India, Indonesia, and Thailand which in 2017 were still located in high growth phase along IU diffusion curve (see Fig. 5.7), the remaining countries successfully head toward full saturation. The latter suggests that across our 12 Asia-Pacific countries, until 2017 individuals started to use the World Wide Web broadly. Available statistics unequivocally suggest that between 1990 and 2017, Internet penetration rates have grown enormously, and this explosive growth in Internet use fuels optimistic expectations for increasing connectivity, offering prospects for the future to eradicate existing huge cross-country inequalities with this regard. Significant rates of increases in Internet assimilation rates are critical, as newly deployed ICT infrastructure creates new types of communication networks leading to economic and social life improvements. IU logistic growth estimates (see Table 5.5) show that all countries steadily follow diffusion paths, inevitably heading toward full saturation—compare respective κ parameters, which speak in support of the supposition that Internet network became widely available in Asia-Pacific region between 1990 and 2017. Naturally the intrinsic growth rates are far less impressive, compared to those—for instance—for mobile-broadband, but we must bear in mind that before 2007 growing Internet usage was preconditioned by deployment of fixed infrastructure. In effect, returned specific duration times resulted to be relatively long; see, for example, India (15.6 years), Australia (14.7 years), or Hong Kong, Malaysia, and New Zealand with slightly above 13 years.

Finally, for better contextualization and more profound understanding of the process of ICT diffusion in 12 Asia-Pacific countries, between 1990 and 2017, in what follows we briefly discuss changing costs of access and usage of various ICT tools. As widely acknowledged, affordability constitutes one of the major prerequisites to unbounded and broad access to and use of technology by all agents (Ayanso and Lertwachara 2015; Lechman 2016). Here below, we investigate key trends in prices and affordability of main ICT services, and then we confront them with changing ICT penetration rates. More specifically we consider mobile-cellular monthly subscription charge (in USD)[6]; fixed-broadband Internet monthly subscription (USD)[7]; handset for 500 MB, for prepaid price of the plan (in USD)[8]; and USB for 1GB, for postpaid price of the plan[9] (in USD).[10] All data are derived from World Telecommunication/ICT Indicators database (22nd Edition 2018). Additionally, we refer to data on costs of access to and use of ICT delivered in Measuring Information Society Report 2016 and 2017.

Figures 5.8 and 5.9 visualize trends in changing prices of access to basic ICT services. Visibly, drops in mobile-cellular monthly subscription charges are most radical across analyzed countries, with only exception of China where between 1995 and 2002, this cost has doubled. Regarding prices of fixed-broadband subscription charge, in case of two countries (Indonesia and Singapore), radical falls are noted, while for the remaining countries, the average prices demonstrate relative stability between 2005 and 2017. In Australia and New Zealand, we even observe increases in costs of monthly subscription of fixed-broadband network. As for prices of 500 MB and 1GB plans, which basically tell about the monthly cost of access to mobile-broadband network, we discover relatively massive decreases in the beginning of the analyzed period, hence between 2012 and 2014.

[6] Data available between 1990 and 2011, but with gaps.

[7] Data available between 2005 and 2017, but with gaps.

[8] Data available between 2012 and 2017, but with gaps.

[9] For detailed definitions, see Appendix A.

[10] Data available between 2002 and 2017, but with gaps.

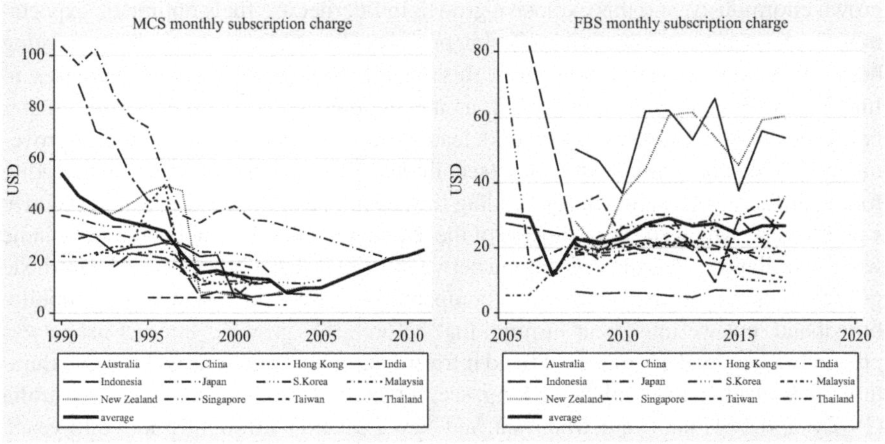

Fig. 5.8 Mobile-cellular telephony and Fixed-broadband monthly subscription charges. Period 1990–2017. For country-wise lines—see Appendix C

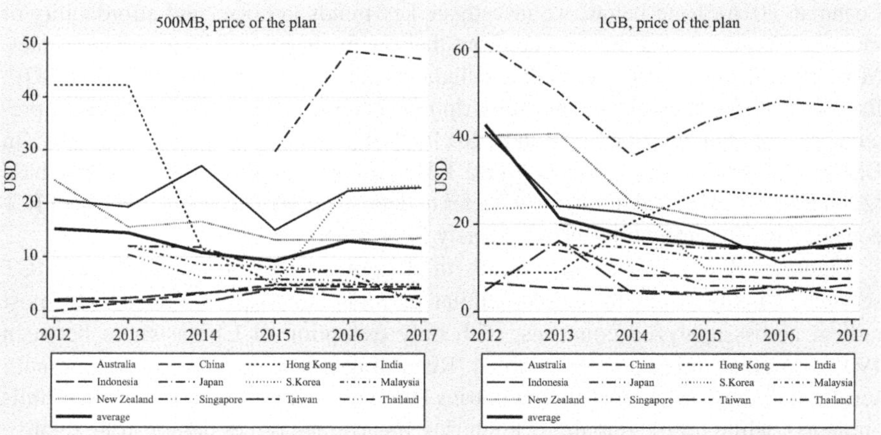

Fig. 5.9 Costs of Internet network access—500 MB and 1GB plans. Period 2012–2017

Since 2014 intime trends stabilize, and no further radical changes (up or downs) are detected. Observed drops in costs of access to basic ICT serviced arguably are claimed as one of the seminal steps forward to provide affordable access to new technological solutions. Making basic ICT services more and more affordable inevitably shall lead to increasing share of society using different types of networks. Recently, among scholars and policy makers emerged a debate on potential "zero-rating" or favorable "price-differentiations" strategies; such business solution on the one hand may significantly enhance growing number of users and more affordable access to ICT for all, but—on the other hand—from purely business point of view is rather a risky solution. Supporters of the "free" access to ICT policy raise arguments that such strategy would allow eradicating digital divides among countries as well as within them. Arguably, low-cost and unlimited access to the Internet, first, encourages demand on ICT devices and further may boost investments in infrastructure and, second, allows societies for better information and knowledge sharing which drives economic development in various aspects. Low cost of access, evidently, eliminates one of the main barriers of ICT access that, especially, materially deprived individuals face to. One of the more advantageous tools to monitor affordability of ICT access are price sub-baskets presented annually in Measuring Information Society Reports issued by the International Telecommunication Union,[11] while the two—mobile-cellular[12] sub-basket and fixed-broadband[13] sub-basket—are the good tools to see changing ICT affordability. For instance, according to ITU (2016) calculations of mobile-cellular sub-basket, in 2015 people in India had to spend 2.11% of their per capita gross national income to buy the basket of standard mobile-cellular services; next, in 2016 (see, ITU 2017) it dropped until 1.81%. Among countries examined, in this respect, Indonesia was the "worst-off economy" as in 2016 a statistical Indonesian had to spend 3.31% of his per capital gross national income[14] to acquire the basket of standard mobile-cellular services, which was far less favorable than in 2015 when it was only 1.80%. Regarding fixed-broadband affordability, also in India and Indonesia, in 2015 people had to spend 4.84 and 10.62% of their per capita GNI accordingly, which especially in case of Indonesia may constitute a significant cost for a household. In 2016, the situation slightly improved for Indonesia as the cost fell until 9.51% of per capita GNI; but in India, it grew up to 5.11%. Apparently, among examined 12 Asia-Pacific countries, in India and Indonesia, the mobile-cellular and fixed-broadband affordability unveiled as relatively low. In other ten countries, the relative costs of buying standard basket of mobile-cellular and fixed-broadband services were low and may not be claimed as real obstacle for broad usage of ICT. In 2016, in all ten countries—with the only exception of South Korea—an individual had to spend less than 1% of his per capita gross national income to buy a basket of standard mobile-cellular services (in South Korea it was 1.24%). In those terms, Singapore

[11] See https://www.itu.int/en/ITU-D/Pages/default.aspx.

[12] "Mobile-cellular sub-basket refers to the price of a standard basket of 30 outgoing calls per month (on-net/off-net to a fixed line and for peak and off-peak times, in predetermined ratios), plus 100 SMS messages. It is calculated as a percentage of a country's average monthly GNI per capita, and also presented in USD and PPP$. The mobile-cellular sub-basket is based on prepaid prices, although postpaid prices are used for countries where prepaid subscriptions make up less than 2 per cent of all mobile-cellular subscriptions" (see Measuring Information Society Report 2016, p.105).

[13] "Fixed-broadband sub-basket refers to the price of a monthly subscription to an entry-level fixed-broadband plan. It is calculated as a percentage of a country's average monthly GNI per capita, and also presented in USD and PPP$. For comparability reasons, the fixed-broadband sub-basket is based on a monthly data usage of (a minimum of) 1 Gigabyte (GB). For plans that limit the monthly amount of data transferred by including data volume caps below 1 GB, the cost for the additional bytes is added to the sub-basket. The minimum speed of a broadband connection is 256 kbit/s" (see Measuring Information Society Report 2016, p.117).

[14] In nominal terms.

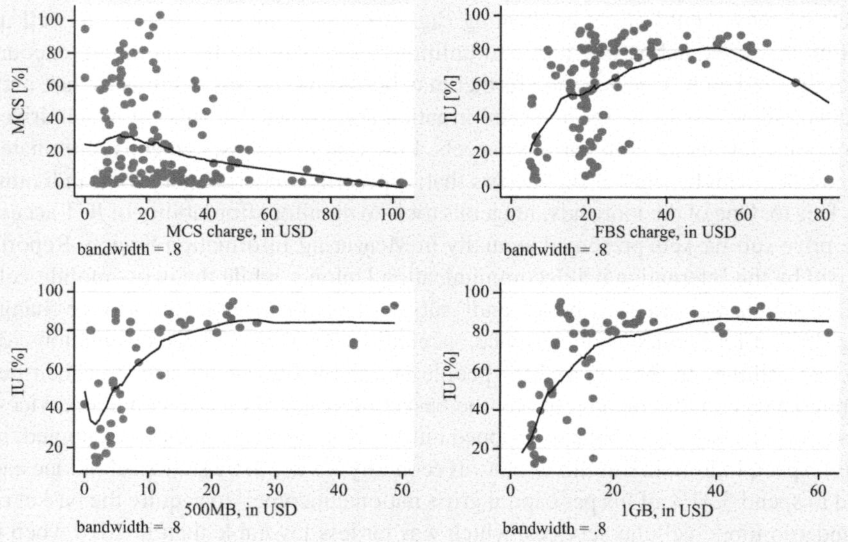

Fig. 5.10 ICT penetration rates versus costs of access and usage. Period 1990–2017

was the best-off country, as only 0.50% of per capita GNI was to spend to acquire a basket of standard fixed-broadband services. Next, in Japan, Hong Kong, or Malaysia, it was 0.62%, 0.63%, and 1.10% accordingly, just to cite few examples.

Another drawing attention observation arises when confronting changes in ICT deployment versus prices of access to basic ICT services. Figure 5.10 graphically displays the statistical relationship between mobile-cellular telephony and Internet penetration rates and prices of access. It would be reasonable to hypothesize on the negative relationship between ICT deployment and usage rates and prices[15]; however in only one case, the examined relationship resulted to be negative—mobile-cellular telephony penetration rates versus mobile-cellular monthly subscription charge. Still, the negative relationship is relatively weak as calculated correlation coefficient is (−0.27), and more detailed examination of the relevant graph shows that high MCS penetration rates are achievable for the mobile-cellular monthly subscription charge ranging between close to zero USD to almost 40 USD.

In other three cases, we observe negative relationships between Internet penetration rates and costs of access to the network. Calculated correlation coefficients are 0.39, 0.56, and 0.59 for the relationship between Internet penetration rates and fixed-broadband monthly subscription charge, 500 MB plan and 1GB plan, respectively. Apparently, in examined Asia-Pacific economies, relatively high (in absolute) terms

[15] See, for instance, works of Gruber and Verboven (2001), Koski and Kretschmer (2005), Grajek (2010), and Baraldi (2012).

cost of access to ICT services did not impede growth of ICT usage. Visibly, demand for ICT services flourished regardless of prices. However, we shall bear in mind the fact that, in analyzed economies, even high prices of access did not worse price affordability to acquire ICT services (see previous paragraphs). Notably, the existence of the positive relationship between increasing ICT penetration rates and costs of access brings to mind the idea on the existence of the unique network effects (network externalities) (Markus 1987; Economides 1996; Geroski 2000; Cabral 2006; Peres et al. 2010; Stoneman 2001), which is observed when pioneering technologies start evading societies and economies. The network effects, in literature, also recognized as the "bandwagon effect" (Farrell and Saloner 1985; Rohlfs 2003) present the unique consumers' behavior associated with prestige-seeking, in here associated with adoption of new technological solutions. The emerging positive externalities phenomenon also suggests that the growing number of users of new technology automatically increases its usefulness and encourages more people to adopt new technological solutions. The network externalities are actually analogous to what we call "imitation effect" in the Bass model (see Bass (1969, 1980)) or the "word-of-mouth" effect (or the "domino effect") (see Geroski 2000; Lee et al. 2010). The network effects demonstrate rather imitative effects, or imitative behavior, unveiled throughout the process of spread of new technologies; the positive feedback arises when society members tend to communicate among themselves, and due to various communication channels, a stock of knowledge on advantages and benefits of new technology is transmitted (see, for instance, in Granovetter 1978; Katz and Shapiro 1985; Cusumano et al. 1992; Jaffe et al. 2005; Bergek et al. 2008; Roper et al. 2013; or Hoy and Polborn 2015). Empirically, the strong network effects are easy to observe when examining price versus demand relationship. In our case, we demonstrate growing demand for ICT usage (demonstrated through Internet users penetration rates) along with the increasing prices of access to ICT services. The latter shows how strong is the network effect and that market agents imitate one another, which effectively boosts demand.

In this chapter we have extensively explored how ICT expanded across 12 Asia-Pacific countries between 1990 and 2017. Evidently, irrespective of cross-country difference in the pace of ICT diffusion or ICT diffusion trajectory shape, we have shown that new information and communication technologies have fast spread across countries in scope, enabling their societies to benefit from new opportunities ICT offer. We have witnessed that Asia-Pacific societies have enormous ability to assimilate new technological solutions, which, undoubtedly, shall have far-reaching socioeconomic implications in the near future. Broad access to ICT gives people an opportunity to "stay connected" and increase their social and economic activity on various fields. The ICT's impact on socioeconomic life may be demonstrated through, for instance, intensification of their market activities. In this line, in what follows, in Chap. 6, we verify if there exists any numerically traceable relationship between ICT deployment and development of financial innovations. Are these two preconditioned?

References

Ayanso, A., & Lertwachara, K. (2015). An analytics approach to exploring the link between ICT development and affordability. *Government Information Quarterly, 32*(4), 389–398.

Baliamoune-Lutz, M. (2003). An analysis of the determinants and effects of ICT diffusion in developing countries. *Information Technology for Development, 10*(3), 151–169.

Banerjee, A., & Ros, A. J. (2004). Patterns in global fixed and mobile telecommunications development: a cluster analysis. *Telecommunications Policy, 28*(2), 107–132.

Baraldi, A. L. (2012). The size of the critical mass as a function of the strength of network externalities: A mobile telephone estimation. *Economics of Innovation and New Technology, 21*(4), 373–396.

Bass, F. M. (1969). A new product growth for model consumer durables. *Management Science, 15*(5), 215–227.

Bass, F. M. (1980). The relationship between diffusion rates, experience curves, and demand elasticities for consumer durable technological innovations. *Journal of Business, 53*, S51–S67.

Bergek, A., Jacobsson, S., & Sandén, B. A. (2008). 'Legitimation' and 'development of positive externalities': Two key processes in the formation phase of technological innovation systems. *Technology Analysis & Strategic Management, 20*(5), 575–592.

Briglauer, W., Schwarz, A., & Zulehner, C. (2011). Is fixed-mobile substitution strong enough to de-regulate fixed voice telephony? Evidence from the Austrian markets. *Journal of Regulatory Economics, 39*(1), 50–67.

Cabral, L. M. (2006). 15. Equilibrium, epidemic and catastrophe: diffusion of innovations with network effects. *New Frontiers in the Economics of Innovation and New Technology: Essays in Honour of Paul A. David*, 427.

Cairncross, F. (1999). The death of distance: how the communication revolution will change our lives. *American Quarterly-Minneapolis, 51*, 160–160.

Comin, D., & Hobijn, B. (2011). Technology diffusion and postwar growth. In *NBER Macroeconomics Annual 2010* (Vol. 25, pp. 209–246). Chicago: University of Chicago Press.

Comin, D., Hobijn, B., & Rovito, E. (2006). *Five facts you need to know about technology diffusion (No. w11928)*. Cambridge, MA: National Bureau of Economic Research.

Cusumano, M. A., Mylonadis, Y., & Rosenbloom, R. S. (1992). Strategic maneuvering and mass-market dynamics: The triumph of VHS over Beta. *Business history review, 66*(01), 51–94.

Economides, N. (1996). The economics of networks. *International Journal of Industrial Organization, 14*(6), 673–699.

Farrell, J., & Saloner, G. (1985). Standardization, compatibility, and innovation. *The Rand Journal of Economics, 16*, 70–83.

Fisher, J. C., & Pry, R. H. (1972). A simple substitution model of technological change. *Technological Forecasting and Social Change, 3*, 75–88.

Garbacz, C., & Thompson, H. G., Jr. (2005). Universal telecommunication service: A world perspective. *Information Economics and Policy, 17*(4), 495–512.

Garbacz, C., & Thompson, H. G., Jr. (2007). Demand for telecommunication services in developing countries. *Telecommunications Policy, 31*(5), 276–289.

Geroski, P. A. (2000). Models of technology diffusion. *Research Policy, 29*(4), 603–625.

Grajek, M. (2010). Estimating network effects and compatibility: Evidence from the Polish mobile market. *Information Economics and Policy, 22*(2), 130–143.

Granovetter, M. (1978). Threshold models of collective behavior. *American Journal of Sociology, 83*, 1420–1443.

Gruber, H. (2001). Competition and innovation: The diffusion of mobile telecommunications in Central and Eastern Europe. *Information Economics and Policy, 13*(1), 19–34.

Gruber, H., & Verboven, F. (2001). The evolution of markets under entry and standards regulation—the case of global mobile telecommunications. *International Journal of Industrial Organization, 19*(7), 1189–1212.

Grzybowski, L. (2011). *Fixed-to-mobile substitution in the European Union*. Working Paper, University of Cape Town, South Africa.

Gunasekaran, V., & Harmantzis, F. C. (2007). Emerging wireless technologies for developing countries. *Technology in Society, 29*(1), 23–42.

Hamilton, J. (2003). Are main lines and mobile phones substitutes or complements? Evidence from Africa. *Telecommunications Policy, 27*(1), 109–133.

Hoy, M., & Polborn, M. K. (2015). The value of technology improvements in games with externalities: A fresh look at offsetting behavior. *Journal of Public Economics, 131*, 12–20.

ITU. (2016). *Measuring Information Society Report 2016*. Geneva: ITU.

ITU. (2017). *Measuring Information Society Report 2017*. Geneva: ITU.

Jaffe, A. B., Newell, R. G., & Stavins, R. N. (2005). A tale of two market failures: Technology and environmental policy. *Ecological Economics, 54*(2), 164–174.

Katz, M. L., & Shapiro, C. (1985). Network externalities, competition, and compatibility. *The American Economic Review, 75*(3), 424–440.

Koski, H., & Kretschmer, T. (2005). Entry, standards and competition: Firm strategies and the diffusion of mobile telephony. *Review of Industrial Organization, 26*(1), 89–113.

Lechman, E. (2016). *ICT Diffusion in Developing Countries*. SPRINGER INTERNATIONAL PU.

Lechman, E. (2017a). *Technological substitution in Asia*. London, Routledge.

Lechman, E. (2017b). *The diffusion of information and communication technologies*. London, Routledge.

Lee, M., Kim, K., & Cho, Y. (2010). A study on the relationship between technology diffusion and new product diffusion. *Technological Forecasting and Social Change, 77*(5), 796–802.

Marchetti, C., & Nakicenovic, N. (1980). *The dynamics of energy systems and the logistic substitution model*. Laxenburg: International Institute for Applied Systems Analysis.

Markus, M. L. (1987). Toward a "critical mass" theory of interactive media universal access, interdependence and diffusion. *Communication Research, 14*(5), 491–511.

Nakicenovic, N. (1987). Technological substitution and long waves in the USA. In *The long-wave debate* (pp. 76–103). Berlin: Springer Berlin Heidelberg.

Narayana, M. R. (2010). Substitutability between mobile and fixed telephones: Evidence and implications for India. *Review of Urban & Regional Development Studies, 22*(1), 1–21.

OECD (2017). *Opportunities and policy challenges of digitalization in Southeast Asia*. OECD Southeast Asia Digital Forum, Sept 2017, Bangkok, Thailand.

Peres, R., Muller, E., & Mahajan, V. (2010). Innovation diffusion and new product growth models: A critical review and research directions. *International Journal of Research in Marketing, 27*(2), 91–106.

Rodini, M., Ward, M. R., & Woroch, G. A. (2003). Going mobile: Substitutability between fixed and mobile access. *Telecommunications Policy, 27*(5), 457–476.

Rohlfs, J. H. (2003). *Bandwagon effects in high-technology industries*. Cambridge, MA: MIT press.

Roper, S., Vahter, P., & Love, J. H. (2013). Externalities of openness in innovation. *Research Policy, 42*(9), 1544–1554.

Sedik, T. A. (2018). *Asia's digital revolution*. Finance and Development IMF.

Srinuan, P., Srinuan, C., & Bohlin, E. (2012). Fixed and mobile broadband substitution in Sweden. *Telecommunications Policy, 36*(3), 237–251.

Stoneman, P. (2001). *The economics of technological diffusion*. Malden, MA: Wiley-Blackwell.

Sung, N., & Lee, Y. H. (2002). Substitution between mobile and fixed telephones in Korea. *Review of Industrial Organization, 20*(4), 367–374.

Ward, M. R., & Zheng, S. (2012). Mobile and fixed substitution for telephone service in China. *Telecommunications Policy, 36*(4), 301–310.

World Telecommunication/ICT Indicators Database 2017 (21st Edition).

World Telecommunication/ICT Indicators Database 2018 (22nd Edition).

Wulf, J., Zelt, S., & Brenner, W. (2013, January). Fixed and mobile broadband substitution in the OECD Countries--A quantitative analysis of competitive effects. In *System Sciences (HICSS), 2013 46th Hawaii International Conference on* (pp. 1454–1463). IEEE.

Chapter 6
New Technologies for Exchange-Traded Funds

6.1 Introductory Notes

In this chapter, we study the role played by the information and communication technologies in the diffusion of exchange-traded funds in the countries of the Asia-Pacific region. We investigate therefore jointly two processes with the potentially profound impact on the local economies, examined separately in the two preceding chapters: development of the ETFs markets and deployment of ICT—both of them were designated as "diffusion," diffusion of the innovative investment funds and diffusion of the new technologies, respectively. In contrast with Chap. 4, in the current part of our analysis, we use exclusively the absolute approach to the evaluation of the ETFs market development (diffusion of ETFs) in order to ensure that our research sample is as comprehensive as possible (utilizing relative approach would mean excluding 6 out of 12 countries); for more details, see Sect. 2.3. For the in-depth analysis of the selected ETFs markets and the results of the analysis conducted using the models of diffusion of innovation, see Chap. 4. Corresponding analysis for the ICT indicators is presented in the Chap. 5. It should be stressed that analysis in the Chap. 4 was based on the monthly data on the turnover of ETFs albeit the analysis in the Chap. 5, due to data availability, focused on the annual evidence. Consequently, we begin the current chapter by "linking" the two previous perspectives and discussing briefly basic evidence on the turnover of ETFs in the annual perspective. The next part of the chapter discusses the evidence on the relationship between ETFs and ICT on the regional level—the conclusions that can be formulated above all with the application of the panel models. Final part covers the results of the country-specific analysis, performed separately for each country.

Analogously to the previous parts of our study, we use data on ETFs and ICT in 12 Asia-Pacific countries, i.e., all in the region in which ETFs were traded for the majority of the analyzed time period. Time period of our analysis in the current chapter is 2004–2016. Annual data on the turnover of ETFs are used, calculated as

A. Marszk et al., *The Emergence of ETFs in Asia-Pacific*,
https://doi.org/10.1007/978-3-030-12752-7_6

the sum of the monthly turnover in a given year in particular country. In case of the ICT indicators, no conversion is necessary as annual data were already utilized and discussed in Chap. 5. Sources of data were provided in the preceding chapters.

It should be emphasized that the topic of linkages between new technologies and the diffusion of ETFs was rarely studied empirically—the scarce evidence presented in Lechman and Marszk (2015) implies that ICT are one of the factors that influence positively the development of ETFs markets in certain countries. We adopt a different approach by analyzing a larger group of countries (more homogeneous—in one region) and focusing on the turnover indicator rather than the asset-based ones. Another important stipulation concerns the direction of the examined relationship as in the current study we analyze exclusively the hypothesized impact of the adoption ICT on the diffusion of ETFs.

6.2 Preliminary Statistics

In the current section, we intend to examine the fundamental statistics of the turnover of ETFs in the 12 countries of the Asia-Pacific region in the annul perspective (rather than based on monthly data as in the previous chapters), a necessary starting point for the analysis of the linkages between ETFs and ICT. First, we discuss the key indicators (minimum, maximum, and average value of turnover) calculated for each country in order to show their key attributes and pinpoint the between-country heterogeneity. Second, we examine the diffusion patterns with regard to the annual turnover of ETFs. Our analysis is concise as both issues were already studied in detail in Chap. 4 using monthly data.

Table 6.1 conveys the basic indicators concerning the development of the ETFs markets in the Asia-Pacific countries. As it may be clearly noticed, there are four countries that clearly stand out in terms of either maximum or average annual turnover of ETFs on the local stock exchanges (in the descending average turnover order): Japan, China, Hong Kong, and South Korea (we classified them previously as the group of the most developed, the designation that seems to be confirmed by the evidence presented in the Table 6.1). What is worth noticing is the substantial difference in terms of both maximum and average value between the two leading countries in this group, Japan and China, and the two relatively smaller ones, Hong Kong and South Korea. It may be to some extent explained by the sizes of their economies—in our study we do not utilize data on the turnover of ETFs in relation to the local GDP (due to the adopted approach to the analysis of the diffusion of ETFs), yet calculation of such indicators clearly confirms this intuition. For Hong Kong, the average value of annual turnover was in the analyzed time period at approximately 25% of the local GDP; for South Korea it exceeded 5%, whereas in case of China and Japan, it was comparable, at about 2%—even the relatively low values for the two latter countries in relation to their GDPs correspond to very high values when expressed in the millions of USD. Finally, the minimum values, referring to the years in the first years in each market's history, show that Japanese ETFs

Table 6.1 Turnover of ETFs in the Asia-Pacific countries (absolute ETFs markets development)—basic statistics

Country	Average [mln USD]	Minimum [mln USD]	Maximum [mln USD]
Australia	5539.7	685.5	12734.8
China	127278.7	0.0	651605.8
Hong Kong	80578.3	2674.8	280061.8
India	2118.9	62.5	7122.8
Indonesia	1.43	0.0	10.85
Japan	155799.0	27247.4	570941.8
Malaysia	74.5	0.0	355.7
New Zealand	70.4	0.0	216.3
Singapore	2500.3	20.7	7941.7
South Korea	75722.6	2460.2	178724.6
Taiwan	13867.3	2309.9	53041.9
Thailand	180.2	0.0	454.2

Annual data for 2004–2016

Note: For New Zealand lack of data for VI 2010–XII 2011—this period is not covered in our calculations

Source: Own calculations

market was already quite substantially developed at the beginning of the 2004–2016 time period—it should be remembered that it is one of the oldest in the world.

In the second group of countries (mid-developed), i.e., Australia, India, Singapore, and Taiwan, the average annual turnover ranged between 2.1 billion USD in India and 13.9 billion USD in Taiwan which may be perceived as the most developed ETFs market in this category (also when minimum or maximum values are taken into account). However, comparison to the market in the most developed category even with the relatively lowest turnover, i.e., South Korea, proves clearly that Taiwan still lags behind in this aspect. Another important conclusion is that, in contrast with the afore-discussed group, the differences in the level of diffusion of ETFs in the four countries in the mid-developed category may not be easily explained by the varying sizes of their economies (or, additionally, the sizes of their financial systems), as proven by, for example, the much lower turnover of ETFs in India than in Taiwan or Australia.

The third group covers the remaining countries, i.e., the least developed ETFs markets in the region, Indonesia, Malaysia, New Zealand, and Thailand, for which the values of turnover of ETFs in the Table 6.1 are the lowest in the entire group of examined Asia-Pacific economies. Minimum values of 0 over 2004–2016 indicate, though, their shorter history than in case of the other studied ETFs markets.

After the discussion of the basic statistics, we focus on the graphical evidence on the diffusion of ETFs in the 12 countries in order to identify the main trends of this process (see Fig. 6.1). As it may be clearly noticed, there are some countries in which the diffusion of ETFs was unambiguous, as proven by the upward trend in the diffusion paths. This group includes Australia, China, Hong Kong, India, Japan, Malaysia, New Zealand, South Korea, and Taiwan. Obviously, the reached levels of

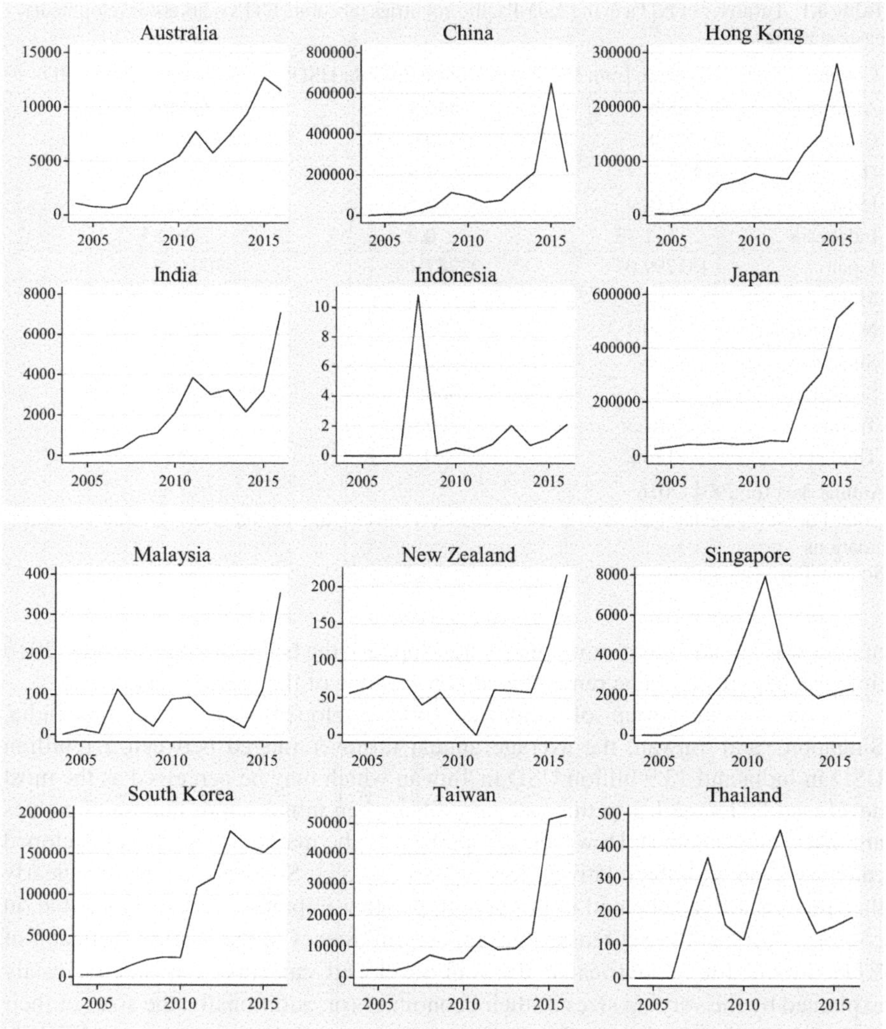

Source: own elaboration.

Fig. 6.1 Diffusion patterns of turnover of ETFs in the Asia-Pacific countries. Annual data for 2004–2016

diffusion in terms of the value of turnover in the USD millions differ considerably, yet in all cases, there is convincing evidence for the expansion of ETFs in the local economic and financial system. This conclusion is not affected by the temporary deviations from the upward trend (e.g., in South Korea). In the remaining three economies, the development patterns of ETFs markets were more complicated. For Indonesia, the growth of turnover of ETFs appears to be short-lived and unsustainable (there are, however, some signs of renewed expansion in the final analyzed years). In case of both Singapore and Thailand, the development patterns can be characterized as reverse u-shaped—after reaching the maximum level of development in approximately 2011, they both experienced a substantial decline, with no evidence for the possible rebound.

6.3 Tracing Empirical Linkages on ICT Versus Exchange-Traded Funds: Panel Regression Estimates

After the reexamination of the basic statistics concerning the development of the Asia-Pacific ETFs markets, i.e., diffusion of ETFs, in the current section, we investigate the evidence for the linkages between ICT and ETFs in order to formulate general conclusions with regard to this region. We begin our analysis by discussing the graphical evidence, and, subsequently, we examine the estimates of the panel models. We analyze the relationships between the value of the turnover of ETFs in USD millions (ETFs—hereafter), indicator of the absolute development of the ETFs market, and three indicators of the ICT adoption, fixed-broadband subscriptions per 100 inhabitants (FBS, hereafter), active mobile-broadband subscriptions per 100 inhabitants (AMS, hereafter), and Internet users per 100 inhabitants (IU, hereafter), each of them representing the different dimension of the spread of the new technologies. Finally, we present the issues that could be regarded as important in the context of the diffusion of ETFs and ICT in the Asia-Pacific region, above all the aspects discussed in the Sect. 3.3, such as robo advising.

Figure 6.2 shows the relationships of ETFs versus ICT across all examined 12 economies between 2004 and 2016. Results provided on the Fig. 6.2 demonstrate that these relationships are not straightforward, regardless of the considered ICT indicator. Nonetheless, it can be stated that they were mainly positive, i.e., increased penetration of ICT appears to affect positively the development of the Asia-Pacific ETFs markets. Still, there are some substantial differences in the strength of these associations, depending on the utilized approach to the measurement of the ICT deployment.

We start our analysis with the broadest indicator of ICT deployment among the considered in this section—IU that represents access to the Internet in the particular country at particular moment in time, regardless of the method and speed of the Internet connection (see graph in the lower-left corner of Fig. 6.2). The applied nonparametric local polynomial function shows that for most values of both ETFs and IU, the relationship is positive; to be more precise, the positive relationship can be observed in case of IU penetration rates below 40 (users per 100 inhabitants; initially, for very low values of IU, it seems basically flat) and above 70. In particular in case of the latter interval, the rapid growth in the turnover of ETFs was demonstrated. In contrast, in case of the IU penetration rates of 40–70, it seems that increases in the access to the Internet in the Asia-Pacific countries were accompanied by the decreasing turnover of ETFs. However, when the actual observed values of IU in the examined countries over 2004–2016 are taken into account, it can be

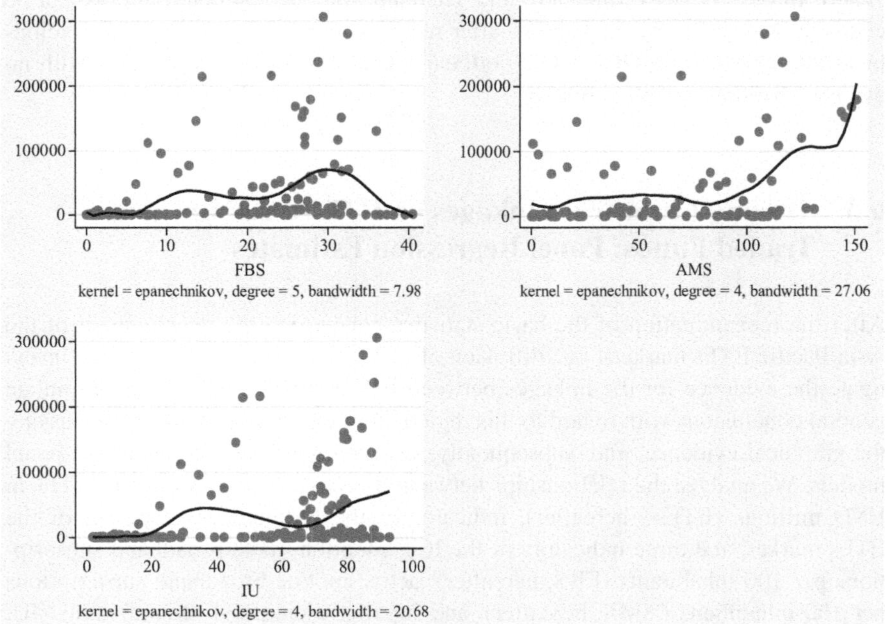

Note: on Y-axis – turnover of ETFs, annual data, in mln USD; extreme observations – excluded; nonparametric local polynomial function applied.
Source: own elaboration.

Fig. 6.2 ETFs versus selected ICT indicators. Annual data for 2004–2016

stated that association between the diffusion of ETFs and share of population using Internet was positive (or at least neutral)—the number of observations within the interval of the negative impact is relatively low. The evident positive relationship refers to the very high IU penetration rates (even close to 100) that were observed in the countries with the most developed ETFs markets—we discuss this issue again with regard to the country-specific evidence.

The remaining two ICT indicators represent two possible ways of accessing fast Internet connections (broadband): first, through fixed telephony (FBS) and, second, through mobile-cellular telephony (AMS). Relationship between ETFs and FBS (see the upper-left graph on the Fig. 6.2) closely resembles and appears to be consistent with the aforementioned association between the diffusion of ETFs and the broadest measure of ICT adoption—IU, the only exception being the apparent negative relationship for the highest values of FBS. Again, two intervals of apparently positive relationship can be distinguished: for the lowest values of FBS (below 10) and in the interval of about 20–30, separated by the weakly negative association in case of FBS of approximately 10–20. In contrast with the IU, the highest values of the ICT penetration measured with regard to the access to fixed-broadband connections were accompanied by the declines of ETFs. It may be explained by some country-specific relationships—high levels of FBS adoption were observed exclusively in case of a few countries in the final years of the examined time period, not necessarily the ones in which the diffusion of ETFs has continued in that time. The vast majority of observations refer, though, to the fragments of the graph that were identified as representing positive linkages.

As discussed in Chap. 5 with regard to the diffusion of ICT in these two dimensions, the evidence on the ICT penetration measured using AMS is much more limited than in case of FBS, due to the shorter availability of this kind of telecommunications services. Consequently, the number of observations is much lower than in case of the previous indicator (see upper-right graph on the Fig. 6.2). Application of the local polynomial function shows that the relationship between AMS and ETFs in the examined countries can be characterized as two-staged. For the majority of values representing the penetration of the active mobile-broadband access to the Internet, there appears to be no clear-cut relationship with the diffusion of ETFs (see the flat part of the AMS graph on the Fig. 6.2); at best it may be described as extremely weakly positive (albeit with some decline for the values of AMS of about 70–80). The second stage of the association between ETFs and AMS refers to the rare high values of the analyzed ICT variable, of approximately 90 and above. Graphical evidence returned with the application of the local polynomial function clearly implies that in the case of the highest levels of the AMS penetration, the increasing access to this type of ICT services may be associated with the growing turnover of ETFs. It should be emphasized, though, that such widespread adoption of the mobile and access to mobile broadband is highly uncommon in the Asia-Pacific region, and, consequently, this apparent positive relationship may be rather unrepresentative as it is based on evidence from a small number of countries.

Important conclusion that can be formulated with regard to the graphical evidence for AMS versus FBS is that the mobile-broadband access to the Internet appears to bear more unambiguous contribution to the diffusion of ETFs than the more established fixed-broadband access. One possible explanation is the broader availability of the mobile-type subscriptions as proven in the Chap. 5—the gap between the mobile- and fixed-broadband subscriptions seems to be increasing, with the potentially more profound impact of the newer type of ICT on the economies of Asia-Pacific countries, including their financial systems (and, accordingly, their ETFs markets). While the availability and thus the influence of the fixed-broadband access to the Internet have remained rather limited, mobile access to the rapid Internet connections has become widespread, and it may be hypothesized that it is used by various participants of the ETFs markets, with possible broad range of applications in this context such as accessing and transferring data on the securities (including ETFs) or conducting operations through online (mobile) brokerage accounts. It can thus be stated that most of these effects can be linked to the demand side of the local ETFs markets, i.e., associated with the decisions of the current and potential investors in the shares of ETFs. In case of the supply side (associated above all with the operations of the providers of ETFs and, more generally, the infrastructure of the ETFs markets), availability of the fixed-broadband Internet

Table 6.2 Turnover of ETFs versus ICT deployment

ETFs						
	RE(1)	RE(2)	RE(3)	RE(4)	RE(5)	RE(6)
FBS	1.31 [0.14][a]	1.31 [0.27][b]				
AMS			0.25 [0.07][a]	0.25 [0.11][b]		
IU					1.82 [0.24][a]	1.82 [0.35][b]
R^2 [overall]	0.23	0.23	0.05	0.05	0.13	0.13
Breuch-Pagan test [prob>χ^2]	646.3 [0.00]		379.9 [0.00]		632.3 [0.00]	
# obs.	154	154	105	105	151	151
Rho	0.91	0.91	0.96	0.96	0.91	0.91
Wald χ^2 [prob>χ^2]	76.05 [0.00]	22.04 [0.00]	12.01 [0.00]	4.52 [0.03]	58.31 [0.00]	26.50 [0.00]

Panel regression results. Annual data for 2004–2016

Note: Panel random effects regression applied; all values are logged; [a]denotes standard errors; [b]denotes robust standard errors; constant included—not reported; all coefficients statistically significant at 5% level of significance

Source: own elaboration

connections seems to be of higher relevance. At the end of the current section, we discuss some issues that may shed light on these relationships.

Preliminary conclusions concerning the linkages between ETFs and ICT, formulated based on the graphical evidence, were further verified more formally by applying the panel models (see the Table 6.2). Single-explanatory variable panel model was estimated separately for each ICT variable: FBS (RE(1)-RE(2)), AMS (RE(3)-RE(4)), and IU (RE(5)-RE(6)). In order to facilitate presentation of the results, model for each particular independent variable is shown in two perspectives: first, with standard errors and, second, with robust standard errors (the other results are identical for both models in case of each variable). For the technical reasons, we do not use models with multiple explanatory variables due to the fact that all three ICT variables are generally strongly interrelated.

Due to the similarity of the conclusions that can be drawn based on the models for each ICT variable, we do not discuss them in-depth separately. In each case, the coefficient of the explanatory variable is positive and statistically significant at 5% level of significance, thus implying the positive impact of the ICT adoption on the diffusion of ETFs in the examined countries.

What is important, estimates of the panel model for the IU variable confirm the positive influence of the broadly defined access to the Internet, regardless whether it is accessed through broadband or mobile channels, and without considering the quality of the Internet connection. Value of the estimated coefficient of this variable is the highest among the three considered ICT indicators, at approximately 1.82—it may be interpreted as implying that the average effect of the 1% change in the access to the Internet measured using the IU indicator can be associated on average with the 1.82% change in the turnover of ETFs (in USD millions); interpretation of the coefficients for the two remaining ICT variables is parallel. It shows that the mere access to Internet was more important for the diffusion of ETFs than the quality or the other aspects of the connection—it may be to some extent explained by the expansion of various fintech services (see the final parts of this section) that in many cases do not require sophisticated technology to be launched and offered to customers (notable example being the high popularity of digital payments in some of the least developed countries and regions of the world (Demirgüç-Kunt et al. 2018)). Robustness of the model with the IU variable is problematic as its R^2 is merely 0.13. Nonetheless, taking into account the high heterogeneity of our sample (both in time and across countries) as well as the fact that we consider only one possible determinant of the diffusion of ETFs, it should be nonetheless stated that explaining approximately 13% of the variability of the dependent variable can be considered a satisfactory result. Obviously, it clearly shows that in spite of the evident positive impact of IU on the turnover of ETFs in the Asia-Pacific region, this determinant may not be regarded as the single factor that affects the spread of the innovative funds—the other with potentially significant impact include the further variables linked to the demand and supply side factors of the development of ETFs markets, e.g., turnover of equities, assets of mutual funds, turnover of stock index derivatives, or rate of economic growth.

Estimates for the two indicators that refer to the broadband connections, AMS and FBS, also suggest their positive influence on the turnover of ETFs in the countries under scope. However, more detailed analysis of the estimated models shows some substantial differences, in particular with regard to both their robustness and the strength of the impact on the diffusion of ETFs. Starting with the latter aspect, the coefficient estimated for FBS is much higher than the one for AMS, thus implying that fixed-broadband connections impacted the turnover of ETFs in the region more positively than the mobile type of fast Internet connections (values of 1.31 versus 0.25). This result may be to some extent surprising taking into account the graphical evidence shown on the Fig. 6.2—the relationship between ETFs and AMS appeared unequivocally positive, whereas for FBS it was more complicated. It may be, though, regarded as proof for the more substantial role of the fixed broadband based on the panel models, in contrast with the aforementioned implications of the nonparametric regression. However, such conclusion would be oversimplified when we consider the robustness of the models for AMS and FBS—in case of the latter explanatory variable, R^2 is much higher; for AMS it is the lowest among all three analyzed ICT indicators, at only 0.05. Consequently, the estimates for AMS should be interpreted with much caution and regarded as highly unconvincing; from the other perspective (in terms of the explained variability of the ETF variables), they may mean that FBS represents a relatively more important aspect for the ICT adoption than AMS. The other interpretation of the returned estimates of the panel models for AMS and FBS may be formulated with regard to the demand and supply side of the development of ETFs markets. As we already explained, AMS can be linked more strongly to the demand-side changes. FBS, whose significance and stronger impact than in case of AMS is implied by the panel models, are, on the other hand, more strongly associated with the development of the infrastructure on the supply side of the ETFs market, because of the types of Internet services used by the entities involved in the launch and distribution (and the trading) of the shares of ETFs—they mainly utilize fixed-type Internet connections rather than the mobile ones (due to, for instance, requirements in terms of the speed and reliability of the connections (necessary for, e.g., processing of transactions)).

As the final step in our discussion concerning the panel models with the ICT variables, we refer to some issues that can make the interpretation of the estimates problematic. The direct comparison of the models estimated for AMS and FBS is hindered by the varying number of observations, much lower in case of AMS as already discussed in the context of the graphical evidence (explained by the shorter availability of the mobile type of broadband Internet subscriptions). Regardless of this stipulation, it may be concluded that in both cases, we confirmed the positive impact of the new technologies on the diffusion of ETFs albeit for AMS this conclusion is based on more limited empirical evidence and less convincing. Finally, it must be stressed that the methodology of the calculation of the three indicators differs; thus they show a slightly varying perspectives of the ICT adoption. IU indicates the relative number of users of Internet, whereas both AMS and FBS represent the relative number of subscriptions. It means that conclusions should be formulated with caution as, for example, each user may have multiple subscriptions—it means that IU may not be perceived as the sum of the various subscription-type indicators because, depending on the country, it may be smaller or (in most cases) higher.

In the preceding paragraphs of the current section, by analyzing the panel data, we presented the empirical evidence on the linkages between the ICT adoption and diffusion of ETFs in the Asia-Pacific region. We conclude our discussion by referring to the selected examples of the ICT applications in the financial systems in the region that can be most strongly associated with the influence on the spread of the innovative funds, i.e., in particular the issue of fintech and its applications in the asset management industry (we discuss social trading and robo advice as they are most relevant in this context). We focus on the aspects on the regional level (common for most yet obviously not all countries), trying to identify the trends that can be observed throughout the region and the features of fintech in Asia-Pacific that are in some ways distinctive in the global perspective. Consequently, country-level issues are not covered here but rather in the Sect. 6.4.

As noted by Barberis (2017), Asia-Pacific is the global leader in terms of the fintech investments (measured using the value of the funds raised by the fintech companies backed by venture capital, as of 2016). The strong position of this region becomes even more apparent when we consider the fact that it was globally the only region with the increasing value of investments in fintech.

There are a number of reasons behind the growth of fintech in this region. Undeniably, one of the key factors is the increasing adoption of the new technologies proven in Chap. 5—without the growing access to various types of Internet services, it would be impossible to offer new services provided online, due to technological limitations or simply lack of customers with adequate means of becoming their users. The other explanations can be formulated with regard to the general macroeconomic attributes of the region on a global scale—the largest population (mostly young, broadly using mobile devices), the most rapid growth of the middle class, and high inequalities in the distribution of wealth (Barberis 2017). It means therefore that there is significant potential demand for the new types of financial services or new ways to provide them that still has not been fulfilled. According to Arner et al. (2016), the development of the fintech industry in the region has been generally boosted by the relatively low IT expenditures of the conventional financial institutions as well as public distrust in the state-owned banks (stemming from, e.g., their inefficiency) and the underdeveloped distribution networks of banks. Consequently, customers are willing to use the services and products of the nonbank financial companies, in particular the mobile-based ones (therefore the crucial role of the mobile ICT services). The other factor that is positive for the fintech companies in Asia-Pacific is the expansion of the private companies in the previously state-dominated markets for financial services and reforms increasing the role of the private sector that are undertaken in some countries of the region.

There are, though, some specific barriers to the growth of the fintech industry in the region (see the discussion in Arner et al. (2016)), in particular when compared to the most advanced European or US fintech sectors: less sophisticated investors (of course, with some exceptions, such as Japan or South Korea), lower level of ICT adoption (see the analysis in the Chap. 5), high regulatory barriers to offer retail banking services, and fragmentation of the regulatory regimes. Another evident attribute that distinguishes the fintech industry in the Asia-Pacific from the other regions (in particular Europe and United States) is its later launch which means that this sector can be expected to undergo similar evolution as in the more mature regions, with the imminent concentration of the companies and bankruptcy of some start-ups (the latter with some negative effects in the short run yet rather positive in the long term).

Apart from the issues linked to the applications of fintech in the asset management industry (that we present in the context of Asia-Pacific in the next paragraphs), there are some other, more general, areas that may identified as potentially indirectly boosting the diffusion of ETFs in the region. One of the most crucial examples of the adoption of the new technologies in the Asia-Pacific financial sector (not limited to the fintech sector) is digital payments (or, more generally, digital banking). Growing popularity of the digital payments in most parts of the region and in particular the mobile payments (due to broad availability of the mobile phones) has already been transforming the local financial systems by, for example, increasing the level of financial inclusion; this topic lies outside the scope of our book; for the detailed overview, see Demirgüç-Kunt et al. (2018) and Ozili (2018). With regard to the diffusion of ETFs in this region, it means that there are increasingly more clients of the formal financial system which leads to the increasing group of the potential users of more sophisticated financial services, such as brokerage accounts or asset management. Moreover, as Karlan et al. (2016) showed, digital financial services affect positively the savings decisions of the households, thus increasing the supply of funds that may potentially be invested in the shares of ETFs.

Furthermore, in the countries of the region, there are other types of digital investment services (or digital banking) such as online investment funds or online brokerage (Mittal and Lloyd 2016) that may also be associated with the undeniably positive influence of ICT on the diffusion of ETFs, due to the increased accessibility of the shares of innovative funds as well as more timely and usually cheaper access to information on the financial markets. These linkages were discussed in detail in Sect. 3.3. As they are widespread in the region and available even in some of the least developed countries in our sample, it seems that their positive contribution to the diffusion of ETFs is unquestionable—they may be regarded as one of the main "transmission mechanisms" between the adoption of ICT and the development of the local ETFs markets.

The other important example is online lending platforms, in particular peer-to-peer (P2P) lending platforms that have also been expanding rapidly in the region—they may be perceived as a possibility to fulfill the needs of retail customers both on the borrowing and investing side, in particular in the countries in which traditional banks focus on the corporate clients (e.g., in China (Cao 2017)). However, their impact on the ETFs markets is difficult to determine—again, it may be positive due to the higher usage of the financial services, i.e., increased financial inclusion (Milne and Parboteeah 2016; Jagtiani and Lemieux 2017) or new sources of entrepreneurship financing (Bruton et al. 2015), but it may also be perceived as an alternative way of investing by the retail clients (Morse 2015; Cai et al. 2016; Wei and Lin 2016) who can opt for it instead of, e.g., ETFs.

Social trading (most briefly understood as following the decisions of the other investors that can be automated and performed by utilizing ETFs) has remained an investment service of minimal importance in Asia-Pacific countries during the analyzed time period. Nonetheless, social trading platforms have been gaining an increasing popularity in certain countries, such as China (Jin et al. 2019). Some of the reasons for their growth in this region are (ForexNewsNow 2016; Fintech News Hong Kong 2017) quick growth in the private wealth (and disposable incomes) of clients, high level of technological readiness to adopt new investment services, popularity of social networks, increasing popularity of the mobile financial services, desire of investors to limit the trading costs, broad range of products offered by the platforms, and risk aversion of the inexperienced clients who prefer to follow the decisions rather than to make their own. It should be stressed that the issue of social trading in this region has been rarely addressed in the academic research or professional reports (with the notable exception of Jin et al. (2019) who studied the Chinese social trading platform, discussed in the Sect. 6.4).

In Sect. 3.3, we presented robo advice as one of the key contemporary examples of ICT adoption in the financial industry. However, there are significant between-regions differences in the usage of this type of fintech asset management services. Asia-Pacific (discussion on robo advisors in this region is based mainly on Phoon and Koh (2018)) is an example of the region in which the spread of robo advisors is still minimal, yet it can be regarded as the third largest market globally, behind the United States and Europe (Sironi 2016). One of the reasons, which indicates the potential problems with determination of the cause-and-effect relationship between diffusion of ICT and ETFs, is the limited availability of the innovative funds on the financial markets in the region. With some exceptions, ETFs markets in Asia-Pacific countries remain underdeveloped, which hinders launch of robo advisors offering passive investment strategies. This problem is particularly noticeable with regard to the clients with limited means who invest small amounts of money through their robo-advising accounts—as Arner et al. (2016) claim, ETFs markets in the region are generally too underdeveloped to facilitate management of the small portfolios with the utilization of the shares of ETFs. Moreover, due to the aforementioned underdevelopment of the Asia-Pacific ETFs industries, most robo advisors in this region offer access to global rather than local financial markets (Phoon and Koh 2018). For instance, in China, robo-advice services, such as Clipper or Youyu, focus on the investors who wish to gain exposure to foreign markets (for more on this topic, see discussion concerning the country-level analysis in the Sect. 6.4).

Robo-advice platforms are not the only example of the online services that can be used to support personal financial management and that are offered by the financial companies in the region. The other related example is various types of digital financial planning services. Their popularity in the Asia-Pacific region has remained limited, analogously to the two other types of fintech applications in the asset management industry presented in the preceding paragraphs. However, in some countries, including China (Bok 2018), Malaysia (Digital News Asia 2018), or Singapore (DBS Bank 2018), such financial services are offered albeit with mixed popularity (usually they remain in the nascent stage of development; therefore it is highly improbable that they could have in any way affected the linkages between ICT and ETFs in the region).

Results of our analysis based on the panel data unambiguously prove that adoption of ICT influenced positively the diffusion of ETFs in the Asia-Pacific region. We confirmed thus the conclusions reached in the previous research on this topic, among them the two studies devoted specifically to the impact of ICT on the diffusion of ETFs—Lechman and Marszk (2015) who analyzed, inter alia, two Asia-Pacific countries, Japan and South Korea, and Marszk and Lechman (2018) who examined all ETFs markets in the world (including the entire group of Asia-Pacific countries). In both cases the significance of the two ICT indicators was clearly identified: FBS and IU (the role of AMS was not previously verified). However, in our study we focused exclusively on the ETFs markets in the Asia-Pacific—the linkages between ETFs and ICT in this group of countries were not studied separately. More broadly, our analysis may be framed within the studies that addressed the issue of the impact of ICT on the financial markets (or in an even broader perspective, the impact on the financial development)—as we showed in the Sect. 3.2, in the majority of the previous studies, it was confirmed to be positive.

6.4 ICT for Exchange-Traded Funds: Country-Specific Approach

In the previous section, we showed that, using data for all 12 examined countries, there is convincing evidence that supports the conclusion concerning the positive impact of the new technologies in the diffusion of ETFs in the Asia-Pacific region, in particular with regard to the analysis conducted with the application of the panel models. In the current section, we investigate the country-level evidence on the linkages between ETFs and ICT, starting with the brief overview of the graphical evidence, followed by the estimates of the country-specific models. In case of each country in our discussion, we refer to the attributes of the diffusion of ETFs and any other issues that may be identified as being significant for the analyzed relationships (in particular, following the analysis in the Sect. 6.3, we take into account the local fintech industries). We present the results on the country-by-country basis, in the alphabetical order; it should be underlined that we devote most attention to the largest ETFs markets in the region: China, Hong Kong, Japan, and South Korea. In some cases we refer to the World Bank Findex database that covers various aspects of financial inclusion (Demirgüç-Kunt et al. 2018); in order to make the analysis concise, we focus exclusively on one of the indicators of the financial inclusion—understood in the World Bank's database as the share of the adult (15+) population that own account at bank (or another financial institution; it includes also people with mobile money accounts). We thus follow the approach of the previous studies of, inter alia, Garg and Agarwal (2014), Brown et al. (2015), Fungáčová and Weill (2015), and Zins and Weill (2016).

First analyzed country is one of mid-developed ETFs markets in Asia-Pacific—Australia. As it can be seen on the Fig. 6.3, it is an explicit example of the country in which the diffusion of the new technologies has been clearly accompanied by the increasing turnover of ETFs. Estimates of the regression models for Australia (see Table 6.3) confirm the positive relationship in case of all three ICT indicators used as explanatory variables, with the strongest identified impact in case of the most encompassing variable—IU. Robustness of the models for Australia is among the highest of all that were estimated for the examined countries, in particular in case of the IU used as the explanatory variable. Consequently, the positive influence of the diffusion of ICT on the development of the Australian ETFs can be hypothesized based on the empirical evidence. However, it should be remembered that Australian ETFs market is not one of the largest in the region—its development has been, though, the most stable in the entire sample. The exact mechanisms through which ICT could have impacted the Australian ETFs market can be related to the high levels of the ICT penetration in this country—regardless of the applied indicator, they were among the highest in the whole region. Moreover, the fintech industry in Australia has been burgeoning in the final years of the considered time period—according to KPMG (2018), the investments in this sector reached 675 million USD in 2016 (compared to 53 million USD in 2012), and both the number of fintech companies and their diversity were among the highest in the region. Development

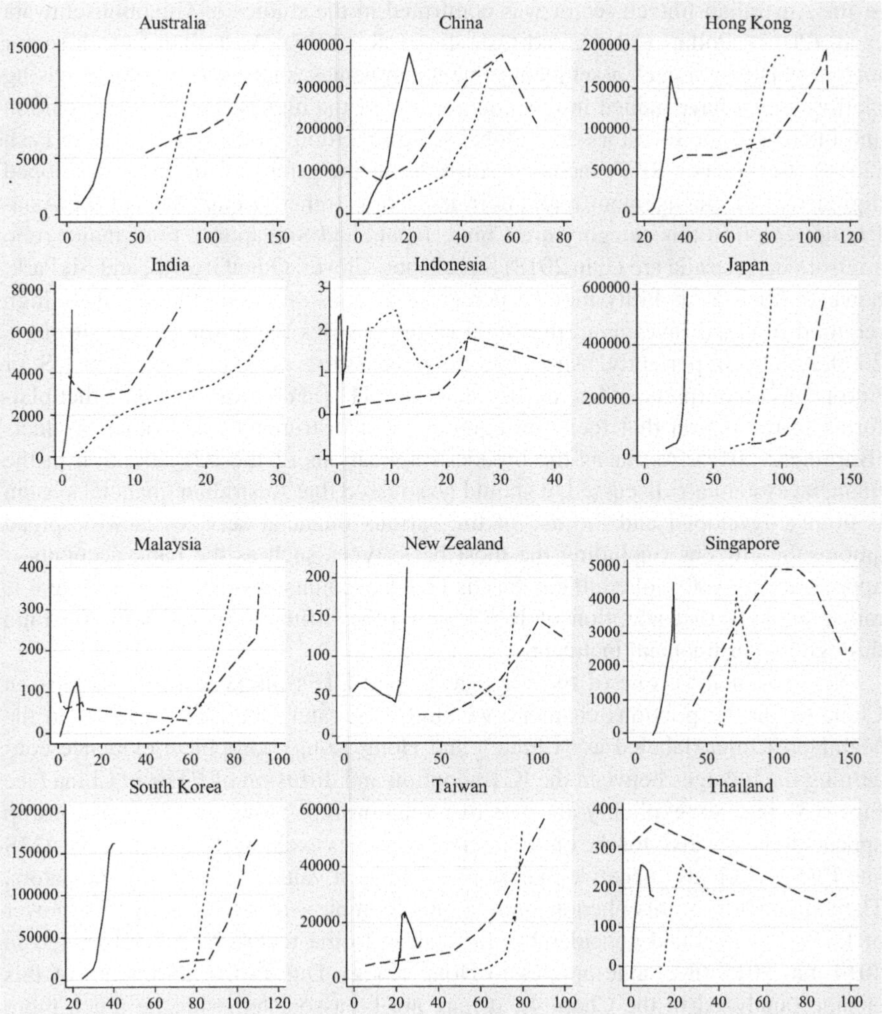

Note: on Y-axis – turnover of ETFs, annual data, in mln USD; on X-axis – ICT deployment per 100 inhabitants: solid line represents ETFs *versus* fixed-broadband subscriptions (FBS); long-dash line represents ETFs *versus* active mobile-broadband subscriptions (AMS); short-dash line represents ETFs *versus* Internet users (IU).
Source: own elaboration.

Fig. 6.3 ETFs versus selected ICT indicators. Annual data for 2004–2016. Country-specific graphical evidence

of the Australian fintech sector was confirmed in the studies of Gulamhuseinwala et al. (2015), Pollari (2016), and Oshodin et al. (2017). Australian fintech sector includes also the fintech asset management companies, such as a few robo-advising platforms that have gained in this country one of the highest levels of recognition and interest of the investors on a global scale according to the report cited in Pash (2018). Burnmark (2017) included Australia in the group of the most developed digital wealth management markets in the world (other countries from the Asia-Pacific region in this category are China, Japan, and Singapore). Four major robo advisors in Australia are (Jain 2018) Strockspot, Clover, QuietGrowth, and SixPark; however, their availability may be perceived as constrained by the relatively high required minimal investment threshold (in most cases the minimal deposit of ca. 2000 AUD). Importantly, Australian robo advisors, analogous to their US or European counterparts, utilize mostly share of ETFs, in contrast with the other platforms in the region that focus on equities, debt instruments, and other products (Burnmark 2017). As far as the broader implications of the ICT adoption in the financial system are discussed, it should be stressed that Australian financial system is highly developed and the use of the various financial services is widespread among the citizens (including the most basic types such as the bank accounts—approximately 100% of adult citizens had bank accounts as of 2017); therefore it is rather unlikely that adoption of ICT boosted the diffusion of ETFs in Australia through higher financial inclusion.

Next we analyze one of the most developed ETFs markets in the region—in China (as in the previous chapters, we study separately the ETFs markets in the Mainland China (labeled as "China") and Hong Kong). Graphical evidence concerning the linkages between the ICT adoption and diffusion of ETFs in China (see Fig. 6.3) implies explicitly the positive relationship. However, the relationship appears to be positive for the entire interval of values exclusively for IU as for AMS and FBS it is clearly negative in case of the highest values of both ICT indicators. The explanation of this phenomenon is rather simple—in 2016 and 2017 turnover of ETFs has declined considerably in relation to the record-high levels noted in 2014 and 2015 (the same applies to Hong Kong). Due to the abruptness of this change (analyzed in the Chap. 4), it may not be associated with the much more gradual diffusion of ICT. Taking into consideration the estimated panel models (see Table 6.3), in case of China, for the two of the ICT explanatory variables, their coefficients resulted to be positive and statistically significant—FBS and IU; mobile-broadband subscriptions appear to be of lesser importance in the context of the Chinese ETFs market as could be deduced from the complicated trajectory of their relationship on Fig. 6.3. Due to the high values of R^2 for both FBS and IU, these two models may be assessed as robust. Insignificance of the AMS variable can be perceived as rather surprising, taking into account the popularity of mobile payments (and some other mobile financial services) in China (such as AliPay)—see the studies of, inter alia, To and Lai (2014), Zhong and Nieminen (2015), Miao and Jayakar (2016), and Yuan et al. (2016). Most likely the results are in this case distorted by the observations in the two final analyzed years.

Table 6.3 ETFs versus selected ICT indicators

ETFs									
	Australia			**China**			**Hong Kong**		
FBS	1.51 [0.41]			1.89 [0.31]			9.42 [1.4]		
AMS		0.77 [0.17]			*0.26* *[0.12]*			8.89 [1.49]	
IU			8.96 [0.89]			2.2 [0.21]			1.21 [0.18]
Prob>F	0.004	0.004	0.00	0.00	0.07	0.00	0.01	0.00	0.00
R^2	0.61	0.59	0.89	0.81	0.33	0.88	0.49	0.81	0.87
Root MSE	0.66	0.21	0.34	0.66	0.61	0.51	0.36	0.64	0.57
# obs.	13	8	13	13	9	13	9	13	13
ETFs									
	India			**Indonesia**			**Japan**		
FBS	1.21 [0.18]			*−0.11* *[1.34]*			3.69 [0.83]		
AMS		*0.32* *[0.17]*			0.56 [0.11]			4.74 [0.91]	
IU			1.48 [0.19]			*0.77* *[1.05]*			7.67 [1.15]
Prob>F	0.00	0.11	0.00	0.93	0.00	0.48	0.00	0.001	0.00
R^2	0.87	0.42	0.83	0.00	0.58	0.09	0.57	0.71	0.81
Root MSE	0.57	0.48	0.63	1.31	0.67	1.24	0.73	0.61	0.48
# obs.	14	7	13	10	9	10	13	9	13
ETFs									
	Malaysia			**New Zealand**			**Singapore**		
FBS	*0.93* *[0.59]*			*0.22* *[0.16]*			6.57 [0.72]		
AMS		*−0.14* *[0.23]*			1.57 [0.26]			*0.46* *[0.42]*	
IU			*1.63* *[4.1]*			*1.26* *[1.14]*			9.85 [3.6]
Prob>F	0.14	0.54	0.69	0.21	0.00	0.29	0.00	0.29	0.02
R^2	0.13	0.04	0.03	0.06	0.71	0.09	0.88	0.11	0.39
Root MSE	1.39	1.34	1.46	0.53	0.41	0.52	0.63	0.63	1.47
# obs.	13	11	13	13	7	12	13	11	13
ETFs									
	South Korea			**Taiwan**			**Thailand**		
FBS	8.98 [0.54]			3.5 [1.03]			*−0.41* *[0.34]*		
AMS		5.51 [1.11]			0.71 [0.14]			*−0.26* *[0.12]*	
IU			17.9 [2.52]			7.08 [1.5]			*−0.94* *[0.49]*
Prob>F	0.00	0.00	0.00	0.00	0.00	0.00	0.25	0.09	0.09

(continued)

Table 6.3 (continued)

R^2	0.93	0.72	0.81	0.34	0.62	0.71	0.14	0.39	0.31
Root MSE	0.42	0.49	0.72	0.86	0.55	0.57	0.59	0.61	0.53
# obs.	13	10	13	13	11	13	11	7	11

Annual data for 2004–2016. Country-specific models
Note: All values are logged; robust standard errors below coefficients; in italics—results statistically insignificant at 5% level of significance
Source: own elaboration

EY report (EY 2017) shows clearly that China has become the country with the globally highest level of the fintech adoption in 2017, surpassing countries such as the United States or the United Kingdom; moreover, it was on a leading position in all examined categories of fintech (except for insurance). According to data on the fintech investments (presented in Barberis (2017)), China is one of the global leaders with regard to the funds allocated to the companies that provide various types of online financial services or other technology-based financial innovations. Some of the Chinese fintech companies that raised most funds in 2016 were Ant Financial, Lufax, and JD Finance (Barberis 2017). One of the reasons for the quick growth of fintech in China is the underdevelopment of the conventional financial sector, with the physical infrastructure notwithstanding the expectations of the customers of, e.g., banks. As Xiang et al. (2017) noted, the fintech industry in China has created significant impact on the traditional financial products and services. According to Xiaofang (2017), Chinese financial authorities have been gradually increasing their oversight of the fintech services.

In China, due to the expansion of the fintech companies, banks are no longer the sole institutions that manage deposits or process payments—such services are offered by a number of other companies; in some fields of fintech, China has even emerged to be the global leader in innovations—the examples include credit-scoring system alternative to the conventional ones (Arner et al. 2016).

Growth of the robo-advisory platforms in China had been very dynamic in the recent years, yet it has not become the major part of the fintech industry in this country—as Mittal and Lloyd (2016) showed, 40% of the Chinese banking and financial services customers used fintech-based payments (14% used lending), whereas only 5% used various kinds of personal wealth management fintech services. According to Phoon and Koh (2018), the first robo-advising platform in China was established in 2015 (the first platform denominated in RMB was launched in 2016). It offers its clients investment recommendations as well as automated risk management. Its reach has been, though, relatively limited as it concentrates on the clients with considerable wealth taking into account the affluence of the local citizens (i.e., it has high minimal investment threshold). More information on the Chinese robo advisors can be found in the comprehensive report by Kapronasia (2017) and in Phoon and Koh (2018).

Despite their later launch than in Europe or in the United States, robo-advisory market in China has been increasing rapidly; as shown by Phoon and Koh (2018) in

2016, it was surpassed only by the US market in terms of the flows of capital to the start-ups in this segment. China can be perceived as the regional leader with regard to this category of the fintech industry. The factors that boost the development of the Chinese robo-advisory platforms include (Wang 2017) growth of the total investable assets (in particular in the middle-class households), increasing awareness of customers, and possibility to fill the gap in the demand for asset management services resulting from insufficient availability of the human advisors. Nonetheless, demand for the robo-advising services in China may be limited by a number of factors including the uncertainty concerning the economic outlook, volatility of the local equity market, and weakening of the local currency (Kapronasia 2017); however, these issues have already been overcome by the Chinese robo advisors through offering access to the foreign financial markets; the other problem are higher fees than in, for example, the United States (Yizhen 2017).

Apart from the robo advisors, the other changes in the Chinese asset management industry linked to the new technologies, with the possible impact on the diffusion of ETFs, is the growing use of the digital technologies among banks, brokerage, and e-commerce companies that is expected to result in the increasing availability of the investment products offered online, both for the mass and high net worth clients (Phoon and Koh 2018). Moreover, various types of online personal wealth management services are available (Mittal and Lloyd 2016).

Social trading services have also been available in China in the analyzed time period and may be regarded as one of the areas of the impact of the ICT adoption on the financial sector that could have influenced positively the diffusion of ETFs. The most notable example of the social trading platforms in China is the largest one—Xueqiu.com (Jin et al. 2019), mostly used by the retail investors. However, its impact on the Chinese ETFs market can be assessed as rather indirect as it does not utilize broadly the shares of ETFs—it could have, though, influenced the turnover of ETFs by increasing the overall activity of investors on the capital markets.

In the broader perspective, the positive impact of ICT on the diffusion of ETFs in China may also be linked to the increasing financial inclusion that was confirmed in some previous studies (see, for instance, Chen (2016), Ding et al. (2017)). According to the Findex database, the share of adult population with bank accounts in China has grown from 64% in 2011 to 80% in 2017. Even more importantly, a substantial share of the Chinese society uses the digital financial services such as payments through the Internet (40% of adults declared in 2017 to have paid bills using such services—one of the highest proportions among all emerging countries; even more (61%) made any type of digital payments). It may thus be expected to be positively contributing to the development of the various segments of financial system, such as ETFs markets.

Both the graphical evidence and estimated panel models show that in case of the next highly developed ETFs market, in Hong Kong, the increasing adoption of ICT was associated with the growing turnover of the shares of ETFs on the local stock exchange; the only stipulation refers to the final years in the examined time period (as indicated within the analysis for China, it can be explained by the sudden decline in the turnover of ETFs). Coefficients of all three ICT explanatory variables resulted to be statistically significant and positive. In contrast with the other examined countries, for Hong Kong the values of both AMS and FBS coefficients were much higher than for IU (at ca. 9 versus 1.2), thus implying, in the context of the development of the local ETFs market, the more significant role of the fast Internet connections rather than the overall access to the Internet. However, the robustness of the FBS model is rather limited as indicated by its R^2. It should be remembered that the case of Hong Kong is in some ways unique in comparison to the other analyzed countries as it is one of the global financial centers, and it can be assumed that the development of the local ETFs market (i.e., its increasing turnover) has to large extent been boosted by the demand (and, in a related process, leading to increased supply) from the nonresidents, including the participants of the local market from the strongly linked Mainland China.

The impact of the ICT adoption on the diffusion of ETFs can be analyzed above all in the context of the infrastructure of the local financial markets (in the entire analyzed time period) and the local fintech industry (in particular in the final years). We focus on the latter area as the stock exchange in Hong Kong was technologically advanced already at the beginning of the examined time period; there have been some improvements over 2004–2016 that can be linked to the increased levels of the ICT penetration, yet, for instance, the access to the Internet was quite widespread as early as in 2004 (there were more than 50 users per 100 inhabitants—see Fig. 6.3). Moreover, the levels of financial inclusion have not increased substantially the usage of the financial services which was prevalent in Hong Kong even prior to the most recent rise of the new technologies.

The example of Hong Kong shows the high dynamics of changes in the fintech industry. As of 2015, it was one of the global leaders with regard to fintech (Lacasse et al. 2016). Data on the increases in the funding of fintech companies presented by Mittal and Lloyd (2016) explicitly prove that in Hong Kong they have been most significant (behind only the Chinese market yet much higher than in, e.g., United States). However, according to the EY report that examined the fintech adoption in 2017 (EY 2017), it lagged behind not only the United States or the United Kingdom but also emerging economies such as China or India. The reason was not the decline of the adoption on the local market but rather more rapid growth in the other countries. Regardless, the use of digital banking services is widespread in Hong Kong—according to the McKinsey's report (2015), as of 2014 digital banking penetration in Hong Kong exceeded 90%. Development of the fintech industry in Hong Kong has been supported by the local authorities. Examples of the support provided to the fintech companies include creation of the fintech accelerators (Arner et al. 2016), regulatory changes (Swartz 2017), and, as one of the most recent initiatives, introduction of the virtual banking licenses (Warelis 2018). Nonetheless, lack of clear regulations on the peer-to-peer lending have hindered the growth of this branch of the fintech industry that has become one of its most prominent parts in, e.g., China (Fong 2015; Mittal and Lloyd 2016).

According to the statistics provided by Statista (2018), size of the robo-advising market in Hong Kong has remained negligible, with assets under management of such companies below 100 million USD as of 2018 (for comparison, according to the same source, in China they exceeded 88 billion USD). Taking into account the size of the local ETFs market, it is thus highly unlikely that the robo-advisory platforms could have contributed in any substantial way to the diffusion of the innovative investment funds (the same applies to social trading). One of the proofs for the insignificant role of the robo advisors in Hong Kong is the very low number of the studies devoted to this topic (with the exception of, e.g., discussion in Phoon and Koh (2018)). First robo-advising platform in Hong Kong was Aqumon (Lu 2018); the other example is Youyu (Phoon and Koh 2018). However, the further development of this segment may be hindered by the introduction of stricter regulation (Mookerjee 2018). Burnmark (2017) classified Hong Kong as an "emerging" digital wealth management market, in spite of its highly developed financial system (in the region it was thus surpassed by, e.g., China or Australia). Some positive influence on the diffusion of ETFs in Hong Kong could have been exerted by the growing share of the online retail trading on the local exchange (Hon 2015).

India is one of the Asia-Pacific countries with the mid-developed ETFs markets—taking into consideration the size of the local economy, the turnover of ETFs on the local stock exchanges has remained very low, despite substantial growth in the evaluated time period. Graphical analysis (see Fig. 6.3) indicates unambiguously positive relationship between adoption of the new technologies considered with the two ICT variables, IU and FBS, and the diffusion of ETFs. These results are confirmed by the estimated panel models (see Table 6.3)—in case of both ICT variables, the coefficients are positive and statistically significant; this evidence can be regarded as convincing as the models are highly robust. However, for the third ICT variable (AMS), no robust conclusions can be reached—analogously to China, the adoption of the mobile-broadband Internet services seems unrelated to the development of the local ETFs market (or, more precisely, the relationships appears to be u-shaped—for the higher values of AMS it was, though, positive).

According to the most recent data available, India has become one of the global leaders with regard to the fintech adoption (even in front of, e.g., the United Kingdom or the United States)—as of 2017, it was surpassed only by China (EY 2017); it was in the top three in all examined categories of fintech services, and in case of insurance, it was the global leader. The growth of the fintech adoption in India has been extremely rapid in the recent years. For example, a few years earlier, in 2014 the digital banking penetration was at 18% (McKinsey 2015). One of the reasons for the fast growth of the fintech industry were the actions of the Indian government such as the demonetization of the large currency notes in 2016 (Sinha et al. 2018) or introducing new types of banking licenses (Arner et al. 2016; Yap 2017). In the context of our analysis of the diffusion of ETFs, the key effect of the increasing fintech adoption (and, indirectly, the adoption of ICT) in India seems the rapidly growing levels of financial inclusion—between 2011 and 2017, the share of adult population with bank accounts has grown considerably, from 35% to 80%. The positive effects of fintech on the financial inclusion in India were confirmed in a number of studies—see, for example, Jutla and Sundararajan (2016), Agrawal (2017), and Malini and Menon (2017). However, the contribution of the digital asset management services to the turnover of the local ETFs can be assessed as negligible due to both their limited size and rare utilization of the shares of the innovative funds. Even though there are several robo-advising platforms that are available in India (19, one of the highest numbers in the world), their assets remain minimal—Burnmark (2017) classified India in the lowest category of robo-advisory markets (in terms of size), "nascent"; according to data provided by Statista (2018), despite reaching the highest levels in the history, their assets under management in 2018 were at merely 24 million USD (in the previous years, they were much lower, thus indicating the minimal importance of this part of the financial sector in the Indian economy). One of the distinguishing feature of the Indian robo advisors is the diversity of the asset classes that are offered to their users through the online platforms (Singh and Kaur 2017), including loans or credit cards that are almost absent in the other countries (Burnmark 2017). The number and reach of the social trading platforms are very limited.

Indonesian ETFs market has been the smallest in our sample over the analyzed time period. It was characterized by the instability in the changes of turnover, with the rapid increase, followed by a sudden decline (see Fig. 6.1). In almost entire period, the monthly turnover has not exceeded ten million USD which proves the marginal development of the local market and extremely limited diffusion of ETFs. Both graphical evidence (see Fig. 6.3) and the estimates of the panel models (see Table 6.3) show that it is difficult to relate the diffusion of ETFs to the adoption of the new technologies. The only exception is the AMS panel model, with the statistically significant coefficient, yet its robustness is rather low (R^2 of 0.58; graphical evidence for AMS shows that this relationship is at best weakly positive). Despite some development of the Indonesian fintech industry (Davis et al. 2017; Kartawijaya and Hamsal 2018; Riyanto et al. 2018), the levels of financial inclusion have remained low (they have been increasing substantially, yet still less than half of adult population had bank accounts), and neither robo advisors nor social trading services have been launched (at least according to data for the 2004–2016 time period (Burnmark 2017; EY 2017)).

Throughout the majority of the 2004–2016 time period, Japanese ETFs market has been the largest in our research sample (in terms of turnover of the shares on the local stock exchange). Diffusion of the innovative investment funds is undeniable and was proven in Chap. 4 with, among other, the application of the diffusion models. As it may be clearly noticed on Fig. 6.3, the relationships between all three examined ICT indicators and development of the Japanese ETFs market were explicitly positive. Estimates of the panel models (see Table 6.3) confirm this conclusion—for all three utilized independent variables, their coefficients are positive and statistically significant. The models are, though, less robust than in case of some of the aforementioned models that were estimated for the other countries in the region. Nevertheless, they may be regarded as convincing proof for the positive role played by the new technologies in the expansion of the innovative investment funds in Japan—as indicated by the highest coefficient for the IU variable, this impact was the strongest in case of the most encompassing indicator, thus implying the importance of the access to the Internet regardless of its further attributes such as speed of the connection (for AMS and FBS, the suggested impact is also substantial).

Identification of the mechanisms of transmission between the adoption of ICT and diffusion of ETFs in Japan is not a straightforward task. Analogously to Hong Kong, it may be hypothesized that it was linked to some extent to the changes in the infrastructure of the capital markets. However, it was already highly developed prior to the analyzed time period; obviously, there were some improvements (e.g., launch and upgrade of the "arrowhead" trading system on the Tokyo Stock Exchange (Kubota and Takehara 2015)). Consequently, we focus on the issues linked to the Japanese fintech industry.

Situation of the Japanese fintech industry is complicated, most simply due to the size and complexity of the Japanese financial system—one of the largest and most diversified in the world with many segments, available financial products and services as well as financial institutions. Despite the relatively low level of the fintech adoption (one of the lowest in the group of countries that were examined in the survey of EY (2017)), taking into account the size of the Japanese economy and financial system, even such limited adoption means that the emerging industry has become substantial in the absolute terms. We focus on the selected aspects, linked to the asset management services (for the more comprehensive overview, see, e.g., KPMG (2016), Ohira (2017), and Gehrke (2018)). It should be stressed that it is rather improbable that the growth of the fintech industry has influenced the diffusion of ETFs through the most basic mechanism, i.e., increased level of the financial inclusion as, at least in terms of the access to the bank accounts, they have been close to 100% of the adult population.

Japan has one of the world's largest robo-advisory markets, in terms of both their assets and number of platforms (Bunmark 2017; Statista 2018). Moreover, according to Bunmark (2017), it is the regional pioneer. The first and still leading ETF-based robo advisor is Money Design Co., Ltd. According to data for 2016 presented in Phoon and Koh (2018), Japan was on the fourth place globally when flows of capital to the robo-advisory start-ups are considered. In contrast with the platforms in most other Asia-Pacific countries, Japanese robo advisors utilize broadly the shares of ETFs within their business model (e.g., Money Design Co., Ltd.), and thus they may be considered to have links to the local ETFs market. According to Fintech Lab (2017), Japanese robo advisors can be divided into two categories: platforms that offer direct investments (minor group) and platforms that offer consultation and advice (the major category; the latter can thus be included in the category of the online personal financial management services rather than the baseline robo advisors). Nonetheless, their popularity remains limited (in particular in comparison to the size of the local ETFs market) when we consider the assets under management of the platforms or the number of their users (Fintech Lab 2017; Thomsen 2017). They may have potential to shape the future development of the ETFs markets due to the broadened accessibility of the asset management services that in case of traditional financial companies are offered mostly to the high-income customers (Fintech Lab 2017; Hallam 2017); for more on the predictions concerning Japanese robo advisors, see Yanagawa (2017). Social trading services in Japan have also not reached the levels of adoption that could be associated with some significant impact on the diffusion of ETFs. Apart from the robo advisors and social trading, there are also other segments of the digital wealth management that could have influenced the diffusion of ETFs in Japan such as increased access to the online brokerage (Uchida 2016) or personal financial management services (Ishiyama 2018), both of which are much more popular than robo advisors.

Malaysia is one of the smallest ETFs markets in the region—for most of the 2004–2016 time period, the monthly turnover of the shares of ETFs has been below 100 million USD. It has increased substantially since the late 2014 which means that diffusion of ETFs in Malaysia is still to be observed. Graphical evidence indicates no meaningful relationship for FBS and positive for the highest values of AMS and IU (i.e., the ones observed in the period of the most rapid growth of the local ETFs market). Estimates of the panel models imply no significant impact of the adoption of ICT on the diffusion of ETFs, yet their robustness is very limited. Local fintech industry has been developing in some fields, as discussed by Ghazali and Yasuoka (2018) or Huei et al. (2018); Malaysia has become one of the regional leaders in the segment of crowdfunding (Arner et al. 2016). However, online asset management services have remained underdeveloped, with, e.g., no robo-advisory platforms.

In spite of the rapid development in the final years of the examined time period, ETFs market in New Zealand has remained very small—in our sample only in case Indonesia the average monthly turnover of ETFs was lower. Graphical evidence presented on the Fig. 6.3 shows that increasing adoption of the new technologies can be associated with the increasing diffusion of ETFs in New Zealand. There was, though, some variability in case of certain values of the ICT indicators—see, for example, the initially negative relationship for the smaller values of FBS and IU (it may be explained by the downward trend in the turnover of ETFs up to 2011 that may not be reliably linked to the increasing penetration of ICT due to the minimal size of the local ETFs market—values of turnover could have been affected by single transactions which means that assessment of some general trends is rather difficult). The panel models lead to no robust conclusions in case of FBS and IU (coefficients of these variables are statistically insignificant, and R^2 of the models are extremely low). However, in case of AMS, the positive impact was confirmed. Again, these differences may be associated with the diffusion trajectory of ETFs in New Zealand rather than convincing proof for the influence of ICT (obviously, such relationship should not be disregarded—our evidence seems simply insufficient to formulate relevant statements). Possible impact of the adoption of ICT on the diffusion of ETFs has most probably not been linked to the increasing levels of financial inclusion (as they were high over the entire period). Local fintech industry has experienced some growth in the analyzed time period (for more information, see, e.g., Pollari (2016), PricewaterhouseCoopers New Zealand (2017), Claessens et al. (2018), and Skinner (2018)), but the segment of the fintech asset management services remains substantially underdeveloped in the areas most important in the perspective of the ETFs market as there have been no local robo-advisory or social trading platforms; some role (yet limited as shown by the negligible turnover of the shares of ETFs) could have been played by the online brokerage services.

Even though the next analyzed country, Singapore, can be characterized as one of the regional leaders in terms of the development of the fintech industry, and it is, analogously to Hong Kong, one of the global financial centers, the local ETFs market is not an example of substantial diffusion of the innovative investment funds. Moreover, as it can be seen on Fig. 6.1, after the period rapid expansion, the turnover of ETFs declined considerably—as we already discussed, this abrupt decrease may be related to the regulatory changes (see Chap. 4). This unusual, reverse u-shaped trajectory of the diffusion of ETFs (for the other example, see the path for Thailand on the Fig. 6.1) is the basic explanation of the complicated graphical evidence presented on Fig. 6.3 that hinders any clear-cut conclusions. Nevertheless, estimates of the panel models imply the statistically significant positive impact of FBS and IU (for the latter the results are, though, weakly robust), thus confirming the possible role of the new technologies in the diffusion of the innovative funds. These results are important as the levels of the ICT penetration in Singapore have been among the highest in the world which means that the contribution of the new technologies can be observed also in case of the countries that are the global leaders in terms of their adoption. Previously we confirmed such relationships in case the other countries in the region with the highest levels of the ICT diffusion such as Australia or Japan—in none there was convincing evidence for the negative impact (on some smaller ETFs markets it was neutral), the same applies to two countries analyzed in the further paragraphs: South Korea and Taiwan.

Taking into account the high development of the local fintech industry, it may be stated that ETFs market in Singapore should have experienced higher rates of diffusion than actually observed over 2004–2016. Despite the relative weakening of its position with regard to the adoption of fintech, it is still among the regional leaders in this field (Gnirck and Visser 2016; Lee and Low 2018); decline took place for the reasons similar to Hong Kong—it was initially on one of the highest positions in the world, yet it was surpassed by countries with more rapidly growing fintech industries; moreover, its projected growth rate is very high (EY 2017). Similarly to Hong Kong, fintech accelerators were subsidized in order to boost the development of the fintech sector (Arner et al. 2016); the other regulatory measures were also undertaken with regard to the regulation of the fintech companies (Fan 2017; Zalan and Toufaily 2017). Fintech industry in Singapore is highly diversified, and it includes all segments that are of particular importance in the context of the development of the local ETFs market:

- Robo-advisory platforms: in Burnmark's report (2017) Singapore was classified as "advanced" market, together with, e.g., Japan or China, there are eight robo advisors (for the detailed description of Bambu, Singaporean business-to-business robo advisor, see Phoon and Koh (2018)); according to the data provided by Statista (2018), their assets were close to 1.8 billion USD as of 2018; as Mittal and Lloyd (2016) noticed, the growth of the robo-advisory market in Singapore should be spurred by the quick increase in the rate of the high net worth clients; nonetheless, due to the underdevelopment of the local ETFs market, most robo advisors in Singapore focus on the funds listed abroad—it may be one of the reasons of the limited impact on the diffusion of the local ETFs.

- Social trading platforms: Singapore may be perceived as one of the leaders in the region with platforms that offer access to various types of financial instruments (Fintechnews Singapore 2017).
- Other services such as online brokerage accounts.

In case of the smallest of the most developed Asia-Pacific ETFs markets, i.e., in South Korea, both the graph presented on the Fig. 6.3 and the estimates of the panel models in the Table 6.3 lead to the same clear-cut conclusion of the explicitly positive impact of ICT on the diffusion of ETFs. In contrast with some aforementioned countries (for instance, China), the relationship between ICT and ETFs appears to be positive regardless of the value of the ICT indicators—it may be linked to the almost uninterrupted growth of the turnover of ETFs on the local stock exchange (see Fig. 6.1). All three specifications of the panel models are highly robust (relatively lowest in case of the model with the AMS variable). What is interesting, the value of the estimated IU coefficient for South Korea is the highest in our entire sample; however, the two remaining ones are also very high, thus implying that the increases in the levels of the ICT penetration in South Korea can be associated with substantial growth in the development of the local ETFs market (measured in terms of the turnover). For example, in case of IU, 1% increase in the relative number of the Internet users can be associated on average with approximately 18% increase of the turnover of ETFs. In the subsequent paragraphs, we attempt to identify the possible mechanisms of transmission—as for the previous countries, we focus on the local fintech industry (we omit the impact on the financial inclusion due to widespread access to the basic financial services).

Generally, the development of the South Korean fintech industry has been rather uneven—in some areas, it has become the regional or even global leader, whereas in most other it has lagged behind. According to the EY's report (2017), in terms of the fintech adoption rate, South Korea was in 2017 in the group of countries with the levels close to the global average. However, one of the distinctive features of the South Korean financial sector is the very high penetration rate of the digital banking services—according to McKinsey (2015), South Korea was in 2014 the regional leader, with ca. 96% penetration rate. Moreover, there have been some initiatives undertaken by the local government aimed at accelerating the growth of the local fintech companies (Arner et al. 2016). For more detailed overview of the South Korean fintech sector, see, e.g., Li et al. (2017).

South Korean fintech industry has remained rather underdeveloped with regard to both types of online services that may offer investments in the shares of ETFs, i.e., social trading platforms and robo advisors. In the former area, despite the vast popularity of the social networks in the South Korean society, no data on the social trading platforms operating in this country can be acquired, thus signaling lack or negligible role of such services. In the latter area, the availability of robo advisors in South Korea can be confirmed—according to Choi (2016), first were launched in the late 2015. The assets under management of the robo-advisory platforms in South Korea reached the record-high level of 331 million USD in 2018 (Statista 2018); the number of their users was merely several thousand. It means that they were much smaller than in Japan or Singapore, not to mention the region's largest robo-advisory market in China; furthermore, their assets were marginal in comparison to the size of the local ETFs market. As Park (2017) notices, the barriers to the development of the South Korean robo-advisory platforms stem from the regulatory requirements that increase their costs as well as lack of customers' readiness.

Additionally, it needs to be mentioned that the other (albeit difficult to evaluate) area of the possible linkages between adoption of ICT and diffusion of ETFs is the application of the new technologies with regard to the infrastructure of the financial markets; for empirical evidence see, e.g., Kim and Seok (2015), Lee (2015), Zhou and Kalev (2019); however, as Kauffman et al. (2015) showed, using the example of the high-frequency trading, South Korea has long lagged behind countries such as Japan due to insufficient investments in the sophisticated trading systems.

For Taiwan, Fig. 6.3 shows the unambiguously positive relationship between two indicators, AMS and IU, and the diffusion of ETFs (in case of the former ICT variable, the evidence is more scarce for the reasons mentioned throughout this chapter). However, for FBS it is much more complicated and can be most briefly characterized as reverse u-shaped-type relationship—positive for the lower value of FBS and negative for the higher ones. The estimates of the panel models (see Table 6.3) imply, though, that in case of all three ICT variables, the impact on the development of the local ETFs market was positive, even for FBS (the robustness of the FBS model is rather limited, as indicated by the low R^2—the explanation may be formulated with regard to the clear nonlinearity of the relationship). Consequently, it may be stated that in the analyzed time period, increasing penetration of ICT has contributed to the diffusion of ETFs. Identification of the more exact mechanisms of this influence is intricate—level of financial inclusion in Taiwan has been high over the entire examined time period (i.e., there is no clear link between adoption of ICT and broader access to the financial services), and the local fintech industry has remained rather underdeveloped as shown by Hung and Luo (2016) and Fulco (2018). There are a number of reasons that hindered the growth of the Taiwanese fintech sector. For example, with regard to robo advisors that may be perceived as the key users of ETFs in the fintech sector, their development in Taiwan has been hindered by the restrictive regulations (Lin 2018).

The final country in our sample is Thailand, in which the development of the local ETFs market over 2004–2016 has been highly limited and the turnover of ETFs on local stock exchange has been characterized by substantial volatility (overall, diffusion path can be described as reverse u-shaped). At the same time, penetration levels of the ICT in Thailand have been rapidly increasing (see analysis in Chap. 5). Consequently, it is impossible to assess the attributes of the relationship between ICT and ETFs, as shown by both the graphical evidence (see Fig. 6.3) and estimates of the panel models (see Table 6.3), all of which lack robustness (relationships appear to be nonlinear which hinders analysis within this framework) and in which all coefficients of the ICT variables are statistically insignificant. It may, thus, be stated that our analysis provides no evidence for the positive impact of the ICT adoption on the expansion of the innovative investment funds in Thailand; however, the possible negative impact was also not identified. To conclude, these two processes appear to be unrelated, even in the light of the development of the local fintech industry, proven in the previous studies of, e.g., Wonglimpiyarat (2017a, b, 2018).

At the end of the Sect. 6.3, we compared the results of our analysis to the conclusions from the previous studies. As we showed in the current section, estimates of the majority of the country-specific models also support the notion of the positive influence of ICT on the diffusion of the innovative funds, in line with the previous findings. The only exceptions are the four countries with the least developed ETFs markets, in case of which the impact of ICT was generally insignificant.

References

Agrawal, R. (2017). Disruption in banking in emerging market economy: An empirical study of India. *Economic Analysis, 50*(3–4), 20–31.

Arner, D., Barberis, J., & Buckley, R. (2016). *The evolution of FinTech: A new post-crisis paradigm?* (p. 62). Sydney: University of New South Wales Law Research Series.

Barberis, J. (2017). The FinTech world is looking fast. In *FinTech 2017: China, Asia, and beyond* (pp. 16–18). Charlottesville, VA: CFA Institute.

Bok, B. (2018). *How is AI shaping wealth management in China?* Retrieved October 24, 2018, from https://blogs.thomsonreuters.com/financial-risk/wealth-management-private-banking/ai-wealth-management-china/.

Brown, M., Guin, B., & Kirschenmann, K. (2015). Microfinance banks and financial inclusion. *Review of Finance, 20*(3), 907–946.

Bruton, G., Khavul, S., Siegel, D., & Wright, M. (2015). New financial alternatives in seeding entrepreneurship: Microfinance, crowdfunding, and peer-to-peer innovations. *Entrepreneurship Theory and Practice, 39*(1), 9–26.

Burnmark (2017). *Digital wealth.*

Cai, S., Lin, X., Xu, D., & Fu, X. (2016). Judging online peer-to-peer lending behavior: A comparison of first-time and repeated borrowing requests. *Information & Management, 53*(7), 857–867.

Cao, L. (2017). Will P2P disrupt the banks? In *FinTech 2017: China, Asia, and beyond* (pp. 47–48). Charlottesville, VA: CFA Institute.

Chen, L. (2016). From fintech to finlife: The case of fintech development in China. *China Economic Journal, 9*(3), 225–239.

Choi, J. -W. (2016). *Robo-advisor almost free to be available in Korea next month.* Retrieved October 29, 2018, from https://pulsenews.co.kr/view.php?year=2016&no=534157.

Claessens, S., Frost, J., Turner, G., & Zhu, F. (2018). Fintech credit markets around the world: Size, drivers and policy issues. *BIS Quarterly Review, 2018*, 29–50.

Davis, K., Maddock, R., & Foo, M. (2017). Catching up with Indonesia's fintech industry. *Law and Financial Markets Review, 11*(1), 33–40.

DBS Bank (2018). *DBS launches Singapore's first holistic digital financial advisor "Your Financial GPS"*. Retrieved October 25, 2018, from https://www.dbs.com/newsroom/DBS_launches_Singapore_first_holistic_digital_financial_advisor_Your_Financial_GPS.

Demirgüç-Kunt, A., Klapper, L., Singer, D., Ansar, S., & Hess, J. (2018). *The Global Findex Database 2017: Measuring Financial Inclusion and the Fintech Revolution*. Washington, DC: World Bank.

Digital News Asia (2018). Maybank2u introduces digital financial planner for customers. Retrieved October 24, 2018, from https://www.digitalnewsasia.com/business/maybank2u-introduces-digital-financial-planner-customers.

Ding, D., Chong, G., Chuen, D. L. K., & Cheng, T. L. (2017). From ant financial to Alibaba's rural taobao strategy–How Fintech is transforming social inclusion. In D. L. K. Chen & R. Deng (Eds.), *Handbook of Blockchain, digital finance, and inclusion* (Vol. 1, pp. 19–35). Cambridge, MA: Academic Press.

EY (2017). *EY FinTech Adoption Index 2017: The rapid emergence of FinTech.*

Fan, P. S. (2017). Singapore approach to develop and regulate FinTech. In D. L. K. Chen & R. Deng (Eds.), *Handbook of Blockchain, digital finance, and inclusion* (Vol. 1, pp. 347–357). Cambridge, MA: Academic Press.

Fintech Lab (2017). *Money design: The first Robo advisory company in Japan*. Retrieved October 25, 2018, from http://fintechlab.pbcsf.tsinghua.edu.cn/english/common/main/newsDetail?id=607.

Fintech News Hong Kong (2017). *Social trading poised to take off in Asia*. Retrieved October 24, 2018, from http://fintechnews.hk/6674/roboadvisor/social-trading-poised-take-off-asia/.

FintechnewsSingapore(2017).*SoutheastAsia'sForexsocialtradingscene.*RetrievedOctober29,2018, from http://fintechnews.sg/9602/personalfinance/southeast-asias-forex-social-trading-scene/.

Fong, A. (2015). Regulation of peer-to-peer lending in Hong Kong: State of play. *Law and Financial Markets Review, 9*(4), 251–259.

ForexNewsNow (2016). *What's fueling social trading in Asia?* Retrieved October 24, 2018, from https://www.forexnewsnow.com/top-stories/whats-fueling-social-trading-asia/.

Fulco, M. (2018). *Taiwan's Conservative Fintech Revolution*. Retrieved October 20, 2018, from https://topics.amcham.com.tw/2018/04/taiwans-conservative-fintech-revolution/.

Fungáčová, Z., & Weill, L. (2015). Understanding financial inclusion in China. *China Economic Review, 34*, 196–206.

Garg, S., & Agarwal, P. (2014). Financial inclusion in India–a Review of initiatives and achievements. *IOSR Journal of Business and Management, 16*(6), 52–61.

Gehrke, N. (2018). *Japanese FinTechs from A to Z.* Retrieved October 25, 2018, from https://medium.com/tokyo-fintech/japanese-fintechs-from-a-to-z-b935a978b90e.

Ghazali, N. H., & Yasuoka, T. (2018). Awareness and perception analysis of small medium enterprise and start-up towards FinTech instruments: Crowdfunding and peer-to-peer lending in Malaysia. *International Journal of Finance and Banking Research, 4*(1), 13–24.

Gnirck, M., & Visser, G. (2016). Singapore, the FinTech Hub for Southeast Asia. In S. Chishti & J. Barberis (Eds.), *The FinTech Book: The financial technology handbook for investors, entrepreneurs and visionaries* (pp. 58–60). Hoboken, NJ: John Wiley & Sons.

Gulamhuseinwala, I., Bull, T., & Lewis, S. (2015). FinTech is gaining traction and young, high-income users are the early adopters. *Journal of Financial Perspectives, 3*(3), 16–23.

Hallam, A. (2017). Arigato Mr. Roboto – Robo-advisors in Japan. Retrieved October 27, 2018, from https://andrewhallam.com/2016/06/arigato-mr-roboto-robo-advisors-in-japan/.

Hon, T.-Y. (2015). An overview online securities trading service in Hong Kong. *Journal of Economics Bibliography, 2*(4), 201–207.

Huei, C. T., Cheng, L. S., Seong, L. C., Khin, A. A., & Bin, R. L. L. (2018). Preliminary Study on consumer attitude towards FinTech products and services in Malaysia. *International Journal of Engineering & Technology, 7*(2.29), 166–169.

Hung, J. L., & Luo, B. (2016). FinTech in Taiwan: A case study of a Bank's strategic planning for an investment in a FinTech company. *Financial Innovation, 2*(1), 15.

Ishiyama, H. (2018). *The Future of Fintech services in Japan and the U.S. identified through consumer trend surveys*. Retrieved October 23, 2018, from https://journal.jp.fujitsu.com/en/2018/03/20/01/.

Jagtiani, J., & Lemieux, C. (2017). *Fintech lending: Financial inclusion, risk pricing, and alternative information.* Federal Reserve Bank of Philadelphia Working Paper, 17-17.

Jain, P. (2019). *Best investing apps & Robo-advisers in Australia*. Retrieved October 12, 2018, from https://skilledsmart.com.au/best-investing-apps-robo-advisers-australia/.

Jin, X., Zhu, Y., & Huang, Y. S. (2019). Losing by learning? A study of social trading platform. *Finance Research Letters, 28*, 171–179.

Jutla, S., & Sundararajan, N. (2016). India's FinTech ecosystem. In S. Chishti & J. Barberis (Eds.), *The FinTech Book: The Financial Technology Handbook for investors, entrepreneurs and visionaries* (pp. 56–57). Hoboken, NJ: John Wiley & Sons.

Kapronasia (2017). *Robo-Advisors in China.*

Karlan, D., Kendall, J., Mann, R., Pande, R., Suri, T., & Zinman, J. (2016). *Research and impacts of digital financial services.* National Bureau of Economic Research Working Paper Series, 22633.

Kartawijaya, R., & Hamsal, I. (2018). FINTECH: FinTech Entrepreneurs versus Banks in Indonesia. *Advanced Science Letters, 24*(1), 264–266.

Kauffman, R. J., Hu, Y., & Ma, D. (2015). Will high-frequency trading practices transform the financial markets in the Asia Pacific Region? *Financial Innovation, 1*(1), 1–27.

Kim, S. G., & Seok, K. J. (2015). Convergence of IT and online security trading: The effects of MTS service quality on customer satisfaction & customer loyalty. *Journal of Digital Convergence, 13*(9), 137–148.

KPMG (2016). *Update on FinTech Development in Japan.*

KPMG (2018). *KPMG Australian FinTech Landscape.*

Kubota, K., & Takehara, H. (2015). *Reform and Price Discovery at the Tokyo Stock Exchange: From 1990 to 2012.* Berlin: Springer.

Lacasse, R. M., Lambert, B. A., Roy, N., Sylvain, J., & Nadeau, F. (2016). A digital Tsunami: FinTech and Crowdfunding. In *International Scientific Conference on Digital Intelligence* (pp. 4–6).

Lechman, E., & Marszk, A. (2015). ICT technologies and financial innovations: The case of exchange traded funds in Brazil, Japan, Mexico, South Korea and the United States. *Technological Forecasting and Social Change, 99*, 355–376.

Lee, D. K. C., & Low, L. (2018). *Inclusive FinTech Blockchain, Cryptocurrency and ICO.* New York: World Scientific.

Lee, E. J. (2015). High frequency trading in the Korean index futures market. *Journal of Futures Markets, 35*(1), 31–51.

Li, G., Dai, J. S., Park, E. M., & Park, S. T. (2017). A study on the service and trend of Fintech security based on text-mining: Focused on the data of Korean online news. *Journal of Computer Virology and Hacking Techniques, 13*(4), 249–255.

Lin, K. (2018). *Taiwan relaxes Robo-advisory rules.* Retrieved October 20, 2018, from https://fundselectorasia.com/taiwan-relaxes-robo-advisory-rules/.

Lu, E. (2018). *Robo-advisers taking the world by storm.* Retrieved October 24, 2018, from http://www.chinadaily.com.cn/hkedition/2018-07/13/content_36566446.html.

Malini, A., & Menon, D. G. (2017, December). Technological innovations in the banking sector in India: An analysis. In *2017 International Conference on Technological Advancements in Power and Energy (TAP Energy)* (pp. 1–5). IEEE.

Marszk, A., & Lechman, E. (2018). New technologies and diffusion of innovative financial products: Evidence on exchange-traded funds in selected emerging and developed economies. *Journal of Macroeconomics.* https://doi.org/10.1016/j.jmacro.2018.10.001.

McKinsey (2015). *Digital Banking in Asia: What do consumers really want?.*

Miao, M., & Jayakar, K. (2016). Mobile payments in Japan, South Korea and China: Cross-border convergence or divergence of business models? *Telecommunications Policy, 40*(2–3), 182–196.

Milne, A., & Parboteeah, P. (2016). *The business models and economics of peer-to-peer lending* (p. 17). Brussels: European Credit Research Institute.

Mittal, S., & Lloyd, J. (2016). *The Rise of FinTech in China: Redefining financial services.* Singapore: Asian Insights Office DBS Group Research.

Mookerjee, I. (2018). *Hong Kong tightening rules for Robo advisors.* Retrieved October 24, 2018, from https://citywireasia.com/news/hong-kong-tightening-rules-for-robo-advisors/a1106164.

Morse, A. (2015). Peer-to-peer crowdfunding: Information and the potential for disruption in consumer lending. *Annual Review of Financial Economics, 7*, 463–482.

Ohira, K. (2017). *FinTech in Japan.* Institute for International Socio-Economic Studies.

Oshodin, O., Molla, A., Karanasios, S., & Ong, C. E. (2017). Is FinTech a disruption or a new eco-system? An exploratory investigation of Banksr response to FinTech in Australia. In *Proceeding of Australasian Conference on Information Systems* (pp. 1–11).

Ozili, P. K. (2018). Impact of digital finance on financial inclusion and stability. *Borsa Istanbul Review, 18*(4), 329–340.

Park, E. -J. (2017). *Need investment advice? Call a robot*. Retrieved October 29, 2018, from http://koreajoongangdaily.joins.com/news/article/article.aspx?aid=3035045.

Pash, C. (2018). *Australian millennials have taken to Robo financial advice*. Retrieved October 12, 2018, from https://www.businessinsider.com.au/australian-millennials-robo-financial-advice-2018-4.

Phoon, K., & Koh, F. (2018). Robo-Advisors and Wealth Management. *The Journal of Alternative Investments, 20*(3), 79–94.

Pollari, I. (2016). The rise of Fintech opportunities and challenges. *Jassa, 3*, 15–21.

PricewaterhouseCoopers New Zealand (2017). *FinTech 2.0. Beyond blurred lines: Have Financial Services Institutions misread the innovation landscape?*

Riyanto, A., Primiana, I., & Azis, Y. (2018). Disruptive Technology: The Phenomenon of FinTech towards Conventional Banking in Indonesia. *IOP Conference Series: Materials Science and Engineering, 407*(1), 012104.

Singh, I., & Kaur, N. (2017). Wealth management through robo advisory. *International Journal of Research-Granthaalayah, 5*(6), 33–43.

Sinha, S., Pandey, K. R., & Madan, N. (2018). Fintech and the demand side challenge in financial inclusion. *Enterprise Development and Microfinance, 29*(1), 94–98.

Sironi, P. (2016). *FinTech innovation: From robo-advisors to goal based investing and gamification*. Hoboken, NJ: John Wiley & Sons.

Skinner, C. (2018). *10 big FinTech trends in New Zealand*. Retrieved October 27, 2018, from https://thefinanser.com/2018/07/10-big-fintech-trends-new-zealand.html/.

Statista (2018). *Robo-Advisors*. Retrieved October 24, 2018, from https://www.statista.com/outlook/337/118/robo-advisors/.

Swartz, K. L. (2017). Stored value facilities: Changing the fintech landscape in Hong Kong. *Journal of Investment Compliance, 18*(1), 107–110.

Thomsen, A. (2017). *Despite the FinTech boom, Robo advisors in Japan have yet to make their mark on the industry*. Retrieved October 27, 2018, from https://sg.news.yahoo.com/despite-fintech-boom-robo-advisors-japan-yet-mark-093333760.html.

To, W. M., & Lai, L. S. (2014). Mobile banking and payment in China. *IT Professional, 16*(3), 22–27.

Uchida, K. (2016). The Characteristics of Online Investors. In S. Ikeda, H. K. Kato, F. Ohtake, & Y. Tsutsui (Eds.), *Behavioral economics of preferences, choices, and happiness* (pp. 667–685). Tokyo: Springer.

Wang, F. F. (2017). Decoding robo-advisors. In *FinTech 2017: China, Asia, and beyond* (pp. 30–33). Charlottesville, VA: CFA Institute.

Warelis, D. (2018). *A digital transformation in Hong Kong Banking*. Retrieved October 12, 2018, from https://blogs.thomsonreuters.com/financial-risk/fintech-innovation/digital-transformation-in-hong-kong-banking/.

Wei, Z., & Lin, M. (2016). Market mechanisms in online peer-to-peer lending. *Management Science, 63*(12), 4236–4257.

Wonglimpiyarat, J. (2017a). FinTech banking industry: A systemic approach. *Foresight, 19*(6), 590–603.

Wonglimpiyarat, J. (2017b). FinTech crowdfunding of Thailand 4.0 Policy. *The Journal of Private Equity, 21*(1), 55.

Wonglimpiyarat, J. (2018). Challenges and dynamics of FinTech crowd funding: An innovation system approach. *The Journal of High Technology Management Research, 29*(1), 98–108.

Xiang, X., Lina, Z., Yun, W., & Chengxuan, H. (2017). China's path to FinTech development. *European Economy, 2*, 143–159.

Xiaofang, J. (2017). The ABCs of financial technology. In *FinTech 2017: China, Asia, and beyond* (pp. 14–15). Charlottesville, VA: CFA Institute.

Yanagawa, E. (2017). Trends and initiatives about Robo-advisers: Pioneering unexplored areas in Japan. *Journal of Digital Banking, 2*(1), 58–73.

Yap, B. (2017). India's new payment banks need a regulatory boost. *International Financial Law Review.*

Yizhen, Z. (2017). China unlikely the next market for Robo-advisors. In *FinTech 2017: China, Asia, and beyond* (pp. 36–38). Charlottesville, VA: CFA Institute.

Yuan, S., Liu, Y., Yao, R., & Liu, J. (2016). An investigation of users' continuance intention towards mobile banking in China. *Information Development, 32*(1), 20–34.

Zalan, T., & Toufaily, E. (2017). The promise of Fintech in emerging markets: Not as disruptive. *Contemporary Economics, 11*(4), 415–430.

Zhong, J., & Nieminen, M. (2015). Resource-based co-innovation through platform ecosystem: Experiences of mobile payment innovation in China. *Journal of Strategy and Management, 8*(3), 283–298.

Zhou, H., & Kalev, P. S. (2019). Algorithmic and high frequency trading in Asia-Pacific, now and the future. *Pacific-Basin Finance Journal, 53*, 186–207.

Zins, A., & Weill, L. (2016). The determinants of financial inclusion in Africa. *Review of Development Finance, 6*(1), 46–57.

Chapter 7
Conclusions

7.1 Introduction

This final chapter is designed to briefly summarize underlying conclusions from the preceding parts of the book. All parts of our extensive study have provided enormous load of knowledge, shedding the light on various aspects associated with the innovative financial products—exchange-traded funds as well as the process of deployment of information and communication technologies. Above all, this research resulted in vast knowledge about some specific aspects of ETFs—their diffusion et alia. In what follows, we try to bring it all together into a single and more comprehensive description, emphasizing major findings of this study.

7.2 Main Themes Covered in the Book

Asia-Pacific region, new technologies, and financial markets are three topics which are currently of global interest. They are of interests of not only academics but also practitioners, people responsible for policy and national development strategies, and even students wishing to broaden their knowledge on the issues discussed during their courses. It seems that combination of these three, seemingly unrelated issues gives solid background for profound, interesting, and up-to-date research.

Countries located in Asia-Pacific region are extremely diversified; not only per capita income varies hugely among them, but they also differ in terms of social and institutional development, political regimes, religion, and social values and attitudes which—to a large extent—constitute important prerequisites for broad socioeconomic development. Asia-Pacific region is where a significant share of global economic growth is generated; there are fast-growing economies like, inter alia, China, India, the Philippines, or Indonesia; moreover, it includes Japan, South Korea, or Australia with well-established economic systems, being claimed as one of the

A. Marszk et al., *The Emergence of ETFs in Asia-Pacific*,
https://doi.org/10.1007/978-3-030-12752-7_7

global core innovators. However, in Asia-Pacific region, we also encounter poor, materially, and technologically deprived countries, which permanently suffer from heavy backwardness. Notably, many Asia-Pacific economies are in the core of global economic landscape. In there, we observe fast-growing financial sector, which is accompanied by rapid and profound transformation of Asia-Pacific financial markets that enhances their complexity and interconnectedness of market agents. Needless to stress, fast economic growth noted across Asia-Pacific economies can be influenced by increasing role of finance and financial markets. Ensuring inclusive growth and development, financial inclusion, and stability is considered as one of the greatest challenges, especially if we bear in mind growing complexity and interconnectedness of the global financial system. As already claimed at the beginning of this book, Asia-Pacific financial systems are worth of interest also for the other reasons. They are effectively dominated by banks that are highly regulated by the governments, banks which tend to focus on traditional bank services rather than the capital markets. Asia-Pacific capital markets are generally characterized by relatively high volatility and high popularity of the financial products linked to commodities as well as products offering leveraged returns. Another important attribute of the Asia-Pacific financial systems is the development of the fintech sector in some countries as shown in Chap. 6.

Asia-Pacific financial markets are increasingly integrated with global financial markets, becoming part of the global financial network. In this context, introducing various financial innovations to Asia-Pacific financial markets becomes seminal. Notably, Asia-Pacific countries are those where, over last several years, rapid spread and growth in use of financial innovations, like ETFs, are observed. Hence, we believe that this part of financial markets deserves special attention. Asia-Pacific region may be regarded as benchmark for the other parts of the world as it encompasses both countries with highly developed ETFs markets and the ones in which the process of their diffusion is still at very early stage. Empirical results presented in Lechman and Marszk (2015) suggest that the process of diffusion of ETFs on the local financial markets follows similar trajectory in many countries and it is shaped by comparable factors, regardless of the region or other specific factors. Therefore, we might conclude that the process of development of ETFs across other countries may follow similar patterns as in Asia-Pacific. We also believe that concentrating on Asia-Pacific countries is far more conclusive than focusing on other regions, as it allows demonstrating cases of countries (financial markets) where ETFs reached their saturation phase as well as countries where the process is still underway or has not even begun, needless to note that such approach allowed us identifying the possible role of information and communication technologies.

Notably, Asia-Pacific region since the early 1990s is overwhelmed by massive diffusion of new information and communication technologies. Explosive growth of ICT in recent years, and particularly rapidly rising share of population using Internet network, has created unprecedented opportunities for all. Fast advances in access to and use of new information and communication technologies can positively affect economic growth and development, improving access to information and knowledge through economy- and society-wide diffusion of new technological solutions and cutting-edge innovations. It can thus contribute to reduction of information asymmetries among market agents and—in the long term—boost productivity. ICT dramatically transform societies and economies, also by creating different forms of networks and new modes of communication and transferring data regardless of physical location of those who wish to communicate. What is important in the context of this book's topic, new information and communication technologies enhance the development of financial systems and markets in various ways (see Chap. 3).

Evidently, financial systems, financial markets, and ICT are closely related (Diaz-Rainey and Ibikunle 2012; Kauffman et al. 2015; Szpringer 2017). Our intention was to combine these issues and provide the exhaustive evidence on aspects related to new technologies diffusion and development of the specific segment of the financial markets (ETFs markets), which—as we claim—is preconditioned by the first. Hence, the central focus of this book was put on examining the relationships between deployment of new information and communication technologies and diffusion of financial innovations in the Asia-Pacific region. More specifically, we have concentrated on exploring the following issues:

- Development of financial innovations diffusion trajectories across the Asia-Pacific stock exchanges.
- Long-term predictions of financial innovations development across examined countries: Trying to establish the possible future path of the ETFs market development in Asia-Pacific.
- Key trends in growing access to ICT as a prerequisite fostering global development and dynamic diffusion of financial innovations (here: ETFs).
- The impact of growing ICT penetration on the development of the ETFs market in countries in scope.

The study was based on 12 economies: Australia, China, Hong Kong, India, Indonesia, Japan, Malaysia, New Zealand, Singapore, South Korea, Taiwan, and Thailand. The core time coverage of this study was fully subjected to data availability; exclusively for the period 2004–2017, the balanced dataset is acquirable for all countries included in the analysis. However, the analysis of the role of ICT in the diffusion of exchange-traded funds (see Chap. 6) covered the period 2004–2016, due to lack of full data for 2017. Intentionally, throughout the book, we focused on the empirical evidence for individual countries (with some basic region-broad analysis) as treating the examined countries as an aggregate would be misleading and could result in loss of information. Moreover, such approach allowed us unveiling unique features of each financial market being in scope, and we were able to present cross-country differences regarding examined processes and relationships. In the following section, we briefly present major findings and conclusions of this exhaustive study.

7.3 Exploring Key Findings

What have we learnt from this book? In this section we comprehensively summarize our contribution to the present state of knowledge with regard to the development and spread of financial innovation—exchange-traded funds, process of diffusion of new information and communication technologies, and the statistical relationships between these two processes across selected Asia-Pacific countries. Our major findings and conclusion are discussed in the subsequent paragraphs.

7.3.1 Financial Innovations Diffusion Trajectories: The Case of Exchange-Traded Funds

First, we have learnt about the process of emergence of innovative financial products—exchange-traded funds (ETFs), i.e., the process of ETFs market development, in 12 examined Asia-Pacific countries. We studied all economies in the region in which ETFs were traded on the local stock exchanges for the majority of the analyzed time period 2004–2017. Our analysis of the process of diffusion of ETFs relied above all on the monthly time series with the values of the ETFs turnover (absolute approach to the evaluation of the ETFs market development (i.e., ETFs diffusion)) and—next—share of turnover of ETFs in the turnover of index instruments (relative approach).[1] Preliminary descriptive statistics regarding general trends in ETFs market development showed how dynamically this financial innovation has spread across analyzed financial markets. Numerical evidence displayed on Fig. 4.1 (see Sect. 4.2), showing total turnover of ETFs in Asia-Pacific countries between 2004 and 2016, demonstrated how radical were the shifts noted with this respect. Total annual turnover has increased from approximately 36 billion USD in 2004 to over 1.1 trillion USD in 2016 (sic!). Although very general, these data show strong growing tendency of the role of this financial innovation on Asia-Pacific financial markets. Clearly, within the analyzed group of countries, some leading countries may be identified and, accordingly, the ones which lag behind. Evidently, when total ETFs turnover in 2016 was considered (the last full year in our dataset), Japan, China, South Korea, and Hong Kong were the regional leaders, accounting for more than 90% of the total turnover. This is obviously associated with economic and institutional strength of these listed countries and their leading position in the region.

Let us now turn to more specific analysis of ETFs turnover and ETFs share in the turnover of index instruments on country level. To provide detailed evidence, we have investigated country-wise patterns of ETFs diffusion by means of monthly time series for January 2004 to August 2017. Using monthly data facilitated capturing both short- and long-run changes in the analyzed values. For each country, we

[1] For details, see Sect. 2.3.

developed diffusion patterns of turnover of ETFs. Separately, for the selected six countries (for the remaining such analysis was impossible), we additionally drew diffusion patterns of shares of ETFs in the turnover of index instruments (see Figs. 4.9 and 4.10 in Sect. 4.3 accordingly). To report on the intime dynamics of the process and identify its unique features, we have provided estimates of logistic growth models (see Tables 4.7 and 4.8 in Sect. 4.3) for each country separately, considering both ETFs turnover and ETFs share in the turnover of stock index instruments.

Figure 4.9 demonstrated huge cross-country variability in terms of ETFs diffusion patterns, not only in terms of values of turnover achieved on each financial market but also with regard to the intime instability. In each examined case, monthly ETFs turnover varied significantly, and the ETFs development paths were generally marked by multiple abrupt ups and downs. Analogous claims are true if shares of ETFs in the turnover of index instruments are taken into account—compare country-wise paths displayed on Fig. 4.10.

Taking closer look at logistic model estimates for ETFs turnover (see Table 4.7), we may conclude that there are substantial differences in expected growth limits of ETFs turnover and intrinsic growth rates. They directly determine the dynamics of the process of diffusion of ETFs across stock exchanges in the examined countries. Notably, in 5 out of the 12 cases, returned parameters were statistically insignificant; thus no valid conclusions can be drawn for India, Indonesia, Malaysia, New Zealand, and Thailand. For the remaining countries, returned estimates were statistically significant and exhibited different characteristics of the process of ETFs diffusion, on which we claim the upper ceiling (growth limit) for ETFs turnover and growth dynamics are of seminal importance. Not surprisingly, the highest values of upper ceiling were returned for Japan and China indicating those stock exchanges as having the highest potential in terms of spread of this type of financial innovation. Next, relatively high values were returned for Hong Kong and South Korea. However, if considering intrinsic growth rates, we note that the highest dynamics of ETFs development was observed in Taiwan (0.397) and China (0.195); thus ETFs turnover was growing there at average speed of 39.7% and 19.5% per annum, respectively. The slowest process of ETFs turnover growth was observed in Australia and Hong Kong—2.7% and 3.8% per annum accordingly (misspecifications not included).

Slightly different in kind, results were generated if ETFs share in the turnover of stock index instruments was considered (see Table 4.8). Statistically significant estimates were returned for three out of six stock exchanges—Hong Kong, Japan, and South Korea. The highest estimated upper ceiling was reported for Japan (6.4%), then for South Korea (4.63%), and for Hong Kong (2.07%). Undoubtedly, Japanese and South Korean stock exchanges (to lesser extent, the one in Hong Kong) are the ones where ETFs play the most significant role compared to the other examined financial instruments. In these two cases, ETFs share in the turnover of stock index instruments diffusion paths resulted to be highest, while in remaining cases, these values remained negligible.

7.3.2 Future of Financial Innovations Development: Formulating Predictions

Second, we have learnt about projections of the diffusion of ETFs across Asia-Pacific countries. In this case we also deployed logistic growth models, previously used to determine specific characteristics of the process of ETFs development. In here we have arbitrarily set five different upper limits of ETFs growth[2] (both for ETFs turnover and ETFs share in the turnover of index instruments), assuming that ETFs development proceeds progressively in the forthcoming periods. Following such approach, basing on past time series and holding rigid assumption that in the next periods the process of ETFs development shall follow the logistic pattern, we have estimated three seminal parameters: prospected midpoint, rate of diffusion, and specific duration (all showing in some way how long it will take to achieve assumed upper ceiling). These estimates provided us more profound insights into potential future development scenarios on the examined stock exchanges. Country-wise forecasts were summarized in Tables 4.9 and 4.10 in Sect. 4.4.

Not surprisingly, the most optimistic development scenarios are for those stock exchanges, which in past periods already demonstrated relative stability and where ETFs diffusion resulted to be relatively dynamic process. For China, Japan, and South Korea, even high imposed values of upper ceilings (in terms of ETFs turnover, see Table 4.9) seem to be achievable in foreseeable time horizon. Relatively reliable predictions for these countries speak in support of our previous conclusions that ETFs development in these countries follows stable patterns and value of ETFs turnover increases steadily. Predictions for Japan imply that Japanese ETFs market will in the upcoming years be still the leader of the Asia-Pacific region. Prospects for Hong Kong are less promising albeit still predicted upper ceilings are potentially achievable in foreseeable time horizon, meaning that it can be expected to remain in the group of the most developed ETFs markets in the region. In the case of the group of mid-developed ETFs markets, for Taiwan the substantial growth of turnover is projected (yet the values reached will probably be still much lower than in the case of the most developed markets), for India the projections show that Indian ETFs market has already started quick growth that can be expected to continue, and in the case of Australia, the diffusion of ETFs is projected to continue, but the projected levels of ETFs turnover are not considerably high. With respect to the remaining economies, no meaningful predictions can be made, mainly due to the high instability of ETFs diffusion processes during past periods.

Finally, regarding predicted diffusion patterns of ETFs share in the turnover of index instruments, we see (compare estimates in Table 4.10) that most promising development scenarios are possible for Japan and South Korea. Japan can be expected to remain the leader in this aspect in the nearest years, but within several years, South Korean ETFs may have the highest share in the turnover of index financial instruments in the region. ETFs in Australia can be predicted to remain marginal

[2] For technical details, see Sect. 4.4.

financial instruments in comparison to the other index instruments. In the case of Hong Kong, India, and Taiwan, the predictions of the market shares of ETFs are highly uncertain (yet they signal some potential for future growth).

7.3.3 Trends in ICT Development

Third, we have learnt about the process of diffusion of new information and communication technologies across 12 countries located in Asia-Pacific Region. We have used annual data extracted from the World Telecommunication/ICT Indicators database 2017 and 2018 (WTI 2017, 21st Edition; WTI 2018, 22nd Edition), tracing back to 1990, on four core ICT indicators—*mobile-cellular telephone* subscriptions per 100 inhabitants, *fixed-broadband* subscriptions per 100 inhabitants, *active mobile-broadband* subscriptions per 100 inhabitants, and *Internet users* per 100 inhabitants. Selected core ICT indicators allow concluding on changing access to and use of basic ICT across countries being in scope of this research. Our research clearly showed that between 1990 and 2017, ICT have spread all over examined economies, and, in fact, none of examined countries was left behind with this respect. According to our calculations, comparing Fig. 5.2 and results summarized in Table 5.1, the average mobile-cellular telephony penetration rate has jumped from 0.78 per 100 inhab. in 1990 to almost 142 per 100 inhab. in 2017, which suggests the average annual rate of growth at around 18.5%. Shifts in deployment of fixed-broadband and active mobile-broadband networks were also high, but evidently the last type of ICT diffused radically faster. Note that between 1998 and 2017, average fixed-broadband penetration rates increased *only* from 0.11 per 100 inhab. to 23.1 per 100 inhab. While with respect to active mobile broadband, from 15.4 per 100 inhab. in 2007 to 104.3 per 100 inhab. in 2017. Fast spread of fixed networks was impeded first by unfavorable infrastructural conditions in some regions of analyzed countries, but above all, once mobile-broadband solutions were introduced to the market, they resulted to be much more favorable technological solution, compared to fixed networks, offering similar telecommunication services. We have also developed country-specific ICT diffusion patterns with respect to each considered ICT indicator, and this exercise has demonstrated that in each country, the ICT diffusion trajectories are rather homogenous and follow the sigmoid-type path. Finally, we have confronted our data on changing ICT penetration rates with data on prices of access to and use of particular telecommunication services (for details, see Chap. 5, Figs. 5.8, 5.9, and 5.10). The evidence shows that at the beginning of analyzed period, prices of access to and use of ICT were falling fast, but then since around year 2000, the average prices stabilized, while ICT deployment accelerated. Nonparametric analysis (see Fig. 5.10) suggests the existence of positive relationship between prices of access to and use of ICT and ICT penetration rates, which supports the hypothesis on the emerging network effects (Geroski 2000; Cabral 2006; Peres et al. 2010; Stoneman 2001) and "domino effect" (Geroski 2000; Lee et al. 2010), when considering the process of diffusion of new information and communication technologies. The numerical evidence on ICT spread across Asia-Pacific economies undoubtedly shows that all examined countries underwent the Digital Revolution, and high level of assimilation and usage of different forms of ICT creates solid foundations to benefit from opportunities that access to these technologies creates.

7.3.4 ICT Versus ETFs Market Development: Tracing the Links

Fourth, we have learnt about the relationship between ICT deployment and ETFs development in Asia-Pacific region, between 2004 and 2016. With this aim, we have used annual time series on ICT deployment, selecting three core indicators: fixed-broadband subscriptions, active mobile-broadband subscriptions, and Internet users. We also used annual data on the value of ETFs turnover in each country. To provide more comprehensive evidence, we have examined this relationship adopting panel regression approach, where all 12 countries were treated as a group, and next—we have deliberately disaggregated the evidence and tested analogous relationships both on regional and country level. Results of numerical analysis of the relationship between ICT adoption and ETFs market development undoubtedly suggest that broad adoption and implementation of new information and communication technologies enhance spread of ETFs in the Asia-Pacific countries (see Fig. 6.2 and Table 6.2 in Sect. 6.3). The evidence generated from panel regression analysis seems to be rather unambiguous and robust, clearly suggesting that higher ICT penetration rates (fixed-broadband network, active mobile-broadband network, and access to the Internet) effectively boost diffusion of exchange-traded funds. Notably these results coincide with the conclusions that may be derived from two other similar studies—compare works of Lechman and Marszk (2015) and Marszk and Lechman (2018). These results, broadly interpreted, generally speak in support of our initial hypothesis that new technologies profoundly impact the development of financial markets and allow for the emergence of novel ICT-based financial innovations; arguably these two are closely interrelated (Varga 2017; Zhou and Kalev 2019). High ICT usage facilitates, at least partial, elimination of information asymmetries, boosting number and volume of transactions mainly by virtually linking geographically separated agents.

Next, to provide deeper insight into investigated interdependency between ICT and ETFs development, we have run country-wise regressions that made it possible to conclude whether this positive relationship is true for each individual country. According to results summarized in Table 6.3 (see Sect. 6.4), we conclude that in majority of cases, the relationships between consecutive ICT indicators and ETFs turnover are positive and statistically significant, the exception being countries with the least developed ETFs markets. Obviously, these findings support our previous evidence generated by panel regression models and give solid fundaments to declare existence of strong and positive relationships between ICT deployment and fast development of ETFs markets across selected Asia-Pacific countries. In the case of each country, we addressed also the issue of the transmission mechanisms between adoption of ICT and diffusion of ETFs, focusing in particular on the financial inclusion and development of the fintech industry.

7.4 Final Note

Hopefully, Asia-Pacific financial markets are less and less lagging behind, gaining important position in the global financial system. Bearing in mind significant changes that are currently observed across Asia-Pacific financial sectors, it becomes obvious that they grow fast, become more complex, and are linked to their counterparts in other regions of the world. At a time, Asian economies demonstrate enormous potential to develop, but this—to a great extent—may be preconditioned by well-structured, stable, and resilient financial sector, which allows mobilizing recourses and boosting productivity and, finally, economic growth.

At the same time, what we observe is enormously fast-growing deployment of various ICT tools across Asia-Pacific countries. This, in turn, provides those economies and societies solid background to escape technological and economic backwardness that some countries in that region still suffer. Considering major aims and scopes of this book, fast advance in the use of and access to ICT generates strong impulses for financial markets to develop. Due to broad accessibility of sophisticated technological solutions, Asia-Pacific financial markets are gradually becoming more technology-based and technology-conditioned. Their complexity is increasing, and radical shifts in their structure are manifested such as development of the ETFs markets (in some cases accompanied by decline of the markets for the competing financial products). Financial markets become more competitive, as—enhanced by ICT—unbounded flows timely of information are freely available and finally more productive which is demonstrated through growing benefits for investors. Undoubtedly, due to ICT adoption, Asia-Pacific financial markets became integrated with the "rest of the world" financial markets; this offers new opportunities but also brings threats and higher exposure to external shocks. Still, our main intention was to provide the audience with the exhaustive evidence on how new technologies deployment and diffusion of financial innovations are interrelated. We do believe that this study not only fills some gaps in the current state of knowledge on the discussed topics but also paves road ahead for further studies. Still much work is to be done and relationships to be discovered.

References

Cabral, L. M. (2006). Equilibrium, epidemic and catastrophe: diffusion of innovations with network effects. *New Frontiers in the Economics of Innovation and New Technology: Essays in Honour of Paul A. David*, 427.

Diaz-Rainey, I., & Ibikunle, G. (2012). A taxonomy of the dark side of financial innovation: The cases of high frequency trading and exchange traded funds. *International Journal of Entrepreneurship and Innovation Management, 16*(1), 51–72.

Geroski, P. A. (2000). Models of technology diffusion. *Research Policy, 29*(4), 603–625.

Kauffman, R. J., Liu, J., & Ma, D. (2015). Innovations in financial IS and technology ecosystems: High-frequency trading in the equity market. *Technological Forecasting and Social Change, 99*, 339–354.

Lechman, E., & Marszk, A. (2015). ICT technologies and financial innovations: The case of exchange traded funds in Brazil, Japan, Mexico, South Korea and the United States. *Technological Forecasting and Social Change, 99*, 355–376.

Lee, M., Kim, K., & Cho, Y. (2010). A study on the relationship between technology diffusion and new product diffusion. *Technological Forecasting and Social Change, 77*(5), 796–802.

Marszk, A., & Lechman, E. (2018). New technologies and diffusion of innovative financial products: Evidence on exchange-traded funds in selected emerging and developed economies. *Journal of Macroeconomics*, https://doi.org/10.1016/j.jmacro.2018.10.001.

Peres, R., Muller, E., & Mahajan, V. (2010). Innovation diffusion and new product growth models: A critical review and research directions. *International Journal of Research in Marketing, 27*(2), 91–106.

Stoneman, P. (2001). *The economics of technological diffusion*. Hoboken, NJ: Wiley-Blackwell.

Szpringer, W. (2017). *Nowe technologie a sektor finansowy [new technologies and financial sector]*. Warsaw: Poltext Publishing House (in Polish).

Varga, D. (2017). Fintech, the new era of financial services. *Budapest Management Review, XLVIII*, 22–32.

Zhou, H., & Kalev, P. S. (2019). Algorithmic and high frequency trading in Asia-Pacific, now and the future. *Pacific-Basin Finance Journal, 53*, 186–207.

Appendix A

ICT Core Indicators. Definitions

ICT indicator	Definition
Fixed-telephone subscriptions	Fixed-telephone subscriptions refer to the sum of active number of analogue fixed-telephone lines, voice-over-IP (VoIP) subscriptions, fixed wireless local loop (WLL) subscriptions, ISDN voice-channel equivalents, and fixed public payphones; this indicator was previously called main telephone lines in operation
Mobile-cellular telephone subscriptions (including both postpaid and prepaid)	Mobile-cellular telephone subscriptions refer to the number of subscriptions to a public mobile-telephone service that provide access to the PSTN using cellular technology. The indicator includes (and is split into) the number of postpaid subscriptions and the number of active prepaid accounts (i.e., that have been used during the last 3 months). The indicator applies to all mobile-cellular subscriptions that offer voice communications. It excludes subscriptions via data cards or USB modems, subscriptions to public mobile data services, private trunked mobile radio, telepoint, radio paging, and telemetry services
Active mobile-broadband subscriptions	Active mobile-broadband subscriptions refer to the sum of standard mobile-broadband and dedicated mobile-broadband subscriptions to the public Internet. It covers actual subscribers, not potential subscribers, even though the latter may have broadband-enabled handsets
Fixed-broadband subscriptions	Fixed-broadband subscriptions refer to fixed subscriptions to high-speed access to the public Internet (a TCP/IP connection), at downstream speeds equal to, or greater than, 256 kbit/s. This includes cable modem, DSL, fiber-to-the-home/building, other fixed (wired)-broadband subscriptions, satellite broadband, and terrestrial fixed wireless broadband. This total is measured irrespective of the method of payment. It excludes subscriptions that have access to data communications (including the Internet) via mobile-cellular networks. It should include fixed WiMAX and any other fixed wireless technologies. It includes both residential subscriptions and subscriptions for organizations

A. Marszk et al., *The Emergence of ETFs in Asia-Pacific*,
https://doi.org/10.1007/978-3-030-12752-7

ICT indicator	Definition
Internet users (%)	This indicator can include both estimates and survey data corresponding to the proportion of individuals using the Internet, based on results from national households' surveys. The number should reflect the total population of the country or at least individuals of 5 years and older. If this number is not available (i.e., target population reflects a more limited age group), an estimate for the entire population should be produced. If this is not possible at this stage, the age group reflected in the number (e.g., population aged 10+, population aged 15–74) should be indicated in a note. If no survey data are available at all, please provide an estimate specifying in detail the methodology that has been applied to calculate the estimate
Fixed-broadband Internet monthly subscription (USD)	Fixed (wired)-broadband monthly subscription charge refers to the monthly subscription charge for fixed (wired)- broadband Internet service. Fixed (wired) broadband is considered to be any dedicated connection to the Internet at downstream speeds equal to, or greater than, 256 kbit/s. If several offers are available, preference should be given to the 256 kbit/s connection. (USD)
Handset_500MB, prepaid, price of the plan (USD)	Price of the plan, in local currency, for a mobile-broadband handset-based prepaid tariffs with 500MB volume of data (USD)
Mobile-cellular monthly subscription charge (USD)	The monthly subscription charge for mobile-cellular service. Due to the variety of plans available in many countries, it is preferable to use the tariff with the cheapest initiation/connection charge. If prepaid services are used (for those countries that have more prepaid than postpaid subscribers), the monthly subscription charge would be zero. If the plan includes free minutes and/or free SMS, this should be put in a note. Taxes should be included. If not included, it should be specified in a note including the applicable tax rate (USD)
Mobile-cellular price of 3-min local call (peak) (USD)	The price of a 3-min peak rate call from a mobile-cellular prepaid telephone to a mobile-cellular subscriber of the same network. Taxes should be included. If not included, it should be specified in a note including the applicable tax rate (USD)
Mobile-cellular price of 3-min local call (off-peak)(USD)	The price of a 3-min off-peak rate local call from a mobile-cellular prepaid telephone to a mobile-cellular subscriber of the same network. Taxes should be included. If not included, it should be specified in a note including the applicable tax rate (USD)
USB_1GB, postpaid, price of the plan (USD)	Price of the plan, in local currency, for a mobile-broadband USB/ dongle-based postpaid tariffs with 1GB volume of data (USD)

Source: Derived directly from the World Telecommunication/ICT Indicators database 2018

Appendix B

Method 1: Kernel Density Estimations

Kernel density estimators belong to a class of nonparametric density estimators. Opposing to parametric estimators, they have no fixed structure and depend on the data points that are supposed to be reached by the estimate. In other words, kernel density estimations may be claimed as a nonparametric method of estimating the probability density function for continuous random data. This highly useful nonparametric technique allows visualizing the underlying distribution of a continuous variable—kernel density curves are generated.

Kernel density curves are plotted by adopting nonparametric estimation of the probability density function holding the form:

$$f(x)=\frac{d}{dx}\mathrm{F}(x), \tag{B.1}$$

where $F(x)$ explains the continuous distribution of random variable X. The density curves that were generated by the kernel density estimator are continuous and show an "empirical" distribution of variables. To estimate density $f(x)$, we use its discrete derivative, and so the kernel estimator takes a general form:

$$f^{\cdot}(x)=\frac{1}{nh}\sum_{i=1}^{n}k\left(\frac{X_i-x}{h}\right), \tag{B.2}$$

where $k(u)$ is a kernel function that satisfies $\int_{-\infty}^{\infty}k(u)du=1$. In our case $f(x)$ shows the percentage of observations located near x. If many observations are located near x, then $f(x)$ is large and the opposite otherwise.

In our study, we apply kernel Epanechnikov, holding a general form:

A. Marszk et al., *The Emergence of ETFs in Asia-Pacific*,
https://doi.org/10.1007/978-3-030-12752-7

$$\frac{3}{4}\left(1-u^2\right)I\left(|u|<1\right). \tag{B.3}$$

Method 2: Inequality Measures—Gini Coefficient, Atkinson Coefficient, and Lorenz Curve

Lorenz curve is used to graphically represent the relative size distribution of a variable, e.g., income or wealth. Technically speaking, if x represents income and $F(x)$ is its distribution that explains the proportion of individuals who have incomes less than or equal to x, then the first moment distribution function may be defined as $F_1(x)$, and $F_1(x)$ explains the proportion of total income that was earned by individuals who have incomes less than or equal to x. In that case, the Lorenz curve demonstrates the relationship between $F(x)$ and $F_1(x)$. The area below the Lorenz curve is widely used to calculate the value of the Gini index (coefficient) (Gini → one minus twice the area below the Lorenz curve). The generalized Lorenz curves are commonly labeled as "concentration curves" and are broadly used as a tool to consider the different aspects of distribution in economic analyses.

Gini coefficient, as one of the common inequality measures derived from the Lorenz curve, measures inequality of income distribution, while 0 corresponds to perfect income equality and 1 total inequality. The Gini coefficient is proportional to the area between the 45° line and the Lorenz curve line for a given variable. The further the Lorenz curve from the 45° line, the higher value of Gini coefficient is reported, which suggests higher inequality.

For given population attributed to values y_i, i=1…n, and if ($y_i \leq y_{i+1}$), the general formula for Gini coefficient is defined as $= \frac{1}{n}\left(n+1-2\frac{\sum_{i=1}^{n}(n+1-i)y_i}{\sum_{i=1}^{n}y_i}\right)$ (Gini 1912). Graphically, the value of Gini coefficient measures twice the surface between Lorenz curve, which shows the cumulative distribution of variable in the sample, and line presenting totally equal distribution.

Gini coefficient ranges from 0 to 1. Perfect equality would yield a value Gini coefficient, 0, while perfect inequality, 1.

Atkinson coefficient (Atkinson 1970), also labeled as inequality aversion parameter, was developed within a class of inequality indexes designed to explicitly introduce value judgments into the inequality measurement. Atkinson coefficient with inequality aversion parameter ε included has a general form, $A_\varepsilon = 1-\left[\frac{1}{n}\sum_{i=1}^{n}\left[\frac{y_i}{\overline{y}}\right]^{1-\varepsilon}\right]^{\frac{1}{1-\varepsilon}}$, where $\overline{y}$ stands for average income of each individual in the sample, y_i is income of an individual, and n is the number of individuals in the sample. The ε parameter represents the degree of inequality aversion. Atkinson coefficients demonstrate high sensitivity to the value of ε; introducing different ε may generate different trends in value of Atkinson coefficient and even produce different rank orders among countries/individuals, if studied. If $\varepsilon = 0$, this suggests no aversion to inequality and if $\varepsilon = \infty$, this suggests infinite aversion to inequality.

Method 3: Technology Diffusion Models, Logistic Growth Model, and Bi-logistic Growth Model

Mathematically, the logistic growth function, which is broadly applied to study technology diffusion, originates from the exponential growth model, and if written as an ordinary differential equation is as follows:

$$\frac{dY_x(t)}{dt} = \alpha Y_x(t). \tag{B.4}$$

If $Y(t)$ denotes the level of variable x, (t) is time, and α is a constant growth rate, then Eq. (B.4) explains the time path of $Y(t)$. If we introduce e to Eq. (B.4), it can be reformulated as:

$$Y_x(t) = \beta e^{\alpha t}, \tag{B.5}$$

with notation analogous to Eq. (B.4) and β representing the initial value of x at $t = 0$.

The simple growth model is predefined as exponential; thus the "resistance" parameter was added to Eq. (B.4). This modification introduces an upper "limit" to the exponential growth model, which instead gives the original exponential growth curve a sigmoid shape. The modified version of Eq. (B.4) is the logistic differential function:

$$\frac{dY(t)}{dt} = \alpha Y(t)\left(1 - \frac{Y(t)}{\kappa}\right), \tag{B.6}$$

where the parameter κ is the imposed upper asymptote that limits the growth of Y. We define $\left(1 - \frac{Y(t)}{\kappa}\right)$ as a "slowing term" ("negative feedback"), which is close to 1 as $Y(t) \ll \kappa$, but if $Y(t) \rightarrow \kappa$, then $\left(1 - \frac{Y(t)}{\kappa}\right) \rightarrow 0$. By adding the slowing-down parameter to exponential growth generates an S-shaped trajectory.

The three-parameter logistic differential equation—see Eq. (B.6)—can be rewritten as a logistic growth function, taking nonnegative values throughout its path:

$$N_x(t) = \frac{\kappa}{1 + e^{-\alpha t - \beta}}, \tag{B.7}$$

where $N_x(t)$ stands for the value of variable x in time period t.

The parameters in Eq. (B.7) are:

- κ—upper asymptote—shows the limit of growth ($N(t) \rightarrow \kappa$), also labeled "carrying capacity" or "saturation."
- α—growth rate—shows the speed of diffusion.
- β—midpoint—shows the exact time (T_m) when the logistic pattern reaches 0.5κ.

To ease the economic interpretation, we replace α with a "specific duration" parameter, defined as $\Delta t = \dfrac{\ln(81)}{\alpha}$, which allows approximating the time needed for x to grow from $10\%\kappa$ to $90\%\kappa$.

In Eq. (B.7), we have three-parameter logistic function, but for estimates of the asymmetric responses, five-parameter logistic functions (5PL) are applied, which follows:

$$y = f(x;p) = d + \frac{(a-d)}{\left[1 + \left[\dfrac{x}{c}\right]^b\right]^g}, \tag{B.8}$$

where $p = (a, b, c, d, g)$, $c > 0$ and $g > 0$. If we restrict $g = 1$, a four-parameter logistic function is generated.

Growth processes are decomposable into *sub*-process; hence the standard logistic growth model can be transformed into a multiple growth "pulses" model. If we have two growth "pulses," this gives rise to the formula:

$$N_x(t) = N_1(t) + N_2(t). \tag{B.9}$$

where, $N_1(t)$ and $N_2(t)$ are $\left[\dfrac{\kappa_1}{1 + \exp\left(\dfrac{\ln(81)}{\Delta t_1}\left(t - T_{m_1}\right)\right)}\right]$ and $\left[\dfrac{\kappa_2}{1 + \exp\left(\dfrac{\ln(81)}{\Delta t_2}\left(t - T_{m_2}\right)\right)}\right]$, respectively. The model defined in Eq. (B.9) is a *bi-*logistic growth equation.

The generalized version of Eq. (B.9) for multiple (→"*z*") logistic growth *sub*-processes follows the *z-component* logistic growth model:

$$N(t)=\left[\frac{\kappa_1}{1+\exp\left(\frac{\ln(81)}{\Delta t_1}\left(t-T_{m_1}\right)\right)}\right]+\cdots+\left[\frac{\kappa_i}{1+\exp\left(\frac{\ln(81)}{\Delta t_i}\left(t-T_{m_i}\right)\right)}\right]=\sum_{i=1}^{z}N_i(t), \tag{B.10}$$

if:

$$N_i(t)=\frac{\kappa_i}{1+\exp\left(-\alpha_i\left(t-\beta_i\right)\right)}. \tag{B.11}$$

Method 4: Locally Weighted Polynomial Smoother

Locally weighted polynomial smoother is a nonparametric method used to graphically fit the curve displaying relationship between two variables. This method of analysis is useful and widely adopted as it allows relaxing rigid assumptions of conventional parametric analysis and regressions, and thus no assumption regarding the form of the relations is made. A huge advantage of using the LOWESS method is that it is outlier resistant, and thus no disturbances in results are introduced.

We approximate the function having a general form:

$$f(.), \tag{B.12}$$

under assumption that all errors e_i generated by the model are identically zero. Having defined x_i as one of the covariates, we can estimate the $f(.)$ by using the multivariate polynomial form where respective x_i is chosen to extrapolate:

$$y_i = f\left(x_i^*\right), \tag{B.13}$$

if $i = 1, \ldots \ldots k$, in the k-nearest neighborhood of x^*, with underlying assumption that f is the locally a smooth function.

Method 5: Panel Regression Models

Fixed effects regression, which allows for heterogeneity across countries, follows the general form:

$$\Psi_{i,y} = \alpha_i + \beta\left(x^{\cdot}_{i,y}\right) + u_{i,y}, \tag{B.14}$$

where α_i is unknown intercept for each entity (country), $\Psi_{i,\,y}$ denotes depended variable, β is the $L \times 1$, and $x^{\cdot}_{i,y}$ stands for the $i$yth observation on L explanatory variables. The subscripts $i = \{1, \ldots\ \ldots\ N\}$ stand for entity (country) and $y = \{1, \ldots\ \ldots\ T\}$ for the time period. In Eq. (B.14), the $u_{i,\,y} = \mu_i + \nu_{i,\,y}$, while the μ_i accounts for the unobservable and time-invariant country-specific effect, which is not captured in the model, and $\nu_{i,\,y}$ is the remainder disturbance (the observation-specific errors).

Fixed effects models can be alternatively presented using binary variables for entity fixed effects, so the Eq. (B.14) becomes:

$$\Psi_{i,y} = \beta_0 + \beta_1 X_{1,iy} + \ldots + \beta_k X_{k,iy} + \vartheta_2 E_2 + \ldots + \vartheta_n E_n + u_{i,y}, \tag{B.15}$$

with notation as in Eq. (B.14), and where E_n is the entity n (with $n - 1$ entities included in the model), ϑ_2 is the coefficient for the binary regressors.

If time fixed effects are added to Eq. (B.15), the time and fixed effects regression model holds the form:

$$\Psi_{i,y} = \beta_0 + \beta_1 X_{1,iy} + \ldots + \beta_k X_{k,iy} + \vartheta_2 E_2 + \ldots + \vartheta_n E_n + \gamma_2 T_2 + \ldots + \gamma_y T_y \quad u_{i,y}, \tag{B.16}$$

with notation as in Eq. (B.15), where T_y is time binary variable (dummy) (with y−1 time periods included in the model) and γ_y is the coefficient for the binary time regressors.

To control for the possibility of emerging heteroscedasticity or within-panel serial correlations, robust standard errors should be specified and reported.

Alternatively, if some differences across examined entities (countries) may have influence on depended variable, we specify random effects model that holds a general form:

$$\Psi_{i,y} = \alpha + \beta\left(x^{\cdot}_{i,y}\right) + u_{i,y} + \varepsilon_{i,y}, \tag{B.17}$$

With notations as in Eq. (B.14), however where $u_{i,\,y}$ explains between-entity error and $\varepsilon_{i,\,y}$, within-entity error.

Appendix C

Changes in costs of access to and use of ICT. County lines. Period 1990–2017

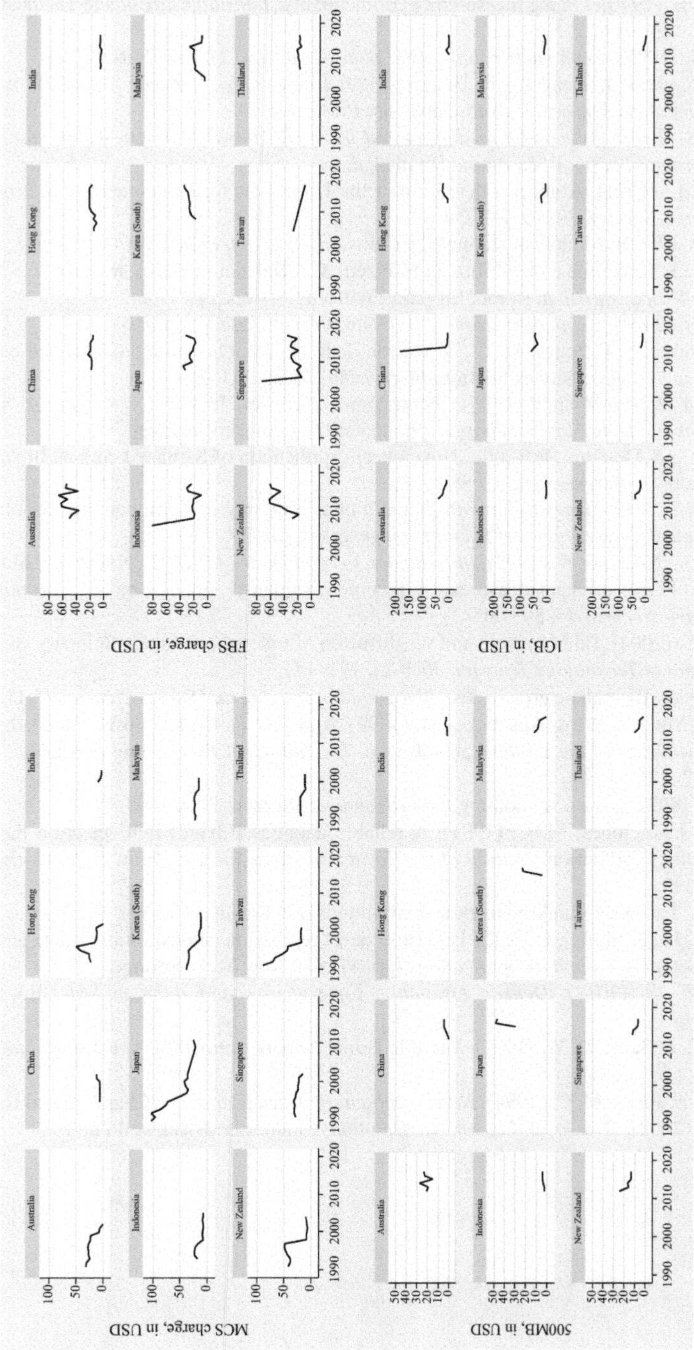

Source: Authors' elaboration.

A. Marszk et al., *The Emergence of ETFs in Asia-Pacific*,
https://doi.org/10.1007/978-3-030-12752-7

Further Reading

Atkinson, A. B. (1970). On the measurement of inequality. *Journal of Economic Theory, 2*(3), 244–263.

Baltagi, B. H. (1995). *Econometric analysis of panel data* (Vol. 2). New York: Wiley.

Diggle, P., Diggle, P. J., Heagerty, P., Heagerty, P. J., Liang, K. Y., & Zeger, S. (2002). *Analysis of longitudinal data*. Oxford: Oxford University Press.

Fan, J. (2018). *Local polynomial modelling and its applications: Monographs on statistics and applied probability 66*. Boca Raton: Routledge.

Gastwirth, J. L. (1971). A general definition of the Lorenz curve. *Econometrica: Journal of the Econometric Society, 39*, 1037–1039.

Geroski, P. A. (2000). Models of technology diffusion. *Research Policy, 29*(4), 603–625.

Gini, C. (1912). Variabilità e mutabilità. In E. Pizetti & T. Salvemini (Eds.), *Reprinted in Memorie di metodologica statistica*. Rome: Libreria Eredi Virgilio Veschi.

Greene, W. H. (2003). *Econometric analysis*. Delhi: Pearson Education India.

Hall, P., Sheather, S. J., Jones, M. C., & Marron, J. S. (1991). On optimal data-based bandwidth selection in kernel density estimation. *Biometrika, 78*(2), 263–269.

Karshenas, M., & Stoneman, P. (1995). Technological diffusion. In *Handbook of the economics of innovation and technological change* (pp. 265–297). Oxford: Blackwell.

Kucharavy, D., & De Guio, R. (2007, November). Application of S-shaped curves. In *7th ETRIA TRIZ Future Conference* (pp. 81–88).

Kwasnicki, W. (2013). Logistic growth of the global economy and competitiveness of nations. *Technological Forecasting and Social Change, 80*(1), 50–76.

Maddala, G. S., & Lahiri, K. (1992). *Introduction to econometrics* (Vol. 2). New York: MacMillan.

Mehran, F. (1976). Linear measures of income inequality. *Econometrica: Journal of the Econometric Society, 44*, 805–809.

Metcalfe, J. S. (2004). Ed Mansfield and the diffusion of innovation: An evolutionary connection. *The Journal of Technology Transfer, 30*(1–2), 171–181.

Meyer, P. (1994). Bi-logistic growth. *Technological Forecasting and Social Change, 47*(1), 89–102.

Meyer, P. S., Yung, J. W., & Ausubel, J. H. (1999). A primer on logistic growth and substitution: The mathematics of the Loglet Lab software. *Technological Forecasting and Social Change, 61*(3), 247–271.

Royston, P. (1992). Lowess smoothing. *Stata Technical Bulletin, 1*(3), 7–9.

Sheather, S. J., & Jones, M. C. (1991). A reliable data-based bandwidth selection method for kernel density estimation. *Journal of the Royal Statistical Society. Series B (Methodological), 53*, 683–690.

Shorrocks, A. F. (1983). Ranking income distributions. *Economica, 50*(197), 3–17.

Shumway, R. H., & Stoffer, D. S. (2011). Time series regression and exploratory data analysis. In *Time series analysis and its applications* (pp. 47–82). New York: Springer.

Silverman, B. W. (2018). *Density estimation for statistics and data analysis*. Boca Raton: Routledge.

Terrell, G. R., & Scott, D. W. (1992). Variable kernel density estimation. *The Annals of Statistics, 20*, 1236–1265.

Wand, M. P., & Jones, M. C. (1994). *Kernel smoothing*. Boca Raton, FL: Chapman and Hall/CRC.

Wolff, E. N. (2009). *Poverty and income distribution*. Chichester: Blackwell Pub.

The manufacturer's authorised representative in the EU is Springer Nature Customer Service Centre GmbH, Europaplatz 3, 69115 Heidelberg, Germany. If you have any concerns regarding our products, please contact ProductSafety@springernature.com

Printed and bound by CPI Group (UK) Ltd, Croydon, CR0 4YY
30/09/2026
02225602-0005